UTM Security with Fortinet

Mastering FortiOS

UTM Security with Fortinet®
Mastering FortiOS

Kenneth Tam
Martín H. Hoz Salvador
Ken McAlpine
Rick Basile
Bruce Matsugu
Josh More

AMSTERDAM • BOSTON • HEIDELBERG • LONDON
NEW YORK • OXFORD • PARIS • SAN DIEGO
SAN FRANCISCO • SINGAPORE • SYDNEY • TOKYO

Syngress is an Imprint of Elsevier

SYNGRESS.

Acquiring Editor:	*Steve Elliot*
Project Manager:	*Mohanambal Natarajan*
Designer:	*Joanne Blank*

Syngress is an imprint of Elsevier
225 Wyman Street, Waltham, MA 02451, USA

Notices
Knowledge and best practice in this field are constantly changing. As new research and experience broaden our understanding, changes in research methods or professional practices, may become necessary. Practitioners and researchers must always rely on their own experience and knowledge in evaluating and using any information or methods described herein. In using such information or methods they should be mindful of their own safety and the safety of others, including parties for whom they have a professional responsibility.

To the fullest extent of the law, neither the Publisher nor the authors, contributors, or editors, assume any liability for any injury and/or damage to persons or property as a matter of products liability, negligence or otherwise, or from any use or operation of any methods, products, instructions, or ideas contained in the material herein.

Library of Congress Cataloging-in-Publication Data
Application submitted

British Library Cataloguing-in-Publication Data
A catalogue record for this book is available from the British Library.

ISBN: 978-1-59749-747-3

Printed in the United States of America
13 14 15 16 17   10 9 8 7 6 5 4 3 2 1

For information on all Syngress publications visit our werbsite at *www.syngress.com*

The statements made herein are not statements made by Fortinet and cannot be construed as a warranty, guarantee, or commitment on behalf of Fortinet. Fortinet®, FortiGate®, and FortiGuard®, are registered trademarks of Fortinet, Inc., and other Fortinet names herein may also be trademarks of Fortinet. All other product or company names may be trademarks of their respective owners. Performance metrics contained herein were attained in internal lab tests under ideal conditions, and performance may vary. Network variables, different network environments and other conditions may affect performance results. Nothing herein represents any binding commitment by Fortinet, and Fortinet disclaims all representations, warranties, or guarantees whatsoever, whether express or implied. Nothing herein shall be considered a waiver by Fortinet of any rights and Fortinet reserves all rights.

Dedications

Kenneth Tam would like to dedicate his work on this book to his wife Lorna for her patience and support throughout this project. Along with his kids Jessica, Brandon, Ethan, and Sophia for the everyday inspiration that gets him through those stressful days and time away on business trips throughout his career.

Martin would like to dedicate his work on this book to his mother Micaela and grandma Guadalupe for the values, education and life example received from both, to his wife Diana for the understanding and support especially while working at nights and weekends on this project, to his daughter Isabella for the inspiration, and to his brothers in arms (the Fortinet Latin American team) for making work a pleasure that he enjoys every day. In-memoriam: Wolfgang Gonzalez.

Bruce would like to dedicate his work on this book to M, R and Y, and to the early inhabitants of the Fortiverse

Rick would like to dedicate his contributions on this book to his wife Lizette for all the sacrifices she has made over the years supporting his career and and to his children who he hopes will learn from his successes and his failures.

Contents

SECTION III IMPLEMENTING A SECURITY (UTM) PROJECT

Acknowledgements

The authors of this book would like to thank the following organizations and individuals:

Fortinet and Founders Ken and Michael Xie: For creating the technology we all love, and for being the organization where the majority of us have enjoyed spending that many years of our professional lives (some of us have been at Fortinet for around 10 years, but we won't say who or Mr. McAlpine, Mr. Matsugu and Mr. Basile will feel old ;-). Not many companies out there have the vibe, the team and the vision to do what Fortinet does.

Michael Xie, Fortinet CTO: for all the support and encouragement we received from him, to work on this project. Yes, we did this in our free time, but knowing Michael had an eye on the project inspired us to do an even better job.

Darren Turnbull, Vice President for Strategic Solutions at Fortinet: For his advice, information and time devoted to review and correct the manuscript. The book is better due to Darren's annotations, comments and critiques.

Samantha Shear, Director of Legal for the Americas at Fortinet: For bridging all the potential legal issues, so the authors could engage on the project and have the freedom to write our thoughts, while ensuring we would not get into trouble.

John Whittle, Vice President General Counsel at Fortinet: For the advice, suggestions and support on the legal issues about our employment at Fortinet and our work on this book.

Sanjeev Sinha for his professional insight and technical review of chapter 11.

Jim Overbeck for his assistance in developing figure 11.2.

Ken Tam, Ken McAlpine and Martin Hoz would like to thank Bruce Matsugu first for taking personal time to review the early manuscripts and then for being brave enough to step up as an author and write chapter 7 and appendix B, and Rick Basile for being another brave man stepping up to write Chapters 9 and 12, very difficult ones. All of us would like to thank Josh More for the time and effort invested correcting and greatly enhancing the manuscript, to the point that he is more than a technical editor, he is really the co-author of the book.

We would like to thank the Syngress Team: Steve Elliot, for all the advice and suggestions. Chris Katsaropoulos, Meagan White, Matthew Cater, Alex Burack, and David Bevans for helping us on different stages in the project. For all, our gratitude for the assistance but also for the great patience and diligence while we worked on the book. We're not sure if our friends at Syngress ever had to deal with so many manuscript delivery date changes:-)

About The Author

Kenneth Tam Fortinet Certified Network Security Professional (FCNSP) is currently with Fortinet as Senior Security Engineer where he provides hands-on installation, support, and training to Fortinet customers in the North Central US states. He has over 18 years experience experience in the networking/security field from working with companies such as Juniper Networks, Netscreen Technologies, 3com, and US Robotics. Mr. Tam has contributed previously on Syngress Books as a co-author of "Netscreen Firewalls"

Martin H Hoz Salvador Fortinet Certified Network Security Professional (FCNSP) and Certified Information Systems Security Professional (CISSP) is currently with Fortinet as Systems Engineering Director for Latin America and the Caribbean. In this capacity he oversees business development from the engineering standpoint, which includes partner readiness, go-to-market strategies and internal enablement. Within Fortinet, Martin is also a member of the FIAT Team, a group of individuals that assist in defining Fortinet R&D Direction. He has almost 20 years experience in the networking security field, as he wrote his first theoretical virus in May 1993 and got his first Internet account in October of the same year. He is a regular presenter at Security Conferences in Latin America and Europe. Martin lives nearby Mexico City and can be reached at mhoz@fortinet.com

Ken McAlpine is a Cisco Certified Internetworking Expert (CCIE) and a Fortinet Certified Network Security Professional (FCNSP)and is currently a Senior Consulting Systems Engineer with Fortinet. His areas of interest and expertise include the overall design, security, implementation and documentation of a secure smart grid network. Within Fortinet, Ken is also a member of the FIAT Team, a group of individuals that assist in defining Fortinet R&D Direction. As an expert in the field, he regularly presents at conferences such as Smart Grid Interoperability Conference.

Bruce Matsugu is currently a consulting systems engineer at Fortinet and has been with Fortinet for over 10-years in a variety of roles including technical support, release management, training, and professional services. A graduate of the University of British Columbia in electrical engineering, Bruce worked previously in hardware design for fibre transport telecom systems and multi-service routers, and in project engineering for wireless messaging systems. He currently lives near Vancouver, BC.

Rick Basile Fortinet Certified Network Security Professional (FCNSP) continues in his tenth year with Fortinet and is currently working as a Senior Network Security Architect. With over 20 years of industrial and information security experience and extensive networking and telecommunications expertise, Rick works with Fortinet's Large Enterprise and Service Provider accounts. Within Fortinet, Rick is also a member of the FIAT Team, a group of individuals that assist in defining Fortinet R&D Direction.

Josh More has over fifteen years of experience in IT, and ten years working in Security. Though today, he primarily works as a security consultant, he has also worked in roles ranging from user to developer to system administrator. He holds several security and technical certifications and serves in a leadership position on several security-focused groups. He writes a blog on security at www.starmind.org and www.rjs-software.com. As security works best from a holistic approach, he works all angles: risk assessments, posture analysis, incident response, malware analysis, infrastructure defense, system forensics, employee training and business strategy. Josh More works at RJS Software Systems, a national data management and security company.

Foreword

Fortinet was founded in a small Silicon Valley garage in November 2000. Today it is a publically traded company (NASDAQ:FTNT) and has more than 1600 employees worldwide. There are many factors that help contribute to the rapid growth of the company; one of the most important factors is that here at Fortinet we are able to continuously react to the demands of the rapidly changing security landscape in which we live creating products and services that truly meet customers' needs and address their concerns. The motivation for founding this company was the realization that content based attacks would become the prevalent tool used by computer hackers and criminals and none of the existing network security vendors would be able to effectively address this fundamental issue effectively.

Our first generation of the FortiGate product family, the Antivirus Firewall, was able to detect and remove content-based attacks. Eradicating these viruses and worms from the network remains a cornerstone of today's FortiGate functionality. With the outbreak of network based worms such as CodeRed, Nimbda, Slammer, this new FortiGate appliance quickly proved to be an essential tool for many a network security administrator protecting universities, finance houses, industrial complexes, retail chains and enterprise customers from these devastating infections.

The landscape changed, and newer threats such as spam, phishing, pharming, browser vulnerability attacks and botnets came one after the other, these unceasing attacks created a nightmare scenario for the network security administrator. Fortunately, the network security industry responded to this change. Various techniques and solutions have now been developed to protect the network from these attacks. Fortinet remains a trusted name in the network security industry. Along the way, Fortinet has evolved its flagship FortiGate product family into a very effective tool to defend against all these attacks and more. The benefit of the FortiGate product is not limited to the individual techniques that are used to protect against each attack a key change was that for the first time an effective multilayer defense was combined in to a single appliance. As more and more of our customers adopted this approach the wider security industry began to take notice. The term Unified Threat Management (UTM) was coined by IDC in 2004 and a new category of network security devices was born.

Today UTM is a multi-billion dollar market and is growing rapidly. Fortinet is proud to be the market leader of this security segment. I believe the real drive for UTM's market growth is the growth in computer network technology. Today, building a computer network is no longer rocket science, no longer a place where only a few highly trained technologists can be successful. There are more and more homes, small offices, retail chain stores that are wired with dozens of devices such as printers, file servers, cash registers, stock control systems and workstations. People from all walks of life, such as doctors, lawyers, grocers, restaurateurs, taught themselves how to build up a network with a book, or some cursory Internet research. Following step-by-step instructions on web sites or stepping through online videos. While professional network security administrators are working on new challenges, creating the super fast networks (100Gbps and beyond) to feed the data centers of tomorrow; or building distributed, high availability virtual networks using load-balanced solutions and VPN technology.

This is why I feel excited about the UTM Security with Fortinet. This book illustrates the UTM concepts in a very clear manner; it provides real-life and immediately relevant examples on how to build a secured network for various types of usage, such as schools, banks, and retail shops. The book shows how the challenges faced by these different types of network can be solved and successful solutions built in easy to follow steps. It has something for both an amateur network administrator, as well as for a seasoned network professional who is willing to learn from his peers.

I've known most of the contributing authors for many years. When they talked to me about their work on this book, it immediately struck a chord with me. The combination of their experience, knowledge and passion make them the dream team to write about this topic. Most of them have had many years of real-life hands-on experience in building secured networks using our FortiGate product within many verticals for some of the most demanding customers in the world. They also share this knowledge running both internal and external master classes.

No matter what business you are in, if you are thinking about building or maintaining a secure network, you can benefit from the concepts and techniques used in UTM Security with Fortinet. Remember, you'll enjoy your network investment much more if it is secured from all those hackers and bad guys out there.

Security is our business.

Michael Xie

CTO, Founder, Fortinet, Inc.

Preface

Reliable documentation resources are always needed when dealing with recent and innovative technologies and paradigms. This book was born as a response to the need of having a document that could cover Fortinet's flagship product FortiGate in detail.

The story goes like this: around 2008 two of the book authors (Martin Hoz and Ken Tam) were together at a company meeting, both being already Fortinet employees. A conversation popped up about the need of a technical book on Fortinet products. To that point there was no general book about Fortinet on the market and several times we had people asking for something that could cover the technology and the UTM paradigm in general. Couple years had past, the book idea went dormant mainly due to busy work schedule, but it remained as part of the to-do list for both of them. As of 2010, Fortinet CTO Michael Xie had brought up the idea of having a published book on Fortinet key selling product FortiGate during one of the FIAT meetings, where Martin was a member of, along with other two co-authors of this book. FIAT is the Fortinet Innovation Advisory Team, a group of individuals that assist the Fortinet CTO Office on defining Research and Development direction. Since Ken Tam already had some experience with co-authoring a book with a previous employer, a company that was also founded by the brothers Michael & Ken Xie, this idea was brought to Ken's attention thus began the book development. The initial thought was the book would need at least a third author, and so Ken McAlpine, a technical genius that had to deal with some of the most complex FortiGate deployments, joined the project which officially started on Summer 2011. What nobody had planned was the amount of workload that takes to write a book combining activities with a main day job that was so demanding due the growth rates Fortinet had been experiencing since its IPO. The team asked Bruce Matsugu to help on reviewing and commenting the manuscripts but then the point was reached where it was necessary to also add him as an author, along with another Fortinet veteran, Rick Basile, who also expressed interest on the project.

At the time we all committed to the project, we all saw the great opportunity we had because of the need of a good Technical FortiGate / FortiOS book. At that point, Fortinet had sold more than 400,000 devices but besides the official documentation, there was not any other written reference. We have to say Fortinet Documentation team is quite good, and the quality of what is produced by them is probably one of the highest in the security industry. But such documentation does not incorporate experience, and we wanted to add value to what it was published already there. With this at sight, the discussion to define the Table of Contents was focused on how could we add value on top of the Fortinet official documentation. We didn't want just to write about the same topics with a different set of words. We truly wanted to add something that someone working with a FortiGate would find valuable as a reference, and something that could give a piece of advice on how to deal with the whole new paradigm that UTM represents in general. UTM allows users to greatly benefit on increased security, enhanced service levels and efficiency, but we believe until this book, there was no text that gave Fortinet the right amount of importance, illustrating that with real-life examples, but above all illustrating UTM is not only for the Small and Medium Business but also for Large Enterprises, Carriers and Service Providers that want to realize the benefits it offers.

This is what we have today here. In every chapter, the author tried to put not only the technical concepts and knowledge that will allow the reader to have a good understanding of the topic at hand, but also tips and tricks, so the reader can benefit of the experience the authors have had through the years of exposure to the technology in different situations, which is usually not covered by the formal Fortinet documentation. We also wanted to add some information on the book about how to handle FortiGate-related projects and how to use this technology to solve issues on some key verticals where Fortinet approach has a clear differentiator over any other technology out there. So, the book you have in your hands is technical in nature, but also gives you some ammo to be better prepared when in the middle of a project related to Fortinet technologies.

Finally, since this book comes after Fortinet sponsored "Unified Threat Management for Dummies", a free book that can be found on Fortinet's website, an effort was made to not overlap with the content offered there.

Intended Audience

Plainly put, this book is for you if you have to work with a FortiGate as an implementer, administrator or support engineer. Whether you work for a Fortinet Partner or a Fortinet User, this book will help you understand a bit more on the UTM world in general and the FortiWorld in Particular.

To make better use of this book, it is assumed that you have at least experience on networking, TCP/IP and some security technology experience. There is an effort to explain in detail as much as possible about the different technologies mentioned, but the book is not to be used as your first one on the topic of Security. Fortinet experience also is not assumed, so it's ok if you are using this book as your first FortiGate text, but you will greatly benefit of having either a Hardware version of the FortiGate or a FortiGate-VM, so you can practice the concepts and commands explained.

Organization of this book

The book is organized in three big parts:

Section I - General Introduction

The chapters in this section are meant to explain what you are going to commonly find as concepts in the UTM world. It introduces you to the story and some debate on UTM versus other security philosophies but also gives you an introduction on how the FortiGate hardware was designed and how the FortiOS operating system was architected, so you can gain a better understanding on those.

* Chapter 1 - Introduction to UTM (Unified Threat Management) - Gives you some history on the UTM term, the philosophy behind it, the advantages versus other approaches such as Best-of-Breed or Next Generation Firewall, as well as how Fortinet differentiates itself versus other UTM proponents.

* Chapter 2 - FortiGate Hardware Overview - Discusses how the FortiGate is designed from the hardware standpoint, and above all it explains the core of the magic behind it: how the different Forti-ASICs (Application Specific Integrated Circuits) work and interoperate to achieve great performance results while keeping the flexibility to accommodate for new features

* Chapter 3 - FortiOS Introduction - Explains the FortiOS architecture, and how Fortinet excelled where others took a long time to catch-up: how the different parts interoperate, how to manage it and how to ensure you are doing things the right way

Section II - UTM Technologies Explained

The chapters in this section discuss how the different technologies offered by the FortiGate/FortiOS duo work, how can they solve problems in your organization, as well as tips and tricks on how to size, deploy and troubleshoot them. There are also a couple of chapters devoted to FortiManager and FortiAnalyzer, the central management solutions to handle configuration management, monitoring, logging and reporting when a large amount of FortiGate devices is deployed.

* Chapter 4 - Connectivity and Networking Technologies - gives you the foundation to understand how networking technologies such as 802.3AD, 802.1q or dynamic routing protocols are used in a FortiGate, how they are configured and some advice on design and troubleshooting

* Chapter 5 - Base Network Security - covers the common security concepts that you can find on most security products. FortiOS Firewall, Identity Based Authentication, Two-factor authentication with FortiToken, IPSec and SSL VPN, Traffic Shaping and SSL Inspection and Offloading are all technologies discussed here.

* Chapter 6 - Application Security - deals with the basic content inspection of the FortiGate. By basic, we mean the content inspection technologies that have been for a long time as part of the FortiGate offer, and thus have a lot of maturity and are commonly used. We work with IPS, Web Content Filter, Application Control and Network Antivirus, but also some time is devoted to review the FortiGuard Network: the cloud-based security updates that feed the FortiOS components to remain updated for greater accuracy and effectiveness.

* Chapter 7 - Extended UTM Functionality - reviews functions that some analysts take as part of a Next Generation Firewall, some as part of eXtended Threat Management (XTM) but all offered as part of the FortiGate featureset. DLP, Endpoint Control, WAN Optimization, Web Caching and Vulnerability Management are reviewed.

* Chapter 8 - Analyzing your Security information with FortiAnalyzer - reviews how to use FortiAnalyzer to get more information out of the logs generated by the FortiGate, how to then discover patterns, get reports, and find relevant information. Information that could be useful in informing executive staff of the benefits of the FortiGate or giving detailed information to a forensics examiner.

* Chapter 9 - Managing your Security configurations with FortiManager - reviews how to use FortiManager to keep a centralized configuration source for your FortiGate deployment

Section III - Implementing a Security (UTM) Project

Here we come to the section that probably makes a difference in this book versus any other.

In chapters 10 to 12 we deal with the project around UTM: how the project should be conceived, what to do to ensure a bigger degree of success when communicating to the non-technical side of the organization, and how to apply all the knowledge gotten in the book when solving problems in an Educational organization, on a Distributed Enterprise and a Financial Organization. Common needs, solutions to them, and typical advice that will help to extract more value out of your FortiGate ecosystem on these specific scenarios. Authors hope that by taking a look on these examples, you can deduct more easily how to approach other scenarios not discussed there.

* Chapter 10 - Designing a Security Solution - deals with some project management issues you might find in your path while working on the installation, configuration or maintenance of a FortiGate solution.

* Chapter 11 - Security on Distributed Enterprises and Retail - details solutions and best practices to the challenges posed by the fact of having a security policy that needs to be enforced in multiple places while it has to be centrally managed to keep compliancy and central enforcement at the same time.

* Chapter 12 - Security on Financial Institutions - Mentions how FortiGates can address typical issues found on financial institutions, where things like low latency or detailed transactional logging are important.

Appendices

Complementing the rest of the book we have some appendices that touch important parts of the FortiGate ecosystem:

* Appendix A - Troubleshooting the project - deals with some suggestions that might impact your work when project is late or budget seems won't be enough.

* Appendix B - Troubleshooting technically - shows you what commands to run when something goes wrong, but above all gives you some ideas on how to approach the issue to find a quicker solution.

* Appendix C - Country codes - Lists the country codes available used for chapter 5. Breakdown of the contributing authors work:

- Ken Tam wrote chapters 2, 5, 11 and Appendix C
- Ken McAlpine wrote chapters 3, 4, 8
- Martin Hoz wrote chapters 1, 6, 10 and Appendix A
- Bruce Matsugu wrote chapter 7 and Appendix B
- Rick Basile wrote chapters 9 and 12
- Josh More technical editor & contributor for all chapters.

General Introduction

Introduction to UTM (Unified Threat Management)

INFORMATION IN THIS CHAPTER:

- Basic Network Security Concepts
  - Computer and Network Security Concepts and Principles
  - Computer and Network Security Technology Concepts
  - Network Security Technology Concepts
  - Commonly used Computer and Network Security Terms
- Unified Threat Management (UTM) Foundations
  - The World before UTM
  - The History of the Unified Threat Management (UTM) Concept
  - UTM vs other Security Architectures
    - UTM vs Best-of-Breed
    - UTM vs Next-Generation Firewalls
    - UTM vs XTM
- Solving Problems with UTM
  - Better Security
    - Consistent Security Policy
    - Protecting against Blended Threats
    - Implementing Clean Pipes
  - More Efficient Security
    - Higher Performance
  - Enhancing Operational Response Times (Meeting and Enhancing SLAs)
  - Getting a Better Support Experience
    - Increasing Network Availability
  - Cost Effectiveness
    - Easier Investment Justification
    - Licensing Simplicity
    - Lowering Operational Costs
- Current UTM Market Landscape
  - UTM a-lá Fortinet
    - Reliable Performance

- Selective Functionality
- Homegrown Technology
- In-house Security Intelligence Unit: FortiGuard Labs
- Single Licensing Cost
- Included Virtualization
- Other Vendors

INTRODUCTION

Internet and Security

It's 4 PM and you realize you forgot today was your wedding anniversary. Some years ago, this would have meant problems back home with your spouse. Today, you can simply go to a site like Google or Bing and search for something to cover for you missing the occasion: look for recommendations for a good restaurant, book seats for a nice show, send flowers, or even buy a gift you can pick up on your way back home. You don't even need to be at your office: you can do it from a cybercafe, a public kiosk, or conveniently from your smartphone while on the train or bus (never while driving your car!). This wouldn't have been possible back in 1999.

Today we do many activities with computers connected to the Internet, and as new users and generations are brought online, many rely on the fact that computers and the Internet are there and will be there. We go to school, shop, do home banking, chat, and interact on social networks everyday and people think the services must be there. They take that for granted. However, the amount of effort, technology, and skill required to keep all the services on the Internet will be a surprise to many. The worst thing is that many of these newcomers begin their online life with little or no education on how to be a good Internet Citizen (or *netizen*), and that also means they don't know the minimum measures they need to take to turn their online experience into a safe and pleasant one.

Among all the disciplines that are used to keep the Internet up and running, Internet Security is of special relevance: the day we began trading over the Internet and money began to be represented by bits flowing on wires, it became attractive to professional attackers and criminals to be online as well. Internet Security is what helps to keep the infrastructure up and running, and it is also the discipline that can keep the Internet as a safe place for us, our kids, and future generations.

Basic Network Security Concepts

Several network security books, especially the ones that are dedicated to firewalls, begin explaining technical concepts right at the first chapter. This book can't be an exception. I would say the material below could be too basic if you are already a computer security master and you are looking to get directly into how Fortinet does things differently with FortiGates. If this is the case, it might be a good idea to jump to *Chapter 2 FortiGate hardware platform* overview of this book. Otherwise, if you are relatively new to computer security or would like to review a different point of view on how to approach the computer and network security challenge, then please keep reading: the author of this chapter enjoyed writing it and tried his best to explain everything in a fun way, whenever possible:-)

But before getting deeper into security, I would like to mention some areas where you might need to get some expertise if you want to really be a network security star. If you are already seasoned, probably this would be a good reminder on areas you should keep updated. If you are new, then this could provide a nice road map to go deeper on the field after you finish reading this book:

- *Programming:* Know at least one third-generation programming language, one fourth-generation programming language, and one script language. The differentiation is made because each one will help you understand different concepts and will teach you to think in different ways when you analyze problems. Some options are C language, SQL, and Korn-shell scripting, but it could also be C#, Ruby or Python, and Oracle SQL. If you want to become a pen-tester, you probably might want to learn a bit of assembler as well. Please note I mentioned "know," which is different from "master." This is important because you probably don't want to become a professional programmer, but you will need to be fluent enough in the language so you can understand code you read (exploit code or source code of Web Applications, for example), modify that to suit your needs or automate tasks.
- *Operating System:* An operating system is the program that is loaded on a device, responsible for hardware and programs management. Every device from a cell phone, to a game console, to a tablet, to a personal computer, has an operating system. You need to understand how it works: memory management; I/O Management in general; processor, disk, and other hardware resources allocation; networking interface management, process management. As with programming, probably you don't need to know how to tune kernel parameters or how to tune the server to achieve maximum performance. However, you need to understand how the operating system works, so you can identify and troubleshoot issues faster, as well as to understand how to secure an environment more effectively. It might not be a must, but experience on at least one of the following operating systems is highly desirable and will always come handy: Microsoft Windows (any version) or a Un*x flavor such as HP-UX, IBM AIX, FreeBSD, OpenBSD, or GNU/Linux.
- *Networking:* One of the reasons why organizations need security is because of the open nature of the Internet, designed to provide robust connectivity using a range of open protocols to solve problems by collaboration. Almost no computer works alone these days. It's quite important to know as much as you can about networking. One example of the networking importance: in the experience of this book authors, at least eighty percent (80%) of the issues typically faced with network security devices (especially devices with a firewall

component like the FortiGate) are related to network issues more than to product issues. Due to this, it's important knowing how switching technologies work, how ARP handles conversions between MAC addresses and IP addresses, STP and how it builds "paths" on a switching topology, 802.3AD and interface bindings, 802.1x and authentication, TCP and its connection states, and how static routing and dynamic routing with RIP, OSPF, and BGP work. All those are important, and I would dare to say, almost critical. And on networking, you will need a bit more than just "understanding": real-world experience on configuring switches, routers, and other network devices will save your neck more than one time while configuring network security devices.

Yes, as you can see, being a security professional requires a lot of knowledge on the technical side, but it is rewarding in the sense that you always get to look at the bigger picture and then, by analysis, cover all the parts to ensure everything works smoothly and securely.

Computer and Network Security Concepts and Principles

Having covered all that we will now review security concepts. We won't explain all the details about them here, since they will be better illustrated in the chapters to come, where all the concepts, technologies, and features mentioned are put to practical use. We will offer here definitions in such a way that have meaning through our book and may not necessarily be the same ones commonly used by other vendors.

Computer and Network Security is a complex discipline. In order to walk towards becoming a versed person, you need to truly understand how many things work: from programming, to hardware architectures, to networks, and even psychology. Going through the details of each field necessary to consider yourself a security professional is way beyond the scope of a single book, let alone a section within a book chapter. If you are interested on knowing more about this field, there are many references out there. In general the Common Body of Knowledge (CBK)[1] proposed by organizations like (ISC)2 or ISACA, and certifications like Certified Information Systems Security Professional (CISSP),[2] Certified Information Systems Auditor (CISA),[3] or Certified Information Security Manager (CISM)[4] have good reputation in the industry, and are considered to cover a minimum set of knowledge that put you right on the track to become a security professional.

This book also assumes that you already have some experience with operating systems, computers, and networks. We won't explain here basic concepts and

---

[1]Common Body of Knowledge by (ISC)2—https://www.isc2.org/cbk/default.aspx.
[2]CISSP Home page—https://www.isc2.org/cissp/default.aspx.
[3]CISA Home page—http://www.isaca.org/Certification/CISA-Certified-Information-Systems-Auditor/Pages/default.aspx.
[4]http://www.isaca.org/Certification/CISM-Certified-Information-Security-Manager/What-is-CISM/Pages/default.aspx.

technologies like netmasks, network segment, switch, or router. We will try to cover any of these concepts in the context of an explanation, if they are affected somehow to achieve a result.

Admittedly, even though effort has been done to keep this book fun, the paragraphs below could be a bit boring if you have already worked with computer security for a while. Having said all the above, we will be discussing here some general security concepts in an attempt to standardize the meaning of these concepts and principles in the context of this book.

Probably the first concepts we need to review are those that are related directly to the Computer, Network, or Information Security fields first. It's very hard to say these days if we should be talking about "Internet Security," "Data Security," "Information Security," "Computer Security," or "Network Security" when we are discussing subjects around this matter. However, for the purpose of this book we will use the terms "Network Security," "Computer Security," and "Information Security" more than the others, since this book discusses a technology whose focus is to be a mechanism to protect computer networks and digital information assets.

The order the concepts are presented is relevant because we try to go from the basic to the most complete and specific ones.

- *Security:* Perhaps this must be the very first term we need to define. For the effects of this book, Security will refer to a set of disciplines, processes, and mechanisms oriented to protect assets and add certainty to the behavior of such protected assets, so you can have confidence that your operations and processes will be deterministic. This is, you can predict the results by knowing the actions taken over an asset. It is commonly accepted that Security is an ongoing process, it consists of Processes, People and Mechanisms (Technology), and it should be integrated to business processes. In that regard, the concept of Security is similar to the concept of Quality.
- *Information Security or Network Security:* It is the concept of security applied to Computer Networks. In other words, it is the set of disciplines, processes, and mechanisms oriented to protect computer network assets, such as PCs, Servers, routers, Mobile devices. This includes the intangible parts that keep these physical components operating, such as programs, operating systems, configuration tables, databases, and data. The protection should be against threats and vulnerabilities, such as unauthorized access or modification, disruption, destruction, or disclosure.
- *Confidentiality:* A security property of information; it mandates that information should be known by the authorized entities the information is intended for. So, if a letter or e-mail should be only known by the e-mail's author and recipient, ensuring confidentiality means nobody else should be able to read such letter.
- *Integrity:* A security property of information; data should always accurately model the represented objects or reality, and should not be modified in such a

way that is unknown by the data owners and custodians. So, if an electronic spreadsheet has a set of values that represent money on a bank account or the inventory of a warehouse, the values recorded in the spreadsheet should accurately represent the money in the bank account and the objects held in the warehouse if you decide to count each coin or bill in the bank deposit or every item in the warehouse.

- *Availability:* A security property of information; data and systems should be ready to be used when authorized users need them. If I need to print a letter from my computer, availability should be the PC, the network, and printer are working ok for me: there is electricity to power the devices, the network is properly configured to carry data from my PC to the printer, and the printer has enough ink and paper. Availability should not be confused with High Availability, which is a related but different concept.
- *Authentication:* It is the process of identifying entity and making such entity prove it is who claimed it is. One of the most common and simple requests of authentication occurs when someone knocks at your door. Before opening the door you may ask "who is this?" Then entity behind your door claims an identity ("It's Joe"), and you are able to verify that by the voice you hear. If you are unsure, you will ask for a second round of authentication: "Joe who?" "Joe the plumber" might ring a bell this time to confirm the identity of the person you were waiting for.
- *Authorization:* It is the process of granting an entity access to resources or assets. So, Joe the plumber is home to help you fix a faucet in the bathroom. You will authorize him to be in the bathroom and perhaps allow him use your wrench or screwdriver. But he won't be on the master bedroom nor allow him use your computer.
- *Auditing:* It is the process of ensuring every activity leave a trace in such a way that someone can reconstruct what actually happened: What was done, by whom, when, and how should be recorded.
- *Threat:* An inherent danger over an object that, due to its nature, will remain constant through the life of that object. For example, a car could be stolen independently if it's well guarded and taken care of, brand new or old. You can increase or decrease the possibility of a danger to happen, but the danger will always be there.
- *Vulnerability:* A specific weakness of an object due to a certain condition of the environment where an object or asset is placed, stored, used, or needed. For example, a car can be stolen more easily if the locks are not placed, it has no alarm, windows are open, or you are parking in a bad neighborhood. All these are vulnerabilities that increase the likelihood of realizing the threat of the car being stolen.
- *Attack:* An action, intentional or incidental, successful or not, performed against an object or an asset, that exploits a given vulnerability in an attempt to realize a threat. An attack is when a thief actually tries to open the car's door using an open window to attempt to take the car away.

Computer and Network Security Technology Concepts

Once we have outlined several important network security concepts, there are several Computer and Network Security Technologies that are worth to define for three reasons: (1) we will be talking about them through the book since Fortinet products, especially FortiGate, the subject of this book, implement these technologies. (2) Since nowadays many vendors offer overlapping features often using different terms to mean the same thing and sometimes working against each other, it is good to set an expectation and define what can be expected out of a feature, how it does complement others, and what you shouldn't expect out of it (and why). (3) All these are typically network border protection technologies, meaning they are typically deployed between the internal (protected) network and the outside network, where we would expect the attackers to sit. We will review this in a little more detailed manner; it is not the case anymore, but in the meanwhile we will study the notion that the technologies below are border technologies to make the explanation a bit easier to understand.

Again, the order in which the concepts appear is meaningful in the sense of going from the fundamental to the most specific.

Firewall: Probably the firewall is the most basic, necessary, and deployed network security technology. The basic firewall responsibility is to allow or deny communications entering or leaving a host, a network, or a group of networks. Communications are allowed or denied based on a set of policies or rules. These rules can be something simple (similar to Access-Control Lists on a switch or router) or something real complex like specifying times, users, network segments, and a lot of more complete connection-context information. The firewall is also responsible for checking some communications integrity, ensuring received connections adhere to network standards, and are not performing suspicious or obviously dangerous activity. The most common Firewall technology used worldwide is Stateful Inspection, which allows tracking connections by state, recorded on a session table. Firewalls are regularly also tasked with authentication duties, since it is a way to track the origin of a connection. Since the firewall is regularly the foundation for other inspections, it is mandatory that the firewall be as fast as possible, preferably wire speed across a broad range of packet sizes because otherwise the firewall would become a network bottleneck raising the temptation to remove it.

VPN (Virtual Private Network): Allows communications between two or more given points to be private. Such points could be a host, or a network, or a group of networks. The communications are secured using one of a range of available encryption algorithms that obscure the information being transferred and also ensure it is not modified while in transit, providing privacy. The most common VPN technologies are IPSec VPN and SSL VPN. Since the VPN could carry most of the traffic, if the information exchange occurs only between specific parties, it is of high importance to have the best possible performance, and wire speed is preferred. A VPN is a perfect addition to a firewall device, since that way the firewall can inspect the traffic going inside the VPN, and the VPN can protect the traffic allowed by the firewall.

Traffic Shaping: It is a module that allows regulation of the way network resources are assigned to entities requesting for them. Once bandwidth-intensive applications such as file sharing or Peer-to-Peer (p2p) applications had to compete with bandwidth-sensitive or latency-sensitive applications such as Voice over IP (VOIP) in a network that had limits, it became necessary to have a way to regulate how bandwidth was assigned. Traffic Shaping mechanisms do this by delaying packets corresponding to applications, users, or IP addresses labeled with low priority under a security environment, traffic found "clean" by security mechanisms could be prioritized according to business rules, which could help to maintain service availability for critical services. For this reason, it makes sense to deploy a Traffic Shaper on the same physical device running a firewall.

IPS (Intrusion Protection System): Also known as Intrusion Prevention System (IPS) or Intrusion Detection and Protection (IDP) System. An IPS should not be confused with an IDS (Intrusion Detection System), since an IDS can only detect but not react, while an IPS can both detect and react to an event. A network-based IPS performs deep analysis on the traffic so network-based attacks can be detected. These attacks are often performed trying to take advantage of a known vulnerability on the operating system or application software. One typical IPS technique is recognizing patterns of known bad behavior, so when an attack is being performed it can be caught by simply identifying its "signature" (the known pattern). This is known as *misuse detection.* Another common technique involves learning or pre-configuring what the common behavior is and then detecting deviations from it, like deviations from a protocol standard or known environment statistics. This is known as *anomaly detection.* Robust Intrusion Protection Systems use both technologies to increase effectiveness. An IPS is a great companion to a firewall because then allowed traffic can be further inspected, and attacks (intentional or accidental) generated by trusted sources can be detected and stopped. Sometimes an IPS is used to measure firewall effectiveness, by measuring attacks before and after the firewall blocks traffic.

Application Control: Is a module that allows or permits traffic from a given application, regardless of the method (port, protocol, application) used to transfer traffic. Since applications increasingly run their traffic over the same network ports to ensure successful behavior of the application, it is important to have a mechanism that could effectively identify and control these applications. Application Control is a mechanism that was created to resolve this need, and it does in a very similar way to how IPS recognizes attacks: by creating "signatures" of the traffic generated by applications and then recognizing these signatures in the traffic flow. Application Control is a great companion to a firewall because it allows deeper enforcement, by extending to the Application level the criteria for allowing or denying traffic.

AntiSpam: Is a module that detects and removes unwanted e-mail (spam) messages. It regularly applies verification mechanisms to determine if the e-mail is spam. Some of these mechanisms are quite simple, like rejecting messages from a list of known offenders. Other mechanisms involve comparing the message received against a database of known bad messages and a centralized list of known mail servers that are used to send SPAM. Since typically SPAM messages come from outside the organization, it makes sense to scan mail traffic on the network border right after it has been authorized by the firewall. It should be noted that preventing spam from being sent becomes important when considered in the wider context of your Internet reputation.

Antivirus: Viruses are probably one of the first problems computer users had once computers became personal. Due to this, viruses are probably the most diverse form of computer problem related to security, and it follows that Antivirus is probably the most widely known protection mechanism. Basically an Antivirus is responsible for detecting, removing, and reporting on malicious code. Malicious code (malware) can be self-replicating code that attaches itself to valid programs (virus), programs that appear to be a valid application so users execute them (trojan horses), or other type of malware like spyware or adware. While Antivirus is typically deployed at host level, a network Antivirus, a mechanism that detects and stops malicious code at the point where content is leaving or entering a network, becomes important when it is necessary to ensure all the computers in such a network have the same level of protection, probably additional to the protection already deployed directly on the hosts. Antivirus is a great companion to a firewall system because it can look for malicious code in very specific ways over traffic that has been allowed, but to do it in an effective way it needs to have high performance so it doesn't become a bottleneck: this is why it needs to be accelerated and this is why it is more effective if it only looks on traffic that has been approved by faster security mechanism, such as a firewall.

DLP (Data Leak Prevention, Data Leak Protection): It is a module that helps tracking specific content entering or leaving the network. It is able to look for very specific contents such as words inside an e-mail message or phrases within a PDF file. As regulation increased, DLP became more important since it can distinguish between attacks and legitimate behavior. One typical example is when an employee sends from his corporate e-mail classified information such as customer lists, checking balances, or credit card numbers: it is not a virus and it is certainly not a network attack. However, if this is done by someone from the technical department and not the accounting department, you might have reasons to be concerned. This is the generic problem DLP is trying to solve: detect bad human behavior that does not necessarily break a rule from the technical standpoint. Due to this, DLP is a great addition to firewall, IPS, and Antivirus devices, because it can complement them by detecting things those mechanisms simply can't due to their nature.

Web Content Filter (URL Filter): Is a mechanism that allows or blocks Web Traffic, based on the type of content. The most common method is classifying the web pages into categories. These generic categories are usually broad such as Games, Finance and Banking, File Sharing, Storage or Phishing websites. It makes sense to deploy a Web Content Filter on the same device where a firewall is running, because the Web Content Filter can greatly enhance the web-surfing policy's granularity. As well, it makes a lot of sense to deploy a network Antivirus and an IPS in conjunction to the web content filter, because this way it is ensured users get clean traffic.

Cache: A cache system stores locally a copy of some content that might be requested by more than one user, so the next time a user requests for it, the content doesn't have to be downloaded from the remote site, saving time and bandwidth.

The most common type of cache is the Web Cache, but it is not the only one. It makes sense to deploy a cache system along with other security technologies like a firewall, an Antivirus, and a web content filter, because it is more efficient to store locally content that was previously authorized and inspected.

WAN Optimization: It is a series of mechanisms that help to reduce the amount of traffic that passes through WAN links, avoiding the usage of expensive bandwidth. Cache is one of the mechanisms used for WAN Optimization, but not the only one, since other techniques are also used, such as TCP optimization, deduplication, and byte-caching. While this is not necessarily a security technology per se, WAN optimization techniques can help to reduce the possibility of certain attacks, such as Denial of Service. The real benefit of this technology, however, is the possibility of reducing WAN link costs, as well as, for certain applications such as Web applications, gives the user the "illusion" that the application is faster than it really is. Since WAN Optimization technologies assume the traffic they will be processing is valid, it is a good idea to ensure that such traffic is, in effect, clean. After all, it makes no sense to "optimize" and make sure an attack or a virus spreading gets better network response times. Due to this, and the fact that WAN Optimization is typically deployed at network border, it makes sense to integrate WAN Optimization to a network security device, especially one that can have Firewall, Network Antivirus, and IPS.

SSL Inspection: Provides the ability to inspect content encrypted by applications using the Secure Socket Layer cryptographic technique. The technique used to perform this function requires the communication to flow through the solution in which it would perform a man-in-the-middle takeover of the SSL session. With this ability, various security inspection features can be applied to the content such as DLP, Web page content filtering, and Antivirus. Example of SSL-based encrypted applications is web browsing session using HTTPS, file transfers with FTPS, and encrypted email with SMTPS, POP3S, and IMAPS.

If you conduct research and take it to some time back, say the mid-1990s early 2000s, you would probably discover that many of the technologies mentioned could be found independent. At some point in time, these technologies began to merge into each other, and since that point an understanding of the security value and efficiencies achieved means that today it is not unusual to find them all integrated into a single device and a single product. But these are not the only ones as we will see now…

All the above-described mechanisms work on different layers of the ISO model, shown in Figure 1.1.

Network Security Technology Concepts

The network security technologies mentioned in the section above are commonly deployed at the network's border, mainly for historical reasons: the first approach to network security was to define an internal network, which was considered protected and secure; and an evil external network where all the bad guys were waiting for an opportunity to attack. This way of thinking meant the natural place to put a device to secure

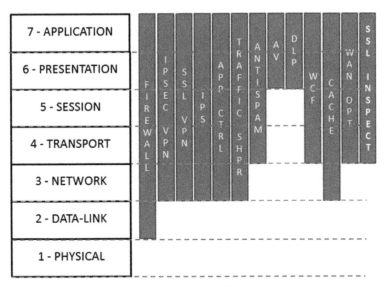

FIGURE 1.1 OSI Model and Security Features Positioning

the defended network was at the network border or frontier. But nowadays this is not the case: increases in the performance of devices doing security inspection that allow protecting higher and higher bandwidths, the need to apply segmentation on networks that increase in complexity with the addition of new services, the struggle in defining where the network starts, and ends, more users and additional applications, the difficulty of identifying good vs evil in all scenarios, added to the always-evolving nature of threats that increase potential attack vectors, have forced the deployment of network-border technologies within what was traditionally considered an internal network.

In addition to the technologies discussed previously, there are some others that adapt better to Internal Security deployments:

- *Wireless Controller:* Wireless networks are popular. The ability to centrally manage the wireless infrastructure for services like roaming for users, avoid signal conflicts or interference are available, becomes more and more important for organizations. Managing all these wireless network functions is the job of a Wireless controller. The importance of having security on such environments increases as well, wireless networks would become an easy target because they don't require potential attackers to be on the same physical premises where the network is: as long as there is signal coverage that's enough. Due to all the above reasons, putting a Wireless controller on a device that also does security makes sense: the secure wireless controller ensures the wireless network is available with good quality services, while allowed traffic is cleaned to ensure no attack, misuse, or abuse is conducted purposely or inadvertently.

- *Network Access Control (NAC) or Network Access Protection (NAP):* This is a concept that was popular some years ago, but was abandoned due to complexities of implementation. However, the concepts remain and are still valid today in a lot of ways. The idea of NAC or NAP is to evaluate each device joining the network to decide whether or not it is compliant with a set of requirements, such as operating system version, running an Antivirus and host firewall enabled. Once the device is evaluated, compliant devices would be allowed and non-compliant devices would be quarantined. It is a good idea to have on a local security device a way to ensure that internal devices meet a minimum security posture, so this internal segment does not represent a problem for the rest of the network, and moreover, in the case that a security problem is detected, the threat can be contained.
- *Vulnerability Management (VM) or Vulnerability Assessment System (VAS):* This technology identifies known vulnerabilities in a set of devices, so they can be solved. Typically, these systems have a list of known vulnerabilities along with their impact ratings (how dangerous the problem is), which is updated periodically. VAS systems are typically used to analyze internal networks and it makes sense to have one along your internal network security device.

As you probably identified at some point while reading, we are mentioning the above technologies because all of them are implemented on Fortinet's FortiGate systems. Once again, we will study all these technologies in detail in the following chapters of this book, but it is important to have an overall view on them from an introductory perspective. Let's now review other concepts that are also commonly used by network and computer security professionals.

Commonly used Computer and Network Security Terms

There are other common concepts which, even though are not necessarily related to products or technologies, are important thorough this book because they will be used frequently. The list does not contain the more obvious concepts and it is by no means exhaustive, but it contains concepts that are more likely to be misunderstood, and we believe it is possible that you will be using them on conversations with customers, suppliers, and colleagues. This is why we believe it is important to standardize them, at least for the scope of this book. To review the list of terms, please refer the glossary section of this book.

UNIFIED THREAT MANAGEMENT (UTM) FOUNDATIONS
The World before UTM

If you think about the last years of past century (1998, 1999), the technology world was different from today in several ways: the Internet had had a steady growth as a new economic platform. Many companies were growing and a lot of people were getting rich just by stating they were doing something new over the Internet. In this Internet-growing economy, there were many things that fostered the growth of IT departments, including budget: the hope that getting market share and a strong brand name would eventually lure customers to buy, made many people invest in companies working somehow with the Internet.

When the year 2000 arrived, many had a lot of hopes, expectations, and fears. But after all, the world didn't end as some religious leaders preached. Also, computers and computer networks didn't really collapse due to the famous Y2K bug as many thought could happen. But then, the so-called Dot-com bubble burst did happen. This event, associated with the fact that the problem happened to companies that somehow were trying to make money with the Internet, lessened people's faith in IT. We won't go deeper here on how or why after a period of fast growth, things went bad. Many books cover that phenomenon from several perspectives. What is important, though, is that things simply never were the same. People and organizations became more cautious and conservative when investing money for online initiatives, and budgets for IT departments began shrinking.

At the same time, another interesting thing happened: Internet Security became more and more important. There were many reasons for this, among them:

- Organizations realized that, despite the dot-com bubble burst, it actually made sense to go online to develop new products and services, reach new customers and markets, or simply keep a stronger relationship with existing ones.
- It was important for companies to build and keep a good reputation. E-Commerce, especially business-to-consumer, was still on its early days, and it was important to give potential customers the confidence they needed to buy.
- The fact that a larger number of people went online, and that the majority of these people were simply not technically educated, was an opportunity for criminals to take advantage of it.

Due to the above, the Internet Security market began to mature. Companies that sold Firewalls, Intrusion Detection Systems, which were considered by many the minimum security technologies that an organization should have, became more specialized—adding robustness, speed, and ease-of-use to their technologies but didn't think of adding new features or protections to them. So, soon other technologies were created to offer protection for aspects of the online corporate. Then solutions like AntiSpam gateways, to "clean" the e-mail flow, were born. We also saw AntiSpyware tools being offered to get rid of programs that informed attackers of our online activities or private information. It seemed at this point that every time attackers found a new way to break things, a new Anti-X technology needed to be developed. Very few thought on the need of developing more protections into existing technologies and combining several of them.

The History of the Unified Threat Management (UTM) Concept

Unified Threat Management is a concept that was used for the first time in a report[5] issued by IDC in 2004 and called "Worldwide Threat Management Security Appliances 2004–2008 Forecast and 2003 Vendor Shares: The Rise of the Unified Threat Management Security Appliance." This report, signed by Charles J. Kolodgy as author, mentioned that UTM was a new category of security appliances and that it was necessary to have at least the functionality of a firewall, a network intrusion prevention system, and a gateway Antivirus to be part of this security appliance category. However, even though the term was first mentioned at this point, the reality is that it actually described what it was already being done by some companies, especially Fortinet, which was already shipping a firewall that included IPS and Antivirus, alongside other functionality.

Fortinet was founded in 2000[6] by Ken and Michael Xie, two brothers that already had a history of innovation: Ken Xie was the previous Founder, President, and CEO of NetScreen, a firm that under his leadership pioneered the ASIC-accelerated security concept, overcoming the performance issues that software-based solutions had shown at the time. Michael Xie is a former Vice President of Engineering for ServGate and Software Director and Architect for NetScreen,[7] and also holder of several US patents[8] in the fields of Network and Computer Security. The original name of the company when it was founded on November 2000 was "Appligation, Inc," which was later changed to "ApSecure" on December of the same year. Later, the name was once again changed (this time for good) to Fortinet,[9] which comes from the combination of two words that symbolize what the company delivers with its technologies: Fortified Networks. The name was decided in an internal company competition.

From its inception, Fortinet had a vision to deliver-enhanced performance and drive consolidation into the Content Security market, developing products and services to provide broad, integrated, and high-performance protection against dynamic security threats, while simplifying the IT security infrastructure. So, the idea was to provide high-performance technology that was secure, consolidated, and simple to deploy and manage. While this concept was relatively easy to understand and a powerful business and technology proposition, it was contrary to what everybody else had been preaching at the time, and this posed some difficulties since the concept was not truly understood initially. Let's see why.

---

[5]IDC 2004 report—http://www.fortinet.com/doc/whitepaper/IDCUTMReport.pdf.
[6]About Fortinet—http://www.fortinet.com/aboutus/aboutus.html.
[7]Fortinet Executive Management—http://www.fortinet.com/aboutus/management.html.
[8]Search query on the US Patent Office Database for the terms "Michael Xie Fortinet"—http://patft.
uspto.gov/netacgi/nph-Parser?Sect1=PTO2&Sect2=HITOFF&u=%2Fnetahtml%2FPTO%2Fsearch-adv.htm&r=0&p=1&f=S&l=50&Query=Fortinet+AND+Michael+AND+Xie&d=PTXT.
[9]Sec Filing—Registration statement S-1 form http://investor.fortinet.com/secfiling.cfm?filingID=1193125-09-169817.

Around year 2000 when Fortinet was born, the biggest organizations with presence on the Internet already had some security solutions deployed: firewalls, IPSec VPNs, Intrusion Detection Systems, Web Content Filters. In the next few years, the same organizations were pushed to purchase new security elements such as SSL VPNs, AntiSpam, Intrusion Prevention Systems, AntiSpyware, and a whole set of additional solutions. While the complexity and cost of this approach increased, this was the accepted *status quo*: since most (if not all) organizations had all these technologies and operated that way, it was accepted that other approaches might be risky. Since the UTM concept was born at a time where people already had purchased some network security components that were working apparently fine, it faced fierce opposition. We say "apparently fine" since despite having all these security components, organizations didn't stop having issues: security technology wasn't making things easier at all and wasn't responding to the challenge of bringing more security to the environments where it was deployed.

UTM vs Other Security Architectures

All the above derived into some "religious wars" between competing "technology fiefdoms" on whether this was the right way to do security or not. The old security architecture where point products were doing specific things had already a large installed base, a large amount of support, and also a long history of working fine (or almost fine). An innovative security architecture was not going to be accepted that easily by people that had a vested interest in keeping the *status quo*, but at the end the clear advantages of the UTM Security Architecture were winning increasing market share.

We will look now at some of those "religious or philosophical wars" that might be of interest to the reader of this book, to understand as well why UTM is still a great technology and business proposition.

UTM vs Best-of-Breed

Consolidation and convergence in Security was not well seen initially, despite consolidation being present in other areas of computing. The PC is probably the most convergent device, since it can be used as a telephone, radio, DVD player, or typewriter, just to give some examples. You have multifunction printers that also can be used for fax, copier, and scanner functions. Today there are convergent networks that carry voice, data, and multimedia at the same time, which wasn't possible in 1990. This convergence took time, but it happened and brought value to our lives. In 2002, when Fortinet launched its first product,[10] convergence in security was clearly not the main trend for existing vendors, who had specific products to solve specific problems and post dot-com bubble revenue stream to protect.

---

[10]About Fortinet, Quick Facts—http://www.fortinet.com/aboutus/aboutus.html.

So, when Fortinet showed up in the arena, with a device called a "Secure Content Processing Gateway"[11] it was clearly disruptive. The device could do at the same time, Firewall, IPsec VPN, Traffic Shaping (all these "standard" functionality in regular firewalls at the time); but also could deliver Antivirus and Worm protection for e-mail and Web traffic, as well as Intrusion Detection and Web Content Filtering (which were traditionally delivered by separate devices). Several questions were raised: Can this device deliver the same quality as a separate device? What happens with performance? How does it compare with what I have today? Is it ok to "put all our eggs into one basket"?

Many opponents to this idea were companies that had been marketing point solutions: Web Filters, Antivirus, Intrusion Protection systems. But without a doubt, the ones that opposed the most were traditional Firewall companies that saw a direct threat here. The firewall had not changed much for about a decade. So, when a new company announced a lot more functionality on the same firewall device, they were immediately perceived as a direct threat.

The questions mentioned above are still asked today, when these lines are being written, nine years after the launch of the "Secure Content Processing Gateway." But now after more than 100,000 customers and 750,000 devices shipped, it is possible to say that:

- Fortinet can deliver all the security functionalities with no real performance compromise, given proper sizing.
- Fortinet can deliver functionalities with the same quality of equivalent separate devices. Moreover, vendors of such separate functionalities are beginning to integrate additional capabilities, further validating Fortinet's approach.
- Fortinet's FortiGuard Labs are capable of providing comprehensive intelligence that feeds Fortinet's customers updated and state-of-the-art security.
- Fortinet has a strong value proposition in both the technical and the business side, and simplifies keeping a highly available environment, so it makes sense to switch from a "best-of-breed" environment to a UTM environment with Fortinet.

Not only that, but UTM can solve issues that a point-product architecture introduces. The section "Solving problems with UTM" below further clarifies this.

UTM vs Next-Generation Firewalls

Another concept brought recently as a contender of the UTM concept, is the "Next-Generation Firewall" (NGFW) one, which is mainly pushed by the research and consultancy firm Gartner, Inc. To understand the roots of this "conflict," we need to take a look at history.

---

[11]Web Archive Showing Fortinet's website in 2002—http://web.archive.org/web/20020610163438/http://www.fortinet.com/faq.html.

One of the first times the term "Next-Generation Firewall" was mentioned by Gartner was on a document published in 2004 titled "Next-Generation Firewalls Will Include Intrusion-Prevention,"[12] which highlighted the importance of coupling technologies like Deep-Packet Inspection, IPS, and in general application-inspection capabilities to a firewall, with the objective of stopping threats like worms and viruses and extending protection to the application layer, so packets with malicious payloads could be stopped. So far, the UTM definition seemed to fit what a Next-Generation Firewall was according to Gartner, but since UTM was a concept brought up initially by IDC, a Gartner competitor, it is unsurprising that Gartner wouldn't adopt the term UTM and probably that's why it came with the Next-Generation Firewall (NGFW) concept instead. Later in the "Magic Quadrant for Enterprise Network Firewalls"[13] document published in November 2008 Gartner mentioned "Next-Generation Firewalls" would be security devices that include Enterprise-grade firewall plus Integrated Deep-packet inspection or IPS, Application Identification, and integrated extra firewall intelligence such as Web Content Filter, while allowing interoperability with third-party rule management technologies such as Algosec or Tufin. The UTM definition still applied and thus far Gartner didn't expressly indicate that UTM was not a Next-Generation firewall.

Later, in October 2009, Gartner published a note called "Defining the Next-Generation Firewall"[14] which mentioned the criteria for choosing a NGFW were standard firewall capabilities, this time including VPN, integrated IPS functions with tight interoperability between the IPS and firewall components, application awareness, and extra-firewall intelligence. If you take a look at this, the UTM definition still applied as it didn't change that much from what Gartner said before. Let's remember that from IDC's definition of UTM, proposed in 2004, a UTM was a security device containing a firewall, an IPS, and an Antivirus as minimum. Fortinet was by then considered an UTM even though it was also offering Application awareness (Application Control) and Web Content Filtering, but it could also be considered a Next-Generation Firewall by Gartner's definition at this point. Then, it happened: in this same document, Gartner expressly mentioned a UTM was NOT a NGFW, and since Fortinet had been by the time the recognized leader on UTM, automatically Fortinet wasn't a NGFW. This of course, caused a lot of confusion.

Having said all that, it seems that according to the concepts proposed by Gartner that Fortinet's flagship product FortiGate could be considered a NGFW by definition, but of course, Gartner is the only one that can officially put or remove a product, brand, or technology on their reports. On the other side, the Next-Generation Firewall definition seems to be close enough to the UTM definition to

---

[12]http://www.gartner.com/resources/121500/121554/nextgeneration_firewalls_wil_121554.pdf—Next-Generation Firewalls will include Intrusion Prevention—Research Document by Gartner.
[13]http://www.gartner.com/DisplayDocument?id=810612—Magic Quadrant for Enterprise Network Firewalls—Research Note by Gartner.
[14]http://www.gartner.com/DisplayDocument?doc_cd=171540—Defining the Next-Generation Firewall—Research Note by Gartner.

wonder if NGFW is actually Gartner's name for UTM, which came around the same time, but got bigger traction at the time. So, what is the answer? The authors of this book all consider the FortiGate to be NGFW and a UTM solution. Bottom line, the feature and functionality offered on the FortiGate meets both NGFW and UTM definitions.

UTM vs XTM

The very same inventor of the UTM term, Charles Kolodgy, in an article for SC Magazine,[15] also coined the term XTM, which is eXtensible Threat Management. According to Mr. Kolodgy, UTM devices will evolve to XTM platforms, which will add even more features, such as reputation-based protections, logging, NAC, Vulnerability Management, and Network Bandwidth Management. All of those are features that are already being delivered by FortiGate, so it is natural to think that if the concept of XTM becomes as strong as the concept of UTM, Fortinet should be considered as part of the brands delivering on this concept.

SOLVING PROBLEMS WITH UTM

Before UTM, the security world seemed to be evolving in such a way that every new threat needed a new protection technology, which led to scenarios that were more complex, more expensive, less effective to manage, and more difficult to operate. When the trend seemed to be clear, and it was when Fortinet's founders decided it was time to do something about it. The success that UTM has enjoyed since then and the way UTM has evolved seem to confirm that it is a very valid proposition in the security world. Let's see why.

Unified Threat Management (UTM) exists because it solves three critical needs: The need of better security, the need of more efficient security (both from the engineering and the cost standpoints), and the need of having cost effectiveness.

Better Security

The first problem UTM can solve really well is the need to increase security. Let's review a couple of examples on how this is achieved.

Consistent Security Policy

Let's face it: even though many organizations have a security policy, a lot of them keep it only in a book but it is actually never enforced with technology. One of the reasons is that it is complex to deploy and configure technology. Why? Let's think on a very basic directive: To avoid infection risks, an organization wants to block Windows executable files entering the network. To make it simple, let's say this means

---

[15]http://www.scmagazineus.com/utms-key-cog-in-infrastructure/article/109728/-.

files with extensions .exe and .com. Where do you do it? Probably your firewall, IPS, network Antivirus, AntiSpam, and web content filter have all the capability to block files; but if you do it on only one probably you will miss some coverage, while if you do it in all of them it becomes harder to maintain, because probably the configuration steps are different. Configuring files blocking on all the devices will also add latency, which will reduce performance which you never want. Now let's assume you have different Firewall, IPS, or Network Antivirus brands in different locations or even different segments in the same network. It becomes increasingly complex quickly.

Now, let's think you have only one place to configure file blocking. And once you configure it there it will be done for Web, Mail, IM, or other traffic that traverses the network. Not only that, but also it will be done only once instead of three times, doing security in an efficient way. Even if you have to apply this policy in several network segments and several branches, it would still be the same policy.

UTM enables consistent security policy deployments.

Protecting against Blended Threats

Today, very few threats consist of a single attack vector: the majority of them consist of at least two or three. Take into consideration for example recent worms that can replicate themselves by exploiting a known vulnerability on a Web server or a web browser or possibly on a file server, while also spreading by e-mail messages sent to your whole address book, as well as messages on social networks like facebook or twitter and finally on messages via Instant Message applications like Microsoft MSN Messenger. Yes, these things exist and they are called *Blended Threats.*

From what we've seen in the recent years, blended threats will only get worse: Conficker, Zeus, and Stuxnet garnered media attention not long ago and proved the blended threat is one of the only ways to make an attack succeed, and the reason for this is because detecting a blended threat is difficult if an organization is using the old security architecture where point products were used to solve point problems, have little or no cooperation between them. Stuxnet is especially interesting because it was a blended threat that could spread in different ways but focused on SCADA environments (infrastructure and grid systems) as a target, making it potentially dangerous even to human lives.

Today, point products that don't cooperate among themselves to share information will be defeated by a blended threat: while the Antivirus could stop some malicious code coming from an IP address and the IPS can detect and stop a network port scan coming from the same source, there is no easy way to correlate the information from these two technologies today: you can use a Security Event Management product, but that is complex and expensive; or you can build scripts to do that for you, but this is difficult and not everybody has the skill to do it. Imagine if you try to integrate your AntiSpam system to your Network Data Leak Prevention while you try to get some Application Control enforced. Even if you had the money and the time to hire the skill (and assuming you could find someone willing to do it), the result likely wouldn't be what you are looking for. Think about it: today, even with all the security products deployed, there are still security issues happening, and this is not because the products being used are not good, but because those products don't help to get an overall big picture and there is no communication among them because they were not built to protect against attacks that would use more than a single attack vector.

Imagine if you had an easy way to tell if a certain IP address is launching viruses and port scans, and also visiting some web pages classified as potentially dangerous or hacker sites while using network control applications via HTTP (port TCP/80). You can accomplish this with a FortiGate, which is why Fortinet can help protect an infrastructure against blended threats. Of course having a UTM is not the Holy Grail of security, but it makes a lot easier to implement an effective defense.

UTM makes protection against blended threats possible.

Implementing Clean Pipes

Today in many countries it is common to use a device to filter water before drinking it. The people using them regularly ask which one purifies water better, and then installs it. Some people ask about how they work, but few understand why carbon filter and reverse osmosis do a good job at purifying water. And certainly very few people care if their own filter is catching mold, bacteria, fungi, or something else: all they care about is the fact that the water they drink is clean so they don't get sick.

The Clean Pipes concept work the same way: the idea is that you have today all kinds of bad traffic in the outside network, which is typically the Internet. Bad traffic could be virus, spam, attacks, bad applications, phishing pages, and a long etcetera list. The reality is that an average user doesn't care if an attack is a worm, a browser exploit, or ransomware: she just wants to have clean traffic she can trust.

UTM can offer the necessary characteristics for effective Clean Pipes:

a. *Security comprehensiveness*: To make the approach effective it is necessary to ensure as many security components as possible are enabled, pretty much like having several water filtering methods together in the same filter. You will need at least Firewall, VPN, IPS, Antivirus, AntiSpam, Web Content Filter, Application Control and DLP features to some degree, in order to have good security to offer.

b. *Optimized analysis*: It is also necessary to establish a pre-arranged order: it would probably not be that good if you filter mold after doing water disinfection with chlorine. Likewise, it would probably not be good to analyze for viruses traffic that will be stopped by a firewall policy.

c. *Holistic solution*: You need to do it everywhere where you have Internet access or it would not be effective protection, and to do that it is necessary to have a cost-effective solution. So, if you have a distributed organization with two or three big locations but tens or thousands of branches, think on the money, time, and resources required to deploy on each branch a network Antivirus, an IPS, an AntiSpam box, a URL Filtering box, and a Firewall/VPN device, not to mention a WAN Optimization device and Vulnerability scanner. But if you only need to place one device, things become increasingly simple quickly.

d. *Scalability*: You might need to add more users to your network tomorrow. Or more sites. Regardless if you need vertical scalability (add more processing power to cover for an increasing amount of users, bandwidth, or services) or horizontal scalability (adding more places where you need inspection), the architecture you choose needs to grow with your needs.

UTM can cover for all of the above, enabling a Clean Pipe service.

More Efficient Security

Overall efficiency is something that is almost never considered when an organization is looking for security technology. The reason for saying this, is that security projects generally focus on performance, cost, and operation of a specific device, not for the organization as a whole. Why is that? Because it is the way things have being done for a good part of the last decade. However, if you look deeper, there are efficiencies that could be achieved by using a consolidated security approach like that which UTM proposes. Let's see.

Higher Performance

Network bandwidth is growing all the time, and it's getting cheaper too. Applications on the other hand, demand more and more bandwidth to work well and many tolerate little or no latency. Due to this, any device that is placed in the network needs to have as much performance as possible so it doesn't become a bottleneck.

The above is especially relevant when border security technologies are used for internal network segmentation: typically the speed required on an Internet connection is significantly lower than the speed on internal networks. It is highly important to achieve as much performance as possible on a security solution, since otherwise users would reject it: whenever a user notices additional delay or additional steps to do something, complaints arise.

One of the ways UTM helps to increase performance is by achieving inspection efficiencies. Think for example on an e-mail message leaving a corporate network: it will probably traverse at least an AntiSpam, a Network Antivirus, an IPS, and a Firewall system. That's four times the same connection is analyzed and three times the connection is inspected at Application Level (by the AntiSpam, Antivirus, and IPS systems). Now imagine a user downloading a file from a web server. Probably a Web Content Filter, a Web Cache, a Network Antivirus, an IPS, and a Firewall will analyze that connection, and that would be at least four devices (or five if you throw a DLP there) doing inspection at application level, which is known to cause delays and be resource intensive.

Now, this is considering that the functions are complementary, but quite often the functions overlap and that increases inefficiency. Think about our "blocking executable files" example mentioned above: several devices trying to block devices is definitely a waste of resources and degrades performance.

What if instead of opening a connection three or four times, it is opened only once? This would be more efficient and even if the time to analyze the same takes the same time, just by the savings on time and resources when opening and closing a connection, it makes worth the effort. Now, think if some of the analysis could be done in parallel. Assuming enough resources are available (i.e. the resources sizing was done properly) that would be even faster, right?

High performance is something UTM architectures can achieve.

Enhancing Operational Response Times (Meeting and Enhancing SLAs)

Increasing dependency on Internet services increases customer demand. People trust the e-mail they send will reach its destination not immediately but in the next minute (have you held a conversation over the phone while sending an e-mail with a document you were going to discuss?). People trust web services to do online payments and students use Google to reduce the amount of time to find information for their school homework. If something fails, everybody wants quick answers and even better quick solutions, right?

Now, imagine an organization that has the old network security architecture. Let's say it consists of three different systems: a Firewall, an IPS, and Web Content Filter to make it simple (organizations today would probably have a Network Antivirus, a Web Cache Proxy, a Network Data Link Prevention system as additional boxes). Now let's imagine a couple of users call the helpdesk with a simple request: "I don't have Internet access because I can't browse Google or Yahoo!" Did this ever happen to you? The engineers working on the network or the security department (or both, depending on how the organization structures the IT function) would need to troubleshoot three different systems. Assuming they are trained and proficient on these technologies, it will still take them time to review the logs on three different boxes, probably with different format, to determine where the problem is. Of course, none of this takes infrastructure troubleshooting (switches, routers, servers, and client systems) into account.

Now let's imagine a modern infrastructure. Let's say there is a device in charge of performing the Firewall, IPS, and Web Content Filter functions. When a user calls with a connectivity problem, there is one console that needs to be reviewed, with a consistent log format and everything in a single place. And if changes need to be applied, there is one device that needs to be reconfigured. Instead of taking N minutes times 3 to review the issue, it takes only N minutes, reducing the response time by 66% (even if it were 50%, that's already something) which enables better service to users.

UTM makes possible to enhance operational response times.

Getting a better Support Experience

If you ever had an environment where three (or more) different products from different vendors were interoperating and you had an issue where it wasn't clear exactly on which device the problem was, probably you were already a victim of the finger-pointing syndrome.

Imagine there is a web connection being blocked and there is interoperation between your firewall, your web content filter, your Antivirus, your Application Control, and your IPS and there is suspicion the connection is being blocked due to a product malfunction because the configuration was working fine and the problem happened out of nowhere. Or think of an e-mail environment where the outgoing messages are analyzed by AntiSpam, Antivirus, Data Leak Prevention, IPS, and Firewall systems and a user simply reports her e-mails are not reaching their destination after several tries and the configuration seems to be ok so everything points to a product malfunction again.

In any of the both cases above, which product's problem is it? Who is going to help you to troubleshoot it? Who should fix it? And all this is without taking into account the troubleshooting you need to do on the underlying infrastructure which has to be reviewed anyway: switches, routers, servers, and also the PCs, laptops, tablets, or whatever client system is being used. Wouldn't you like to reduce the amount of potential failure points and also the potential finger-pointing to where the problem might sit?

With UTM, since the functions reside on a single box, you have only one support you need to call, and there is only one entity that should give you the answer.

UTM helps you reduce the stress of technical support finger-pointing.

Increasing Network Availability

One of the recurrent arguments against UTM is the fact that it might decrease availability because it's like "putting all your eggs in one basket." The assumption here is that if one component fails, the whole solution will be down. But let's take a closer look.

Once again, let's say an organization has a firewall, an IPS, and a Web Content Filter system. The general assumption would be that having a separate product architecture is better from the availability standpoint because if one of them goes down, the others are still active. This is only partially true because if the device fails there will be a network outage. If there is a planned maintenance window, there will still be some service outage. Now, let's assume each device fails or is brought down for maintenance reasons twice per year. Remember since they are separate devices they probably won't fail or be maintained at the same time, but at different times. That is a total of six times the network service is disrupted within a year.

Now, think you have a UTM device that covers for the Firewall, IPS, and Web Content Filter functions. Let's assume this device fails three times instead of just once or twice: that's still 50% less outages that you had with three separate products. Even if the UTM had four or five failures, that would still be more availability than with point products (Figure 1.2).

All of the above is, of course, not considering redundancy. Remember UTM solutions can be placed in High Availability like any other network security solution. Assuming that you have the same three point products mentioned above, you would need to deploy six boxes if you want to have high availability, and probably you would need more if you wanted availability of five nines. This has not only a bigger cost but also more complexity and additional maintenance overload, which is also increased because you might need some additional infrastructure elements like load

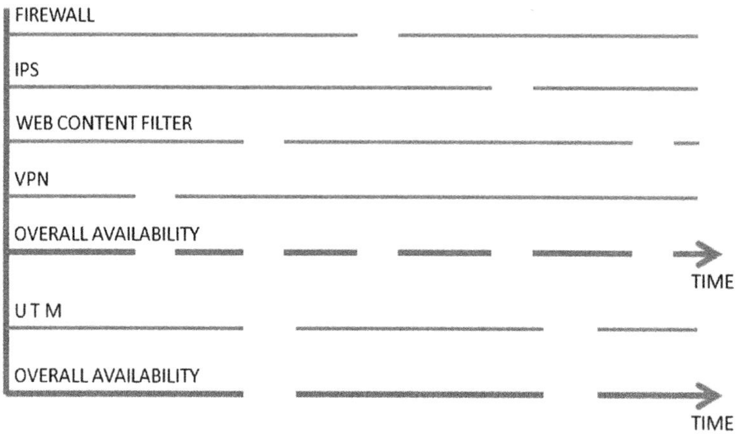

FIREWALL

IPS

WEB CONTENT FILTER

VPN

OVERALL AVAILABILITY

TIME

U T M

OVERALL AVAILABILITY

TIME

FIGURE 1.2 Best-of-Breed vs UTM Availability Comparison

balancers or probably additional switches also, which if configured in a fully meshed topology (where all network elements are connected to each other) could become unnecessarily complex. With UTM you would need only two boxes to cover for your availability needs, which would make a simpler, cleaner, and more elegant network design while helping increase network service time. If you need redundancy, in most of the cases an additional box (for a total of three) will cover your needs.

UTM helps you increase your network availability while keeping your security.

Cost Effectiveness

There is a famous Spanish saying that goes "nobody is in fight with his wallet," meaning that most of the people try to save some money whenever you can. And certainly in crisis times, when IT budgets are not abundant as they used to be, and we need to squeeze as much value as we can out of the money we have, it is always wise.

Granted, probably you dear reader, being this is a (mainly) technical book, have little or nothing to do with the way budgets are planned and exercised in your organization. But probably you have to convince someone on why the technology product you are recommending is the best one for your organization, or you have to help your boss to support the purchase decision of a UTM product. This is where this information becomes handy. Now if you are a reader that has the direct budget authority then this information would only help further justify your UTM purchasing decision.

Easier Investment Justification

So, your organization needs a firewall. Someone needs to ask for money to buy it. You could probably mention "network security" as one of the reasons to buy it and it will be approved. Then an IPS is required and the same person might go for the second time to request money to enhance "network security." By the time money is requested to purchase an AntiSpam, DLP, Network Antivirus, or some other network security component, someone might wonder why so much money is being invested in network security components: "Didn't we just buy something to do network security? Why do we need to keep buying more of these things?" Explaining the difference between network-based attacks and application-level attacks, or between HTTP and SMTP, to somebody on the business side might not be an easy conversation, and today it isn't a necessary conversation.

This is a completely different situation than when you only need to ask for money for Network security once. Maybe twice if you are doing High Availability (HA) in two phases, but that's pretty much of it. It would be an easier conversation to have with people that don't understand bits and bytes (and probably don't need to and thus don't care).

Oh! and finally imagine how easier the security purchase justification would be if you can print a single executive report showing how many security policy violations the firewall stopped, how many attacks the IPS prevented, how many viruses the Network Antivirus prevented, and how many threats the other security systems protected against. Imagine that: a single two page executive report that you can hand to someone showing the value behind your security system. UTM can definitely do this.

Licensing Simplicity

When security functions are in different boxes, quite often they are licensed in different ways: Firewalls by performance or protected IP addresses. Antivirus by performance or users. AntiSpam by mail boxes. Web Content Filters by the amount of seats. This makes purchasing security solutions complex and expensive: what happens if you need High Availability? What happens with the renewal price if the amount of users or services increases next year? Exactly how much money do you need to schedule on your next year budget to pay for the renewal?

When all the security functions are on the same box it makes sense to have a single licensing model. Most UTM vendors follow this simplified model. Some of them charge separately for different security functions, but it is still simpler than dealing with different vendors and different licensing schemes.

By the way, licensing is never an issue with Fortinet since all features become included as part of the price when a Bundle is purchased, and there is no limit in the amount of users, connections, or other criteria. So, as long as the UTM solution is sized appropriately to meet today's and tomorrow's potential growth environment, what to use or what not to use is only a matter of technical configuration, not licensing.

Lowering Operational Costs

Probably you have heard the concept of Total Cost of Ownership (TCO). But you may not have been too convinced by their arguments on why they had an advantage from the Cost Perspective in the long term.

TCO is what you pay for a product not only for the purchasing price but adding the amount of money you need to spend on its maintenance. Talking about network devices you have electricity and cooling from the physical perspective, the maintenance cost you pay to be entitled to support and upgrades, and also the money you invest on people so they can keep the products running well, which means the salary and training an organization pays to its engineers or the fees paid to a consultant. All this adds up.

From simple math, it will be cheaper to power and cool one box instead of three (or more). It will be easier to pay for support and upgrades for a single box than to pay for three. And of course, it is cheaper to pay for an engineer to attend the training for a single technology than to pay for three courses. Moreover, with a single technology an engineer will have the chance to become an expert, which would allow him to solve issues more quickly and be proficient in tuning the configuration to extract the maximum value out of a product, avoiding the common case of having a product that does 100 things but you only use 20 of them. Besides, with IT budgets shrinking it is quite common to find IT engineers tasked with several responsibilities, and having less technologies to be worried about will create time for them to focus on other equally important things.

UTM allows an organization to lower operational costs.

CURRENT UTM MARKET LANDSCAPE

The Unified Threat Management (UTM) market has matured in the last couple of years, with new players in the arena trying to capture market and with Fortinet continuously leading with innovation.

Below you will find some notes about how different UTM implementations work and how Fortinet's offer compares against them. We have to place here a disclaimer: the Authors of this book are Fortinet employees at the time these pages are being written, so there is a potential conflict of interest in that regard. However, we are sticking strictly to points that can be verified using public sources, so the reader can confirm everything being mentioned here.

UTM a-lá Fortinet

Fortinet was named UTM market leader for the 25th consecutive quarter by analyst firm IDC[16] in July 2012. This is an important accolade for the company and its flagship product FortiGate because it recognizes Fortinet's continued efforts to keep innovation, service, and strong value proposition. It also shows the market has being

---

[16]http://www.fortinet.com/press_releases/120703.html—Fortinet Named Leader of Worldwide Unified Threat Management Market for 25th Consecutive Quarter by Leading Market Research Firm.

recognizing this for more than five years in a row now, which is a further validation of the previous statement.

Fortinet's UTM implementation is called FortiGate. It is actually the product this book is about. Let's analyze some of the main features that make it unique and valuable when it comes to UTM.

Reliable Performance

Security processing is resource intensive. This is one of the reasons why Fortinet chose to create a security architecture that would use Hardware Acceleration as an integral component.

Application Specific Integrated Circuits (ASICs) make it possible to achieve wire-speed performance in some of the underlying functions like Firewall or VPN. This is important because if the foundation technologies are slow, everything else will be slow. As it will be discussed in Chapters 2 and 3, FortiGate makes use of ASICs both for Network Processing (Layers 1–4 of the OSI model) and Content Processing (Layers 4–7 of the OSI model), which results on hardware accelerations of pretty much all the security functions FortiGate delivers. With Fortinet, the Firewall and the VPN components (essential components that must be present in a network security solution) will never be the bottleneck.

ASICs bring another benefit: predictable performance. Since the processors are 100% dedicated to the task they are doing, they are not "distracted" with something else. Security technologies running over generic CPUs, for example, need to use the main CPUs for everything: from security inspection functions to administrative and resource management functions. So, if an administrative function takes some resources they won't be available to security inspection functions, and since probably the amount of administrative load changes over time, there is no reliable way to get exactly the same resources to the inspection function and thus it will never be exactly the same performance. ASICs in the other end will only be doing one thing: security inspection. So, to give an example with the firewall function: even if the main (generic) CPU of the FortiGate is busy adding users, showing statistics, sending SNMP traps, or browsing logs for the administrator, the Network Processor ASIC (the one used to accelerate firewall functions) will always and only doing firewalling, which will allow to be certain that the performance shown will always be the same regardless of the amount of administrative load in the device.

Selective Functionality

Security policies often discriminate between different user or application categories. This is necessary especially when trying to enforce a well-known security principle: need-to-know. Users or applications will often be allowed to flow in certain network segments, but depending on what their purpose and target audience is, their behavior might change. You already know this: marketing needs access to Social Network sites but they need games blocked there, and also need to put appropriate IPS and AV inspections for the Web traffic passing through. Web Applications need access to backend Databases but only to certain ports, and while protecting this traffic by an IPS that covers threats against the operating system and the database. And the list goes on...

As discussed previously, UTM implies the fact that several functions running separated previously, will now run together. One of the concerns administrators have is that if they deploy a FortiGate, they will need to use all the features, and they will be enabled for all the users. This is not true at all.

FortiGate is flexible enough to allow an administrator to enable or disable a feature in the box at will. The Protection Profile concept, which will be explained with more detail in following chapters, allows a security administrator to define a criteria on where, when, and how a security feature like Antivirus, IPS, Web Content Filter, DLP, or other, will be used. All the features can be enabled or disabled at will, but can also be customized to in some cases the Antivirus only inspects web traffic, while in other segments it inspects Web, FTP, and Mail traffic for example. The IPS can be customized to protect against HTTP browser attacks in one segment, while it protects against GNU/Linux and Windows operating systems and database traffic for another segment. You can be granular to say for example, Antivirus is only applied when a user connects via VPN. Or you can have different Web Content Filtering settings depending on whether the user is on a wired or a wireless network. The range of possibilities is as big as your imagination (or your security policy) allows.

Some other vendors might use an all-or-nothing approach limiting the options you have to enforce your security policy, but certainly not Fortinet.

Homegrown Technology

A common question customers ask is if Fortinet licenses technology, or has an OEM agreement with other security vendors in order to provide some of the security functions like Antivirus or Web Content Filtering. The answer is no.

Fortinet has developed in-house all the security technologies included on its FortiGate product line. This means the IPS, Antivirus, Web Content Filter, Data Leak Prevention, and other technologies were created from the ground-up at Fortinet. All the technologies were created with the premise that they would be part of a device that was doing already other functions, so they were not "glued" at some point, but rather architected as part of an overall solution.

There are several advantages of this approach of not doing OEM agreements. It is more efficient because the components were designed to interoperate among themselves from day zero. Performance, usability, and effectiveness could be affected when you "glue" a technology into an existing architecture that was not designed to interoperate with other components. It also avoids the vendor finger-pointing problem when issues arise and vendor's technical support needs to be engaged. It provides customers the certainty the feature will keep a quality standard, because when an OEM agreement changes over time the quality of the product may change as well. The future of the technology is under control, since the road map depends exclusively on the own needs and requests from the own customers, and there is no potential conflict of interest with other parties which might refuse to create an enhancement if it poses some sort of threat to the business strategy of the OEM vendor. Creating the technology also provides Fortinet with a far more fundamental understanding of the solution provided, and functional requirements of a given technology.

Some vendors choose to do OEM agreements for their UTM offers, but not Fortinet, for the reasons above.

In-house Security Intelligence Unit: FortiGuard Labs

Yes, Fortinet develops all the inspection technologies: The Antivirus and IPS engines, the DLP motor, the firewalling kernel, the web filtering categorization, and AntiSpam defenses. But several of these inspection technologies require constant evolution due the always-changing threatscape: Antivirus needs updates in the engine to adapt to new forms of malware. IPS needs new signatures that could cover for new attacks and engine updates that catch new evasion techniques. Application Control needs signatures for new applications but also constantly refined engines to adapt to applications that change behavior like Skype or proxies like tor or Ultrasurf. And this is only a small amount of examples.

Now, let's recall that some security technologies might overlap in functions and you need to decide the best place to do an inspection or how to use the different functions to complement the inspection and achieve greater effectiveness. The only way to cope with all these challenges is if you have in house enough researchers in enough disciplines, so you really get the big picture and decide what the best approach to attack the problem is.

FortiGuard Labs[17] is the Fortinet's Threat Research and Response unit, responsible for keeping all the security inspections offered by the Fortinet product portfolio efficient, accurate, and up-to-date. It is a team of security professionals distributed worldwide that are continuously researching on new threats and how to fight them. This team is responsible for updates on these areas: Antivirus, Intrusion Prevention System (IPS), Database Security, Web Filtering, AntiSpam, Web Security, Application Control, and Vulnerability Control and Management. This intelligence is later distributed to Fortinet's customers worldwide using a network of content servers called FortiGuard Distribution Network (FDN), which ensures entitled customers are always up-to-date. The reports[18] written by the FortiGuard team also help to determine trends on attacks and protections, and review the current status of the Internet security in general.

Some companies prefer to partner, use OEM agreements or outsource the Security Intelligence function. Fortinet believes it is important to keep the Security Intelligence unit in-house, so higher efficiencies can be achieved and higher security can be delivered, with better quality, more speed, and broader coverage. It also creates

---

[17]http://www.fortiguard.com.
[18]http://www.fortiguard.com/fortiguard_labs/threat_monitor.html—FortiGuard reports.

valuable feedback in to the product development as changes to the threat landscape are detected.

Single Licensing Cost

Another spread myth is that FortiGate is licensed per feature. This is only partially true, because it is one of the ways the product can be purchased, but it's not the only way. Fortinet has a license that is called "Bundle" which includes the hardware being purchased, FortiOS software updates, security updates for all the security features FortiOS has and also entitled to 8×5 support. All FortiGate products are licensed this way because it highly simplifies licensing, reduces costs (bundles are often cheaper than buying licenses for security features a la carte) and also helps to better plan for next year's budget.

With some UTM vendors, it is quite difficult to determine what features need to be purchased, and since sometimes the UTM features come from technologies that are produced by another vendor, the licensing depends on many factors, making it unnecessarily difficult. Fortinet makes it easy including on a single SKU, which means a single price, all features and licenses required to have the boxes running with all features enabled from the licensing perspective without worrying about having to cover additional costs.

Included Virtualization

The entire FortiGate ecosystem includes virtualization. From the FortiGate as the inspection point, to the FortiManager as the management piece and FortiAnalyzer as the reporting and auditing piece; all of them support virtualization.

Fortinet's main products include virtualization since version 1. Not only this, but the majority of FortiGates allow for 10 virtual instances with no license at all. FortiGate virtual instances are called Virtual Domains (VDOMs). High-end models (FortiGates with a four-digit model number) allow for additional virtual instances with the purchase of additional licenses. Also, most of FortiManager and FortiAnalyzer include the capability of virtual instances. Virtual instances in administrative products are called Administrative Domains (ADOMs). Things may go even more interesting because Fortinet offers Virtual Editions (i.e. virtual appliances for VMWare) of these products, with the possibility of having VDOMs and ADOMs within a virtual product. So the flexibility is there and the possibilities open.

NOTE

The FortiCulture

There is something you should know about Fortinet: There is a FortiCulture. All the products in Fortinet begin its name with the "Forti" prefix. So, a new product for network Load Balancing would become FortiBalancer or a product to do Database Security would be FortiDB. These products, by the way, exist. There are also FortiShirts and FortiPens usually delivered as giveaways at conferences and expos. So, everytime you hear or see something with "Forti" as prefix, in red-colored letters, probably that has something to do with Fortinet.

Other security vendors think of virtualization as an additional product line, charge for it, or are just beginning to explore the area. At Fortinet, virtualization is a mature feature and part of the value proposition given to customers since day one.

Other Vendors

In the last couple of years, after noticing it was a Security Architecture worth considering and with several advantages over the old paradigms, several traditional vendors jumped to the UTM bandwagon.

A study called "Worldwide Network Security 2010–2014 Forecast and 2009 Vendor Shares" authored by John Grady and published in November 2010[19] by IDC, analyses the Unified Threat Management (UTM) market in several ways, including the amount of devices shipped, revenue, and price bands. Since IDC was the analyst firm that brought up the UTM concept by the first time, they are a reliable source to determine who the players on the market are. Names that appear on top places depending on how the analysis is done are Fortinet of course, but also SonicWALL, McAfee, Check Point, Cisco, WatchGuard, and Crossbeam Systems.

Gartner on the other hand, finally published a UTM Magic Quadrant[20] authored by John Pescatore and Bob Walder in October 2010, and it is the most recent at the time this text is being written.

If we take Gartner as reference, the vendors mentioned in the "leaders" quadrant are Fortinet, SonicWALL, Check Point, and WatchGuard. Cisco and Juniper appeared in the "challengers" quadrant. McAfee and Crossbeam Systems do not appear.

McAfee discontinued its UTM offer (a product called SnapGear) in March 2010,[21] leaving it without a product in this market. Crossbeam Systems is a hardware vendor that provides a platform for other security vendors like Check Point, Source-Fire, IBM, McAfee, Sophos, or Imperva, so they can run in a single platform. Crossbeam doesn't really have a security product on its own, just hardware and an operating system.

As a disclaimer, we have to say that all the authors of this book work at Fortinet and are biased, but please take our word that we tried to remain objective. To be fair on the analysis, and because technology constantly evolves, we didn't want to be outdated by the time the book goes to press. So, what we are saying here is that if you really want to compare UTM products, you need to develop your own evaluation criteria.

We truly believe security is not a "one-size fits all" type of thing, as everybody has unique needs, environment, challenges, and also preferences. Two companies, even if they are on the same vertical, will never have an identical approach to everything.

---

[19]http://www.idc.com/research/view_lof.jsp?containerId=225381—Worldwide Network Security 2010–2014 Forecast and 2009 Vendor Shares by IDC.
[20]http://www.gartner.com/DisplayDocument?doc_cd=206923—Magic Quadrant for Unified Threat Management.
[21]https://community.mcafee.com/docs/DOC-1263—McAfee SnapGear EOL Announcement.

It needs to be remembered, a solution is "best-of-breed" only if it's best-of-breed for you and it solves your specific problems, and even the best-of-breed can become extinct.

After all, that's why competition exists: to provide a market with choices, so a customer can enjoy the best possible service.

EVOLUTION AND FUTURE OF UTM

Consolidation is a trend that is here to stay due to the powerful value proposition it makes to all kinds and sizes of organization. Consolidation in network security is not the exception. We will see more consolidation with more features on the same box, better integration among them, and more speed to cope with new network speeds.

FortiGate Hardware Overview

2

As information technology matures, the threats against it evolve ever more quickly and increase in complexity. It's not just a firewall component that is needed in today's networking environment but several products are needed to help mitigate potential threats towards and most dominantly from within a company's networks [1]. Network components such as Application aware firewall controls, Intrusion Detection & Prevention, Anti-virus/Anti-spyware, Anti-spam, Web content filtering, and Data Loss

Detection & Prevention systems are just some the needed components to help mitigate potential threats. Fortinet have and continue to reshape the network security world with the concept of combining majority of these key network security components into one cohesive solution for the constant changing security landscape of threats. The solution Fortinet developed created a new category of network component in which market researcher, IDC called a UTM (Unified Threat Management) solution. The FortiGate UTM appliances and system products were formed and are considered Fortinet flagship products line. The purpose of this chapter is to provide insight from the beginning to the current FortiGate products line. In addition, we will cover topics surrounding the FortiGate solution that are not entirely covered by Fortinet own documentation such as its proprietary hardware and software features and sizing the solution. Lastly, we'll provide a high-level overview of Fortinet's remaining products portfolio.

FORTIGATE HARDWARE OVERVIEW
The Fortinet Way

Fortinet product focus has always been an appliance-based solution. So why was the appliance based-solution chosen over a typical software-based approach? We can see from the evolution of routers and firewalls, appliances provided a more focused way of handling these functions with through custom software & hardware features. From a business standpoint, we could see this approach has been a successful model for many companies such as Cisco, Juniper, Netscreen, and Fortinet. Now although you can have hardware customized into an appliance form factor it does not always mean there are also further customized circuitry within an appliance. Most security appliances out there are built from a general purpose computer foundation. The biggest limiting factor in general purpose computers for any security network performance handling capabilities are the circuit board bus and CPU. From a very high level, Figure 2.1 shows a typical general purpose computer designed appliance in which the CPU handles all network communication. Competition with this architecture would suffer performance constraints as additional UTM features are enabled.

Throughout the evolution of firewalls, companies that are more focused on developing software to operate on general purpose machines also leverage special add-on hardware acceleration components installed within the computer ISA, EISA, or PCI slots. Generally these types of cards could provide additional memory expansion, or additional dedicated processors such as ASIC (Application Specific Integrated Circuits) to offload encryption algorithm computations used for IPSec. Although the additional add-on cards do help boost performance they do not provide higher performance when compared to dedicated appliances with specialized custom hardware that are integrated into a close system architecture design.

So how does Fortinet addresses performance concerns on their UTM platforms, especially when additional features are enabled? Besides providing a turn-key

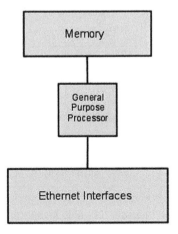

FIGURE 2.1 High-Level CPU only Architecture

THE FORTINET WAY

Tighter integrations with Close system architectures

Fortinet's FortiGate UTM solution is built from the ground up with the idea of a close system architecture providing the ability to tightly integrate proprietary software with custom hardware technology. Case in point, a single packet could flow through multiple inspection engines all in one pass through their solution without having to disassemble and reassemble each time it has do apply Anti-virus/spyware, Web Filtering, IDS, IPS, Application Controls, DLP or Anti-spam. In addition, each security engine component for these inspection technologies is modular with fault-tolerance capabilities. This protects against scenarios where resources are consumed or for some reason an inspection process goes offline (see Chapter 6 for additional information). Many vendors who claim to support a single-pass architecture are limited to an all or nothing approach. So if one module fails, the entire inspection flow fails.

---

solution in which the custom hardware design is combined with proprietary software, Fortinet appliances also include various proprietary custom chipsets known as FPGA (Field Programmable Gate Array) along with custom circuit boards to help boost performance. From a FPGA/ASIC architecture, let's examine the advantage it has with Fortinet solution to performance handling at the application layers of their UTM FortiGate solutions. Using the high-level diagram in Figure 2.2, we'll illustrate the packet flow handling with Fortinet's Content Processor (CP) ASIC. When packets arrive into the Ethernet interfaces, a general purpose processor would direct traffic to the CP ASIC when application layer inspections are required to assist with content inspection. The CP ASIC was specifically developed to help offload content inspection capabilities from the general purpose processor(s) against threat patterns loaded into memory for comparisons. Patterns are also dynamically loaded into memory to

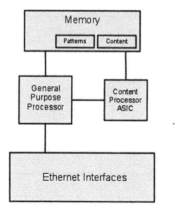

FIGURE 2.2 High-Level Content Processor (CP) ASIC Architecture

be used by the CP ASIC for comparisons. These processors can perform protocol recognition and parsing providing a quicker way of reassembling data streams to be inspected for potential malicious content. CP ASIC are primarily used to offload application controls, Anti-virus/spyware, intrusion detection & prevention, and other application level security functionalities.

In addition, the CP ASIC provides additional cryptography acceleration which will be outlined in detail in the hardware accelerations section. Cryptography accelerations help increase performance for IPSec and SSL capabilities on the product. Besides CP ASIC, Fortinet has also incorporated another content level FPGA/ASIC called a SP (Security Processor). The security processor combines FPGA logic with multi-core/multi-threaded CPU operating at the interface level. This provides additional intrusion detection & prevention, IPv6, and Multicast accelerations. These types of ASIC were originally offered as add-on modules but have since been migrated into newer FortiGate models.

So we understand Fortinet has developed custom hardware to help with application level inspection but how about network level accelerations? Network acceleration hardware was also another area Fortinet has invested in with the development of the NP (Network Processor) ASIC. Given the name of network processor, its purpose is similar to other network processors on the market used for high speed processing of network level flows. These processors are typically designed in-line with the network flow communications path as illustrated in Figure 2.3—High-Level Content Processor (CP) ASIC and Network Processor (NP) ASIC Architecture. With the NP ASIC positioned in-line it helps reduce load on the overall system. In addition, Fortinet's custom NP ASIC design provides multi-gigabit speed when processing in stateful firewall traffic filtering, Network Address Translations (NATs), protocol anomaly detection, and expedited delivery of latency-sensitive traffic at the interface level. These processors can also be used for IPSec VPN traffic offloading capabilities.

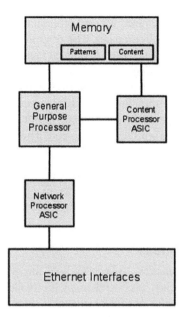

FIGURE 2.3 High-Level Content Processor (CP) ASIC and Network Processor (NP) ASIC Architecture

Evolution of FortiGate

Fortinet first appliance product release was the APSecure 300 which was launched as a network-based Anti-virus, IPSec VPN, and Firewall solution. The first product name was derived from the company's previous name of APSecure which was later changed to Fortinet. With the new company name, Fortinet product naming convention has been pretty straight forward and obvious with using a portion of the company name thereby all of its current product naming convention starts with Forti…! Before any sales were made the first Fortinet appliance was quickly renamed from APSecure 300 to FortiGate 300. Eventually additional models came about such as the FortiGate 50, 100, 200, and 400.

The initial appliance incorporated both a proprietary harden OS, called FortiOS (v2.16 was the first official release) and a proprietary hardware circuit board designed with a general purpose CPU along with a chipset design that provided performance offloading capabilities using a FPGA (Field Programmable ASIC). The original FPGA was from a third party and was used in the first hardware releases of the FortiGate 50, 100, 200, 300, and 400 models. Within a year the third-party FPGA was replaced with the first Fortinet custom developed FPGA called a CP1 (Content Processor v1). The initial CP1 provided offloading accelerations capabilities related to content (Layer 7) inspection and encryption algorithm accelerations. Because the CP1 was based on a programmable ASIC rather than a static ASIC, it was not limited to the functionality designed into the silicon. To assist with the constant change in method of content inspection, Fortinet cleverly designed it's own proprietary language used to reprogram the CP via it's FortiOS firmware updates. The proprietary language use to communicate with the CP ASIC is called CPRL (Compact Pattern Recognition Language).

Throughout the years, Fortinet came out with several iterations of the Content Processor ASIC and eventually additional types of ASIC(s) use to offload additional functionalities. As of this writing, the Content Processor has been through its eighth generation. An ASIC design and development is not an easy task, it's generally involves 1–3 years process from beginning to end. The cost in developing an ASIC is not low. The initial cost of developing a single ASIC technology from scratch requires a multi-million dollar investment and generally takes years in development cycle. That Fortinet has gone through eight cycles of this development effort is a testament to Fortinet's industry leadership.

Current FortiGate Solutions

As with any innovative company, to keep up with the evolution of technology and market demands Fortinet had produced many FortiGate models since their first product in late 2002. Besides hardware changes, there were also accompanying software changes. From a hardware stand point, newer circuit board designs with faster bus speeds and more memory along with newer ASIC(s) that had evolved with additional performance handling features and faster processing power. As of this writing, Fortinet has developed four different types of ASIC each with two or more revision enhancement such as the CP8, NP4, SP2, and SoC ASICs which we'll go into further detail on the following sections. From a software standpoint, additional feature enhancements were added in almost every major and minor release of FortiOS.

The FortiGate operating system, FortiOS, is considered firmware—encompassing not only a proprietary kernel used to operate the entire solution but all the necessary programming for the everyday operation of the solution. FortiOS is stored and loaded from on-board flash during boot-up of the solution. The FortiOS firmware itself is upgradeable via its graphical interface or command line interface over the network or via a USB-connected device. Additional details of the firmware release cycles and upgrade process would be outline in the next chapter.

We're not going to outline every hardware product release and features per release as the majority of this information can be founded at the following web links:

For latest Fortinet product releases:

Fortinet website (www.fortinet.com).

For End of Sale/End of Support products references:

With a valid support login, this information can be founded at https://support.fortinet.com/EndUser/ProductLifeCycle.aspx.

For current and past feature FortiOS releases:

There are two locations this information can

a. At Fortinet main documentation website which is publicly available at: http://docs.fortinet.com.

b. Each FortiOS firmware release includes release notes. Release notes are a good source of information on new features added, upgrade & downgrade processes, FortiGate models the firmware is supported on, bugs that were addressed, and any known bugs pending resolution. Firmware release along with release notes do require a valid support login to access them at: http://support.fortinet.com.

As of this writing, the current FortiGate appliances ranges from the FortiGate 20C at the low end appliance models to the 5000 series modular system chassis solutions. The FortiGate solution is the only solution in the market as of this writing with the most third party certifications. Certification such as ICSA Labs certifications on Gateway Anti-Virus Detection, Network Firewalls, Network IPS, and SSL-TLS VPN. In addition, Virus Bulletin 100, IPv6 Ready Phase 2, NSS UTM, Common Criteria EAL-4+, and FIPS-140-2. It's safe to state that Fortinet pretty much have all market sizes covered with their breath of FortiGate platform offerings.

Virtualized Appliances

To keep up with the industry movement towards virtualization, Fortinet has also ported over the FortiGate UTM into a Virtual Machine offering. Virtualized versions of the FortiGate UTM solution are provided in a Virtual Machine Open Virtualization Format (VM OVF). VM versions are also available with most of Fortinet product portfolio offerings that would be highlighted towards the end of this chapter. Benefits of moving to a virtualized solution are beyond the scope of this book but this information can be founded at any virtualization vendor website such as VMWare website: http://www.vmware.com/virtualization/.

Although virtualization might be a viable option for some of the Fortinet product offerings such as their central management solutions, FortiManager and FortiAnalyzer, there are sacrifices to consider when virtualizing the FortiGate itself. One sacrifice encountered with a VM version of FortiGate would be related to performance. Based on our discussion earlier in this chapter, the FortiGate appliance and system solutions incorporate custom hardware to help accelerate performance and reduce load concerns when compared to other competitors developing their solution off of general purpose computers. The same idea of custom hardware goes out the window with a VM version of the FortiGate.

FORTIGATE CUSTOM HARDWARE ACCELERATIONS OVERVIEW

The purpose of the section is to highlight Fortinet key differentials of their various ASIC technologies used within their FortiGate UTM solution. For complete technical details of Fortinet hardware accelerations please reference their "FortiOS Handbook:

Hardware" documentation located at Fortinet public documentation site [2] under the FortiGate section.

Fortinet custom ASIC development milestones:

2002—Started out with the first development of the Content Processor (CP) ASIC. This was the first phase in hardware performance acceleration for content level scanning along with IPSec VPN cryptography and key exchange acceleration.

2005—Development of the first Network Processor (NP1) ASIC. Originally named the FortiAccelerator (FA2 ASIC), was developed as an interface based processor to provide firewall acceleration and additional IPSec VPN offloading capabilities.

2008—Security Processor (SP) ASIC came about providing additional accelerations for IPS, IPv6, and Multicast.

2009—System on a Chip (SOC) ASIC was an industry first of combining a CPU and two different ASIC technology (CP & NP) into a single chip. This type of ASIC are primarily marketed in the low end units to reduce footprint of the circuit board design thus providing high performance firewall and VPN accelerations in a smaller package.

Features of the Last Four Generations of Content Processor (CP) ASIC Functionalities

CP4 ASIC

- DES/3DES/AES in accordance with FIPS46-3/FIPS81/FIPS197.
- SHA-1 and MD5 HMAC with RFC1321 and FIPS180 compliance.
- HMAC in accordance with RFC2104/2403/2404 and FIPS198 compliance.
- IPSEC protocol processor.
- Random Number generator.
- Public Key Crypto Engine.
- Content processing engine.
- ANSI X9.31 and PKCS#1 certificate support.

CP5 ASIC
Provides the following addition to the previous version:

- High performance IPSEC Engine improvements.
- Random Number generator with ANSI X9.31compliance.
- Public Key Crypto Engine supports high performance IKE and RSA computation used in IPSec and SSL accelerations.
- Script Processor.

CP6 ASIC
Provides the following addition to the previous version:

- Dual CPRL Content Processors.

- SSL/TLS protocol processor for SSL content scanning and SSL acceleration.

CP8 ASIC

Provides the following addition to the previous version:

- Over 10 Gigabits throughput IPS Content Processor for packet content matching with signatures.
- ARC4 in compliance with RC4.
- Public key exponentiation engine with hardware CRT support.
- Primarily checking for RSA key generation.
- Handshake accelerator with automatic key material generation.
- Sub public key engine (PKCE) to support up to 4094 bit operation directly.
- Message authentication module offers high performance cryptographic engine for calculating SHA256/SHA1/MD5 of data up to 4G bytes.
- PCI express Gen 2 four lanes interface.
- Cascade Interface for chip expansion.

Features of the Network Processor (NP) ASIC Functionalities

NP1 ASIC

- 4 Gbps of IP packet forwarding throughput (bi-directional with 2×1 Gigabit interfaces).
- 1 Million+ sessions of searching and dynamic network address translation (DNAT).
- 350Mbps+ of IPSec ESP encryption/decryption processing (3DES+MD5 only).
- Support for session timeout.
- IP/TCP/UDP checksum calculation offloading.

TIP

CLI command to determine which CP version

The command use to determine whether a CP ASIC exist or what version of the CP ASIC is 'get hardware status'. Example output:

```
# get hardware status
Model name: FortiGate-200B
ASIC version: CP6
ASIC SRAM: 64M
CPU: Celeron (Covington)
RAM: 1009 MB
Compact Flash: 3838 MB/dev/sda
Hard disk: not available
USB Flash: not available
Network Card chipset: mvl_sw Ethernet driver1.0 (rev.)
#
```

- Up to 512 Virtual Domain support.
- Traffic shaping capabilities.
- Firewall policy checks.

NP2 ASIC

Provides the following addition to the previous version:

- 8 Gbps of IP packet forwarding throughput (bi-directional with 4×1 Gigabit interfaces or 11 Gbps with 10 Gigabit interface).
- 1 Gbps+ of IPSec ESP encryption/decryption processing (DES, 3DES, AES-128, AES-192, AES-256) and AH (MD5, SHA-1).
- Enhanced Extension Interface (EEI) support between NP2 providing $8\times$ Gigabit interfaces to scale up to 16Gbps IP packet forwarding throughput.
- Jumbo frames support up to 9000 bytes.
- Packet fragmentation & de-fragmentation.
- TCP offloading.
- DSCP support.
- IPS anomaly filtering and logging.
- Increased of up to 4096 Virtual Domain support.

NP4 ASIC

Provides the following addition to the previous version:

- 40 Gbps of IP packet forwarding throughput (bi-directional with 2×10 Gigabit interfaces).

TIP

CLI command to determine which NP version

There no direct way to determine whether a NP ASIC exists or what version of the NP ASIC is but there is a CLI command that can be used in a trial and error fashion to confirm these two questions. This command would be the 'get hardware npu <npu version> list'. Where <npu version> could be np1, np2, or np4—if either entry takes then this provide the answer otherwise there's no NP ASIC in the product.

Example output:

 # get hardware npu np2 list

ID	PORTS
--	-----
0	port13
0	port14
0	port15
0	port16
#	

Note: Command only works on FortiGate appliances and system models with built-in ASIC chipset therefore FortiGate VM versions would not have this CLI option.

- 10 Million+ sessions of searching and dynamic network address translation (DNAT).
- 12 Gbps+ of IPSec ESP encryption/decryption processing (DES, 3DES, AES-128, AES-192, AES-256) and AH (MD5, SHA-1).
- Seamlessly scalable system with switch chips to support any throughput.
- Policy-based & Per-IP Traffic shaping and counter per session/per VLAN.

FortiGate Hardware Accelerations Behaviors

In this section we'll highlight some of the intricacy involved when using the Fortinet ASICs. The following outline is based on the more recent ASIC versions. There are three security acceleration technologies with FortiGate platforms supporting these types of ASIC we will dig into.

Firewall Acceleration using NP ASIC

"Fast path" is a term use to indicate a session or a flow is being processed by the ASIC. The alternative is "slow path" which is traffic handled by the main process unit processor (CPU).

Fast path session offloading requirements:

- NP based ASIC provides firewall accelerations at wire speed for all packet sizes. With a single NP4 ASIC, it can scale up to 40 Gbps (bi-directional) stateful firewall offloading.
- There are a limited number of interfaces on each FortiGate model that are tied to certain NP ASIC versions. Given the NP ASIC is designed to sit in-line with the flow of communication (as noted in Figure 2.3—High-Level Content Processor (CP) ASIC and Network Processor (NP) ASIC Architecture), the NP1 can support up to 2×1 Gbps interfaces and NP2 up to 4×1 Gbps. *For optimal performance, ingress and egress interface should be terminated to the same ASIC.* See Table 2.1 on NP Shared port mappings on various FortiGate models. There also existing FortiGate modules such as the double-width AMC module, ADM-XB2 with an NP2 ASIC that leverages dual 10 Gbps interfaces thus ingress and egress needs to reside within the module in order to achieve the NP2 maximum IP forwarding rate of up to 11 Gbps (bi-directional).
- The NP2 ASIC provides an EEI (Enhanced Extension Interface) to connect two NP2 communication paths together. This pair of NP2 ASIC can be found in limited FortiGate models therefore the ingress and egress interface pairs can be spanned out between the two NP2 supported in-line interfaces. See Figure 2.4 on various FortiGate models with EEI.
- The NP4 ASIC eliminates the EEI requirement to span multiple supported interfaces. Enhancements to the circuit board design combine multiple interfaces for leveraging the NP4 ASIC offloading capabilities.

Table 2.1 FortiGate models and Modules with ASIC types & Interface Mappings

Fortinet Product	Content Processors	Network Processor	NP Shared Ports (inherent that all ports would use CPx ASIC)
FortiGate 20C	SoC	SoC	All ports
FortiGate 30B	N/A	N/A	N/A
FortiGate 40C	SoC	SoC	All ports
FortiGate 50B	CP5	N/A	N/A
FortiGate 60B	CP5	N/A	N/A
FortiGate 60C/CM	SoC	SoC	All ports
FortiGate 80C/CM	CP6	N/A	N/A
FortiGate 110C/111C	CP6	N/A	N/A
FortiGate 100D	CP8	N/A	N/A
FortiGate 200B	CP6	1 × NP2	Ports 13–16
FortiGate 300C	CP6	2 × NP2	NP2 #1: Ports 1–4 NP2 #2: Ports 5–8 EEI between NP2 #1 & #2
FortiGate 310B/311B	CP6	2 × NP2	NP2 #1: Ports 1–4 NP2 #2: Ports 5–8 EEI between NP2 #1 & #2
FortiGate 620B/621B	CP6	4 × NP2	NP2 #1: Ports 1–4 NP2 #2: Ports 5–8 NP2 #3: Ports 9–12 NP2 #4: Ports 13–16 EEI between NP2 #1 & #2 EEI between NP2 #3 & #4
FortiGate 600C	CP8	1 × NP4	Ports 1–20
FortiGate 1000C	CP8	1 × NP4	Ports 1–24
FortiGate 1240B	CP6	2 × NP4	NP4 #1: Ports 1–24 NP4 #2: Ports 25–38
FortiGate 3016B	CP6	4 × NP2	NP2(#1 & #2): Ports 3–10 NP2(#3 & #4): Ports 11–18 EEI between NP2 #1 & #2 also NP2 #3 & #4
FortiGate 3040B	CP7	2 × NP4	NP4 #1: Ports 1–4, 9–13 NP4 #2: Ports 5–8, 14–18
FortiGate 3140B	CP7 & SP2	2 × NP4	NP4 #1: Ports 1–4, 9–13 NP4 #2: Ports 5–8, 14–18 SP2: Ports 19–20
FortiGate 3240C	CP8	2 × NP4	Ports 1–28

Table 2.1 FortiGate models and Modules with ASIC types & Interface Mappings (*continued*)

Fortinet Product	Content Processors	Network Processor	NP Shared Ports (inherent that all ports would use CPx ASIC)
FortiGate 3950B/3951B	CP7	1 × NP4	All ports
FortiGate 5001A-SW/DW	CP6	N/A	N/A
FortiGate 5001B	CP7	2 × NP4	(see note A)

FortiGate Modules	Content Processors	Network Processors	NP shared ports
RTM-XB2	N/A	2 × NP2	All ports
RTM-XD2	N/A	1 × NP4	All ports
ADM-XB2	N/A	2 × NP2	NP2 #1: Ports 1–2 NP2 #2: Ports 3–4 EEI between NP2 #1 & #2
ADM-XD4	N/A	1 × NP4	All ports
ADM-FB8	N/A	2 × NP2	NP2 #1: Ports 1–4 NP2 #2: Ports 5–8 EEI between NP2 #1 & #2
ASM-FB4	N/A	1 × NP2	All ports
ADM-XE2	SP1	N/A	All ports on module for SP1 only
ADM-FE8	SP1	N/A	All ports on module for SP1 only
ASM-CE4	SP1	N/A	All ports on module for SP1 only
FMC-XD2	N/A	1 × NP4	All ports
FMC-XG2	SP2	N/A	All ports on module for SP2 only (see note B)
FMC-C20	N/A	1 × NP4	All ports
FMC-F20	N/A	1 × NP4	All ports

Note A: The NP4 processors on the FortiGate 5001B are linked internally using 2 × 10 Gbps Attachment Unit Interface (XAUI) links (XAUI-link1 and XAUI-link2). For optimal performance, ingress and egress traffic should traverse the same XAUI link and NP4 processors. The NP4 ASIC shared ports are:

- *port1, port3, and fabric1 are connected to NP4-1 and XAUI-link-1.*
- *port2, port4, and base1 are connected to NP4-1 and XAUI-link-2.*
- *port5, port7, and farbic2 are connected to NP4-2 using XAUI-link-1.*
- *port6, port8, and base2 are connected to NP4-2 using XAUI-link-2.*

Note B: FMC modules supports internal facing interfaces connected to FortiGate models with ISF (Integrated Switch Fabric) supporting these modules such as the FortiGate 3950B. With the ISF, all on-system-based ports (excluding management ports) on these FortiGate models (e.g. on 3950B port1-6) could leverage the SP2 ASIC for its related acceleration functions.

FIGURE 2.4 Fortinet's First Appliance, The APSecure 300 Model

---

> **TIP**
>
> **High Availability (HA) offloading capabilities**
> In a configured Active/Active High Availability FortiGate cluster using FGCP (FortiGate Clustering Protocol), TCP base traffic are load balanced to other Active FortiGate cluster members by a designated FortiGate device within the cluster. Once the load-balanced traffic qualifies for the NP ASIC traffic characteristics, all subsequent traffic designated to be load balanced to corresponding cluster member devices continues to use the fast path. NP ASIC fast path session are not synchronized through heartbeat interface in a HA cluster thereby providing additional offloading capabilities without adding any addition burden on FortiGate main processor.

- In order to be processed as fast-path using the NP2 or NP4, the traffic flow must have the following characteristics:
    - Ingress and egress interface must traverse through same NP ASIC.
    - Layer 2 Ethernet frame type & length of 0x0800 (IPv4), 0x8100 (IEEE 802.1Q), 0x8809 (IEEE 802.3ad LACP).
    - When using link aggregation (IEEE 802.3ad LACP), the links needs to be defined within the same NP ASIC port mapping.
    - Layer 3 protocol must be IPv4.
    - Layer 4 protocols must be TCP, UDP, or ICMP.
    - Traffic originating from FortiGate itself does not qualify.
    - Qualified Layer 3 or 4 traffic must not require session-helpers usage.
    - Firewall policy must not have application layer inspection features enabled such as Anti-virus, Web filtering, Anti-spam, Application controls, DLP, or IDS/IPS.
    - Per policy Traffic shaping profiles are supported whereas Per-ip traffic shaping profiles are only supported on NP4.
    - Port-based traffic bandwidth definition such as the interface CLI-based command for inbandwidth and outbandwidth are not supported on NP2. NP4 only supports outbandwidth setting.

Fast Path subsequent packet requirements: In order to maintain the existing session to be processed by the NP ASIC, the following traffic characteristics must continue to be met otherwise traffic would be processed via slow path with FortiGate main processor (CPU).

- Subsequent inbound packets into NP must not be fragmented.
- Subsequent outbound packets from the NP must not require fragmentation to a size less than 385 bytes. Thus, the MTU (Maximum Transmission Unit) for the NP interfaces should also meet or exceed 385 bytes setting.

> **TIP**
> **Disabling NP ASIC offloading**
> For testing or troubleshooting purposes, the offloading of traffic to the NP ASIC can be disabled per ASIC with the following command:
>
> # diag npu <npu version> fastpath disable <NPx ID>
>   The <npu version> could be substituted for 'np1', 'np2', or 'np4' whereas <NPx ID> is the NP ASIC id—if you substitute the <NPx ID> with a '?' it would provide the NP ASIC ID list then re-issue the command and replace <NPx ID> with the corresponding ID, e.g. if the FortiGate model has 2 × NP2 ASIC then the ID starts out with '0' for the first NP2 and '1' for the other NP2.
>   This command is a temporary global command. When system is rebooted it would default back to 'fastpath enable'. To confirm whether fastpath is disabled or enabled, use command of:
>
> # diag npu <npu version> performance <NPx ID>
> <snipet output>...
> NAT Performance: BYPASS (Disable) BLOCK (Disable)
> <snipet output>...
>
>   Look for the above example of 'NAT Performance:'—if BYPASS shows 'disable' that means fastpath is disable—otherwise if it shows 'BYPASS (Enable)' then fastpath is enabled.
>   *Note:* Command only works on FortiGate appliances and system models with built-in ASIC chipset therefore FortiGate VM versions would not have this CLI option.

VPN Acceleration using NP and CP ASIC

The FortiGate main processor, along with the CP ASIC, assists with IPSec tunnel IKE setup. Once the tunnel is established, IPSec ESP payload packets are offloaded to NP ASIC. To meet the fast path requirements of NP ASIC, the following configuration and traffic characteristics are required:

- IPSec tunnel has to be configured as a tunnel interface and not as the default policy-base IPSec setup.
- In IPSec phase1-interface setting, the Local Gateway IP must be defined as the IP address of the local terminating interface. For example, if the IPSec tunnel is being terminated on port1, it's the port1 IP address that needs to be defined.
- In IPSec phase2-interface settings, the configuration should consist of:
  - Encryption algorithm must be DES, 3DES, AES (128 | 192 | 256 bit), or null
  - Authentication algorithm must be MD5, SHA1, or null
  - If encryption is null then authentication must be null
  - If Anti-Replay detection is enabled then the following settings must be defined within CLI to enable Anti-replay offloading onto NP:

config system npu
  set dec-offload-antireplay enable
  set enc-offload-antireplay enable
  end

Note: Command only works on FortiGate appliances and system models with built-in ASIC chipset therefore FortiGate VM versions would not have this CLI option

• Packets originating from FortiGate itself (local host address within FortiGate) can be offloaded by enabling the following CLI command:
config system npu
  set offload-ipsec-host enable
end

• Authentication algorithm such as MD5 and SHA1 used for HMAC checking is by default enabled to offload to NP but can be disabled with following CLI command:

config system global
  set ipsec-hmac-offload disable
end

UTM Acceleration using CP and SP ASIC

• Inherently, all traffic processed by the FortiGate main processors works in conjunction with CPx ASIC for additional offloading capabilities. This functionality are dependent on the version of CP ASIC capabilities as outlined in the above section titled 'Features of the last four generations of Content Processor (CP) ASIC functionalities'.
• SP ASIC provides acceleration of traffic with characteristics related to the features it supports such as Multicast traffic, Intrusion Protection, Application Controls, flow-base Anti-virus/spyware flow-base Web Filtering, flow-base DLP, and IPv6. The following traffic characteristics are required for this acceleration:

  ◦ Ingress and egress Ethernet connectivity has to reside within the same SP ASIC interface port mappings (see Table 2.1 on modules and FortiGate models with this ASIC).
  ◦ For Multicast acceleration, multicast firewall policies must be defined on the interface port mappings support by the SP ASIC.
  ◦ For IPv6 acceleration, IPv6 firewall policies are required to be defined on the interface port mappings supported by the SP ASIC.
  ◦ For Intrusion Protection, Application Controls, flow-base Anti-virus/spyware flow-base Web Filtering, and flow-base DLP: IPv4 firewall policies with related UTM profiles and sensor for these application layer inspection are required to be defined on the interface port mappings supported by the SP ASIC.

THE 'BLACK ART' OF FORTIGATE SIZING

FortiGate sizing has always been considered as a black art we will try to tackle this subject in this section. Sizing any network product depends on various network elements with the environment's current and potential growth requirements.

First and foremost, knowing the need for the product will help identify the elements surrounding the integration of the product in your environment. This includes such things as placement of the solution in your architecture and performance requirements. If there's an expectation to have the solution in place long enough to create a return on investment then the solution needs to be sized not just for today's environment but also for growth over × number of months or years. When sizing a UTM solution, the elements involved in determining the proper solution is far greater to that of a typical network device such as a router or a switch. Given that a UTM solution can potentially replace multiple security stand-alone point products, each of these security product functions needs to be considered into the sizing of the proposed UTM solution. As with any investment, it's imperative a sizing exercise be done prior to any purchase. Besides figuring out which device best fits your current and future network environment, further diligence is needed to verify that the proposed solution does fit and work in your environment. You may wish to acquire the actual proposed UTM solution for a hands-on evaluation. At the end of the day, you do not want an incorrectly sized complex security & networking device in your environment that could potentially cause issues and cost more money to correct the problem.

To help determine which FortiGate UTM solution best fits your environment, there are two steps:

> Step 1: Sizing Data Gathering — Gather as much information as possible to help with sizing the appropriate solution
>
> Step 2: Assessing The FortiGate Solution—Taking that gathered data from Step 1 and apply the responses to several areas of information to identify the appropriate FortiGate model.

Sizing Data Gathering

Let's go over questions that should be answered to size a FortiGate UTM solution. The questions are separated in two general parts, Security Requirements and Network Requirements:

(1) *Security Sizing Requirements Questions:* The purpose of these security related sizing questions is to determine the actual needs of the UTM solution. Each FortiGate UTM solution has fixed limit of resources allocated to certain functionalities. We'll outline some of these fixed resources to consider for each service with the below questions.

a. What are the security feature requirements today?

b. What are the security feature requirements that could be needed over the time for the purchase will be amortized and should this be considered in sizing the

---

TERMINOLOGY

In-line vs. Sniffer mode

In-line mode: Traffic flows through solution for inspection.

Sniffer mode: Monitoring only mode on a switch port configured for Port Mirroring.

solution? Given the benefits of a UTM handling multiple features at an overall lower TCO (Total Cost Ownership) there could be the possibility of replacing an existing stand-alone point security solution when the service contracts expires e.g. an existing firewall, web filtering, intrusion protection system, etc.

c. How many network users or devices expected to traverse through UTM solution?

Here's a high-level checklist of security features currently offered on FortiGate UTM solutions along with related resources that could affect sizing:

- Firewall
  - Number of expected firewall policies and objects
  - Concurrent connections (or sessions) support
  - New session setup per second handling
  - Packet size handling

- VPN
  - The type of VPN protocol used e.g. IPSec vs. SSL
  - If IPSec: encryption requirements, number of site to site (device to device VPN), # software remote VPN clients, or both
  - If SSL: encryption requirements, # of web-mode termination, # of tunnel-mode termination

- Network Anti-virus/Spyware
  - Methods used:
    - In-line: Flow-based method (faster performance) vs. proxy-based method (more secure). If proxy-based method, number of connections (or sessions/users) expected to be scanned
    - Sniffer mode for monitoring only

  - Protocols needed for scanning
  - Custom block/warning message usage
  - Quarantine usage
  - SSL inspection usage

- Web Filtering
  - Methods used:
    - In-line Transparent (transparent in a way there's no modified needed on client end to support this) Flow-based method (faster performance) vs. proxy-based method (more secure). If proxy-based method, # of users expected
    - Sniffer mode for monitoring only
    - Explicit (want client to adjust web browser proxy settings to point to UTM) web proxy support. If so, number of explicit web proxy users
    - Redirection with WCCP

  - Custom block/warning/disclaimer message usage
  - SSL inspection usage

- Application Controls
    - Methods used:
        - In-line with prevention capabilities
        - Sniffer mode for monitoring only

- Intrusion Detection or Prevention
    - Methods used:
        - In-line with prevention capabilities
        - Sniffer mode for monitoring only

- Anti-Spam
    - Email protocol usage
    - Custom block/warning message usage
    - SSL inspection usage

- DLP
    - Methods used:
        - In-line Transparent (transparent in a way there's no modified needed on client end to support this) Flow-based method (faster performance) vs. proxy-based method (more secure). If proxy-based method, # of users expected
        - Sniffer mode for monitoring only
    - File filtering usage
    - SSL inspection usage

- Web Cache
    - Hard disk usage
- Wan Optimization
    - Hard disk usage
    - Wan optimization expected protocol usage

- NAC/Endpoint controls
    - Number of FortiClient usage
- Vulnerability Management
    - Expected number of hosts/subnets used
- Historical logging & reporting
    - Number of UTM devices to support logging
    - Types of logs from UTM devices
    - Hard disk usage

- Centralized management

    - Number of UTM devices to be managed

    (2) *Network Sizing Requirements Questions:*

a. Where's the UTM expected to be placed within your network architecture? Possible locations include the network perimeter, the access layer, distribution, or core of your network.

b. What are the expected overall network performance requirements for the related security requirements for the placement of the solution?

c. What is the current network performance where the UTM solution will be placed? Some of this data can be gathered from existing security or network solutions. The more complete answer on these questions the more accurate sized UTM solution could be proposed. Such as:

- What is the current peak and/or average network throughput in bits or bytes per second?
- What is the current peak and/or average new connections per second?
- What is the current peak and/or average network volume?
- What is the network packet size distribution?

d. Will the UTM solution operate in-line, off-line, or a mixture of both in-line and off-line? If in-line, what's the planned operational mode such as Transparent (layer 2) mode, NAT/Route (layer 3) mode, or both?

e. How many physical (including any redundant interface or 802.3ad LACP connectivity needs) and expected logical interfaces (802.1q VLANs)?

f. What are the required physical interface requirements? e.g. Fast Ethernet, 1G fiber or copper, 10G.

g. If there are multiple network physical or logical interfaces, what are the expected performance requirements for communications between these in either in-line or off-line?

h. Is there a need for path or device redundancy? e.g. redundant interface support and High Availability clustering.

i. Is there a need for jumbo frame?

j. Is there a need to virtualize the UTM components into their own isolated UTM function via virtual domain (VDOM) (see Chapter 4 on VDOM description)? If so, which ones are likely to be used now and in the future?

k. Are there any power supply requirements such as AC vs. DC? Is redundant power needed (depending on whether device redundancy is required redundant power may not be a critical requirement).

Assessing the Recommended FortiGate Solution

With the majority of the previous questions answered, the next step is to assess which FortiGate platform best meets the above requirements. To provide a more accurate decision on the platform of choice, we will need to analyze three areas:

I. Feature Capabilities—To determine which platform would meet the requirements features

II. Feature Capacity—To determine which platform would handle the requirement features based on current and future growth feature requirements

III. Performance Capabilities—To determine which platform would meet current throughput & load requirements as well as expected future growth

Feature Capabilities

From a supported feature capabilities standpoint, the majority of the features are supported across all FortiGate platforms but there are a handful of features that are not. The information is maintained in the FortiOS documentations found at http://docs.fortinet.com/fgt.html.

Here's a quick reference of supported features that are limited to certain FortiGate models:

- VDOM (virtual domains) are supported FortiGate 50B and higher models. By default it includes up to 10 VDOM license. FortiGate 1240B and higher has the ability to scale above 10 VDOMs (see those datasheets for maximum VDOM capacity).
- WAN optimization and Web caching are supported only on FortiGate models with on-board storage (4G or higher) or with solid state hard drives options. WAN optimization requires both ends of a connection to be FortiNet technology. For example FortiGate to FortiGate or FortiClient to FortiGate.
- 802.3ad link aggregations are supported on FortiGate 200B and higher models.
- High Availability is supported on FortiGate 40C and higher models.
- Localized SQL logging is supported on FortiGate models with solid state drives.
- SSL inspection and SSL offloading are supported on FortiGate models with SoC or CP6 & higher ASIC. Certain models maybe software restricted from leveraging this feature even though the hardware model supports this chipset. For example, FortiGate 20C has a SoC but function is disabled.

Feature Capacity

To find the feature capacity of each FortiGate platform, Fortinet provides publicly a Maximum Value Guide of all FortiGate platforms which can be found at: http://docs.fortinet.com/fgt/handbook/40mr3/fortigate-max-values-40-mr3.pdf (as of this writing, FortiOS 4.0 MR3 was the most current version — in general the max value guide can be found in the related FortiOS version section under FortiGate products).

Review of this Maximum Value Guide will provide insight as to any feature settings that might affect current and future requirements.

Examples of such feature capacity limits include:

- firewall rule limits
- VPN capacity
- Objects capacity
- Routing capacity
- UTM settings capacity, etc.

Some of the feature capacities can also be founded in the product datasheets.

The FortiGate datasheets and Maximum Value guide refer to System level vs. VDOM level capacity. Technically, all devices by default operate in a single VDOM instance even without VDOM enabled. So the capacity for VDOM denotes the capacity of the device. If VDOM is enabled then the combined capacity would equal the System level capacity. For example, a FortiGate 1240B can handle 10,000 gateway-to-gateway IPSec tunnels at the System level and 5000 at a VDOM level: If no VDOM configuration exists then the overall number of supported gateway-to-gateway tunnels would be 5000 (by default a device without VDOM enable is treated like a single VDOM instance). If two configured VDOMs exist then the number of gateway-to-gateway tunnels between the two VDOMs (max 5000 per VDOM) would be no more than 10,000 supported tunnels. Further, if there are three VDOMs, VDOM-A has 2000 tunnels configured, VDOM-B has 5000 tunnels configured then VDOM-C cannot have more than 3000 tunnels configured because it would reach the System level capacity of 10,000.

Performance Capabilities

The majority of FortiGate platform performance characteristics can be found on their main website. For a quick reference product matrix showing each FortiGate model specifications in a single area see: http://www.fortinet.com/doc/FortinetMatrix.pdf.

For a more in-depth specification, individual FortiGate datasheets are located at: http://www.fortinet.com/products/fortigate/.

Reviewing datasheets quickly helps to determine the potential FortiGate model ranges; in particular which FortiGate platform would meet the network throughput requirements:

- Feature performance capabilities such as Firewall, IPS, Anti-virus, and IPSec & SSL VPN throughput numbers.
- Concurrent sessions (connections) supported.
- New session setup (TCP base) per second.

TIP

Additional general performance numbers

All performance testing are done in house using testing tools such as BreakingPoints [4] to provide the results. Not all performance metrics are highlighted in datasheets but here are some general rules regarding this missing features:

-For supported security features configured or using flow-base inspection methods such as Anti-virus, Web Filtering, DLP, and Application control, the expected performance should be slightly higher then published IPS throughput numbers.
-Supported security features that are configured for proxy-based inspection such as Web Filtering, DLP expected performance should be slightly higher then the published Anti-virus throughput numbers.

Also note, when particular security features are enabled it is not assumed that all traffic would fall into that throughput range. It is only the policy definition with the related security feature setting which could be affected by the stated performance throughput. For example, on a FortiGate 1240B, the anti-virus (proxy-based) throughput is noted as 900Mbps. There exists a policy in which anti-virus is the only security inspection service enabled within a policy, traffic that triggers the supported anti-virus proxy-based ports would be limited to 900 Mbps whereas other traffic that does not trigger the proxy listening ports would not have this limit.

Narrowing down the FortiGate platform based on the above criteria would help provide the minimum platform model but in most cases this is not enough. As the traffic load increases, the traffic patterns would vary (e.g. various packet sizes, more internet usage during a certain time, large file transfers occurring at various time, etc.), having varying traffic loads and patterns does not provide a predictable way of determining what effects this has on various features therefore finding the proper FortiGate platform is difficult to predict. The goal of the sizing exercise is to find a solution that best fits in your environment at the cheapest possible cost. Anyone can oversize the solution as a precaution but from a cost perspective this is generally not advised. Further discussion throughout the chapters will provide additional insight to help narrow down the FortiGate platform of choice.

Given the innovative capabilities at Fortinet, features may change after the writing of this book. It's always best to consult the latest published Fortinet documentations and, if possible, a certified Fortinet reseller or Fortinet sales engineer.

CENTRALIZED MANAGEMENT PLATFORM OVERVIEW

Fortinet centralized management solutions include the FortiManager and FortiAnalyzer products. FortiManager provides the centralized management of multiple FortiGate devices in a single management view. The FortiAnalyzer provides a centralized view of real-time & historical logging along with reporting capabilities of logs collected from FortiGate devices and various Fortinet products. Fortinet's approach in offering two separated components for centralized management provides a scalable and flexible option for consumers. For example, a customer may not want to centrally manage their solution but want the historical logging and reporting capabilities. Rather then paying extra for central management capabilities and/or having to work through the management interfaces to get to the historical logging & reports, the solutions may be purchased separately. In our opinion, having your management capabilities, especially with historical logging and reporting residing in the same solution, would not only burden the overall solution but also run the risk of running out of storage space on the local disk. Having the centralized management solution (both policy management and logging & reporting) separated provides the following benefits:

1. Improves scalability. Ability to move to higher disk capacity drives.
2. Provides flexibility. Can manage and log/report separately without having to depend on each operation.
3. Reduces performance burdens and increases reliability. Relieves additional system burden on overall UTM architecture. With central management is built into UTM/NGFW solutions, when unit goes offline i.e. power reasons, defective device, network outages then central management along with logging & reporting could be inaccessible or lost.

As of this writing, here are some key features available for each of the management platform:

FortiManager provides:

- Web GUI management for all features. In addition, a java client for policy management.
- Centralized security policy management of multiple FortiGate UTM solutions.
- Centralized security policy management of multiple FortiClient end point solutions.
- Role-based administration.
- Administrative Domains (ADOM) providing a virtualized group of managed devices within a single separated management view. In addition, administrator can be restricted to their assigned ADOM for management.
- Customizable administrative web portal.
- Global object database support, providing use of common configuration across global policy and/or unique policy per managed UTM solutions.
- Policy & Device auditing.
- Manual & scheduled pushes of policies and firmware updates to UTM solutions.
- CLI and TCL scripting support with manual or scheduled push capabilities to managed UTM solutions.
- XML API support for third-party integration.
- Mini-FDN (FortiGuard Distributed Network) support to provide Anti-virus/Spyware and IDS/IPS signature updates. In addition, support for a localized Anti-Spam RBL and Web URL categorization database.

FortiAnalyzer provides:

- Centralized logging and reporting management for various Fortinet products.
- Real-time log viewer.
- 300+ predefined reports along with report customization capabilities.
- SQL database support locally or externally. Integrated SQL query & schema tools for further customizable reporting.
- Role-based administration.
- Administrative Domains (ADOM) providing a virtualize group of managed devices within a single separated management view. In addition, administrator can be restricted to their related ADOM for management.
- Network Event Correlation.
- Centralized quarantine capabilities for FortiGate UTM solutions. Providing a centralized repository for infected and blocked files.
- DLP archive & data mining capabilities.
- Network Analyzer.
- Vulnerability and Compliance Management scanning.

FORTINET PRODUCT PORTFOLIO

Besides Fortinet's offering of their FortiGate UTM solutions and their related central management capabilities, there are several other products Fortinet offers. We'll highlight the purpose and key points on each of their product offerings.

High-level overview of Fortinet's service and other non-UTM product offerings:

FortiGuard

FortiGuard is Fortinet's threat research and response service for the FortiGate UTM platforms and for most of the other offerings. The services offered here are primarily subscription based, providing signature updates for anti-virus, intrusion prevention, and application controls. In addition, direct access to real-time anti-spam reputation databases and web filtering URL categorization databases for the FortiGate UTM solution. The FortiGuard service is maintained and updated by security researchers around the world. Upon discovery of new threats, research and development of the related service signatures are synchronized with over two dozen global data centers where updates are distributed hourly to hundreds of thousands Fortinet UTM devices. Besides actively tracking global threats, developing, and maintaining security services for their UTM offerings, Fortinet security researchers also actively find exploits. To see both current and historical discovered vulnerabilities, see the FortiGuard web site [3]. For further details on FortiGuard, please reference Chapter 6.

FortiCarrier

The FortiCarrier solution is an extension of the FortiGate solution. It leverages the same features as in the current FortiGate FortiOS but adds features used in service provider infrastructures such as GTP firewall, secure MMS (MulitMedia Messaging Services), and IMS SIP signaling firewall capabilities. As of FortiOS 4.0 MR3, all of the SIP related features in FortiCarrier was ported over leaving GTP and MMS features as the main differences for the FortiCarrier product line. The FortiCarrier platforms are limited to the FortiCarrier 3810A, 3950B, and the 5000 series system products with the FortiCarrier 5001A-DW and 5001B blades. For further details on the FortiCarrier products visit: http://www.fortinet.com/products/forticarrier/.

FortiBridge

FortiBridge is a stand alone product used in conjunction with the FortiGate UTM platforms to provide a bypass method when the UTM solution goes offline. The FortiBridge bypass capabilities provide a automatic bridging of traffic by routing traffic around an inline FortiGate UTM in an event of a power outage or a system fault. There are three version of this product:

FortiBridge-2002: Provides two segment bypass protection with
$8 \times 10/100/1000$ copper interfaces.

FortiBridge-2002F: Provides two segment bypass protection with $4 \times$ GbE SFP (fiber or copper) and $4 \times$ GbE fiber interfaces.
FortiBridge-2002X: Provides two segment bypass protection with 4×10 GbE SFP+ and 4×10 GbE LC Fiber interfaces.

Given this is an external bypass solution; it only works with a FortiGate UTM solution deployed in a transparent (layer 2) mode. This could be a cheaper alternative network redundancy solution then purchasing another FortiGate device for a high availability configuration. The only downsides to this solution are the transparent mode requirement (typical with any bypass solution on the market) and when the FortiGate UTM solution goes offline then there are no security enforcement in place. Since the FortiGate is offline and the external bypass solution is in bypass mode therefore bypassing security inspections usually performed by the FortiGate solution. For further details on the FortiBridge products visit: http://www.fortinet.com/products/fortibridge/.

FortiAP

FortiAP is an 802.11x wireless access point (AP) offering. As of this writing there are three commercial grade FortiAP models offered by Fortinet, FortiAP-210B, FortiAP-220B, and FortiAP-222B. All three models support 802.11a/b/g/n standards and operate on both 2.4 GHz b/g/n and 5 GHz a/n spectrums. The 210B has single radio whereas the other two have two radios. The 222B can be used outdoors unlike the other two models which are indoor only. Each radio supports multiple wireless clients with ability to span across multiple wireless network segments each with its own SSID and with different access rights. Having multiple radios in a single FortiAP provides options for dedicating certain wireless frequency spectrums to specific uses. A radio could also be dedicated for wireless rogue AP (Access-Point) detection. Rogue detection provides another layer of defense by detecting unauthorized access points being used in your network environment. In addition, on-wire rogue AP detection is possible by leveraging the dedicated wireless radio detected rogue AP MAC address and correlating the FortiGate wireless controller MAC entries from potential wireless user client using the rogue AP on the network. If a rogue AP is detected on your physically connected network (on-wire), the FortiGate has the ability to suppress and block network activities coming from the discovered rogue AP. These APs are used in conjunction with the FortiGate UTM solution acting as a wireless controller for the AP and providing fast roaming capabilities between FortiAPs. The wireless controller function is included in almost all FortiGate models (check datasheet to confirm support). With the FortiGate providing the wireless controller functionality, it adds additional benefit for a secure wireless infrastructure by leveraging all the FortiGate offered UTM features. For further details on the FortiGate built-in wireless controller feature will be covered in Chapter 7 of this book.

FortiToken

FortiToken provides a two-factor authentication solution for use with the FortiGate platforms administrative access, IPSec VPN, SSL VPN, and Identity Policy Authentications.

It provides another layer of security with a one-time password (OTP) capability used in conjunction with an existing single-factor authentication, such a static password. The seeding of the OTP is managed by our FortiGuard Center as a cloud-based repository. The FortiToken can also be used as a stand alone external authentication method used in conjunction with the FortiAuthenticator product (see description on this product below). Further details on this product will be covered in Chapter 5.

FortiAuthenticator

FortiAuthenticator is a user-based identity management solution, used for user authentication, two-factor authentication with FortiToken, and identity verification network access. The user authentication credentials use a build-in standardized RADIUS or LDAP server configuration. It may also be integrated with third-party authentication servers such as Microsoft Active Directory by using LDAP. For further details on the FortiAuthenticator product visit: http://www.fortinet.com/products/fortiauthenticator/.

FortiMail

FortiMail is a comprehensive messaging security solution. It provides Anti-Virus, Anti-Spam, Data Loss Prevention, and Identity-Based Encryption for email. The product can operate in Gateway (MTA), Transparent and also offer a full email server mode capability. As of this writing there are four appliance models (FortiMail 200D, 400C, 2000B, 3000C), a chassis blade (5002B) version, and a Virtual Machine (VM) version. For further details on the FortiMail product visit: http://www.fortinet.com/products/fortimail/

FortiWeb

FortiWeb is a WAF (Web Application Firewall) that is used to protect, load balance, and accelerate content to and from web server(s). As a WAF, it provides protection for web applications and related database content by mitigating common threats like cross-site scripting, buffer overflows, denial of service, SQL injection, and cookie poisoning. It addresses the OWASP Top 10 web application vulnerabilities. FortiWeb also provides server load balancing, content-based routing, data compression, and SSL encryption accelerations. The product is ICSA Labs certified and also provides a built-in vulnerability scanner module that helps with PCI DSS compliance requirement 6.6. As of this writing there are three appliance models (FortiWeb 400C, 1000C, 3000C) and also a Virtual Machine (VM) version. For further details on the FortiWeb product visit: http://www.fortinet.com/products/fortiweb/.

FortiScan

FortiScan is a vulnerability management solution which provides a central network-level and OS-level vulnerability scanning of devices throughout the network. In addition, it provides patch & remediation management, asset management, and compliance reporting capabilities that are compliant with regulatory and best practices for FDCC, NIST SCAP, SOX, GBLA, HIPAA, PCI/DSS, FSIMA, and ISO 17799. For further details on the FortiScan product visit: http://www.fortinet.com/products/fortiscan/.

FortiDB

FortiDB is a database security and compliance product which provides a central management view of policy compliance and vulnerability management for databases. It supports majority of the commercial databases such as Oracle, MS SQL Server, Sybase, and DB2. As of this writing the product comes in three models (FortiDB-400B, 1000C, and 2000B) and also in a Virtual Machine (VM) version. The main difference between the FortiDB models are the licensing structure each model supports which are based on number of database instances used for the product. For further details on the FortiDB product visit: http://www.fortinet.com/products/fortidb/.

FortiBalancer

FortiBalancer is an application delivery controller. It provides Layer 2 through Layer 7 load-balancing capabilities. In addition, it provides a built-in caching supporting HTTP 1.1, in-line HTTP compression, TCP connection multiplexing, TCP accelerations, IPv6 support, and SSL offloading/acceleration. The product can be deployed in proxy and transparent mode configuration. As of this writing there are three versions of the FortiBalancer (FortiBalancer-400, 1000, and 2000). For further details on the FortiBalancer products visit: http://www.fortinet.com/products/fortibalancer/.

FortiClient

FortiClient is a software-based endpoint security client providing various security features for enterprise and mobile devices. As of this writing there are four versions of the client offering various features for several different OS platform and mobile devices. The versions of FortiClient and supported features are:

FortiClient (standard)—Provides IPSec & SSL VPN, two-factor authentication support, Wan Optimization, and Application detection & enforcement along with Policy compliance enforcement when used with FortiGate UTM devices.

FortiClient Premium—Provides all of the above features and adds Anti-Virus, Anti-Spam, Application-based firewall, and Web Filtering.

FortiClient Lite—Is a free edition that only provides Anti-virus/spyware functionality.

All versions of the FortiClient are supported on most Windows versions in 32 bit or 64 bit. At this time, only the standard FortiClient is support on OSX.

Fortinet also offers a stand alone SSL VPN client for tunnel mode usage to a FortiGate solution. This stand alone SSL VPN client can be installed separately with no additional cost. Although, access to this client is available at Fortinet support website with a valid FortiCare support contract login. This endpoint SSL VPN client can support Linux and Mac OS besides Windows OS.

For further details on the FortiClient products visit: http://www.fortinet.com/products/endpoint/ or http://www.forticlient.com.

REFERENCES

[1] <http://www.pcworld.com/businesscenter/article/148653/network_managers_fear_security_threats_from_within.html>.
[2] <http://docs.fortinet.com/>.
[3] <http://www.fortiguard.com>.
[4] <http://www.breakingpointsystems.com/>.

FortiOS Introduction

FORTIOS ARCHITECTURE

The firmware used on FortiOS is delivered as a single consolidated image containing the kernel, user-space applications, and initial signature databases. By not having to download modules for installation, the FortiGate appliance can immediately provide application layer protection.

The kernel follows the POSIX standard and includes the traditional separation from user-space applications. The kernel provides enough services to support a security-focused system and interface for more flexible applications to use. Fundamentally, the role of the kernel is to serve as a bridge between the hardware and the applications. As mentioned in the previous chapter, FortiOS devices include general hardware like Ethernet interfaces and custom-built ASICs.

Like a networking stack that's based on the OSI seven-layer model or a server with dedicated hardware, kernel, and user-space applications, the FortiOS is layered. The first layer consists of the actual hardware that makes up the appliance. All FortiGate appliances contain at least the following hardware: CPU, RAM, network interfaces, ASIC Content Processor, and a form of permanent storage. Further details on hardware can be found in Chapter 2. Recently, Fortinet has introduced a System-on-a-Chip (SoC) design for entry level. This design includes all of the hardware mentioned as well as integrates elements of the Network Processor (NP) and Content Processor (CP) hardware to accelerate firewall performance.

The second layer includes all software components that provide access to the hardware layer. These are often referred to as "device drivers" and may be compiled into the kernel itself (layer 3). As the hardware components will slightly differ from model to model, the drivers will as well. For example, lower-end systems may use Intel or Broadcom network devices, while higher-end systems will rely on an ASIC. Different hardware will require different drivers. Since some drivers are compiled in, this means that different FortiGate models will necessarily require different firmware. In addition, the FortiNPU layer provides a common interface to FortiOS for the various hardware combinations.

The third layer is the kernel or Operating System (OS) layer. Like kernels in other OSs, it has direct interaction with the device drivers at Layer 2 and provides interfaces to the user-space applications. This enables Fortinet to rapidly deploy new features onto the FortiGate devices. To provide maximum performance, the firewall engine is implemented in the kernel. This allows it to efficiently interact with the interrupt handling, task scheduling, and memory management subsystems. Integration between the kernel and the firewall engine allows for other applications to communicate with layer 3 through pipes and shared memory access.

The fourth layer is composed of the user-space applications. These applications access the kernel using the internal Application Programming Interface (API). These APIs are internal and intended for Fortinet developers. They are not made available to third parties as they might change without notice. Most of the remaining functionality in FortiOS devices is implemented in individual applications at this layer. Commonly used applications include transparent proxies and the AV and IPS engines.

The final layer is the configuration layer, which consists of the Web and Command Line Interfaces (WebUI and CLI). Whether accessing the configuration through the web interface running on the built-in web server or through shell commands, the configuration itself is stored internally as a text file. CLI configuration commands can be entered in via SSH or on the console port during the POST process.

Console access requires your terminal emulator to be set for 9600-N-8-1. For systems that support multiple FortiOS images, the config file is stored with each corresponding image.

Multiple Image Support

Modern FortiGates include permanent storage that is used for both the firmware image and the configuration of that image. While the type of storage may either be Flash or NAND RAM and the amount varies by hardware model, the storage itself is divided into three separate file systems. The first two contain copies of the firmware image and associated configuration file. This provides a backup and recovery system, should a firmware update experience difficulty. During normal operations, only the active file system is mounted by the OS.

You can define which firmware image is Active image via the Web UI, or the CLI. From the Web UI, navigate to System → Dashboard → Dashboard then click on 'Details' at the end of the Firmware Version line. From the CLI you can use the "diag system flash list" to list the images on each of the partitions, and "exec set-next-reboot primary | secondary" and to select the partition to boot from during the next reboot. When displaying the partitions, partition number 1 is considered the primary and partition number 2 is the secondary. You can also select the firmware image to boot from the system BIOS during boot via the console port. When you boot, simply press a key when prompted and select to boot the "Default" or "Backup" from the menu.

The third file system contains the most recently downloaded signature database for each service that is licensed and activated. In order to provide a baseline level of security, each firmware image incorporates the AV and IPS database that was current when the firmware was released. Thus, even if there is a problem downloading the latest set of AV and IPS protections, some protection is available.

Firmware Image Versions

All Fortinet firmware images follow a standard naming/numbering convention. The named scheme includes the Major, Minor, and Patch release numbers. The alternate, and more common, naming scheme simply consists of those three numbers separated by periods. Major number releases, the first of the set, are released approximately every four years. Minor numbers, generally every six months and patch releases as needed. Major releases typically contain new functionality. Minor releases include enhancements to the existing feature set and patch releases simply fix known issues. An alternative method long form for describing the release is also found, for the previous example this method would be written 4.0 MR3 Patch 2, MR denoting Minor Release.

There could be as much as 20 months after the initial 4.0.0 release to the 4.3.2 version, as three Minor releases must have been released and two patches for the current version. A Fortinet Major release has a relatively long lifespan.

These releases all correlate to a specific build, and this build number is references where the firmware is displayed (WebUI system information widget, CLI "get system status" command, and the configuration backups). This number is considered the most accurate information regarding the firmware that you're running, so Fortinet support may ask for this number in preference to the Major.Minor.Patch number. To speed things up, it would be wise to always run the "get system status" command and copy the output to the technical support engineer. This way, they will have access to all hardware details, serial number, firmware version, and BIOS level.

Fortinet makes every attempt to keep the releases consistent across all models. Thus, when a new Minor release is available, it is released on all currently supported systems. When a new Major release becomes available, the Minor versions for the older Major releases are usually halted at their current level. Patches may be released as needed, but any feature enhancements will focus on the most current Major releases. Fortinet's policy is to maintain the current and immediately previous Minor releases.

FortiOS Operational Modes

FortiGate devices can run in two modes: Layer 3 or Layer 2. Layer 3 is the more traditional operating mode and works much like other firewall products. In this mode, which Fortinet refers to as "NAT/Route", each interface has an IP address and makes routing/forwarding decisions like a traditional router.

However, Layer 2 mode is much less common. Referred to as "Transparent", it allows the Fortinet to be introduced to a network without requiring changes (IP addressing, routing) to the surrounding Layer 3 environment. This is particularly helpful when the FortiGate is providing security augmentation or visibility beyond traditional Layer 4. In other words, if device is being used to provide UTM features, but should not interfere with the filtering capabilities on the existing firewalls, it can easily supplement the network with Web Content Filtering or IPS functions.

Another interesting outcome of the transparent mode configuration is that the FortiGate can now be placed in the middle of an existing 802.1q trunk and provide security for multiple VLANs (Virtual LANs) at the same time. The 802.1q specification provides a method for allowing multiple distinct networks to operate on the same physical infrastructure, creating a virtual infrastructure on top of the physical one. Packets are identified as belonging to a specific virtual infrastructure (or VLAN) by the value of the VLAN tag added to the packets, if there is no VLAN tag in the packet header then the packet is commonly referred to as being untagged, or as some vendors refer to it, being in the Native VLAN. The FortiGate uses these tags the same way, identifying packets belonging to a specific virtual infrastructure by the value of the VLAN tag. For more specific details on the 802.1q specification, please see the standard documents from the IEEE (International BLAH BLAH BLAH) where configuring VLANs is covered in some detail in Chapter 4. Of course appropriate sizing is required for this to work without providing unacceptable latency on all the traffic.

There is even a CLI configuration option that tells the FortiGate to forward all VLAN-tagged packets as-is without any type of inspection. Thus, all traffic is passed, but if a particular VLAN-tagged communication needs to be inspected, the administrator can add a pair of interfaces. By defining ingress and egress interfaces for a specific VLAN, that traffic can be inspected without slowing down the rest of the network.

When configured in Transparent mode, the FortiGate operates like a very smart Layer 2 bridge or switch. For example, when an ARP request is received on an interface, the FortiGate consults its MAC table and if it is not already known, the FortiGate sends the ARP request out to all other operating interfaces in that VDOM. Once an ARP reply is seen on an interface, the MAC address is added to an internal table. Then, since the source and destination addresses are known, the firewall policy can be evaluated. If the firewall policy allows the traffic, then the packets received on the ingress interface are rewritten to the egress interface with no changes. This means that the MAC addresses remain the same, so the FortiGate is effectively invisible to the network.

This bridge/switch like behavior also allows end systems to directly connect to the FortiGate, so all security enforcement is performed on the FortiGate itself. This greatly simplifies the process of maintaining security on multiple systems with various OSs. Transparent mode also includes the ability to terminate IPSec tunnels and perform NAT operations, this is configured as an advanced configuration but basically these operations are performed by treating the management IP address assigned to the VDOM like a gateway, this is the address that the IPSec tunnels originate from or are destined to, for example.

Packet Flow Handling

Like everything else, network speeds have increased over time. As a result, security operations must be performed at ever-increasing rates. To help address this, Forti-Gate appliances that include the SP module can offload not just Layer 3/4 firewall processing, but also full Layer 7 processing. This speeds up analysis by the IPS and Application Control engines.

Generally, FortiOS will process packets in layer order. Thus, Layer 2 checks happen first, followed by Layer 3 processing and all the way up the OSI model. Layer 2 checks include evaluating the packets for integrity (checksum), identifying whether the packet is IP-based and, if so, forwarding it up the processing stack. Non-IP packets are processed if the FortiGate is configured to do so, usually only in Transparent mode.

As soon as the Layer 3 information is available, FortiOS compares the destination IP address to the routing table in order to determine the egress interface. The destination IP address is also compared against other possible terminations: IPSec tunnels, SSL VPNs, and WAN routes. Packets that must be decrypted are processed first, using the cryptographic engine present in the NP or SP or, if neither are available, by the CP. The decrypted packet is then passed along to the firewall engine.

At this point enough information is available to evaluate the packet against the firewall policies. The packet's Layer 3 and 4 information is evaluated against the rules in each policy, in top-down order with the first match winning. While security policies that are source and destination-specific are considered more secure, FortiOS allows you to define non-interface-specific rules by setting the policy to the "any" interface. This is often considered easier to manage, albeit at the cost of decreased processing efficiency and a slightly higher chance of unanticipated results in edge cases.

If the packet matches an identity-based policy, then further evaluation occurs. The next process checks the user-authentication database, matching the source IP address against the known users, if no match is found then the traffic is matched against the Guest Access group.

Once a policy has been matched for a packet, the type of processing is determined. This is where packets are optionally passed on to UTM processing. If there is no UTM configured for the matching policy and the hardware platform has a Network Processor (NP), then a session-key is pushed down to the NP so that any future packets associated with this session can be accelerated. If a UTM feature is active and it makes use of the IPS Engine and there is a Security Processor (SP) present, then the session information is pushed down to the SP so that the session can be locally processed. If the policy requires the intervention of a transparent proxy or if a SP is not present, then the traffic is handled by the main CPU. The CPU also processes other features such as SSL-VPN, WAN optimization, etc.

WebUI Management Interface

The most-often used administrative interface for FortiGate devices is accessed via a standard web browser. The interface is wholly contained within the FortiGate and does not rely on any external systems or services. Most operations can be performed with this WebUI, however a small number of advanced operations require the command line interface (CLI). This can be accessed directly over SSH or through a widget located within the WebUI itself.

By default, FortiGate devices have either the internal or port1 interfaces configured to have an IP address of 192.168.1.99/24 and to listen for the HTTPS on port 443. For reasons of simplicity, the devices created for the smaller market (SOHO, Remote Office, and Small Enterprise... all devices smaller than the 200B) also listen for HTTP on port 80. These devices also simplify setup by running a DHCP server. If they are added to an environment that already has a DHCP server, two problems could arise. If the local network is 192.168.1.*, the possibility of conflicting IP addresses exists, which could take one or both systems offline. If the local network is anything else, there is the possibility that the wrong IP address could be assigned, which would prevent that system from accessing the network.

These are classic security vs convenience tradeoffs. So, if you have one of these units, it would be wise to disable the unneeded services once the FortiGate is initially configured. Note, though, that changes on a FortiGate are made immediately once the "OK" or "Apply" buttons are clicked. Thus, if you disable the HTTP access and you are using that access, you will need to reconnect over HTTPS as soon as you disable HTTP.

The WebUI also supports widgets other than the option to embed the CLI. These widgets are user configurable and can be added to the system dashboard or to any custom dashboard that you create to provide specific views into your network activities.

CLI Management Interface

Advanced users often prefer the command line interface to a WebGUI. The CLI is exactly the same regardless of how it is accessed, whether that is via the physical console port, across the network using SSH or telnet, or via the integrated WebUI console widget. CLI commands follow a branching model, with four primary areas: config, diag, exec, and get/show.

config	Precedes any command that alters the Operating Configuration. These changes are stored to the permanent configuration
diag	Precedes commands used to perform troubleshooting operations, if the command results in a change to the operating configuration of the FortiGate these changes are not saved to the permanent configuration, so if you reboot the device, they will be undone
exec	Precedes the CLI commands used for routine operations. Some are related to troubleshooting such as ping and traceroute while others are related to system operations and maintance, such as performing a backup or requesting signature updates
get	Used to view the current operating value for all options of a configuration element. Unlike "show", this includes all values, whether they are defaults or changed
show	This option allows for the current settings for a configuration element to be displayed, but unlike "get", only displayed the values that have been changed from the defaults

To help you navigate the CLI, you can use the "?" and [Tab] shortcuts. Entering "?" at any point will give you a context-sensitive list of valid options and the "Tab" key will cycle through those options.

The CLI is highly structured and is intended to match the layout implemented in the WebUI as much as possible. For example, the "config" suboptions mirror the main menu options in the WebUI: config system, config firewall, config router, etc.

A number of configuration elements are stored and accessed in a list-like structure. This is mostly true for elements which are one of many, such as interfaces (port0, port1, port2, etc.), policies, addresses, and services. When configuring these elements, the "next" command indicates that you are done configuring the current element in the list and are ready to move on to the next one. The "end" command indicates that you are done configuring that list and are ready to go back to the previous level.

```
config system address
edit "port1"
    set ip 1.2.3.4 255.255.255.0
    set allowaccess ssh https ping snmp
```

```
next
edit "port2"
  set ip 5.6.7.8 255.255.255.0
  set allowaccess ssh https ping snmp
next
end
```

It should be noted that the CLI syntax is case-sensitive, so the word "this" is not the same as the word "This". Since the system is object-based, you can therefore create objects that differ only in capitalization. This can obviously become very confusing, so it is recommended that you decide on a standard style (such as lowercase, Initial Caps, CamelCase, or ALLCAPS) and stick to that as much as possible. This way, you can use an alternate case to highlight items as exception or out of the norm. An example of this would be having rules like: "block inbound http", "allow outbound ssh", and "DEBUG – ALLOW HTTP TO SERVER2".

When working with the CLI it is important to note that, as and when you click "OK" or "Apply" in the WebUI, the configuration changes are immediate when you run a "next" or "end" command. In some cases there is also the option to abandon a partial set of changes by issuing the "abort" command.

If you enable VDOMs, be aware that you are adding a layer of complexity. To manage this additional layer, you will see a separation at the top of the CLI command tree that isolates global configuration options from VDOM-specific configuration options. So the highest level of the CLI tree consists of only the config option, and a single get command (get system status), the config option then accepts only two suboptions: "global" and "vdom", so you can choose which mode to enter. To keep you from being confused, the CLI prompt also changes to reflect the mode that you are in.

```
FGT # config global
FGT (global) # ?
config
diag
exec
get
show

FGT # config vdom
FGT (vdom) # edit <vdom_name>
FGT (root) # ?
config
diag
exec
get
show
```

SYSTEM OPTIONS
Recommended Configuration Options

There are some configuration options that in their default configuration don't really result in a very secure implementation, some of these are more related to ease of use and should really be disabled. There are other options that are often considered to be best practices for configuring security devices.

Configuring Logging

FortiOS has extensive logging support. This is used, not just for generating traffic and security logs, but also for system operations and auditing system configuration changes. Log messages can be sent to many different types of servers, including Fortinet's own FortiAnalyzer (see Chapter 8 for more information), industry standard Syslog Servers using either unreliable UDP transport[1] or reliable TCP transport[2] as well as the WELF log format as originally specified by Webtrends Corporation. Though the WebUI only supports one target, both FortiAnlyzer and Syslog messages can actually be specified to up to three logging servers, each with their own configuration (see Figure 3.1). However, only one Webtrends server is supported within FortiOS and that configuration is CLI-only. In addition to remote logging, the FortiGate also has the ability to save log messages in memory or local storage, if space is available. Of course the amount of log messages that can be stored in memory is very small (approx 128 logs per message type) and they roll out the bottom when a new message appears, with local storage the log files are rolled out periodically with the oldest logs automatically deleted when the storage space reaches 80% of it's available capacity.

Fortinet also offers a cloud-based/SaaS logging solution known as FortiGuard Analysis & Management Service (FAMS). This is intended for smaller organizations, as they are unlikely to have invested in central logging infrastructure. In addition to logging, this service also offers a configuration repository to allow you to track your configuration changes over time.

You can specify the type and severity of log messages sent to each log destination. This allows you to only send the appropriate log messages, simplifying analysis and reducing storage requirements. For example, if your Security Event and Incident Management (SEIM) system is only reporting on Security events, there is no point sending Network (traffic log) messages to it. The same goes for network-trending analysis that has no need for Security logs.

There is very granular configuration of what logs are sent to each destination. Each log message also has a severity level and you can configure what level messages are

---

[1]RFC 5424 The Syslog Protocol (obsoletes RFC 3164).
[2]RFC 3195 Reliable Delivery for Syslog.

FIGURE 3.1 Configuring Logging

sent to each destination. This allows you to leverage, for example, an existing Syslog system that can be used to send SMS messages or emails on critical events. Setting that destination to only receive messages of warning or greater severity will reduce the number of false alarms. You can review the severity available for log messages in the Log Reference Guide on http://docs.fortinet.com.

The CLI configuration commands for each destination vary slightly as they have different capabilities and therefore different configuration requirements.

```
config log syslogd setting
  set status enable
  set server 'X.X.X.X'
  set reliable disable        ← enabling this turns on reliable
  set port 514                  syslog (syslog over TCP)
  set csv disable             ← some systems prefer the keyword=value
                                pairs to be comma seperated
  set facility local7         ← allows the syslog server to seperate
                                out the log messages
end
```

```
config log fortianalyzer setting
  set status enable
  set ips-archive enable            ← send IPS triggered packets to
                                      FortiAnalyzer
  set address-mode static
  set server X.X.X.X
  set conn-timeout 10
  set monitor-keepalive-period 5
  set monitor-failure-retry-period 5
  set source-ip 0.0.0.0
  set upload-option realtime         ← send logs in real-time,
                                      they can also be uploaded
                                      periodically
end
```

Starting with FortiOS 4.3 it is possible to have a separate logging configuration for each VDOM. By default the values configured at the Global level are used. However, if you wish to have a specific VDOM send its logs to a different FortiAnalyzer or Syslog server, or if you wish to have a different filter configuration for that VDOM you'll need to configure that from the CLI. Please see Chapter 8 for more information on configuring logging with VDOMs.

SNMP Configuration

The most common method for most organizations to obtain real-time information on the operational status of their network infrastructure is via the Simple Network Management Protocol (SNMP), it has a long history and is very well defined. The FortiGate devices support the two most common SNMP versions, commonly referred to as v2c and v3. Since the FortiGate is a security device, it is suggested that SNMPv3 be used since it provides better security than it's predecessor v2c. From a purely informational perspective, both versions provide the same level of detail, v3 just provides a better level of security, but due to it's slightly increased complexity it's not supported by all SNMP tool sets.

Configuring the SNMP agent on the FortiGate involves two basic steps, the first is enabling the agent, it is not enabled by default, to do so navigate to System → Config → SNMP and select the checkbox labeled SNMP Agent and fill out the

---

TIP

Additional Detail Logging Options

As the FortiGates have additional capabilities beyond the standard Network and Security protections, the FortiAnalyzer has the capability to analyze the data that the UTM functions return. If you are using a FortiAnalyzer, you can also pass non-standard information such as IPS Packet Logs, attachments that were detected to contain malware and files that violate the Data Leak Protection settings.

information for the Description, Location, and Contact fields, these correspond to the standard SNMP MIB values of sysDescr, sysLocation, and sysContact, respectively, do not forget to press the apply button before proceeding to configure the SNMP community settings.

SNMP v2c uses a simple access control mechanism referred to as a "community." This value needs to be configured on both the SNMP management/query tool as well as the FortiGate, this string is case-sensitive, multiple distinct communities can be configured if required. For each community a set of Hosts and interfaces are defined, these are the systems that the FortiGate will accept SNMP queries from and send SNMP traps to, you can enter either a subnet definition or a host definition, if no subnet mask is provided then it is assumed to be a /32 or host address. If you enter a value of 0.0.0.0/0.0.0.0 here any host can perform an SNMP query as long as the other requirements as described in Controlling Administrative Access below are met. It is however suggested to configure only the addresses required in this hosts list, only host definitions (/32 netmask) will be sent traps since it would be impossible to know what hosts on a /24 subnet are supposed to receive the traps, and we certainly don't want to send the same trap to every possible host in that subnet. You can also configure the types of traps that are sent as well as the option for sending original v1 style traps and accepting v1 style SNMP queries. If you have trouble performing an SNMP query against the FortiGate, you may need to change the setting for the query versions based on how they behave, normally it's safe to leave both enabled, if you are planning on collecting a significant amount of SNMP data, then it is suggested to only use the v2c format as it supports the ability to receive multiple queries in a single transaction as well as return multiple results in a single transaction.

Configuring SNMPv3 is very similar to configuring SNMPv2, however you have options to enforce strong authentication and to encrypt the payload in the SNMP transactions, the entire v2c transaction is all-clear text so it brings a small potential risk for information leakage. There are three options available, no authentication or payload encryption (noAuthNoPriv), only strong authentication (authNoPriv), and both strong authentication and payload encryption (AuthPriv), select the desired option from the WebUI, note that these are per User Name, multiple User Names can be defined and are synonymous with the SNMPv2c community. For each User Name you can define a set of Notification Hosts, also known as trap receivers and just like SNMPv2c the types of traps that are sent to each of the defined Notification Hosts.

Configuring SNMP from the CLI is slightly more complicated than one might expect, in particular, defining the permitted SNMP query hosts and trap receivers requires a second set of config and edit branches within the one for configuring the SNMP community.

The basic information that is common between both SNMPv2 and SNMPv3 as well as the option to enable SNMP in the first place:

```
FGT # config system snmp sysinfo
  set contact-info "NetOps and SecOps"
  set description "FortiGate Security Enforcement Poin"
```

```
   set location "Somewhere, Someplace"
   set status enable
end
```

Now you can configure SNMPv2 and/or SNMPv3, note that they are configured separately.

```
FGT # config system snmp community
 edit 1
    set name "SOC-mgmt"
    set query-v1-status disable
    set trap-v1-status disable
      config hosts
        edit 1
           set ip 172.30.25.161 255.255.255.255
        next
        edit 2
           set ip 172.31.21.161 255.255.255.255
      end
  next
  edit 2
    set name "NOC-Mgmt"
    set query-v1-status disable
    set trap-v1-status disable
      config hosts
        edit 1
           set ip 10.10.10.0 255.255.255.0
        next
        edit 2
           set ip 10.11.12.161 255.255.255.255
    end
FGT #
FGT # config system snmp user
 edit "StrongSNMP"
    set notify-hosts 172.25.25.162 172.25.35.162
    set security-level auth-priv
    set auth-pwd <password up to 32 characters>
    set priv-pwd <password up to 32 characters>
end
```

Both of the above examples use the default configurations for the types of traps to send (all possible options), if the administrator has configured only some of the traps to be sent to a specific trap receiver then there will be a configuration option listing all the options on a single line, similar to the following, you can specify the types of traps to send on a per-community basis (use the ? key when configuring to get the current list of available options), not a per-receiver basis, all hosts configured for the same community receive the same set of traps.

```
set events cpu-high mem-low ha-switch ha-hb-failure ha-member-up ha-
    member-down
```

If you are deploying the FortiGates in an FGCP HA configuration, then there is an additional option that you may want to enable. By default only the primary FGCP cluster member has the ability to send and receive data since the virtual IP and virtual MAC are allocated to that device, this means that FGCP has to proxy the SNMP queries to the subordinate cluster members, and the SNMP management tool has to be able to configure to send multiple SNMP queries, the queries need to use a community that has the desired subordinate units serial# appended to the configured community string. An alternative configuration is to reconfigure the cluster to run with reserved management ports enabled (discussed elsewhere in this book), when this is done you will need to inform the SNMP agent to accept SNMP queries on these dedicated management interfaces, to do so for SNMPv2 add the configuration option "set ha-direct" to each host definition for each community, for SNMPv3 it's a little easier, it's done once for each User Name.

```
FGT # config sys snmp community
  edit 2
      config hosts
        edit 1
            set ha-direct enable
            end
  end
FGT #
FGT # config sys snmp user
  edit "StrongSNMP"
    set ha-direct enable
  end
```

Controlling Administrative Access

Since the FortiGate is a security device that can be locally configured, it is very important that you appropriately control access to the system. The first and most obvious method is to use strong credentials. Additionally, FortiOS versions prior to 4.3 have two extra methods of controlling access, Administrative Access is controlled at the interface level and Trusted Host access is controlled at the administrative account level.

The interface-based Administrative Access determines what protocols run on an individual interface. This way, a security-conscious administrator can enable only the minimal protocols required on the specific interfaces needed. Even though FortiOS supports HTTP and telnet access to the interface, it is highly recommended that these are not enabled as they pass credentials in clear text. Thus, if an attacker got access to your network, they could read the credentials, access the FortiGate device, and make configuration changes.

You can even disable the ability to send an ICMP echo (Ping) request to an interface, although that will make future troubleshooting more difficult. This is another tradeoff, ease of troubleshooting for you vs ease of gathering data for your attacker.

In addition to the interface-based Administrative Access controls, you can also change the TCP ports that the administrative protocols listen on. This is highly recommended as it hides the access from the less skilled attackers and weeds out failed login events to only those you need to pay attention to. Of course, you do have to choose port numbers that you can remember so you can still access your device. From the WebUI you can navigate to System → Admin → Settings → Administration Settings. Changing the ports here affects all interfaces and will disconnect your current session if you change the port that you are using. As noted earlier in this chapter, the changes are immediate once you click the "Apply" button (see Figure 3.2).

You can also make this change via the CLI:

```
FGT # config system global
FGT (global) # set admin-port <integer>          ← the port
                                                    for HTTP access
FGT (global) # set admin-sport <integer>         ← the port
                                                    for HTTPS access
FGT (global) # set admin-ssh-port <integer>      ← the port
                                                    for SSH access
FGT (global) # set admin-telnet-port <integer>   ← the port
                                                    for telnet access
FGT (global) # end
```

You may also need to change the administrative port if you want to have the FortiGate provide a port-forwarded config that uses the FortiGate's actual IP address. For example, you wish to provide access to a secure web server on an internal network on the de facto standard port of TCP/443, if you leave HTTPS administrative access enabled on the interface connected to the Internet and don't change the port then when an external user attempts to connect to the FortiGate Internet IP address on TCP/443 the user will receive the FortiGate WebUI login prompt instead of the desired web page from the internal web server.

In addition to controlling the port and protocol by which you can access the WebUI and CLI, you can also limit access at the IP level for each of the

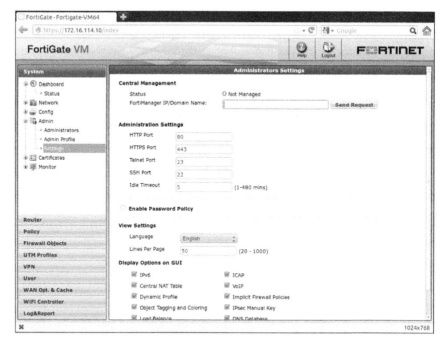

FIGURE 3.2 Controlling Administrative Access

administrative accounts. These are known as the Trusted Hosts settings. Using the WebUI, navigate to System → Admin → Administrators → Trusted Hosts. If you are running FortiOS 4.3 you'll need to select the checkbox labeled "Restrict this Admin Login from Trusted Hosts Only" before you will be able to configure them. If you are using a remote authentication service such as RADIUS, LDAP, or TACACS+ you will need to ensure that the set of trusted hosts for the administrative account covers all users that will be logging in via that method. Remember that if you have administrators logging in from home, they might have dynamically assigned IP addresses from their ISPs. If this is the case, and their external IP address changes, they may be locked out from administrating the device. You can work around this issue by only allowing access to the administrative functions from a VPN range or from statically assigned internal systems.

FortiOS Default Behavior to Non-Service Ports

Once upon a time, before security of networked equipment became a concern, there was a protocol known as ident[3] that was intended to associate a username with a port. A number of legacy applications (and newer ones built on top of these legacy apps)

---

[3]RFC1413—Identification Protocol.

> **TIP**
>
> **Login Banner Support**
>
> It's normally considered a best practice to warn someone when they are attempting to access a secure system. In some legal jurisdictions, this is required, as otherwise people can claim ignorance that what they are doing is illegal.
>
> Typically this is performed via some type of banner. FortiOS supports access banners for both CLI and WebUI access. You have full control over the content of these banners; they are part of the Replacement Messages configuration at System → Config → Replacement Message → Administration → Login Disclaimer. Once you have messages that you are satisfied with, you will need to enable this from the CLI.
>
> ```
> FGT # config system global
> FGT (global) # set access-banner enable
> FGT (global) # end
> ```
>
> The access banner is only displayed after you have successfully supplied a valid set of administrative credentials.

still make an attempt to use this protocol. If the protocol is unavailable, there may be a long timeout and as a result most modern systems return a TCP RST packet to any attempts to connect to this service. This terminates the connection on the system that sent the original ident packet, so it doesn't have to wait for the request to time out. This is also the default behavior for FortiOS. However, this is another tradeoff. It speeds up the dropping of connections that would not be useful anyway, but it also leaks information about the system. This is usually useful to an attacker during a probe or fingerprinting phase. You can optionally configure FortiOS to not send a TCP RST packet when a connection attempt is made, making it harder to determine the network devices in use. This is configured on a per-interface basis, so it would be most applicable on your external interfaces.

```
FGT# config system interface
FGT (interface) # edit <name>
FGT (<name>) # set ident-accept enable
FGT (<name>) # end
```

The behavior of the FortiGate for connections to any other IP/port combination for an IP Address configured on the FGT will depend on the FortiGate configuration, such things as the combination of administrative access and trusted hosts, or a Virtual IP associated with a firewall policy.

Network Time Protocol (NTP)[4]

If you will never need to use the log information generated by the FortiGate for legal or HR purposes, it is essential to ensure that the local clock is accurate. This is also

---

[4]RFC 1129—Internet Time Synchronization: The Network TIme Protocol.

essential if you plan to use a two-factor solution, as this will help to avoid problems with clock skew between the FortiGates and the tokens. Time synchronization also makes it much easier to analyze the timeline of an event if the clocks on all the systems involved are synchronized.

You can configure the system time and time zone manually from the Web UI dashboard System Information widget. You also configure an NTP server here, so the FortiGate can pull it's time from a trusted source. Fortinet supplies pool.ntp.org as a default which should be fine for most uses. However, if your company runs an internal NTP server, it may be more appropriate to use that. While the Web UI allows you specify only a single NTP server, FortiOS actually supports the configuration of multiple servers through the CLI. Configuration of time servers based on the NTPv3 protocol is also available from the CLI, this version of the protocol requires an authentication string for access, so it is disabled by default and is normally only used when connecting to an internal NTP server.

```
config system ntp
   config ntpserver
     edit 1
        set ntpv3 disable
        set server "pool.ntp.org"
     next
     edit 2
        set ntpv3 enable
        set server "privateNTP.example.com"
        set authentication enable
        set key-id 1
        set key <passphrase>
     end
   set ntpsync enable

set syncinterval 60
end
```

Specifying the Source IP Address for FortiOS Originated Traffic

A FortiGate has many interfaces and, therefore, can have many source IP addresses. This can create problems in some situations. Consider a case where a large organization is using IPSec for site-to-site communication. In an environment like this, there could be multiple logging servers located at various points throughout the network. By default, when the FortiGate sends a message to local log server, it will use the IP address of the interface nearest the server. However, this means that the same device shows up in the logs under multiple IP addresses. This can make for difficulty when correlating log events. Similarly, if you use remote authentication (RADIUS, TACACS+, or LDAP), there often are hard limits on which IP addresses can request access. This provides protection to the authentication server, but means that every time an interface on the FortiGate is altered, the authentication configuration must also be changed or risk being locked out.

For most of the traffic that originates from the FortiOS, it is now possible to specify the source IP address that the device will masquerade as. You can specify any address you want, typically though, the IP address of the loopback or internal interface is used. This option is only available from the CLI and is configured within the specific service that you wish to masquerade, such as DNS, NTP, or logging. As of this writing, all traffic that originates from FortiOS can have the source IP changed except for sflow collectors and SNMP traps.

```
FGT # config system dns
FGT (dns) #set status enable
FGT (dns) #set source-ip <a FortiGate interface IP>
end
config system ntp
   set status enable
   set source-ip <a FortiGate interface IP>
end
config log syslogd setting
   set status enable
   set source-ip <a FortiGate interface IP>
end
```

Dealing with Administrative Operations

Once deployed, the FortiGate becomes a critical part of your security infrastructure. Of course as a prudent administrator you need to be able to cope with a system failure. To be prepared, you should periodically back up the FortiGate configuration, understand how to upgrade the firmware, and know how to quickly get a replacement unit up and running.

Performing Backups

Since the system configuration may contain confidential information, only administrative accounts with sufficient privileges (such as the superadmin) are allowed to perform backup operations. Backups can be initiated from either the WebUI or the CLI. When performing the backup from the CLI, you can save the configuration in many places: on a TFTP server, an FTP server, a locally installed USB memory device or, if available, a FortiManager (see Figure 3.3).

Method	CLI Command	Comments
TFTP	exec backup [config | full-config] tftp <ip address> <filename.	
FTP	exec backup [config | full-config] ftp <ip address> <filename> <username> <password>	
USB	exec backup config usb <filename>exec backup full-config usb <filename>	The file referred to by <filename> must be on the first partition of the USB memory stick and this partition must be formatted as FAT32

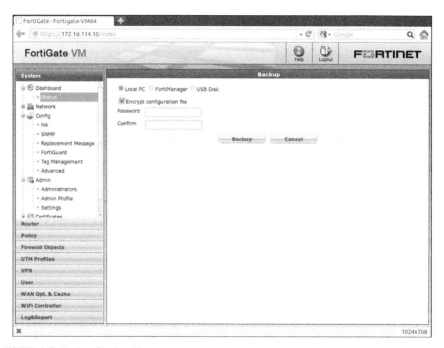

FIGURE 3.3 Performing Backkups

If you are using any type of certificate-based service on the FortiGate (IPSec/SSL-VPN tunnels using certificates for authentication, certificate-based user authentication, or any of the SSL inspection services), you will want to provide a backup password. The SSL Certificates stored on the FortiGate are only backed up when a password is provided. This way, there is reduced risk of losing control of the private keys, which could allow an attacker to intercept traffic the same way the FortiGate can. Needless to say, it is critical that you know the password to restore the configuration. There is no way to recover any information from password-protected backup file if that password is not known.

As of FortiOS 4.3 it is also possible for a VDOM Administrator to back up the configuration for just their VDOM(s). This works exactly the same as the methods described above, except that the backup only contains information for that particular VDOM.

Restoring the Configuration

Restoring a configuration is one of the few operations that requires the FortiGate to reboot. The process will replace any current configuration information on the FortiGate, including network configuration and administrative accounts. Thus, if you have changed your administrative access since the backup was performed (disabled HTTP, changed the SSH port, etc.), you will have to access the system the old way after the restore is complete. Be sure to check all of your settings after a restore to ensure that you don't inadvertently lose hardening configuration.

You can restore a configuration using all of the same methods mentioned for performing a backup. If a password was used to backup the configuration, you will need to provide the correct password for the restore to be successful.

The restore process also checks the FortiOS version and model number used when the backup was originally performed. If they don't match, FortiOS will refuse to restore the configuration. This avoids unexpected results, as there are occasionally CLI config command changes between FortiOS versions. When restoring a backup from a FortiOS version that is more recent than the version of FortiOS currently running, the backup may contain configuration statements that are inaccurate, invalid, or simply unsupported.

It is possible however, if necessary, to restore a configuration backed up from one version of FortiOS to a system running a different version of FortiOS, or even to restore a backup from one FortiGate model to an unrelated FortiGate model. This often occurs during an upgrade.

If you need to restore perhaps a backup made a while ago, when your FortiGate was running a different version of FortiOS, it is best to go through the downgrade/upgrade process, downgrading to the version of firmware from which the backup was made, then upgrading to the desired release following the process in the Release Notes for that version. However, if this is undesirable for some reason, you can manually edit a copy of the configuration backup and change the first line in the file to reflect the version of FortiOS that you are currently running. If the backup was performed using a password, then this method will not work, as the backup will be encrypted and not editable.

The first line of a configuration backup should contain a line that looks something like this:

```
#config-version=FG5A01-4.00-FW-build315-110330:opmode=0:vdom=1:user=admin
```

You will need to change the firmware version information to match that of the current firmware. The simplest way to get this line correct is to perform a backup from the current firmware running on your FortiGate and then copy that first line over the first line in the configuration file you wish to restore. If you do not have access to the FortiGate to perform the restore, you will have to edit it manually. To do this, you must know the build number and the date code that follows, so in the above example, the "build315-110330" text is the complete version information.

If you are doing the restore, errors will be logged to the console. Follow the instructions in the "Multiple Image Support" section earlier in this chapter to connect. If there are any issues interpreting the configuration file, they will be output on the console, or if not of a critical nature they will be logged to a logfile and a message similar to the following will appear on the console

"Configuration errors found, please review the output of *diag debug config-error-log read*"

If you don't have the option to view the console output during the restore, then you should definitely review the output from the above command at your earliest opportunity. This will highlight any configuration statements that could not be correctly applied to the currently running configuration.

If you are attempting to restore a configuration from one model FortiGate onto another model FortiGate, even if it's the same version, you will need to make sure that the configuration is modified to reflect the physical characteristics of the target model. The most common changes required are interface names. Some of the entry-level models have interfaces named things like: wan1, wan2, internal, DMZ, etc. While other models have simply port1, port2, port3, port4, etc. Luckily, since the configuration is a text file, this is normally a simply search and replace exercise. Once you've looked after all the physical items, you'll also need to modify the configuration file's first line to reflect the new model. The above example was for a FortiGate 5001A, if we are attempting to install that config to a FortiGate 5001B as part of an upgrade, then the first line needs to become:

```
#config-version=FG5B01-4.00-FW-build315-110330:opmode=0:vdom=1:user=a
  dmin
```

Note the only change was to the model information (FG5A01 became FG5B01). The rest of the line remains the same since, in this case, the new FortiGate 5001B will be running the same version FortiOS.

Upgrading/Restoring Firmware

It's almost inevitable that at some point in your time with the FortiGate device, you will need to change the firmware image stored on the FortiGate. This could be to recover a failed unit or to upgrade/downgrade the firmware on a currently operating unit.

If the FortiGate is operating and you know the credentials for an administrative account with sufficient privileges, you can restore a firmware image from either the WebUI or the CLI. If the FortiGate is non-operational (powers up and loads the BIOS but cannot load the firmware from flash), or you no longer have valid administrative credentials, you can install a firmware image from the FortiGate BIOS.

To restore a firmware image from the WebUI, simply navigate to the System Information widget on the System Dashboard, select the restore option, and locate the file on your local PC.

When restoring a firmware image from the CLI, you can select from multiple different methods for transferring the firmware image to the device: TFTP, FTP, USB, FortiGuard and, if available, from a FortiManager.

Finally, you can restore a firmware image to an operating FortiGate device by power-cycling the FortiGate with a USB memory device installed. For this to work correctly, you will first need to copy an appropriate firmware image (obtained from the Fortinet Support website, http://support.fortinet.com) to the USB memory device and save it as a file named "image.out" in the root directory of the first partition (which must be formatted as whether FAT16 or FAT32) of the USB memory device.

When the FortiGate boots, the original firmware image will load, but during the initialization phase it will check to see if there is a USB memory device present. If the first file system contains a file called image.out, this file is then copied into RAM, the checksum verified, and the platform and version IDs checked. If all of these checks are valid, then the new image is copied to either the alternate boot partition (for devices with multiple boot partitions) or the primary boot partition (replacing the current firmware image). Once the copy completes, the FortiGate will automatically reboot to load the new firmware image. If the USB memory device is still installed after the reboot, the image won't be reinstalled as the firmware version on the USB memory device will match the version that just booted.

If your FortiGate device is no longer able to boot the firmware image stored in flash memory, your only recourse is to install a new firmware image from the systems BIOS. This operation also overwrites the unit's configuration file and is one method of recovering a unit for which you do not know the administrative credentials. This method requires that you have physical access to the FortiGate to connect to the console, and a computer running a TFTP server that can be directly connected to the FortiGate. The ethernet interface that you will need to connect to the TFTP server varies from model to model, but is typically either the port1 or internal interface.

Connect to the FortiGate's serial console port using the Fortinet supplied console cable, your terminal emulator should be configured for 9600 baud, no parity, 8 data bits, and one stop bit, commonly known as 9600 N81.(see Figure 3.4)

Now, when you power up the FortiGate you should see output similar to the following from the console port:

```
Ver:03006000
Serial number:FG300A2904500319
RAM activation
CPU(00:00000f29 bfebfbff): Do MP initialization
Total RAM: 512MB
Enabling cache...Done.
Scanning PCI bus...Done.
```

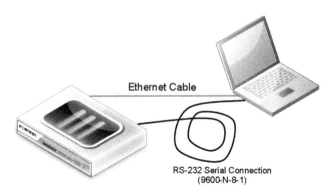

Ethernet Cable

RS-232 Serial Connection
(9600-N-8-1)

FIGURE 3.4 Connections Required for Firmware Installation via Console Port

```
Allocating PCI resources...Done.
Enabling PCI resources...Done.
Zeroing IRQ settings...Done.
Verifying PIRQ tables...Done.
Boot up, boot device capacity: 61MB.
Press any key to display configuration menu...
......
```

The only important piece of information in the output at this time is the prompt to "press any key to enter menu", when you do so a very simple text menu will be displayed. This prompt only appears for approximately five seconds, if you don't press a key soon enough the FortiGate will continue the boot process, so power-off and try again.

```
[G]: Get firmware image from TFTP server.
[F]: Format boot device.
[B]: Boot with backup firmware and set as default.
[C]: Configuration and information.
[Q]: Quit menu and continue to boot with default firmware.
[H]: Display this list of options.
```

One of the most common reasons for a FortiGate to no longer boot from its flash storage devices is that these memory chips only have a limited number of read-write cycles. Sometimes very minor manufacturing flaws result in failure, though for most systems this is beyond the expected lifecycle. Due to this, when doing a manual recovery, it's always a good idea to format the flash storage device. This ensures that any sectors that have gone bad will not be used for data storage. To format, select the "F" option from the menu. This will only take a very few seconds to complete.

```
All data will be erased,continue:[Y/N]?
Formatting boot device...
..............
Format boot device completed.
Enter G,F,B,C,Q,or H:
```

At this point, the system will no longer have a firmware image or configuration, and so will be unable to participate as a network filter. The only method for getting a firmware image onto the system at this point is via the BIOS and a local Ethernet connection.

To upload the desired firmware image to the FortiGate via TFTP, select the "G" option. This option will prompt you for the TFTP server IP address, the IP Address to assign to the FortiGate's interface and the name of the file to download from the TFTP server. As the device no longer does routing, there is no option to enter a default gateway. Thus, the system that is running the TFTP server needs to be either directly connected to the FortiGate or be on the same Layer 3 subnet.

```
Enter TFTP server address [192.168.1.168]:
Enter local address [192.168.1.188]:
Enter firmware image file name [image.out]: FGT_300A-v400-build0482-
   FORTINET.out
MAC:00090F8542E1
##################
Total 20941933 bytes data downloaded.
Verifying the integrity of the firmware image.
Total 28000kB unzipped.
Save as Default firmware/Backup firmware/Run image without saving:[D/
   B/R]?
Programming the boot device now.
.........................
Reading boot image 1405524 bytes.
Initializing firewall...
System is started.
FG300A2904500319 login:
```

The exact output on your FortiGate appliance may differ slightly from the above, depending on the exact BIOS and model, but the steps remain the same. The above output is from a system that supports two firmware partitions, so we are prompted for the partition in which to install the image. If you have formatted the flash as suggested above, then it doesn't matter which partition you choose (they're both empty) so you might as well choose the Default (also called Primary). If you have not formatted the flash, then "Default" refers to the partition already marked as bootable.

This could be either the Primary or Secondary flash partition. If your system is an older one that does not support multiple firmware partitions, then you are prompted to either write the image to flash or directly run the image.

Password Recovery

If you like many users there will, unfortunately, come a time when you will be unable to login to and administer a device. There are many reasons that this could occur: the remote authentication system is unreachable, your credentials are incorrect, you don't have the credentials, or you've restored a configuration and do not know what the restore reset the access credentials to.

There are two methods available for performing a password recovery. The first method is described above. Installing a firmware image from the BIOS overwrites everything in the partition, including the configuration, and therefore all the authentication details. Of course this means you have also lost all of the rest of the configuration as well.

If you need to recover the administrative credentials without losing the configuration, you must have physical access to the FortiGate. To perform the password recovery process, follow these steps:

1. Connect to the console port and make sure that you have access by pressing [Enter] a few times to get a system prompt.
2. Power the FortiGate off. This will interrupt any traffic passing through the FortiGate, so plan accordingly.
3. Power the FortiGate back on.
4. When you see the BIOS in the console, get a copy of the serial number, either by using copy/paste or writing it down.
5. Once the login prompt appears, login using a special account "maintainer".
6. The password for this account will be the concatenation of "bcpb" and the systems serial number. Thus, if your serial number was "434522", the password will be "bcpb434522".
7. You only have 30 s from the time the login prompt appears to enter the correct username and password information, after that the account is automatically disabled. Thus, it is wise to use copy/paste on your system.

For most deployments, the fact that you need physical access to the FortiGate should avoid any abuse of this option. However, as of FortiOS 4.3, it is possible to completely disable this feature. The following parameters would disable the password recovery:

```
config system global
  set admin-maintainer disable
end
```

Be aware, though, that if this is done, resetting the administrative credentials will require a complete reinstallation of firmware from the BIOS.

Automatic FortiAP Firmware Updates from FortiGate

To simplify the operation and maintenance of a Fortinet-powered secure wireless infrastructure, you can have the distributed FortiAP update their own firmware images directly from the system acting as the Wireless Access Controller. To enable this, you need first to add the FortiAP firmware to the FortiGate that is the Access Controller. You do this via TFTP or FTP in a similar manner as applying a firmware update.

```
FGT # exec wireless-controller upload-wtp-image tftp <image name>
   <server IP>
```

```
FGT # exec wireless-controller upload-wtp-image ftp <image_name>
   <server IP><:port> <username> <password>
```

You can upload multiple firmware images to the FortiGate, but only one per FortiAP model.

To view the current images on the Access Controller, you must use the "wireless-controller list-wtp-image" command.

```
FGT # exec wireless-controller list-wtp-image
```

WTP Images on AC:

ImageName	ImageSize(B)	ImageInfo	ImageMTime
FAP222-IMG.wtp	3848808	FAP222-v4.0-build219	Fri Sep 30 15:19:12 2011
FAP22B-IMG.wtp	3744564	FAP22B-v4.0-build219	Fri Sep 30 15:08:31 2011

By default, when the FortiAP reboots, it will automatically update the firmware image. If you want to disable this capability, you will need to update the configuration for the FortiAP from the CLI.

```
FGT # config wireless-controller wtp
FGT (wtp) # edit <FAP>
FGT (<FAP>) # set image-download disable
FGT (<FAP>) # end
```

Finally, by default when you access the FortiAP from the console port, there is no password defined. This is typically not a problem, as they aren't very easy to physically access. However, it is still recommended that you change the password. At this time, this can only be done from the CLI.

```
FGT # config wireless-controller wtp
FGT (wtp) # edit <FAP>
FGT (<FAP>) # set login-passwd-change yes
FGT (<FAP>) # set login-passwd <string>
FGT (<FAP>) # enable
```

Enabling VDOMS

One of the nice implementation features of FortiGate's VDOMs is that you don't need to decide at installation time whether or not you will use them. They can easily be enabled at a later date. You can even enable VDOMs while the firewall is running without affecting traffic. The only impact is that administrators be logged out of the administrative interfaces when VDOMs are enabled.

When VDOMs are enabled, all initial security-related configurations are automatically moved to the default VDOM, which is named "root". This VDOM is automatically created when VDOM's are enabled and cannot be deleted. All system-level (cross-VDOM) configurations are performed outside of the VDOMs in what is referred to as Global mode.

The simplest way to enable VDOMs is from the WebUI. Navigate to the System → Dashboard page and look at the "System Information" widget. This widget should indicate whether VDOMs are enabled. If they are not yet enabled, clicking on the "Enable" link will present a dialog warning the Administrator that this action will log them out. Selecting "OK" will trigger the enable process and log you out. When you log back into the WebUI, you will immediately notice that there are significantly fewer options in the left-hand menu. The bottom of this menu is a selector that allows you to toggle between "Global" and "root". All of the configuration that you had on the FortiGate previously will now be found in the "root" VDOM.

For administrators considering a complicated configuration utilizing multiple VDOMs, it is recommended that you use the default root VDOM for Out-of-Band management. This VDOM would contain a single interface so it would be unable to function as a firewall. However, it would provide a good way to access the system. All actual user traffic would be via interfaces tied to other VDOMs.

UTM Technologies Explained

Connectivity and Networking Technologies

INFORMATION IN THIS CHAPTER:

- Operating Modes
  - Layer 2 (Transparent)
  - Layer 3 (NAT/Route)
- Connectivity
  - Dynamically Addressed Interfaces
  - VLAN Interfaces
  - 802.3AD
  - Redundant Interfaces
  - Wireless
  - Modems
  - IPv6 Interfaces
- Routing
  - Static Routing
  - Policy-Based Routing
  - Dynamic Routing
    - RIP (Routing Information Protocol)
    - OSPF (Open Shortest Path First)
    - BGP (Border Gateway Protocol)
    - IS-IS (Intermediate System to Intermediate System)
    - Route Redistribution
    - Multicast
    - ECMP (Equal Cost MultiPath)
    - BFD (Bidirectional Forwarding Detection)
    - Information and Troubleshooting
- Servicing Users
  - DHCP
  - DNS Server
- Virtual Domains (VDOM)
- High Availability

OPERATING MODES

As noted previously, a FortiGate can be configured to operate either in Transparent mode, like a switch (L2 based forwarding) or in NAT/Route mode, like a router (L3 based forwarding). Thus, the way in which packets are treated will depend on which of these two modes the device is in.

Layer 2 (Transparent)

This mode of operation is also commonly referred to as bridged mode, as the operation is very similar to that of a Layer 2 bridge or switch. The default operating mode for a FortiGate or a newly defined VDOM is always L3 mode. Changing the mode is as simple as using the link in the System Information widget on the main status page. Once selected, you will be prompted to specify the IP address and default gateway information for the device to use after the mode has been changed. This IP address will be used for accessing the FortiGate administrative interfaces. As noted in previous chapters, changes like this take place immediately, so it is important to use an address that will remain reachable. It would also be a good idea to verify that the planned network interfaces over which the WebUI will be accessed have sufficient administrative protocols configured at System → Network → Interfaces. If you are using the CLI, you will also need to configure the IP address and the default gateway.

```
FGT# config system setting
FGT (settings) # set opmode transparent
FGT (settings) # set manageip <ip: x.x.x.x> <subnet: x.x.x.x>
FGT (settings) # end
```

When operating in Transparent Mode it is critical that you install and configure the FortiGate in configuration that avoids creating network loops. Much as L2 switches do, a FortiGate tracks all ARP request/reply transactions and builds a table of IP/MAC/interface values. This table is consulted for each new packet received so the correct egress interface can be determined and, therefore, linked to correct firewall policies. When the FortiGate receives a packet with a destination IP and/or MAC that is not in the current table, the FortiGate will flood the packet out to all allowed interfaces.

In some networks the Spanning Tree Protocol (STP) may be used to avoid creation of network loops, the FortiGate device itself does not participate in STP, it can however forward STP packets, this is enabled from the CLI by setting the option stpforward to enable for the appropriate interfaces.

```
config system interface
 edit <interface name>
   ...
   set stpforward enable
   ...
 next
end
```

Layer 3 (NAT/Route)

Layer 3 is the traditional operating mode for most firewalls. In this mode, the interface from which a packet is forwarded is based on the routing table.

CONNECTIVITY

The FortiGate product family supports a number of different types of network interfaces. While these are primarily 802.3 Ethernet interfaces, 802.11 Wireless, ADSL2/2+ modems, Analog Modem, RS232 and USB connected modems are also supported. At this time, there is currently no support for any of the traditional wide area connection technologies such as ATM, T1/T3, etc.

Some models support modularity, allowing for different types of physical interface to be combined. These include RJ45, Short-Haul multimode fiber, Long-Haul multimode, and/or singlemode fiber. Some of the more recent models also support SFP (1 Gbps) interfaces. The top end of the product line also supports SFP+ (10 Gbps) interfaces. The SFP+ interface is physically plug-compatible with its predecessor, the SFP. These are often incorrectly referred to as GBIC's, but are not the same as Cisco's older socket technology.

Dynamically Addressed Interfaces

Any Ethernet interface on the FortiGate can be configured to support dynamic IPV4 addressing via DHCP or PPPoE. Both of these protocols normally provide next-hop gateway information which the FortiGate can either accept or ignore depending on the setting of the "Retrieve default gateway from server" option. When enabled, the default route provided is installed into the local routing table. If the option is disabled, the provided route will not be installed. In the CLI, this setting is defined as "set defaultgw enable" under the interface parameters.

When using dynamically addressed interfaces, it won't be possible to configure your DNS to allow access to the device by name, as the addresses will periodically change. A simple solution to this is to enable the FortiGate's integrated support for Dynamic DNS. When this is enabled, the FortiGate will update a Dynamic DNS system on every address change. Support includes a number of commercial providers and one generic service. The Dynamic DNS configuration can be edited from both the WebUI and the CLI.

VLAN Interfaces

All of the FortiGate units with the exception of the smallest of the entry-level models support the use of VLANs (virtual LANs) as defined by the IEEE 802.1q specification.

A VLAN is a method of allowing multiple distinct networks to operate over the same physical infrastructure, the packets associated with each of these distinct networks are identified by the use of additional data in the packet, commonly referred to as a VLAN tag, these tags are used by the physical network components to isolate the packets for each distinct (or virtual) network, this includes the FortiGate.

A virtual VLAN interface is needed for each VLAN that needs to have security enforcement performed, these can be created from the WebUI by navigating to System → Network and clicking on the Create New button, in the edit page change the interface type option to VLAN interface and specify the physical interface this VLAN is to be associated with and then specify the VLAN tag that identifies the traffic. From the CLI, you will need to set the interface type to VLAN in order for the remaining required configuration options to become available, you will also need to assign the new interface to a VDOM, if you do not have VDOMs enabled then you will still need to assign the interface to the root VDOM.

```
FGT # conf sys int
FGT (interface) # edit port1.10
new entry 'port1.10' added
FGT (port1.10) # set type vlan
FGT (port1.10) # set vlanid 10
FGT (port1.10) # set vdom root
FGT (port1.10) # set interface port1
FGT (port1.10) # end
```

You can use the same VLAN number only once per physical interface, however you can use the same VLAN number on different physical interfaces.

If you are configuring your FortiGate to operate in Transparent mode there is a potential challenge with VLANs. A packet received on one VLAN could potentially be flooded out to all the other VLANs interfaces, resulting in looping. ARP requests, in particular, are a common cause of this type of loop since they are L2 broadcast packets that need to be forwarded. To prevent this type of loop, it is critical that you ensure those packets are contained to their correct broadcast domain. This isolation is ensured with the "forward-domains" FortiOS feature, defining groups of interfaces that belong to the same L2 broadcast domain. This option is currently only available from the CLI. Normally, to configure this feature, you would have the VLAN pairs on the corresponding 802.1q trunks configured into unique forward-domains.

```
FGT # config system interface
FGT (interface) # edit "port1.10"
FGT (port1.10) # set vdom "root"
FGT (port1.10) # set forward-domain 10
FGT (port1.10) # set interface "port1"
FGT (port1.10) # set vlanid 10
FGT (port1.10) # next
FGT (interface) # edit "port2.10"
```

```
FGT (port2.10) # set vdom "root"
FGT (port2.10) # set forward-domain 10
FGT (port2.10) # set interface "port2"
FGT (port2.10) # set vlanid 10
FGT (port2.10) # end
FGT #
```

When creating a firewall policy that references an interface in a forward-domain, the only other valid interfaces are those in the same forward-domain. An attempt to use a combination of interfaces that aren't in the same forward-domain will result in an error.

Beginning with FortiOS 4.3, there is a simplified version of the forward-domain configuration, referred to as a "port-pair." Only two interfaces can be configured into a port-pair and all lookup functions are disabled. Thus, it is assumed that a packet received on one port-pair interface has only one egress option: the other interface in the pair. Therefore, there is no need to perform any IP/MAC table lookups. This feature can be created from the WebUI by navigating to System → Network → Interface→, there is a small arrow on the right of "Create New," click on it and select port-pair, select the two interfaces to use in the newly defined port-pair. When creating a firewall policy for traffic transiting the port-pair interfaces, the correct alternate interface is automatically filled in when either interface is selected.

There may also be situations where you are only interested in providing security controls on some VLANs within an 802.1q trunk. By default, when a packet is tagged for a VLAN that is not configured for a specific interface, it is dropped. However, you can configure the FortiGate to simply forward the non-matching packets out the corresponding interface without being processed by the FortiGate. This is accomplished using the "vlanforward" option on both interfaces.

```
FGT # config system interface
FGT (interface) # edit port1
FGT (port1) # set vlanforward enable
FGT (port1) # next
FGT (interface) # edit port2
FGT (port2) # set vlanforward enable
FGT (port2) # end
```

802.3AD

Commonly referred to as Link Aggregation, this widely implemented industry standard allows the network architect to design an infrastructure that increases potential throughput and resiliency without the additional complication of the Spanning Tree protocol.

To avoid communication mismatches, a Link Aggregation interface must be created using identical physical interfaces. Once a physical interface is added to an aggregate interface, it is no longer available for any other configuration.

Aggregate interfaces can be created from either the WebUI or the CLI. From the WebUI:

1. Navigate to System → Network → Interfaces → small arrow on the Create New button.
2. Select the interface option from the pull-down list.
3. Use the displayed dialog to

    a. Define a new interface.
    b. Give the interface a name.
    c. Set the type to "802.3ad link aggregation."
    d. Select the physical interfaces that you wish to use in the bundle.
    e. Define the remaining interface parameters as required.

From the CLI, the configuration steps would be similar to the following:

```
FGT # config system interface
 edit "Bundle1"
  set vdom <vdom name>
  set type aggregate
  set member <intf name> [ <intf name> ....... ]
 <other interface parameters as required>
```

When an aggregate interface is created, there are a few additional configuration options available that provide for control over the behavior. These will be explained later in this chapter.

```
set lacp-mode [active|passive|static]
set lacp-speed [fast|slow]
set algorithm [L2|L3|L4]
```

Once created, the Aggregate Interface can be used just like a physical interface, including adding VLANs, defining policies, etc.

A Link Aggregation interface can be optionally configured to support the LACP protocol, as defined by the IEEE. By default, when a new Link Aggregation interface is created, LACP is disabled. Enabling LACP is only possible from the CLI. This is where you define support for both Active and Passive modes as well as slow and fast LACP PDU intervals. You can also choose the algorithm used for distributing packets across the member interfaces, based on the L2, L3, or L4 information.

When using Link Aggregation in conjunction with an HA cluster configuration, there are few additional factors to keep in mind. If both units in an Active-Active cluster are connected to the same external Link Aggregation, then it is important that both units send/receive LACP packets so that all the interfaces are operational. The default behavior is for the slave unit to not send LACP PDUs. If the cluster is configured as an Active-Passive cluster then it is important to ensure that the slave unit does not send LACP PDUs to the external systems, as that would indicate to it that the path is valid. This would result in packets being sent to the Passive unit as well as the Active and since the Passive unit would not be passing traffic, the connection could experience high latency or outright disruption.

```
FGT # config system interface
 edit <aggregate interface>
  set lacp-ha-slave [ enable | disable ]
```

Redundant Interfaces

This configuration option provides some of the benefits of 802.3ad Link Aggregation without the complexity and potential interoperability challenges. It addresses the common requirement to deploy security products with as much resiliency as possible, providing physical link resiliency.

Much like an aggregate interface, a redundant interface is a virtual interface that is composed of a set of physical interfaces. Once a physical interface is assigned to a redundant interface, it is no longer available for use anywhere else in the configuration such as routing or firewall policies.

Creating a Redundant Interface is similar to creating a Link Aggregation interface. If using the WebUI:

1. Navigate to System → Network → Interfaces → small arrow on the Create New button.
2. Select the Redundant Interface option from the pull-down list.
3. Use the displayed dialog to

   a. Select the interfaces you wish to add to the Redundant Interface definition. If using the CLI, you can issue the following commands:

```
FGT # config system interface
FGT (interface) # edit <new interface name>
FGT (port1) # set vdom <vdom name>
FGT (port1) # set type redundant
FGT (port1) # set member <intf name> [ <intf name> ....... ] <other
interface parameters as required>
```

Once created, the Redundant Interface can be used just like a physical interface.

FortiOS performs dependency checking to ensure that an object can be safely added/deleted/modified. If you do not see the physical interfaces that you wish to use, it means that it must be in use in the configuration of another object such as DHCP server, firewall policy, or even address objects. If you are unable to locate a dependency for an interface, you can use the following command to locate all the references: *diagnose sys checkused system.interface.name <intf name>*

Wireless

The most straightforward way of implementing a secure wireless solution for a small physical location is to deploy a single FortiWifi appliance rather than a FortiGate appliance. These devices are essentially regular FortiGates with the addition of an integrated 802.11 wireless radio. By default, the wireless radio appears as a unique physical interface. Firewall policies control the traffic that is allowed to and from this interface. It is sometimes desired to have the wireless and wired networks bridged together to create a single Layer 3 network that spans both physical media. Because this is a rare use case and, in some cases, is considered dangerous, it cannot be configured through the WebUI. However, it is possible to do via the CLI.

```
FGT# config system switch-interface
FGT (switch-interface) # edit <new interface name>
FGT (interface name) # set members wlan internal
FGT (interface name) # set vdom root
```

For a larger implementations, where the physical area needing to be covered is greater than the range of a single FortiWIFI, there Fortinet lightweight access points (LWAPs) should be considered. These lightweight access points are connected to a FortiGate (or FortiWifi) via an ethernet connection and accept their configuration from the FortiGate/FortiWifi. Traffic is received on these LWAPs and sent back across the wired connection via an encapsulating protocol based on CAPWAP. CAPWAP is an open standard.

Regardless of the deployment method used (standalone or LWAPs), the configuration process is pretty much the same. There is support for multiple SSIDs, each SSID appearing as a separate interface, allowing the administrator to configure unique security policies per SSID. Each SSID can also have unique configuration for various wireless parameters, such as encryption type, whether a portal is in use, etc.

To create a new SSID and its accompanying virtual interface, navigate to the Wireless Controller section of the WebUI, then to Wifi Network → SSID → Create New. At this point, you will be presented a page that looks very similar to the regular interface page, but also includes the configuration of the wireless parameters such as SSID, security mode, authentication requirements, and even the possibility of a custom authentication portal.

If you are deploying a LWAP configuration you will have to assign the LWAPs to the SSIDs before they are able to provide service.

Modems

Some of the FortiGate models such as the 60CM and 80CM are available with integrated wireline modems, other FortiGate models also support a variety of 3G/4G cellular data modems connected to their USB interfaces.

Both types of modems have nearly identical methods for configuration and use. The modem can be used as a standalone interface for locations where there may not be any traditional broadband connectivity available. They can also be configured as a backup interface for a regular physical interface.

IPv6 Interfaces

All of the above interface types, as well as the physical interface, can be configured with an IPv6 address. If both are configured, the interface is essentially in dual stack mode. If you only want an IPv6 address on an interface, simply set the IPv4 address to 0.0.0.0 or use the *unset ip* configuration option. The IPv6 configuration for an interface is implemented as a sub-table within the existing interface configuration, all IPv6-related parameters are configured here, including administrative access to the FortiGate via IPv6. You can also configure the IPv6 information from the WebUI, however you will first have to enable the display of this in the WebUI, by default the IPv6 configuration options are disabled to keep the WebUI simple. To enable the display of IPv6 in the WebUI, navigate to System → Admin → Settings, under the Display Options in GUI section there is a checkbox for IPv6, selecting this and clicking on apply will result in the IPv6 configuration options being displayed where appropriate in the WebUI.

```
FGT # config system interface
FGT (interface) # edit port1
FGT (port1) # config ipv6
FGT (ipv6) # set ip6-address <IPv6 address and prefix>
FGT (ipv6) # set ip6-allowaccess [http|https|snmp|ping|telnet|ssh|fgfm]
FGT (ipv6) # end
FGT (port1) # end
FGT (interface) # end
```

If you want the FortiGate to send IPv6 router advertisements, you cannot use the interface as a SLAAC (StateLess Address Auto Configuration) client interface.

```
FGT (ipv6) # set ip6-send-adv enable
```

You can configure IPv6 addresses for the interface much like IPv4:

```
FGT (ipv6) # config ip6-extra-address
FGT (ip6-extra-address) # edit <additional IPv6 address and prefix>
FGT (<additional IPv6 address> # next
```

IPv6 StateLess Address Auto Configuration of the interfaces is not enabled by default, but is supported on any interface once the *autoconf* parameter is used to enable IPv6 on the interface. This method is normally only used on client devices, not multi-homed devices such as the FortiGate.

The normal configuration has the FortiGate providing auto configuration information in response to a SLAAC request from other devices. To enable this, you will need to add the prefix and set the autonomous flag on that interface. Obviously, this prefix should include the address assigned to the FortiGate interface.

```
FGT # config system interface
FGT (interface) # edit port1
FGT (port1) # config ipv6
FGT (ipv6) # config ip6-prefix-list
FGT (ip6-prefix-list) # edit <IPv6 Prefix>
FGT (<IPv6 Prefix>) # set autonomous-flag enable
FGT (<IPv6 Prefix>) # set onlink-flag enable
```

The onlink-flag parameter above indicates that the prefix applies to the physically connected network, as opposed to prefixes that are indirectly connected.

ROUTING

This section is not intended to provide a detailed explanation routing protocols. That is far beyond the scope of this book, and there are many very good books available that deal solely with these routing protocols. The focus is to help the administrator get started with routing, and cover issues that are more specific to FortiOS.

It is important to understand how FortiOS internally handles routing updates, particularly when it comes to planning a HA configuration. The software that implements routing runs in what is commonly referred to as "user space." This prevents faults or attacks on this component from impacting the kernel. In such instances, the user space applications will crash and be automatically restarted. Since the firewall engine runs inside the kernel, it is necessary to import the route information from the various routing protocols into the kernel's Forwarding Information Base or FIB. The FIB is the kernel structure that is used to determine the correct egress interface and next-hop gateway for every packet flow. This implementation also allows the kernel to learn the best route for a destination regardless of the routing protocol from which the information is obtained. To view the kernel routing table you use the CLI command "diagnose ip route list."

With the exception of Static Routes, which apply regardless of layer mode, this section only applies to FortiGates running in L3 NAT/Route mode.

Static Routing

When the FortiGate is deployed as a perimeter device, static routing is the most common routing implementation. This is particularly true when there is limited internal L3 network segmentation. Typically, one default route points toward the Internet and any other routes exist to route internal traffic toward the internal routers.

When running in Transparent mode, this is the only method of routing supported. In some situations, particularly when there are internal routers, you will need to be careful about how you define the static routes. If you use a single default route pointing toward an Internet router, it may become possible for the FortiGate's firewall engine to view the data path as asymmetric. This will result in dropped packets. To avoid this, it is wise to always configure an internal static route that uses the correct internal interface of the FortiGate and a default route that directs Internet traffic to the external interface. The default route toward the Internet is also required for the FortiGate to be able to retrieve service updates from the FortiGuard network (see Figures 4.1 and 4.2).

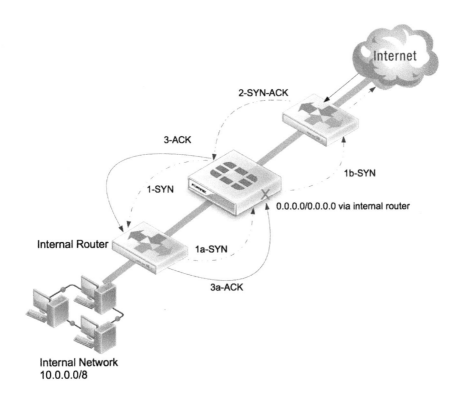

1-SYN : TCP SYN sent from FGT mgmt interface to internal router based on static route
1a-SYN : Router send TCP SYN back thru FGT to FGD server on Internet
1b-SYN : TCP SYN fwd'd thru FGT session entry created with state SYN_SENT
2-SYN-ACK : TCP SYN-ACK reply sent by FGD server received by FGT mgmt interface
3-ACK : TCP ACK sent from FGT mgmt interface to internal router based on static route
3a-ACK : Router sends TCP ACK back thru FGT to FGD server on Internet
X : Packet dropped by firewall engine since it is out of state, firewall engine did not see SYN-ACK as it was processed by FGT mgmt interface

FIGURE 4.1 Two Different TP Mode Scenarios where a Single Default Route will Result in Traffic Problems

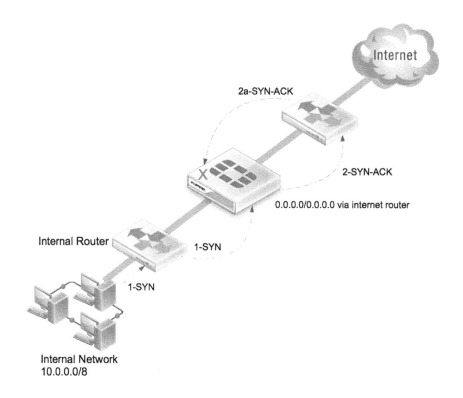

1-SYN : TCP SYN sent from internal client to FGT mgmt interface
2-SYN-ACK : FGT mgmt interface sends SYN-ACK reply to internal client via internet router
2a-SYN-ACK : router sends SYN-ACK packet back thru FGT to internal router to reach client
X : Packet dropped by firewall engine since it is out of state, firewall engine did not see original SYN
as it was processed by FGT mgmt interface

FGURE 4.2 Two Different TP Mode Scenarios where a Single Default Route will Result in Traffic Problems

When you initially change a FortiGate to operate in TP mode, you will be prompted to enter a default gateway. When using the CLI, adding additional static routes as required is no different than when routing in NAT/Route mode. However when running in TP mode, you must add the required static routes under System → Network → Routing Table (see Figure 4.3).

Policy-Based Routing

Most commonly used in a perimeter deployment when there are multiple connections to the Internet. Policy-Based Routing (PBR) allows the network architect to alter the normal routing behavior for traffic flows in ways that are not limited only to the destination IP address. This routing can include the destination port, the source address (or range/subnet), the IP protocol number, or even the incoming interface.

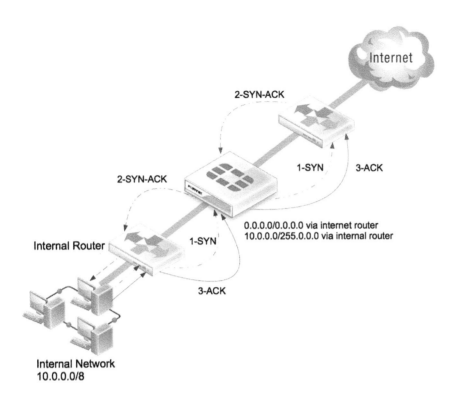

1-SYN : TCP SYN sent from FGT mgmt interface to internet router based on default route
2-SYN-ACK : TCP SYN-ACK reply sent by FGD server received by FGT mgmt interface
3-ACK : TCP ACK sent from FGT mgmt interface to internet router based on static route

FGURE 4.3 Both Solutions can be Solved by Specifying both a Default Route to the Internet and Specific Routes for the Internal Networks that are behind the Internal Router

For example, you may prefer all Web Browsing and similar (perhaps user interactive) traffic to access the Internet via one Internet provider while all other traffic is sent via an alternate provider. This can be useful when one provider charges a premium for a very low-latency service, which you would use for traffic that requires this low latency, such as VOIP.

When you are creating a Policy Route for a specific protocol, such as SMTP, it is important to specify both the protocol (6 for TCP) and the port (25 for SMTP). If the route only involves a single port, both the start and end port will be the same. If you attempt to create a Policy Route for a specific port and you neglect to specify a specific protocol, the system will not understand your meaning. As a result, your changes will not be accepted and will be lost.

Polity route statements are processed in a similar manner as firewall policies—top-down, with the first match winning. New policy routes are always added to the bottom of the list. If you need to change the position of a statement, you will need to select the new policy route using the checkbox and then use the "Move To" option from the menu bar to change its position. From the CLI, you use the "move" command followed by the "before" or "after" keyword and then the ID number of the policy to which you wish to move the policy route.

In this example, we assume that there is an existing policy route configuration that forces all HTTP traffic out the WAN2 interface. However, we need to change the system such that traffic from a specific source exits WAN1. However, when we create this rule, the traffic continues to follow the original path, due to the top-down processing.

```
FGT # show router policy
config router policy
 edit 1
  set input-device "internal"
  set protocol 6
  set start-port 80
  set end-port 80
  set output-device "wan2"
 next
 edit 2
  set input-device "internal"
  set src 192.168.1.1 255.255.255.255
  set protocol 6
  set start-port 80
  set end-port 80
  set output-device "wan1"
 next
end
```

To resolve this, we need to use the "move" command to change the ordering of the policy routes.

```
FGT # config router policy
FGT (policy) # move 2 before 1
FGT (policy) # show
config router policy
 edit 2
  set input-device "Bundle1"
  set src 192.168.1.1 255.255.255.255
  set protocol 6
  set start-port 80
  set end-port 80
```

```
    set output-device "Bundle2"
  next
  edit 1
    set input-device "Bundle1"
    set protocol 6
    set start-port 80
    set end-port 80
    set output-device "Bundle2"
  next
end
```

Now the policy routes are in the desired order and traffic will be forwarded as expected.

Dynamic Routing

FortiOS, when configured in L3 (NAT/Route) mode, has supported the most common open routing protocols since version 3.0. The support for these routing protocols has been enhanced over time, and newer protocols have been added. Another significant area of improvement has been the addition of support for IPv6 information.

These dynamic routing protocols are commonly broken into two major categories: Interior routing protocols or IGP (Interior Gateway Protocols) and Exterior routing protocols or EGP (Exterior Gateway Protocols). An IGP is typically used within a single organization, while an EGP is typically used to connect disparate organizations or large Enterprises to the Internet. RIP and OSPF are examples of IGP, while BGP and IS-IS can be used as either an IGP or EGP.

RIP (Routing Information Protocol)

Unlike the other routing protocols, there are actually two different versions of RIP. The original RIP v1/2 protocol handles IPv4 routing. RIPng as the next generation, however, supports IPv6. Each is configured independently.

It is commonly assumed that RIP is no longer appropriate as a routing protocol, primarily due to its behavior of frequently sending the entire local forward database to all peers. However, there are still architectures where it is appropriate. It is particularly appropriate in architectures that require dynamic routing support but also a very fast convergence time. For example, consider a distributed IPSec hub-and-spoke topology that leverages dialup as well as redundant tunnel configurations.

> When VDOMs are implemented on a FortiGate, the routing information is isolated per VDOM. This allows for complete independent configuration and for overlapping or duplicated IP address space to be used by various VDOMs.
>
> If your configuration consists of multiple L3 VDOMs and you want to exchange routes, you'll need to set up peering across inter-VDOM links connecting the VDOMs. For example, a service provider might have a routing VDOM that connects to a number of customer VDOMs.

OSPF (Open Shortest Path First)

The most common use of this routing protocol is to facilitate route updates within a single organization, often to support an IPsec-based distributed network. It is designed to support large distributed networks via "areas". These areas are numbered with a dotted quad notation, much like IPv4 addresses. These areas are always connected to 0.0.0.0, which is commonly referred to as the backbone area.

BGP (Border Gateway Protocol)

As the de facto routing protocol of the Internet, BGP has two common deployment models. When used for internal routing within a single administrative domain, BGP is also referred to as iBGP. When used to send routes outside of this domain it is commonly referred to as external BGP.

BGP provides extensive control over the propagation of network topology information... so much so that it is often viewed as overly complicated.

The BGP routing protocol uses a TCP connection to each peer to both transmit routing information and ensure the viability of the peer. This also means that there is a requirement for the administrators of each end of the connection to cooperate. It is not normally possible to establish a BGP peer by configuring the IP address of the peer on only one side of the connection.

While there is support for configuring BGP in the WebUI, this is really only sufficient to get the most basic BGP configuration up and running. You can define your local Autonomous System (AS), router ID, interfaces and networks to be propagated. More advanced configuration will require the CLI.

One of the original design requirements was that BGP be extensible. This is implemented via "capabilities". There are a number of capabilities defined by various RFCs. The most commonly used are the "route-refresh" and "graceful-restart" capabilities. Capabilities are negotiated between the peers during the initial establishment of a BGP session and can be disabled or enabled on a per-neighbor basis. The graceful-restart capability can also be enabled/disabled globally.

One useful configuration parameter that is disabled by default is the ability to generate log messages whenever there is a neighbor change. If you are using BGP, you should seriously consider enabling this. Otherwise, a routing change could occur invisibly and be extremely difficult to troubleshoot.

```
FGT # config router bgp
FGT (bgp) # set log-neighbor-changes enable
FGT (bgp) # end
```

> Native IPv6 peering is supported in BGP. To configure an IPv6 peer, you enter an IPv6 address when configuring the neighbor and specify the networks using the "config network6 option" instead of the IPv4-based "config network". Similarly, there are separate IPv6 versions of commands that must be used to define things like aggregation and redistribution.

When deploying a FortiGate solution in a HA configuration, the graceful-restart capability should be enabled on both the FortiGate and the appropriate peers. This capability allows for one peer to notify another when there will be a temporary failure. The result is that, for a period of time, the peer should not drop any routes learned from the failing router. This allows traffic to continue to be forwarded by the routers (using the old routing information) until the TCP peer connection can be rebuilt. When the FortiGate cluster is undergoing a role change, such as during a firmware upgrade, before failing over, the FortiGate sends a graceful-restart message to the configured peers. This way, they will continue to use their old routing information until the peer can be re-established.

```
FGT # config router bgp
FGT (bgp) # set graceful-restart enable
FGT (bgp) # config neighbor
FGT (neighbor) # edit <IP Address>
FGT (<IP Address>) # set capability-graceful enable
FGT (<IP Address>) # end
```

IS-IS (Intermediate System to Intermediate System)

Primarily seen in carrier networks and large enterprise private WAN implementations, IS-IS is considered a possible successor to BGP.

At this time, there is no WebUI support for configuring IS-IS. It is CLI only. However, routes learned via IS-IS are displayed in the WebUI Route Monitor.

Route Redistribution

It is fairly common to have multiple routing protocols running on the same router, since the routing protocols are independent; the routes learned are also independent. Route Redistribution allows routes learned via one routing protocol to be propagated by a different protocol.

One of the more common uses of redistribution is for resilient VPN configuration when using a dial-up or dynamic VPN gateway. When an IPsec Phase2 Security Association is negotiated, and you have enabled redistribution of connected routes, it will be redistributed into your internal routing protocol.

You can configure a route-map to control what routes are redistributed into the target routing protocol. For example, if you are learning both RFC-1918 addresses and public Internet address information for internal networks, you won't want to publish the RFC-1918 addresses into your Internet BGP peering connection.

Route redistribution is enabled on a per-protocol basis.

Multicast

Multicast is usually only required when the FortiGate is being deployed at perimeters for internal security zones and not at the Internet perimeter. PIM Sparse and

Dense modes are both supported when the unit is operating in NAT/Route mode. When running in Transparent mode, there are two deployment options. One is to have the FortiGate forward any multicast packets without evaluating them against the security policies. The other option is to explicitly configure multicast firewall policies to allow only those desired. The first option is enabled from the CLI using the following command:

```
FGT # config system settings
FGT (settings) # set multicat-skip-policy <enable|disable>
```

Currently, the only way to create multicast firewall policies is via the CLI. They are separate from the regular firewall policies.

```
FGT # config firewall multicast-policy
FGT (multicast-policy) # edit 1
new entry '1' added
FGT (1) # set srcintf port1
FGT (1) # set dstintf port2
FGT (1) # set srcaddr 192.168.0.1 255.255.255.255
FGT (1) # set dstaddr 224.0.0.5 255.255.255.255
FGT (1) # set protocol 89
FGT (1) # set status enable
FGT (1) # set action accept
FGT (1) # next
FGT (multicast-policy) # edit 2
new entry '2' added
FGT (2) # set srcintf port1
FGT (2) # set dstintf port2
FGT (2) # set srcaddr 0.0.0.0 0.0.0.0
FGT (2) # set dstaddr 0.0.0.0 0.0.0.0
FGT (2) # set status enable
FGT (2) # set action deny
FGT (2) # end

FGT #
```

This would only allow the OSPF router with the interface address of 192.168.0.1 to forward multicast packets through the FortiGate.

If you are using multicast security policies in Transparent mode, you may run into an issue with the Multicast TTL value. Some multicast protocols require the TTL value to be a known value. By default, when a packet is processed by the security policy, the TTL value in the packets gets decremented. This will break the protocol. To avoid this situation, you can use the "set multicast-no-ttlchange" option from the CLI.

ECMP (Equal Cost MultiPath)

ECMP is less a protocol than a method for improving utilization of multiple paths to the same destination network. As the intent is to ensure that the same session or flow always uses the same egress interface, ECMP examines more than just the destination address when making a forwarding decision. The default method for making this decision is to track the source IP address and alternate through the list of eligible egress paths for each unique source/destination IP address pair. There are two other methods available as well. The first method (Weighted Load Balance) allows you to configure a weight for each interface. This determines the ratio used to split the flows across the interfaces. For example, if you set the weight on one interface to 100 and the weight on another to 50, this will result in twice as many flows being handled by one interface. The second method is referred to as "spillover". This method ignores the less-preferred interfaces until the preferred interface hits a specific bandwidth utilization level. This is most appropriate when the egress interfaces have dramatically different performance characteristics, such as a 10 Mbps Metropolitan LAN type connection with an ADSL2 alternate connection.

You can choose the ECMP method via the WebUI by navigating to Router → Settings and selecting the desired configuration from the set of radio button options. If you are using either the weighted or spillover options for ECMP, you will need to configure the weight or spillover amount for each interface in the same location as the other interface specific configuration options: System → Interface → interface_name (see Figure 4.4).

Similarly, the configuration from the CLI is performed in two separate locations. The ECMP mode is configured under system settings, and the weight or spillover values are configured within the interface parameters.

```
To enable Weighted Load Balance ECMP
FGT # config system settings
FGT (settings) # set v4-ecmp-mode weight-based
To enable Spillover ECMP
FGT # config system settings
FGT (settings) # set v4-ecmp-mode usage-based
To reset to the default of source-IP based ECMP
FGT # config system settings
FGT (settings) # set v4-ecmp-mode source-ip-based
Per interface configuration when using Weighted Load Balance ECMP
FGT # config system interface
FGT (interface) # edit <interface name>
FGT (port1) # set weight <integer for ratio, 0-255>
Per interface configuration when using Spillover ECMP
FGT # config system interface
FGT (interface) # edit <interface name>
FGT (port1) # set spillover-threshold <integer for rate in Kbits/second>
```

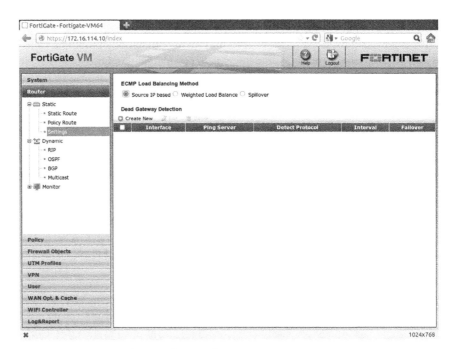

FGURE 4.4 ECMP (Equal Cost Multiple Path)

You can have both weight and spillover options configured for an interface. The one that will actually be applied depends on the current setting of the "v4-ecmp-mode" variable in systems settings.

[VDOM Note] When a FortiGate is operating with multiple NAT mode VDOMs, the ECMP method can be specified per VDOM
[IPv6 Note] The ECMP configuration is the same for both IPv4 and IPv6

You will still need to correctly configure your firewall policies for all interfaces being used. If you are using two interfaces, you will need to configure the policies twice, once for each interface. You can optionally configure the interfaces into a Security Zone to simplify this. This would require the administrator to only configure a single set of egress policies. However, when interfaces are configured into a Security Zone, you lose the ability to use the interfaces independently within a firewall policy. You must choose one way or the other. The primary reason for wanting separate firewall policies would be that you don't want all traffic to pass over all interfaces. For example, if you have configured a modem as a backup interface to a low-latency and high-bandwidth Internet connection, when failure occurs, the routing decisions must differ. Since VOIP is unlikely to work across a high-latency modem and general web browsing will quickly consume the limited bandwidth, these protocols could be blocked from that route. This would leave capacity free for critical credit card and inventory search transaction.

BFD (Bidirectional Forwarding Detection)

This protocol is defined by two IETF drafts, the purpose of which is to allow a given device the ability to detect whether the path to the next router is valid in both directions. This protocol needs to be implemented on both ends of a physical link and is specific to that link only. In other words, it validates the reachability of the router and its ability return traffic, thereby verifying the underlying L2 connectivity.

Information and Troubleshooting

To retrieve the current operating status for routing protocols, you will use the "get router info" or "get router info6" commands. There are a large number of sub-options available to show you the status and information appropriate to each routing protocol. For example, "get router info bgp summary", or "get router info ospf status". The sub-options vary by routing protocol.

You can obtain run-time information for the various routing protocols from the CLI via the "get router info <protocol> <options>" command. If you are concerned about IPv6, the command differs by only one character: "get router info6 <protocol> <options>". The type of information available depends on the routing protocol. For example, with OSPF, you can obtain information on the adjacencies, the interfaces running OSPF, the database, etc. In contrast, for BGP, you can get information based on Autonomous System info, community information, neighbor information, the application of route-maps, and prefix-lists, etc.

```
FGT # get router info ospf ?
database show ospf database information
interface    show ospf interfaces
route show ospf routing table
neighbor show ospf neighbors
border-routers show ospf border routers
status    show ospf status
virtual-links    show ospf virtual links
FGT # get router info bgp ?
cidr-only    display routes with non-natural netmasks
community    display routes matching the communities
community-info list all bgp community information
community-list display routes matching the community-list
dampening    display router dampening infomation
filter-list display routes conforming to the filter-list
inconsistent-as display routes with inconsistent AS Paths
```

```
neighbors   show BGP neighbors
network  show BGP info for network
network-longer-prefixes       show BGP info for route and more
   specific routes
paths path information
prefix-list display routes conforming to the prefix-list
regexp   display routes matching the AS path regular expression
quote-regexp   display routes matching the AS path "regular expression"
route-map   display routes conforming to the route-map
scan  display BGP scan status
summary  summary of BGP neighbor status
memory  BGP memory table
```

There are also debug options available under "diagnose ip router <protocol>". Generally speaking, you enable debugging for the type of information that interests you and then you define the level of detail that you want.

```
FGT # diagnose debug enable
FGT # diagnose ip router bgp level info
FGT # diagnose ip router bgp events enable
FGT # diagnose ip router bgp updates in enable
FGT # diagnose ip router bgp updates out enable
```

To see what level and type of debug messages are being generated:

```
FGT # diagnose ip router bgp show
BGP debugging status:
 BGP events debugging is on
 BGP updates debugging is on (outbound)
 BGP debug level: INFO
```

To disable all currently enabled debug information

```
FGT # diagnose ip router bgp all disable
```

SERVICING USERS

There are many technologies today that are intended to simplify the lives of network administrators. Of course, even with these technologies, managing, and administering a widely distributed IP-based network becomes even more complicated. The two most important services are DHCP and DNS. The former allows a device to automatically configure its network parameters while the latter allows a system to be able to connect to another system without having to remember numerical IP addresses. DNS also allows the services to move around fairly transparently, as DNS changes can be made within the DNS list and not on each individual client. A stable and reliable DNS deployment becomes even more important as people migrate to IPv6. This is not simply because IPv6 addresses, being up to four times longer than IPv6, are hard to remember, but also to facilitate the transition from IPv4 to IPV6 for both clients and servers.

DHCP

A FortiGate unit can make use of DHCP services in a one of two methods, as DHCP Client and as a DHCP server. Any interface can be configured to obtain its address via DHCP. This is mostly used on the entry-level products, so they can be connected to a broadband Internet provider. Configuring this is as simple as selecting the option in the WebUI. If needed, there are a few of additional options. "Override internal DNS" will replace the statically configured DNS details with the DNS servers provided in the DHCP process. The "Retrieve default gateway from server" controls whether or not the default gateway obtained via the DHCP process is installed in the routing table. You may not want to enable this option if you are using DHCP to assign an address to an internal interface.

When running as a DHCP Server, the FortiGate can provide DHCP services for multiple interfaces simultaneously. When operating as a DHCP Server and configured in an HA cluster, the lease information is synchronized between cluster members so that a failover between cluster members will not result in duplicate leases being handed out.

The DHCP server supports configuration options that should be sufficient for nearly any environment. This includes the ability to assign all the expected values to a client: IP Address, domain name, default gateway, subnet mask, up to two WINS servers, up to three DNS servers. The DNS servers can either be manually configured addresses or the addresses currently in use by FortiOS. It also supports address reservations and exclusions, as well as custom option fields. These custom fields are most commonly used for devices like VoIP phones, to provide information for the device to load its firmware and configuration.

The FortiGate can provide DHCP services to not just locally connected devices but also to remote client systems connecting to the FortiGate system via IPSec tunnels. Leveraging this capability allows internal systems or firewalls to treat traffic that originates from the IPSec gateway differently from other traffic. It also allows all the remote users to be sourced from a specific range of IP addresses.

In larger customer environments, an IPAM (IP Address Management) appliance or application is often deployed to allow for simpler management of DHCP configuration. To take advantage of this, the FortiGate must be configured to forward locally occurring DHCP requests to this centralized service. This is done by configuring the FortiGate interface as a DHCP relay and specifying the IP address of the IPAM system.

DNS Server

DNS (Domain Name Services) is one of the most important services for users on a network. Most users remember services by name, not number. Also, the use of names makes the physical location of a service portable. As the deployment of IPv6 becomes more prevalent, the use of DNS will pretty much become a requirement as the length of the new addresses makes them very difficult to remember.

There are a number of different ways that DNS can be configured on a FortiGate. The simplest is to have the FortiGate transparently forward DNS requests received to the DNS servers configured on the FortiGate. This process is referred to as DNS-forwarding. If the FortiGate is connected to the Internet via a service that uses dynamically assigned addresses, then it is important to configure the FortiGate to accept and use the DNS servers advertised by the provider rather than the default DNS servers. This happens by default when the interface is configured via the WebUI. If, however, you are configuring the interface from the CLI, then you should include the CLI command "set dns-server-override enable" in the interface parameters. This option will appear in the WebUI as "Override internal DNS" when the interface is configured to use either DHCP or PPPoE.

Efficient DNS are important not only for accessing Internet sites, but as the corporate infrastructure grows; the DNS environment becomes more critical. This growth often involves the deployment of DNS Servers in remote locations. In a server-centric environment, this typically results in an increased burden on operations and maintenance. As of FortiOS 4.3, however, this functionality can now be off-loaded to the FortiGate appliance.

VIRTUAL DOMAINS (VDOM)

The separation of VDOMs is so complete that you can have both Transparent and NAT/Route mode VDOMs on the same physical device. This leads to some interesting possibilities, such as using some of the FortiGate to provide NAT/Route perimeter firewall functions while using a different set of interfaces to provide a focused in-line IPS/Application Control solution for an internal segment.

HIGH AVAILABILITY

There are a wide variety of options when deploying or designing a Highly Available FortiGate solution. The most common of these being the Fortinet-specific HA feature. The FGCP (FortiGate Gateway Clustering Protocol) consists of two or more identical FortiGate units. In addition to the more traditional Active-Passive configuration, the cluster can be deployed in an Active-Active mode, where all the cluster units are used to perform content layer inspection on the traffic. Regardless of the

> One current limitation that may prevent the use of FGCP HA is that currently FortiOS cannot operate in either a Active-Active or Active-Passive HA cluster if any of the interfaces are configured to obtain their addresses dynamically, such as via PPPoE or DHCP, all interfaces must have statically configured IP addresses.

mode, the configuration consists of a number of components including: configuration synchronization, session synchronization, and cluster membership monitoring.

For FGCP to function, you must configure a few parameters. This configuration is performed via the WebUI by navigating to System → Config → HA or via the CLI as follows:

```
FGT# config system ha
  set mode a-a | a-p | standalone              (setting mode to
    standalone disables FGCP operation)
  set cluster-id <integer>
  set hbdev <interface> <priority> [ <interface> <priority> .......... ]
```

The default cluster-id is zero, and the priority value is used to force the selection of the preferred heartbeat interface to use for configuration and session synchronization. This may be a requirement if you are using different speed interfaces or a combination of accelerated and non-accelerated interfaces. The interface with the highest priority value that also has valid link integrity and is receiving heartbeat packets from the other cluster units is selected for the transmission of the configuration and session synchronization data. These heartbeat interfaces are also used to perform the election of roles within the cluster. There is always a primary unit that is responsible for all topology-related activity such as sending/receiving ARP request and reply packets as well as running any dynamic routing protocols. Other units operate as secondary units, receiving the MAC and route information from the primary unit.

It is highly recommended that a minimum of two heartbeat interfaces be configured to prevent the creation of a split-brain cluster in the event of a connection failure. These split-brain clusters result in both units believing that the other unit is no longer operational. If you are using an Active-Passive configuration, the use of crossover cables is sufficient. If, however, you are deploying an Active-Active configuration consisting of more than two units, you must connect the heartbeat interfaces of all units via a Layer 2 network. When using multiple HA interfaces, they should be connected to separate L2 networks.

Configuration Synchronization—this process keeps the configuration of all units in the cluster synchronized, with the exception of a small number of items that are unique per device. These include the unit's hostname and HA priority values. In addition to the system configuration, this process is also responsible for synchronizing the AV and IPS signature updates, X.509 certificates, and even the DHCP lease database. This process occurs on one of the heartbeat interfaces.

Session Synchronization—Unlike the configuration synchronization process described above, Session Synchronization consists entirely of run-time information. This includes the state information for sessions as they are created, updated, and deleted as well as topology information such as MAC address and routing information. The session-table information is only synchronized if the session-pickup option is enabled in the HA configuration. Like the Configuration Synchronization traffic, the Session Synchronization traffic also runs across the heartbeat interfaces.

Interface Monitoring—There are two methods used to monitor the operational health of the cluster devices. The first is the heartbeat interface configuration. These interfaces are used to connect the cluster units together, typically via a crossover cable. This connection is used by one cluster member to verify the presence and health of any other cluster members. A heartbeat packet is sent periodically that contains the units serial number as well as other health information such as the number of monitored interfaces that are operational. The second method is interface monitoring, based on the presence (or lack thereof) of link integrity on the configured interfaces. The intent is to quickly cause a cluster failover if any of the connected infrastructure becomes disconnected. Obviously, you need to carefully consider the interfaces to monitor. If you have interfaces that are occasionally reset as part of normal operations, or are not critical to continuous operation, you may not wish to monitor them.

Unit election is controlled by the following:

HA Uptime—This is most common determining factor. When a unit begins running, it compares its local HA Uptime to that of other units that wish to be part of the same cluster. If the unit's HA uptime is lower than that of the current master, it becomes a secondary unit and begins the configuration sync process. Once that process completes, it is considered to be fully operational.

This HA uptime is not the same as the system uptime. It can be manually reset to zero by issuing the CLI command "diagnose sys ha reset-uptime". Doing so will result in that unit changing its role to secondary, allowing another device to take over the primary role. This mechanism is useful if you wish to force a failback after a previous cluster member's failure has been resolved. This mechanism is also handy if you wish to test the HA failover functionality after making changes to either the FortiGate HA configuration or something in the connected infrastructure.

However, be aware that the granularity used when comparing the HA uptime defaults to 5 min (300 s). If both uptime measurements are within this window, failover will occur. This is done to prevent a repetitive failover situation where the devices rapidly cycle between primary and secondary. This interval can be configured via the CLI, config system ha → set ha-uptime-diff-margin.

Unit Priority—This option controls the behavior of the unit as HA is starting. If the HA Uptime values are within the interval defined by "set ha-uptime-diff-margin", then the unit with the higher priority value will be elected as the cluster primary.

This is most often used when the devices are located in the same facility. However, for operational reasons it is preferred to "know" in advance which physical unit should by default be the primary unit.

Override—This configuration option is used to force a specific unit to operate as the cluster Primary unit. This is usually only used when the cluster units are geographically separated and it is preferred that traffic pass thru one location if that location is fully operational. It is also recommended to use a ping server with this configuration.

Unit Serial Number—This is the final tiebreaker in the event that two identically configured units are powered up at exactly the same time.

It is strongly recommended that multiple heartbeat interfaces are configured to avoid the unfortunate situation of a split-brain cluster in the event of failure. Unlike more traditional HA clusters, the FortiGate cluster configuration does not require any additional addressing to be performed. All the cluster maintenance functions are handled by the FGCP protocol. When configured in Layer 3 mode, the cluster uses a floating/virtual MAC and IP address design. The virtual MAC is unique per physical interface and is constructed as follows:

00:09:0f:00:<groupID>:<interface index>

"GroupID" is the cluster ID as assigned during configuration. Customizing this groupID allows multiple FGCP-based clusters to be connected to the same Layer 2 network without running into MAC address conflicts. The cluster primary unit is responsible for this MAC address and will use it in an any packet that should be processed by the firewall, either for user-traffic or even administrative traffic.

There are instances when the complete HA functionality is either not required or applicable. Most of these individual HA features can be used individually. For example, the session-sync capability can be configured to support a geographical separation of the FortiGate devices where the configurations may not necessarily match due to different Layer 3 transit addressing. However, it may be desired that the session information be copied while an external function is used to determine the active data path.

```
FGT # config system session-sync
FGT (session-sync) # edit <idx>
FGT (session-sync) # set peerip <ip_address>
FGT (session-sync) # set peervd <vdom_name>
FGT (session-sync) # set syncvd <vdom_name list>
```

HA LICENSE REQUIREMENTS

When configured in a cluster, not must all members be the same model; they must have equivalent licensing for subscription services and any optional VDOMs. This is true even when configured to run in an Active-Passive configuration. If you are considering adding VDOMs to your configuration you will need to purchase the VDOM licenses for all cluster members. Similar requirements apply to the subscription services.

The "peervd" and "syncvd" parameters are optional and specify the VDOM from which to originate the connection and the VDOMs whose session details are synchronized. An empty list results in all session details being synchronized.

Conversely, it may be desired to have only the configuration synchronized between the FortiGate devices, with no session synchronization, or even heartbeat detection. This may be the case when the devices are geographically separated and resiliency is provided by controlling which unit is actively passing traffic.

The FortiGate Operating System also supports the RFC-based VRRP protocol to support resilient designs. This allows for forwarding traffic even if the security functions provided by the FortiGate are not available (such as for maintenance). This would be a configuration where the FortiGate is the preferred VRRP peer, and something like a third-party router is providing the resilient path.

Base Network Security

INFORMATION IN THIS CHAPTER:

- Misc NAT Functionalities
  - NAT within multicast firewall rule
  - NAT in Layer 2 (Transparent mode)
  - NAT in VPN
- Identity-Based Authentication
  - Firewall Authentication
    - Local Authentication Database
    - External Authentication Databases
  - Defining a External Authentication Server
    - External Authentication via RADIUS
    - External Authentication via TACACS+
    - External Authentication via LDAP
    - Adding The External Authentication Server to FortiOS User Group
      - Local or External Authentication Server Firewall Authentication Identity-Based Policies
    - FSSO (Fortinet Single Sign On)
    - FortiOS FSSO Agent Communication Setup
      - Adding FSSO FortiOS User Groups
      - FSSO Identity-Based Policies
  - VPN
    - IPSec
      - FortiOS IPSec Key Points
      - FortiOS IPSec Phase 1 Tips
      - FortiOS IPSec Phase 2 Tips
      - FortiOS IPSec third-party Interoperability Tips
    - SSL VPN
      - Web Mode
      - Accessing the FortiGate Web Portal
      - Functions within the FortiGate Web Portal
      - Tunnel Mode
      - Configuration Checklist for Tunnel mode
      - Port Forwarding Tunnel Mode
      - Virtual Desktop Mode
    - Misc VPN
      - PPTP
      - L2TP
      - L2TP over IPSec
      - GRE
      - GRE over IPSec
  - Traffic Shaping
    - Shared Policy Shaping
    - Per-IP Shaping
    - Application Control Shaping

- SSL Inspection
  - Antivirus SSL inspection
  - Web Filtering SSL inspection
  - DLP SSL Inspection
  - Anti-spam SSL Inspection
- Two-Factor User Authentication
  - Two-Factor Hard or Soft Based FortiToken
  - Two-Factor Certificate Based User Authentication
  - Two-Factor Email Based
  - Two-Factor SMS
    - External Two-Factor Authentication with FortiToken
- Load-Balancing Capabilities
  - IP and/or Port Range load balancing
  - Server selection load balancing

This chapter's intent is not to provide a step-by-step instruction manual, but to be more of an overview of the basic security features offered by the FortiGate solution. We will explore several common configuration scenarios that are not fully covered by the existing Fortinet documentation. The goal is to provide a high-level overview along with insight into configuration and save you troubleshooting time.

FIREWALL

The base functionality of the FortiGate is the firewall. This monitors all traffic that traverses the solution, and so it is a good connection point for the other features. As we stated in Chapter 2, the FortiOS operating system handles all decisions and, with the specialized ASIC hardware, UTM functionality can be offloaded.

To permit or deny traffic through the FortiGate, you must use firewall policies. In this context, the term "policy" is intended technically and refers to a group of one or more rules within the FortiGate. This is not to be confused with the more management-related meaning that dictates what is and should not be done. Policies in FortiOS are organized based on flow direction—how traffic moves between interfaces (physical or virtual) or security zones. Sometimes, we use the terms "policy" and "rule" inter-changeably, as a policy that consists of a single rule is logically identical. The FortiGate

---

TIP

Default Policies

By default, a FortiGate in Transparent (Layer 2) or NAT/Route (Layer 3) mode denies all traffic. The lower-end models, such as the 80C and lower, all come with a predefined outbound rule that allows traffic. This makes them easier to use in smaller businesses, but at the cost of a stronger security policy. For more information on this, please see the FortiGate Quick Start Guide: http://docs.fortinet.com/fgt_qsg.html

requires policies to be in place for traffic to flow, and because it is a stateful firewall, all state information for IPv4 and IPv6 up to Layer 4 is maintained throughout each session. See Figure 5.1 for a graphical representation of how this works.

The order of processing is important to understand. Policies are matched based first on the source and destination interfaces and the rules within the matching policy are processed from the top down. In other words, they are compared from top to bottom according to the following matching criteria:

1. Source and destination firewall addresses.
2. Services.
3. Schedule.

If no rules are matched, the FortiGate defaults to the implicit Deny rule which drops the connection. By default, this rule does not log its actions. If you wish to view the actions of this rule, perhaps for troubleshooting purposes, you can create an explicit rule at the bottom of your policy and set it to Deny all traffic, but with logging enabled. This will create a rule above the implicit Deny rule that has the same effect, but turns on logging. Therefore, no traffic will ever match the implicit rule and every denial will be tracked.

If you are using the additional UTM functionality that the FortiGate provides, the fact that the device will maintain state information provides an additional layer

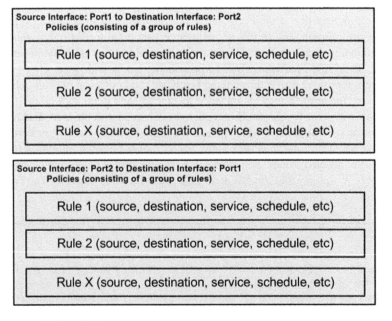

FIGURE 5.1 A Policy of Rules

of security. In addition, filtering out unwanted traffic can help reduce processing, thereby saving resources for the traffic that is allowed. As we discussed in Chapter 2, stateful inspection helps reduce the management of rules while it also uniquely tracks individual sessions. This improves security by reducing the chances of session spoofing or hijacking... a common technique used in man-in-the-middle attacks.

An example is the IPS processing capability. By maintaining the state of a session, if an attack is detected, only that session need to be blocked. This can be useful to block attacks from a source network without blocking any other legitimate connections that might be sharing that source, perhaps through a NAT rule.

Interface-Based Rules

When access control first came about, ACLs (Access Control Lists) were generally applied on the ingress or egress interface within the router such as on a Cisco router. Management of ACLs can get pretty complicated. An administrator would need to understand their network environment, protocol, and communications paths. They would also need to create access controls permitting the original and all related responses and then apply those lists at each interface. This increases the administrative overhead, and therefore runs the risk of being inflexible and security weakening over time.

When commercial firewalls came about, vendors began to simplify the process of management. One common solution is to do management at a global level and have the firewall itself apply the policies to the individual interfaces. However, for this to work, the device must be trusted to handle the underlying Layer 2 to 3 transition. Using global firewall policies and trusting the firewall to maintain session state helps reduce the amount of work needed to manage the firewall rules.

Another common concept is that of security zones. With security zones, firewall policies can be tied to one or more interfaces that are, in turn, tied to unique network segments. If communications take place between two networks, the firewall simply references the policies associated with each of the two network zones to make the comparison. This layer of abstractions greatly simplifies the management of the firewall.

Firewall policies in the FortiGate are based on similar concepts. By default, FortiOS uses the physical or the logical interface like a zone. Based on the interface name, firewall policies are tied to these interfaces and to the direction of the communication flow.

For example, a FortiGate 310B has ten interfaces named "port1" through "port10". If traffic is to communicate from the internal LAN "port1" to the WAN "port2", then a firewall policy would need to be created with a source interface of "port1" to a destination interface of "port2". As FortiOS maintains the session state, there is no need to create an opposite rule, e.g. from "port2" to "port1" for the return/reply traffic.

Zone definitions are also supported within FortiOS. Similar to the security zone concept, a zone in FortiOS represents one or more interfaces, like a group definition.

There are many advantages to using Zones:

- Provides an easy way to reference firewall policies.
- Provides the ability to group interfaces together.

This last advantage is useful in scenarios where multiple network paths must share the same policy definitions. For example, port1 and port2 could be connected to different ISPs. Grouping port1 and port2 into a Zone then applying policies to and from that Zone means that you do not have to duplicate firewall rules. Multiple IPSec tunnels can also be tied to a zone this way.

When there are multiple physical or logical interfaces within a Zone, communication between these interfaces is blocked, by default. To allow communication, you either define intra-zone firewall policies:

```
config system zone
    edit "testzone"
        set interface port1 port2
    next
end
config firewall policy
    edit 1
        set srcintf "testzone"
        set dstintf "testzone"
        set action accept
        set schedule "always"
        set service "ANY"
    next
end
```

You can also change the default behavior to always allow communication:

```
config system zone
    edit "testzone"
        set interface port1 port2
            set intrazone allow
    next
end
```

TIP

Zone vs. Alias

Technically, you can define an Alias for the interface. This places the alias name next to the physical interface name within the Web UI, however, this is limited to physical interfaces only. Once an interface is part of a zone, the interface cannot be named specifically in another policy. An interface may also not be in more than one zone.

Building Blocks of a Rule

A typical firewall rule generally contains a source network, destination network, and service port as well as either a permitted or denied action definition. However, since FortiGates offer more than just firewalling capabilities, most of the UTM capabilities can also be defined within a rule. These can include identity policies, where user activities are tied to user names; traffic shaping profiles, where the traffic for the triggered rule would be passed on to other constricting rules; and end point controls, leveraging FortiClient application for further security restrictions.

Rules in FortiOS require, at minimum, the following attributes:

- Source Interface | Zone
- Source Host(s) | Network(s)
- Destination Interface | Zone
- Destination Host(s) | Network(s)
- Service(s)
- Schedule
- Action (Permit, Deny*, SSL-VPN, or IPSec-VPN)

* When left undefined the Action setting defaults to "deny", so while it is required, it does not need to be specified.

TIP

CLI syntax hint on required settings
To see what settings are required prior to committing a rule via the CLI, issue a "set ?".
This command outputs of all available settings. However, you'll notice an asterisk (*) next to some of the Set settings. This asterisk denotes a setting that must be specified in order to create the rule.

This is not limited to just rule creation. The asterisk is used consistently throughout the CLI to indicate requirements.
Example CLI output:
 # conf firewall policy

FGT (policy) # edit 1
new entry '1' added
FGT (1) # set ?
*srcintf   *source interface name*
*dstintf   *destination interface name*
*srcaddr   *source address name*
*dstaddr   *destination address name*
rtp-nat use   *this policy for RTP NAT*
action   *policy action*
...
In this example, you can see that *srcintf, dstintf, srcaddr,* and *dstaddr* are required, whereas *rtp-nat* and *action* are not. Please also note that a non-required item will take its default setting if another value is not provided.
To view all settings, including those set by default, perform a "get" or "show full".

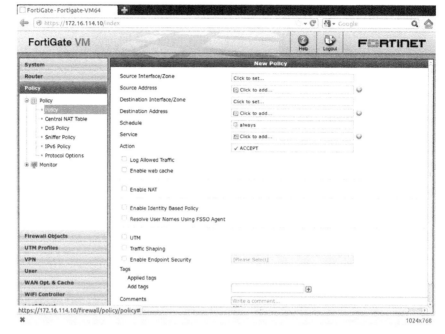

FIGURE 5.2 Web UI Policy Setting

The CLI syntax for a minimum firewall rule required settings are:

```
config firewall policy
    edit <id #>
        set srcintf <interface or zone name>
        set dstintf <interface or zone name>
        set srcaddr <address object name>
        set dstaddr <address object name>
        set schedule <schedule name>
        set service <service name>
        set action <action>
    next
end
```

Address Objects

Address objects are used within a firewall rule to represent the source "srcaddr" and destination "dstaddr" settings. An address object can be defined in various ways, including the IP base (Host or Networks), IP ranges, Domain Name, Geography, or Wildcard format.

Host IP or Network Address Object

```
config firewall address
    edit <address object name>
        set associated-interface <interface name>
        set type ipmask
        set subnet <IPv4 address> <mask> or <IPv4 address/mask>
    next
end
```

When using the "set subnet...." syntax, the mask definition can be denoted in bits. For example, when using the 10.10.10.0 network, you'll have an entry of "10.10.10.0/24". Alternatively, you could use the full four octet mask definition of "10.10.10.0 255.255.255.0". For individual host address, a mask of "<host ip>/32".

Address objects with IPv6 format would be configured under:
config firewall address6

IP range Address Object

```
config firewall address
    edit <address object name>
        set type iprange
        set start-ip <IPv4 start IP range>
        set end-ip <IPv4 end IP range>
    next
end
```

This address object provides the ability to define an IP range using the "set start-ip..." and "set end-ip..." syntax to specify the range (see Figure 5.3).

DNS Named Objects via FQDN (Fully Qualified Domain Name)

```
config firewall address
    edit <address object name>
        set type fqdn
        set fqdn <domain name>
        set cache-ttl <0 to 86400 seconds>
    next
end
```

The setting specific for the domain name must be resolvable by the FortiGate in order to translate it to the IP that will be used to match a rule or policy. Thus, it must be a "fully qualified" domain name (FQDN) that can be passed to the DNS systems

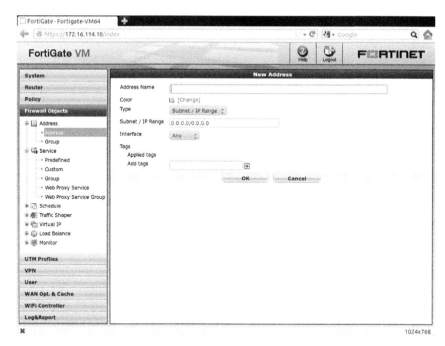

FIGURE 5.3 Web UI Address Object Setting

that the FortiGate will reference. This may be either the defined network DNS servers or the local DNS database. Local DNS records are resolved with priority, so only those entries not locally defined would be forwarded to the network DNS servers.

The setting of "set cache-ttl" is used to define the cache expiration time for the resolved FQDN. By default, this value is defined at 0 therefore the cache does not expire (until FortiGate is rebooted).

Configuration for the local DNS server is defined under with "*config system dns-database*" (see Chapter 4 for further details).

Configuration for the system level DNS servers is:

```
config system dns
    set primary <dns server IPv4 address only>
    set secondary <dns server IPv4 address only>
end
```

TIP

FQDN address object cache timer

It is recommended to define the "set cache-ttl" to a reasonable value rather then leaving this value at default of 0. In a scenario when a DNS record is updated for the FQDN host entry, previous resolved entry would still exist in cache therefore affecting traffic.

If using IPv6, you will need to use "set ip6-primary" and "set ip6-secondary" instead of what is used in this example.

Geography (Country)-Based Address Object

```
config firewall address
    edit <address object name>
      set type geography
      set country <two character country code - see Appendix D.>
    next
end
```

The two character country code is case sensitive and, as of this writing, expects the codes to be in upper case. This code is matched against a GeoIP database that links IP addresses to country codes. This database is maintained by Fortinet and updated via the FortiGuard center.

Wildcard Address Object

```
config firewall address
    edit <address object name>
      set type wildcard
      set wildcard <IPv4 host address/mask>
    next
end
```

Wildcard address objects provide a flexible way of defining network objects than conventional subnet masking can accomplish. For example, assume you have various networks that have similar first and third octets. A good example is 10.x.10.x, where "10" is the similarity. If you want to add an address object to encompass these similar networks, typical subnet masking would require that you add an individual address object for each one, e.g. 10.1.10.0/24, 10.2.10.0/24, etc. With wildcard masking,

---

TIP

System level DNS source-ip
If there's a need to have FortiOS, send its DNS request from another address rather than the default egress interface, the following CLI command can be added:
    config system dns
     set source-ip <IPv4 address only>
    end
    The source-ip needs to be a valid IP address assigned on one of the FortiGate interface. As of this writing, only IPv4 source-ip is supported.

this could simply involve one address object entry such as "set wildcard 10.0.10.0 255.0.255.0".

If you are used to the way other vendors do masking, be aware that this approach may seem backwards to you. From a binary view with wildcard masking, consider the bit values representing the following:

0 = match bit
1 = ignore bit

Applying the bit values with the above wildcard example of 0.0.0.255 would translate to the binary of:
00000000.00000000.00000000.11111111
So first three octets are matched whereas the last is ignored. Therefore, when applied to 10.10.10.0, only 10.10.10.x is matched and the "x" could be anything.

Miscellaneous Address Object Options

Some settings can be defined on any address object, regardless of type.

"set associated-interface <interface name>", defines the physical or logical interface tied to the address object. When this setting is undefined, it defaults to "any", indicating a match for all interfaces.

"set color <color #>", defines the color used to identify the object in the WebUI. The default value of "0", sets the color to orange. For complete list of color numbers, see Fortinet's FortiGate CLI manual.

"set comment <comment string - up to 64 characters>", defines a comment for the address object.

"set tags <tag string - up to 64 characters>", defines a tag which can be used as a custom identifier for filtered views. It may also be used for object references.

Address Group Objects

Address groups allow the configuration to quickly reference a set of addresses as if it was a single object. This simplifies maintenance because a change to the group will cause the change to affect each rule that references that group. This can be particularly useful if there is a set of addresses that serve as a load-balanced pool or a set of addresses that represent other networks.

```
config firewall addrgrp
    edit <address group object name>
        set member <name of address object - multiple entries delimited
        by a space>
    next
end
```

When defining the members of an address group, multiple addresses can be defined by listing them on the same line and placing a space between each item. For example: "set member address1 address2 address3 address4" to add four address objects to the address group.

Address group objects take the same settings that address objects do.

If a group of IPv6 addresses is required, you must use the command "config firewall addrgrp6".

Service Objects

Service objects are objects within the FortiGate that reference services. It is often easier to reference a name like "web" within a configuration instead of specifying that it is a TCP communication that runs on ports 80, 443, and 8080. You can also blend different protocols in a single service definition and define ranges of ports.

```
config firewall service custom
    edit <service name>
        set protocol TCP/UDP/SCTP
        set tcp-portrange <destination low port>-<destination high
        port>:<source low port>-<source high port>
        set udp-portrange <destination low port>-<destination high
        port>:<source low port>-<source high port>
        set sctp-portrange <destination low port>-<destination high
        port>:<source low port>-<source high port>
    next
end
```

While TCP and UDP are generally known in the industry, it is worth mentioning that SCTP stands for Stream Control Transmission Protocol, and should be used for streaming protocols.

To customize a ICMP service the CLI syntax would be:

```
config firewall service custom
    edit <service name>
        set protocol ICMP
        set icmpcode <icmp code number>
        set icmptype <icmp type number>
    next
end
```

To customize an IP protocol the CLI syntax would be:

```
config firewall service custom
    edit <service name>
        set protocol IP
        set protocol-number <protocol number>
    next
end
```

FortiOS includes several predefined service objects which can be viewed with "get firewall service predefined ?". To see the detail predefined service settings use the command of "get firewall service predefined <name of service>" (see Figure 5.4).

Service Group Objects

One or more services can be grouped together within a Service Group. The service group can then be applied to a rule rather than having to define each individual services.

```
config firewall service group
    edit <service group name>
        set member <name of service object - multiple entries delimited
        by a space>
    next
end
```

Schedule Objects

Schedule objects define, when a rule can be activated based on either a recurring or one time definition. This is often used to allow less strict control over web browsing

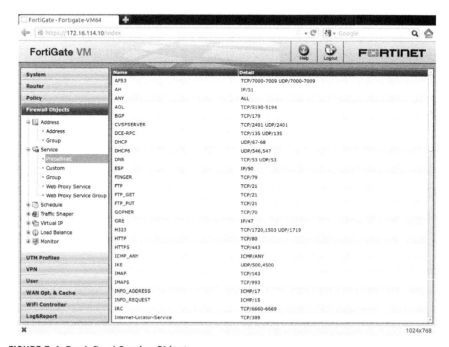

FIGURE 5.4 Predefined Service Objects

during off-hours. However, if you are using this feature to loosen restrictions at certain times, be careful to only loosen productivity restrictions and not actual security rules.

To help keep different schedules straight, the "set color <color #>" configuration setting can be defined here.

Recurring Schedule

```
config firewall schedule recurring
    edit <name of schedule>
        set day < sunday | monday | tuesday | wednesday | thursday |
        friday | saturday >
        // additional days would be separated by a space
        set start <hh:mm>
        set end <hh:mm>
    next
end
```

One Time Schedule

```
config firewall schedule onetime
    edit <name of schedule>
        set start <hh:mm> <yyyy/mm/dd>
        set end <hh:mm> <yyyy/mm/dd>
    next
end
```

Schedule Group Objects

```
config firewall schedule group
    edit <name of schedule group>
        set member <one or more schedule (one time or recurring),
        separated with a space>
    next
end
```

"set color <color #>" option can also be defined here.

Multicast Rules

Firewall policies are based on unicast traffic. If you need to handle multicast traffic, the process is very different. Unlike unicast, multicast traffic control can only be configured via the CLI. The way this traffic handled depends on the mode in which the device is deployed. In Layer 3 (NAT/Route) mode, multicast traffic is not natively forwarded, thus any rules that might exist will not be honored. If you must run in this mode and must forward multicast traffic, "multicast-forward" must be explicitly enabled.

```
config system setting
   set multicast-forward enable
end
```

Due to the way that the TTL specification is written, a FortiGate will only forward multicast traffic with a TTL greater than 2. To increase the chance that the TTL will not expire before reaching the multicast router, you need to configure the device to not decrement the TTL value.

```
config system setting
   set multicast-ttl-notchange enable
end
```

In Layer 2 (Transparent) mode, traffic with multicast destination addresses is blocked by default. A multicast firewall rule is required to permit the traffic through. If there's a need to change the default behavior to forward any multicast traffic without multicast rule definitions, then multicast rules must be explicitly skipped.

```
config system setting
   set multicast-skip-policy enable
end
```

Whether you're in Layer 2 or Layer 3 mode, once you have allowed the FortiGate to handle multicast traffic, you should tighten your control. Otherwise, you run the risk of generating more traffic than your network can handle. At minimum, to permit all multicast traffic simply add an entry within the multicast policy section:

```
config firewall multicast-policy
   edit <id #>
   next
end
```

Multicast rules differ from unicast rules. Here are some key points to keep in mind.

- Like unicast, when no multicast rules are defined and forwarding is enabled, then all multicast-related traffic is blocked. Thus, an "accept" multicast rule is required to permit multicast traffic.
- There are no dependent settings within a multicast rule. For example, when working with unicast, you must define the source/destination interface & networks and services (ports). However, in a multicast rule, no settings are

dependent on each other. For example, a multicast rule with a single source address with the "set srcaddr" setting would only permit the particular source defined to any destination.

- Unless specifically defined, a multicast rule will default to working on all interfaces.
- Source and destination addresses are explicitly defined in IP address format only. There's a limit of up to 2 address entries per source or destination.
- The "set protocol" setting limits the number of protocols used within a multicast rule. This setting is not the same as when used for unicast, where it provides the ability to restrict services (ports).
- Multicast rules are only definable via CLI.
- IPv6 multicast rule definitions are not currently supported.

If you need to restrict multicast to only a specific source, destination, protocol, and port, consider the following example.

```
config firewall multicast-policy
    edit <id #>
        set srcintf <interface or zone name>
        set dstintf <interface or zone name>
        set srcaddr <IP address format only - up to 2 (space delimited)>
        set dstaddr <IP address format only - up to 2 (space delimited)>
    next
end
```

IPv6 Rules

Due to the relatively newness of IPv6 and its increased complexity, firewall rules for IPv6 traffic are defined in a separate set of policies. These policies may be defined via either the CLI or the WebUI. As IPv6 is not being adopted very widely and to minimize the management costs that come with additional complexity, the ability to configure IPv6 via the WebUI is hidden, by default. To enable this feature, you must use the CLI.

```
config system global
    set gui-ipv6 enable
end
```

The rules and default options when configuring IPv6 generally match those of IPv4 unicast, with the exception of:

- Policy-based IPSec options are not supported and must be done with interfaces.
- The UTM features of IDS/IPS and Application Control are not supported.
- Network Address Translation (NAT) is not supported.

- Web caching is not supported.
- WCCP (Web Cache Control Protocol) is not supported.
- Disclaimer/Policy usage messaging is not supported.
- Identity policies only support authentication that is prompted by the firewall.

  - This means that Fortinet Single Sign -on (FSSO) is not supported.

IPv6 rules also have the same dependent settings as IPv4: source & destination interfaces and addresses, schedule, and services.

Local-In Firewall Rules

Local-in firewall rules provide the ability to restrict traffic that is specifically related to the FortiGate interfaces. A common example would be management traffic directed towards the IP address of a specific (physical or logical) FortiGate interface. Local-in rules may only be configured via the CLI.

Example of minimum configuration for a IPv4 Local-In firewall rule:

```
config firewall local-in-policy
    edit <id #>
        set intf <source interface name>
        set srcaddr <address object name>
        set dstaddr <address object name>
        set schedule <schedule name>
        set service <service name>
        set action <action>
    next
end
```

The default action for a local-in policy is deny, so any traffic that does not explicitly match a rule will be dropped.

Be very cautious when defining local-in policies. It is possible to inadvertently block access to the management portion of the FortiGate, effectively creating a denial of service condition. For example, if a local-in rule was created that matched the IP used to manage the FortiGate, and the service was set to ANY with default action of deny then all management access to the FortiGate management IP address would be denied. To correct this self-inflicted deny management access would require a direct physical console access to FortiGate to login and correct the rule.

Miscellaneous Firewall Settings
Session-ttl (Session Timers)

Idle timeouts are defined with session-ttl. Each established session is assigned a timer. This allows the FortiGate to expire a session if no activity occurs within the allocated time limit. If activity occurs during the timeout session, the counter will reset itself to the initial value defined, and restart the count when the session again becomes inactive.

Default session-ttl for following protocols:

ICMP$=60$s
UDP$=180$s
TCP$=3600$s

Session-ttl can be adjusted per VDOM, per firewall rule, or per custom service level. The following from top to bottom are the session-ttl presence order:

1. Custom service session-ttl.
2. Firewall rule session-ttl.
3. VDOM session-ttl.

The default value for the custom service and rule level session-ttl is 0 s therefore would use the VDOM level session-ttl value. Once the custom or rule level session-ttl values are defined then those values would take the presence order.

CLI configuration for VDOM level session-ttl:

```
config system session-ttl
    set default <seconds>
        config port
            edit <index number>
                set protocol <protocol number>
                set start-port <port number>
                set end-port <port number>
                set timeout <seconds>
            next
        end
end
```

"set default" defines the global session-ttl for TCP traffic. By default this value is 3600 s.

To customize a session-ttl, you must use "config port". This is where you'll define an entry that is tied to a particular protocol. If the protocol is TCP or UDP then you can further customize a port range or specific port with the start-port and end-port setting. The session timeout value is then defined in seconds. While there are many possible protocol numbers, the most common are 1 (ICMP), 6 (TCP), and 17 (UDP). While reasonable defaults are defined for these protocols, they can be changed. To do this, simply add a custom session-ttl.

```
config system session-ttl
    config port
        edit 100                    // choose a non-conflicting index number
```

```
            set protocol 1              // defines the protocol as ICMP
            set timeout 30              // change ICMP protocol timeout
            to 30 seconds
        next
        edit 200
            set protocol 17            // defines the protocol as UDP
            set start-port 69          // defines the starting port
            range
            set end-port 69            // defines the ending port range
            set timeout 1200           // change UDP port 69 (TFTP)
            timeout to 1200
seconds
        next
    end
end
```

CLI configuration for firewall rule level session-ttl:

```
config firewall policy
    edit <rule number>
        ...
        set session-ttl <seconds>
        ...
    next
end
```

CLI configuration for custom service level session-ttl:

```
config firewall service custom
    edit <service name>
        ...
        set session-ttl <seconds>
        ...
    next
end
```

Session Helpers/ALG (Application Level Gateways)

FortiOS maintains state information up to Layer 4 on all IPv4 and IPv6 traffic that is allowed by the firewall. However, some traffic requires additional inspection in order to properly control the traffic. For example, to properly communicate through NAT, it may be necessary to define additional network address translation within a packet stream. The firewall feature that handles further inspection for this type of communication is called "Session Helpers". This feature is also known in the industry as ALG (Application Level Gateways). To reduce the need for administrators to manually tweak common protocols, the following are already defined within the FortiGate.

Protocol Name	Protocol Type	Listening Port
FTP	TCP	21
DNS-UDP	UDP	53
TFTP	UDP	69
PMAP	TCP/UDP	111
DCERPC	TCP/UDP	135
RSH	TCP	514
TNS	TCP	1521
PPTP	TCP	1723
H323	TCP	1720
RAS	UDP	1719
MMS	TCP	1863
RTSP	TCP	554, 7070, 8554
SIP	UDP	5060
MGCP	UDP	2427, 2727

FortiOS session helpers are protocol-specific and written to follow their respective standards. However, not all communication is standards-compliant. Traffic that is not fully complaint could be interrupted when the session helper are triggered. If you experience problems with a session helper, you can disable it to facilitate troubleshooting.

config system session-helper
show // To display session-helper index number to delete
delete <the session helper index number>
end

If you do not want to completely delete the helper, you may also change the listening port. This will prevent a match on the communication port that you are using, and therefore prevent the helper from triggering. If choosing this method, be careful to only move the helper to an unused port. After all, you wouldn't want to interrupt legitimate traffic.

```
config system session-helper
  edit 13              // this is the default session helper index for SIP
    set port 35000     // changing from default listening port of 5060 to 35000
  next
end
```

Asymmetric Handling

When the FortiGate is expected to process asymmetric traffic, you may need to disable some features. In order for the firewall to store a TCP session in a state table, it must first see a complete three-way TCP handshake and then the remainder of the session traffic. In an asymmetric traffic flow scenario, the client would send a TCP SYN along a route that includes the FortiGate, but the TCP SYN/ACK from the server could be sent along another route that would bypass the FortiGate. Since FortiGate would not see the TCP SYN/ACK from server, it would drop the packet, thereby preventing the session from being established.

There's an option to disable the firewall's stateful nature, effectively turning it into a stateless ACL. The CLI setting is:

```
config system settings
    set asymroute enable
end
```

For IPv6 related traffic, the CLI syntax would be:

```
config system settings
    set asymroute6 enable
end
```

Both of the IPv4 or IPv6 asymmetric settings are configurable per VDOM. Therefore, it's important to note that if this feature is enabled, it will affect all traffic within the VDOM, though not all traffic to the device. Thus, if you need this feature, but still need to statefully track other connections, it may be wise to create a dedicated VDOM for asynchronous connections only.

NAPT (Network Address & Port Translation)

Network address and port translations are enabled with individual firewall rules. There are several ways to perform address translation:

- Source IP and source port translation using egress interface.
- Source IP Pool with source port translation.
- Source IP and source port translation using central NAT table.
- Destination IP.
- Destination IP and destination port.
- Destination IP range.
- Destination IP groups.

Address translation is only possible with IPv4. Given the amount of space available, there is a limited demand for IPv6 address translation. Therefore IPv6 NAT is not currently supported by FortiOS.

In the next section, we will review the settings required to define different address translation scenarios and specific firewall settings. NAT is not a global setting, and it must be controlled with individual rules to properly manage traffic.

Source IP and Source Port Translation Using Egress Interface

```
config firewall policy
    edit <existing rule number>
```

```
        set nat enable
    next
end
```

When "set nat" is enabled, the default translated address will be the IP address of the egress interface. This will also activate port address translation (PAT) for the source port. With NAT and automatic port translation, a single NAT IP address can handle 32,768 TCP sessions and 32,768 UDP sessions. When a session is added to the state table, the client defines the original source port, so when the packet exits the FortiGate, the translated port is automatically reassigned to a non-conflicting random source port. If a single NAT IP port resource is consumed, subsequent traffic will fail to establish, and thus, generate a "NAT port is exhausted" message from FortiOS.

Some legacy applications may require the communication to use the same originating source port. To disable PAT and have the session use the same originating port, the following command can be added to the NAT rule:

```
config firewall policy
    edit <rule number>
        set fixedport enable
    next
end
```

Source IP Pool with Source Port Translation

```
// Defines the source IP pool ranges
config firewall ippool
    edit <ip pool name>
        set startip <starting address >
        set endip <ending address >
    next
end


// To apply the source IP pool, it must be enabled on the related
    traffic firewall rule
config firewall policy
    edit <rule number>
        set nat enable
        set ippool enable
        set poolname <ip pool name>
    next
end
```

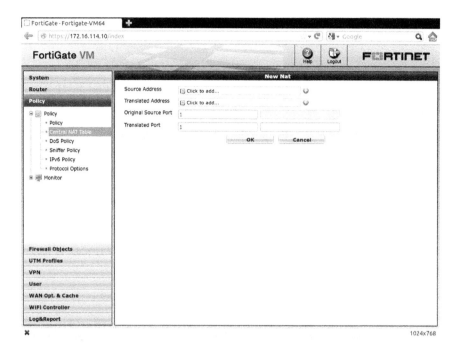

FIGURE 5.5 IP and Source Port Translation Using Central NAT Table

The above example would allow traffic to NAT off a range of IP addresses. In addition, source port NAT is enabled inherently. This helps to scale sessions above 32,767 per protocol (see Figure 5.5).

Source IP and Source Port Translation Using Central NAT Table

```
// Defines the central-nat entries
config firewall central-nat
    edit <index number>
        set status enable
        set orig-addr <address object name>
        set nat-ippool <ip pool name>
        set orig-port <starting source ip port number 1-65535 range>
        set nat-port <translated port or port range>
    next
end
// To apply central NAT entries to traffic, it must be enabled on
    related traffic firewall rules
config firewall policy
```

```
     edit <rule number>
        set nat enable
        set central-nat enable
     next
end
```

The Central NAT table provides an organized listing of explicit source NAT definitions. When creating a central NAT entry via the CLI, the "set orig-addr" command requires a predefined address object. Similarly, the "set nat-ippool" command requires a predefined IP pool. When using the Web UI, new objects can be created within the central NAT creation view.

The "set orig-port" command defines the starting source port, while the ending range is defined with "set nat-port". For example, consider the command "set nat-port 1024-65535". When "orig-port" is defined as 1024 then the ending range would be "65535". On most systems, ports 1–1024 are reserved for system services. This allows for more streamlined security, as listening on these ports typically requires administrative access. Thus, best practice involves defining the "orig-port" and "nat-port" within the non-reserved port ranges (1024 through 65535).

To use the central NAT table, it must be explicitly enabled within a firewall rule.

Destination IP

Destination NAT and port forwarding are configured via the VIP (Virtual IP) settings. Once the VIP has been created, it must be applied to a firewall rule for the translation to be triggered. Despite its name, the VIP setting has nothing to do with HA clustering or VRRP (Virtual Router Redundancy Protocol). Later, in this section we'll also discuss how VIP settings within FortiOS are used for load balancing. Since VIPs are used for destination only translation, they are always defined under the destination address.

A destination one-to-one NAT (or static NAT), would consist of the following minimum settings:

```
// create destination NAT IP (VIP)
config firewall vip
   edit <name of vip>
      set type static-nat
      set extintf <inbound external interface name>
      set extip <inbound IP address>
      set mappedip <destination IP address>
   next
end
// Tie VIP to firewall rule
config firewall policy
```

```
    edit <rule number>
        set dstaddr <name of vip>
    next
end
```

The "set type" setting defines the VIP type which by default is "static-nat". Static-nat provides the following covered function related to destination IP and/or port forwarding. The other options are "load-balance" and "server-load-balance" which will be covered later in this chapter, The "set extintf" setting defines the interface expecting the incoming traffic. The interface can be explicitly defined or set to "any".

"set extip" defines the destination address to be translated. By default, this is defined as "0.0.0.0" and will match all addresses. If left at the default setting, any connection hitting the rule with this assigned VIP definition would be translated to the address defined in "set mappedip". This default behavior could be useful in situations where the external interface has a dynamically assigned IP address. Other than cases when multiple addresses share the default of 0.0.0.0, extip addresses cannot overlap with one another.

"set mappedip" define the actual translated destination address.

Destination IP and Destination Port

The translation used for ports is defined along with the destination address. When you must perform a one-to-many NAT, where the destination address is translated to different ports, you must link the VIP to a firewall rule.

```
// create destination NAT IP and port forwarding (VIP)
config firewall vip
    edit <name of vip>
        set type static-nat
        set portforward enable
        set extintf <inbound external interface name>
        set extip <inbound IP address>
        set mappedip <destination IP address>
        set extport <port number>
        set mappedport <port number>
        set protocol <tcp | udp | sctp>
    next
end
// tie VIP to firewall rule
config firewall policy
    edit <rule number>
        ....
```

```
      set dstaddr <name of vip>
      ….
   next
end
```

The following settings provide the destination port translation:

"set portforward enable" turns on the port forwarding for the VIP definition. Therefore, the following settings are also required:

"set extport <port number>" defines the destination port to be translated. Each port/extip address combination must be unique.

"set mappedport <port number>" defines the translated destination port. This port must also be unique in combination with the extip address.

"set protocol <tcp | udp | sctp>" defines the protocol used for the port mapping.

Destination IP and/or Port Ranges

A single VIP definition can consist of a destination range and/or corresponding port ranges. When defining an IP-only range (no port forwarding), it must be continuous and not overlap with the existing "extip" address. Once the range has been specified, the "mappedip" range should equal the size of the range to which it is being mapped. For example, if "extip" is defined as 172.16.1.10–172.16.1.15 which represents seven IP addresses, then the "mappedip" would also have to represent seven IP address, such as 192.168.1.24–192.168.1.29.

extip "translates to"	_mappedip
172.16.1.10	192.168.1.24
172.16.1.11	192.168.1.25
172.16.1.12	192.168.1.26
172.16.1.13	192.168.1.27
172.16.1.14	192.168.1.28
172.16.1.15	192.168.1.29

The CLI syntax for this sort of mapping would be as follows:

```
// create destination NAT IP ranges (VIP)
config firewall vip
   edit <name of vip>
      set type static-nat
      set extip <starting ip address range>-<ending ip address range>
      set extintf <inbound external interface name>
      set mappedip <starting ip address range>-<ending ip address
      range>
   next
```

```
end
// tie VIP to firewall rule
config firewall policy
    edit <rule number>
        set dstaddr <name of vip>
// Given VIP are used for destination only translation, the VIP defined
    setting are always chosen under the destination address
    next
end
```

When using port forwarding, you may also define port ranges. Like the IP address ranges, a port range must be continuous with the "extport" and "mapped-port" ranges containing equal number of ports. When defining the mappedip, if only the starting address for a range is defined, FortiOS automatically adds the ending IP address.

```
// create destination NAT IP and port forwarding ranges (VIP)
config firewall vip
    edit <name of vip>
        set type static-nat
        set extip <starting ip address range>-<ending ip address range>
        set extintf <inbound external interface name>
        set portforward enable
        set mappedip <starting ip address range>-<ending ip address
        range>
        set extport <starting port range>-<ending port range>
        set mappedport <starting port range>-<ending port range>
    next
end
// tie VIP to firewall rule
config firewall policy
    edit <rule number>
        set dstaddr <name of vip>
    next
end
```

To avoid mapping confusion, external and mapped port ranges must be continuous. Also, as with ranges, FortiOS will automatically add the ending port number to correspond to the extport range mapping.

For example, if the extport range is 80–81 and the mappedport is 8080–8081 then the destination translation results would be:

extip "translates to"	mappedip	extport "port forward to"	mappedport
172.16.1.10	192.168.1.24	80	8080
172.16.1.10	192.168.1.24	81	8081
172.16.1.11	192.168.1.25	80	8080
172.16.1.11	192.168.1.25	81	8081
172.16.1.12	192.168.1.26	80	8080
172.16.1.12	192.168.1.26	81	8081
172.16.1.13	192.168.1.27	80	8080
172.16.1.13	192.168.1.27	81	8081
172.16.1.14	192.168.1.28	80	8080
172.16.1.14	192.168.1.28	81	8081
172.16.1.15	192.168.1.29	80	8080
172.16.1.15	192.168.1.29	81	8081

Destination IP groups

Destination IP groups are simply grouping one or more VIP definitions.

```
config firewall vipgrp
   edit <name of vip group>
      set interface <inbound external interface name>
      // multiple members are delimited by a space
      set member <VIP name or VIP group name>
   next
end
// Tie the VIP group to a firewall rule
config firewall policy
   edit <existing rule number>
      set dstaddr <name of vip group>
   next
end
```

Misc NAT Functionalities
NAT within Multicast Firewall Rule

```
config firewall multicast-policy
   edit <rule number>
      set nat <IPv4 source NAT address>
      set dnat <IPv4 destination NAT address>
   next
end
```

Within a multicast firewall rule, the source and/or destination NAT is definable per rule.

NAT in Layer 2 (Transparent Mode)

When FortiOS is deployed in Layer 2 (Transparent) mode, NAT is still possible at a per rule level: source NAT with IP Pools, Central NAT, or destination NAT with VIP one-to-one or port forwarding support. All NAT functions in transparent mode are configurable via CLI only.

NAT with VPN

NAT is possible with both IPSec and the SSL VPN and can be configured with both the CLI and the GUI. This will be discussed further in the section on VPN.

Identity-Based Authentication

Identity-based authentication provides user authentication at a firewall rule level. When identity-based authentication is enabled within a firewall rule, it allows you to further control traffic based on user identities. When this feature is enabled, identity rules can be defined as simply as a single rule linking traffic processing to identify or as more complex groups. In order for the traffic to trigger the identity policy within firewall rule, the traffic first must qualify based on the rule source interface/zone, source network(s), destination interface/zone, and destination network(s).

Prior to creating an identity-based rule, you must first define where authentication credentials will be referenced. There are two methods of identity authentication: firewall authentication, which would prompt the end user for their login credentials, and Fortinet Single Sign On (FSSO) which is used in conjunction with Microsoft Active Directory or Novell eDirectory infrastructure. This allows users to authenticate without being prompted for credentials if they have already logged in to the infrastructure.

Firewall Authentication

Firewall authentication credentials can be stored locally or configured to use external authentication servers such as Radius, TACACS+, LDAP, or Fortinet's two-factor authentication.

Local Authentication Database

Locally stored credentials for firewall authentication require a two step configuration process.

```
// First, define the local login and related password
config user local
   edit <login name>
```

```
      set type password
      set passwd <password>
   next
end
```

```
// Second, link the locally created login credentials to a FortiOS user
   group. This user group name is referenced in the identity firewall
   rule for firewall authentication
config user group
   edit <local database group name>
      set group-type firewall
      // multiple login(s) are delimited by a space
      set member <local user name1> <local user name2> <...>
   next
end
```

"set group-type" should be set to "firewall" to enforce the firewall authentication method. The other choice of "fsso-service" would be used for MS AD integration, which will be discussed later.

External Authentication Databases

Using login credentials from an external authentication server also requires a two step process.

1. Define an External Authentication Server (Radius, TACACS+, or LDAP).
2. Add an External Authentication Server to a FortiOS User Group. Further external groups can then be defined within the FortiOS user group definitions.

Defining a External Authentication Server

External Authentication via RADIUS: To configure a FortiGate to authenticate against a RADIUS server, you must, at minimum, define the type, shared secret, server, and port.

```
config user radius
   edit <radius server name>
      set auth-type { auto | chap | ms_chap | ms_chap_v2 | pap }
      set secret <radius secret key>
      set server <radius server ip address>
      set radius-port <radius port number>
   next
end
```

"set auth-type { auto | chap | ms_chap | ms_chap_v2 | pap }" defaults to "auto" which negotiates in the following order: pap, ms_chap_v2, then chap. If auto-negotiation is not desired, it can be explicitly defined (see Figure 5.6)

External Authentication via TACACS+

To configure a FortiGate to authenticate against a TACACS+ server, you must, at minimum, define the type, server, port, and key.

```
config user tacacs+
   edit <tacacs+ server name>
      set authen-type { ascii | auto | chap | ms_chap | pap }
      set server <tacacs+ server ip address>
      set port <tacacs+ server port>
      set key <tacacs+ secret key>
   next
end
```

"set authen-type" defaults to "auto" which negotiates in the order: pap, ms_chap, then chap. As with RADIUS, this authentication type can be explicitly defined.

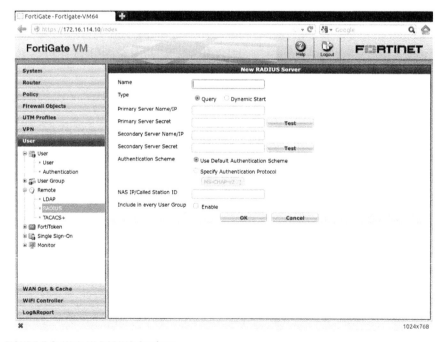

FIGURE 5.6 Web UI RADIUS Settings

External Authentication via LDAP

Due to the complexity inherent in LDAP, it is somewhat more difficult to configure.

```
config user ldap
    edit <ldap server name>
        set server <ldap server ip address>
        set port <ldap server port>
        set type { simple | anonymous | regular }
// if 'type' is defined as 'regular' then 'username' & 'password' are
    required
// 'secure' is an option and, if defined, Requires 'ca-cert'
            set username <ldap 'regular' login name>
            set password <ldap 'regular' login password>
            set secure <disable | ldaps | starttls>
            set ca-cert <certificate name on FortiGate>
        set cnid <common name identifier>
        set dn <distinguished name path>
        set member-attr <attribute string>
        set group-member-check <group-object | user-attr>
// if 'group-member-check' is defined as 'group-object' then 'group-
    object-filter' is needed
            set group-object-filter <group object filter string>
    next
end
```

As of this writing, you can define up to ten LDAP server definitions. FortiOS supports the LDAP protocol (RFC2251) for looking up and validating user credentials. It is compliant with all servers that support up to LDAP v3. As Microsoft's Active Directory service (AD) is based on LDAP, FortiOS's LDAP can reference it. However, FortiOS does not support any proprietary extensions, such as password expiration notifications, etc.

"set cnid <common name identifier>" defaults to the LDAP Canonical Name or "cn". In an AD environment, this is the "Display Name" identifier of an AD user. If there's a need to reference the actual AD logon name, this value can be changed to "sAMAccountName" via "set cnid sAMAccountName"

To check the "Display Name" (cn) vs. a "Logon Name" (sAMAccountName) on a Microsoft Directory server, run the following commands from the Microsoft Windows Command Prompt.

```
// to show the Display Name (cn) linked to a sAMAccountName
# dsquery user -name <sAMAccountName>
//to show the Logon Name (sAMAccountName) linked to a Display Name (cn)
# dsquery user -samid <display name>
```

"set dn <distinguished name path>" defines the hierarchy of the LDAP database object classes above the common name identifier (cnid setting). In an AD infrastructure, the root is defined by "dc", organizational unit is defined with "ou", and the container or user group are defined by "cn".

For example, to query the LDAP server for a user named "fortiuser" who belongs in a user group named "Users" under domain.test.com, you must specify the dn path as: "cn=Users,dc=domain,dc=test,dc=com". This restricts the LDAP server to query only the "Users" group. Alternately, the dn path can be defined as: "dc=domain,dc=test,dc=com" which would encompasses any other ou or cn beneath it.

"set member-attr <attribute string>" defaults to "memberOf" for MS AD or Open LDAP use. If you are using Novell's eDirectory server, this value should be changed to "groupMembership", e.g. "set member-attr groupMembership".

"set group-member-check <group-object | user-attr>" defaults to "user-attr". If set to "group-object" then the "set group-object-filter" would need to be defined. By default, group-object-filter is defined as "(&(objectcategory=group)(member=*))" which works well with a Microsoft network. Other examples of group-object-filter are:

(&(objectclass=groupofnames)(member=*))
(&(objectclass=groupofuniquenames)(uniquemember=*))
(&(objectclass=posixgroup)(memberuid=*)) // typically used with Open LDAP

See *Appendix B—Troubleshooting* for additional details on using CLI debug commands to test the external authentication servers. You can run a debug test on a username to discover group membership information. This can be used to further tune the definitions (see Figure 5.7).

Adding an External Authentication Server to a FortiOS User Group

```
config user group
    edit <user authentication group name>
        set group-type firewall
        // Multiple external servers are delimited by a space
        set member <external server name1> <external server name2> <...>
        config match
            edit <entry number>
                set service-name <external server name>
                set group-name <name of external server group>
            next
        end
    end
end
```

To enforce the firewall authentication method, the command "set group-type" should be set to "firewall". The other choice of "fsso-service" would be used for AD integration and will be discussed later.

Besides external servers, "set member" can also reference local accounts. The section preceding "config match" defines the external authentication server groups

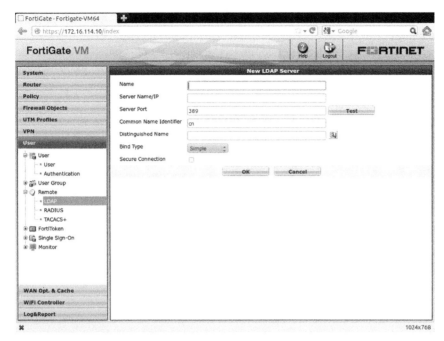

FIGURE 5.7 Web UI LDAP Setting

that are tied to a specific external authentication server. Each "edit <entry number>" is processed from top to bottom for login searches. Each entry defines the external server and the respective external groups.

External group definitions vary based on the type of external authentication servers used. For RADIUS and TACACS+, the external group name should match the group name passed in the Vendor Specific Attribute (VSA) Fortinet-Group-Name. Table 5.1 shows an example of the FortiOS RADIUS VSA dictionary on the supported attributes. However, this can change with technology. Updated versions of

Table 5.1 FortiOS Radius VSA Dictionary

# FortiOS v4.0 MR3 RADIUS VSA Dictionary		
VENDOR	**Fortinet**	**12356**
BEGIN-VENDOR Fortinet		
ATTRIBUTE Fortinet-Group-Name	1	string
ATTRIBUTE Fortinet-Client-IP-Address	2	ipaddr
ATTRIBUTE Fortinet-Vdom-Name	3	string
ATTRIBUTE Fortinet-Client-IPv6-Address	4	octets
ATTRIBUTE Fortinet-Interface-Name	5	string
ATTRIBUTE Fortinet-Access-Profile	6	string
END-VENDOR Fortinet		
#		

this dictionary are available under the support site within the GA or MR download directories.

The external group definition for an LDAP server should consist of a full dn path for the login credential in question. As noted in the above example, the group-name would be "set group-name cn=Users,dc=domain,dc=test,dc=com".

Local or External Authentication Server Firewall Authentication Identity-Based Policies

```
config firewall policy
   edit <rule number>
      set srcintf <interface or zone name>
      set dstintf <interface or zone name>
      set srcaddr <address object name>
      set dstaddr <address object name>
      set action accept
      config identity-based-policy
         edit <id rule number>
            set groups <FortiOS user group>
            set schedule <schedule name>
            set service <service name objects(s)>

            ...

         next
      end
   next
end
```

Creation of an identity rule is done within an existing firewall rule. Once an identity-based policy is enabled, rules must be added, otherwise all traffic would be implicitly denied.

When an identity-based policy is enabled, the only required settings are the source and destination interface and the network objects needed to trigger further inspection.

"config identity-based-policy" defines the sub-rule section for identity-based rules. Within this section, rule entries are created much like the FortiOS firewall. Each identity rule starts with "edit <id rule number>", where a single FortiOS user group is specified along with the related service access controls: "set service <service name object(s)>", schedule, and any related UTM security inspection requirements.

When using identity-based rules, order is important, as the rules are processed top to bottom. Prior to FortiOS 4.0 MR3, if a user does not belong in one FortiOS user group then the each next rule would be inspected in turn until a match is made, otherwise the session would be denied. Starting in FortiOS 4.0 MR3, this behavior was changed with the following setting:

```
config user setting
    set auth-multi-group {enable | disable}
    set auth-timeout-type {idle-timeout | hard-timeout | new-session}
    set auth-timeout <seconds>
end
```

"set auth-multi-group" is enabled by default, allowing inspection for users belonging to multiple user groups.

In addition to the "config user setting", there are authentication timeout settings that can be defined for authenticated user sessions. The "set auth-timeout-type" provides three types of authentication timeout methods defined by "set auth-timeout". All user settings are defined per VDOM.

"set auth-timeout-type idle-timeout" forces the user to re-authenticate their session if it goes idle. The timeout length is set under "set auth-timeout <seconds>". If you need to force the user to re-authenticate regardless of idle or non-idle traffic, you must use the hard timeout as set in "set auth-timeout-type hard-timeout".

If you need a timeout that functions like a hard timeout, but only forces new sessions to be re-authenticated, you must use "set auth-timeout-type new-session". This can be useful for cases where the security of re-authentication is needed, but users balk at the difficulty of a hard timeout.

FSSO (Fortinet Single Sign On)

Originally FSSO was named Fortinet Server Authentication Extension, but it was renamed in FortiOS 4.0 MR3. FSSO provides a transparent authentication experience for users that have already authenticated to a Microsoft or Novell environment. It is transparent in that, from an end user perspective, users are not prompted for credentials if they are already logged into the directory service.

FortiOS communicates directly with an FSSO agent. This agent is installed on the authentication infrastructure and determines whether the user is logged in. It also correlates the user's IP information so the session may be tracked within FortiOS.

In the next sections we'll go over the basic configuration needed to get FSSO working. However, before this can be done, you must decide in which mode you will run the FSSO agent.

IPV6 TIP

IPv6 Identity Base Authentication support
As of this writing, FortiOS MR3, FSSO, & NTLM authentication is not supported for IPv6. Only firewall authentication where the user would be prompted for credentials.

The FSSO agent can be deployed in one of two modes: DC Agent or Polling. In a Novell eDirectory environment, only the Polling mode is supported. For AD environments, the differences between these two modes follow.

DC (data collector) Agent Mode:

- Requires the installation of a file (dcagent.dll, 100 KB) on each of the domain controllers within the domain being monitored. This file is installed within the Windows\system32 directory of the domain controller server.
- No services run in this mode.
- After this file is installed, the domain control must be rebooted. When using multiple domain controllers, the reboot may be staggered to prevent downtime for the domain.
- The agent sends logon events to the Collector Agent and requires a minimum of 64 kilo bits per second of bandwidth added to the network load
- Provides an accurate capture of all logon events

Polling Mode:

- Does not require any software to be installed on domain controllers. Only requires that a Collector Agent be installed on any machine on the domain.
- The CA will poll logon events from each individual domain controller. In an AD infrastructure, communication from CA to domain controllers requires that TCP port 445 be opened to the DC servers.
- Polling mode is less reliable then agent mode, as the events are only seen once they are polled. During heavy system or network load, the polling timeframe may need to be increased, thereby further decreasing reliability.

In an AD infrastructure, events do not indicate when a user logs off. To accurately track whether a user is still logged onto a computer, it is recommended that all end user workstations be allowed to communicate with the CA server on TCP ports 139 or 445. This allows access to registry information to determine whether the user is still logged onto the computer. This is defined by the CA workstation verification interval, which defaults to five minutes. If your internal policy does not allow communication on these ports, then you should disable workstation verification by changing the interval setting to zero.

FortiOS FSSO Agent Communication Setup

Once the FSSO agent method has been determined and the agent configured on the server, the next step is to define the FSSO communication between FortiOS and the FSSO Collector Agent. For both AD and eDirectory, the FSSO Standard mode can be configured. Use of the Advanced FSSO mode requires AD. In contrast to the standard mode, where the user group filter is defined on the CA server, the advanced mode allows for group filters to be defined on the FortiGate using LDAP queries. This provides the ability to support nested or inherited user groups.

```
// If using FSSO Standard mode
config user fsso
                edit <name>
        set server <IPv4 address of server with FSSO collector agent>
        set port <server port - default 8000>
        set password <password to match FSSO collector agent settings>
    next
end
// If using FSSO Advance access mode
config user fsso
            edit <name>
        set server <IPv4 address of server with FSSO collector agent>
        set port <server port - default 8000>
        set password <password to match FSSO collector agent settings>
        set ldap-server <LDAP server name>
    next
end
```

Adding FSSO FortiOS User Groups

```
config user group
        edit <user authentication group name>
            set group-type fsso-service
            // Multiple AD/Novell groups are delimited by a space
            set member <group name1> <group name2> <...>
end
```

To enforce FSSO authentication, "set group-type" should be set to "fsso-service".

FSSO Identity-Based Policies

```
config firewall policy
        edit <rule number>
            set srcintf <interface or zone name>
            set dstintf <interface or zone name>
            set srcaddr <address object name>
            set dstaddr <address object name>
            set action accept
            config identity-based-policy
                edit <id rule number>
```

```
            set groups <FortiOS FSSO user group>
            set schedule <schedule name>
            set service <service name objects(s)>
                ...
        next
      end
    next
end
```

FSSO identity rules are similar to those used for firewall authentication except the "set groups" definition would reference the FSSO user group name rather than a FortiOS firewall authentication user group name.

When AD authentication does not match any of the identity-based rules but non-authenticated users must still be controlled, you must create a default "bottom" rule. This default rule needs to be assigned to the "FSSO_Guest_Users" for the "set groups" definition.

VPN

FortiOS supports various VPN (Virtual Private Network) functions such as IPSec, SSL VPN, GRE, PPTP, and LT2P.

IPSec

There are two IPSec methods available in FortiOS: policy- or interface-based. The first method is policy-based where a single firewall rule defines access control to and encryption and decryption within an IPSec tunnel. Policy-based IPSec is defined when the action for a firewall rule is set to "ipsec" and given a VPN tunnel profile selection. Both inbound and outbound traffic is controlled by the single rule.

In contrast, an interface-based IPSec configuration provides a virtual encrypted interface which traffic can be routed based on firewall rule definitions. In this mode, as there is a virtual IPSec interface, dynamic routing protocols such as RIPv1/v2, OSPF, BGP, and multicast related protocols (IGMP, PIM) can be tied used to perform routing. Most users find this a more robust VPN method then policy-based IPSec. IPv6 is only supported on Interface-based IPSec configurations.

With either method, configuration for the IPSec tunnel requires defining both phases 1 and 2 for the tunnel. Policy-based IPSec settings are configured under:

config vpn ipsec phase1
config vpn ipsec phase2

Interface-based IPsec is configured with:

config vpn ipsec phase1-interface
config vpn ipsec phase2-interface

Once the phase 1 and phase 2 IPSec settings are configured, the next steps depend on the type of IPSec method used:

Policy-based IPSec:

- Defines firewall rules for the policy-based IPSec tunnel. The destination interface for the rule must match the "local interface" setting in phase 1. To apply to the IPSec tunnel, the rule action must be set to "ipsec" and match the phase1 name of the tunnel. Once complete, the rule would dictate the source network, destination network, services, and time (schedule) for the traffic used by the policy-based tunnel.
- Ensures that inbound IPSec packets are destined to the policy-based IPSec "local interface" and that the encrypted destination network traffic is routed towards the corresponding interface of the policy-based IPSec rule.

Interface-based IPSec:

- Defines a firewall rule for the interface-based IPSec tunnel by binding the IPSec interface name to either the source or destination interface of a rule. The rule would then dictate the source network, destination network, services, and time (schedule) for the type of traffic used for the interface-base IPSec tunnel.
- Configures a static route for the interface-based IPSec tunnel interface for the remote networks. Optionally, a dynamic routing protocol can be applied to this interface. In this case, routes would be dynamically learned and added to the FortiGate's routing table to determine what network(s) are routed through the tunnel.

FortiOS IPSec Key Points

IPSec can be complicated. While the following sections explain some common ways to deploy IPSec, you may need to reference the Fortinet IPSec VPN handbook (http://docs.fortinet.com/fgt.html) for additional details.

FortiOS IPSec Phase 1 Tips
To ensure a successfully negotiated phase 1, the following settings generally need to match the remote end settings:

- IKE mode negotiations method (Aggressive or Main)
- Methods used to authenticate remote VPN peers such as:
  - Certificates
  - Pre-shared key
  - Local ID match with remote Peer ID

- IKE version (1 or 2)
- Phase 1 Encryption (DES, 3DES, AES) and Authentication (MD5, SHA) cipher proposals
- DH (Diffie-Hellman) Group level (1,2,5, or 14)
- Keylife timers. The lowest keylife timer is chosen during the IKE negotiations
- NAT Traversal version

> **NOTE**
>
> **Encryption Exportation Restrictions**
>
> If you are based in the United States of America and are dealing with FortiGate products outside the country, be aware of the laws covering encryption technologies. For some countries, it may be necessary to use Fortinet's "low encryption" offerings to comply with local laws. These products have a product SKU noted as LENC (low encryption). Consult Fortinet sales for additional information.

The remote gateway can be a static IP, but this is not required. If the remote gateway is not static, consider using dynamic DNS with a fully qualified domain name. This way, the tunnel will rely on the DNS name to identify the remote end. You can also use dial-up to connect to the FortiGate and initiate the IPSec VPN.

When negotiating aggressive vs main modes of IKE, be aware that the main mode provides more secure negotiation since that portion is encrypted. However, for such connections to work, the other end of the connection must be static. In contrast, aggressive mode is used when the IP address is unknown or changeable. This mode is specifically needed when local ID and peer ID settings are used with dynamic end points. When using IKEv2 option:

- Aggressive vs. Main mode only supported IKEv1 and not IKEv2
- Local and Peer ID not supported
- Only one DH group supported
- XAuth is not supported

When the phase 1 keylife timer expires (28,800 s by default), rekeying is done only when tunnel is in a non-idle state. If you need to prevent the tunnel from rekeying between IKE peers, use the following global setting:

```
config system global
    set phase1-rekey {enable | disable}
end
```

Note: If set to "disable", rekeying does not occur. Therefore the IPSec tunnel session would be torn down. The tunnel would then need to be re-established with a new SA (security association) when traffic is seen for the IPSec tunnel.

To ensure that the tunnel is always up, the following setting can be enabled to always force tunnel establishment:

```
config vpn ipsec {phase1 | phase1-interface}
    edit <name of phase1 tunnel>
        set auto-negotiate enable
    next
end
```

By default, auto-negotiation is disabled, so if the tunnel is disconnected, it will only be re-established by traffic destined for the tunnel. This can happen, when the local end of the tunnel is rebooted, the session is torn down manually, or when the keylife timer expires but rekeying is disabled.

Any time the tunnel is re-established, there will be a delay and packets will be lost during the tunnel negotiations. Enabling auto-negotiation will automatically cause a re-establishment attempt of the tunnel regardless of traffic usage. This is more efficient, as it reduces the delay and makes it more likely that the tunnel will be up when it is needed. It is recommended that auto-negotiation be enabled for both phases.

When using Xauth (Extended Authentication):

- Each phase 1 Xauth server configuration is limited to one user group definition; If more than one user group is required for Xauth, you will need a separate phase 1 definition for each user group.
- Multiple tunnels are determined based on unique IPSec phase 1 configurations. Using matches between peer and remote client IDs can help to distinguish between IPSec configurations. If multiple user groups are used in Xauth, multiple IPSec tunnels exist. Therefore peer/local ID will determine the tunnel to use.
- Aggressive mode is required to help distinguish between peer IDs.

The DPD (Dead Peer Detection) setting is available to ensure that the IPSec tunnel is successfully established with a peer. By default, DPD sends a probe packet every 5 s (based on "dpd-retryinterval") and if there's no response to the probes after three attempts (based on "dpd-retrycount"), then the tunnel session would be cleared and re-establishment would be attempted. This prevents non-operational tunnels from lingering due to remote issues. However, the remote end needs to support DPD in order for this to work properly.

If the IPSec connection must traverse a NAT device, NAT Traversal (NAT-T) can be enabled to allow the IPSec connection to establish. Given that IPSec does not use a specific port, NAT-T wraps the IPSec packet into a UDP packet. This allows the NAT to occur on the UDP header address and port. Version 1 of NAT-T communicates on UDP port 500 whereas version 3 communicates on UDP port 4500. Both versions are supported by FortiOS. In most cases, the NAT device that provides state on the session or has an idle timer could potentially interrupt the session when no traffic is flowing. To prevent this, the NAT-T keepalive feature can be enabled. This will periodically send packets to simulate activity on the session. By default, such a packet is sent every 10 s. The NAT-T setting and NAT-T keepalive setting can be defined as followed:

```
config vpn ipsec {phase1 | phase1-interface}
    edit <phase1 vpn name>
        set nattraversal enable
        set keepalive 10
```

```
        next
end
```

To take advantage of hardware acceleration offered in FortiGate models with a NPx ASIC, first verify the hardware offloading requirements as found in Chapter 2 under "VPN Acceleration using NP and CP ASIC". Next, make sure that you are using an interface-based IPSec configuration, as use of the ASIC is determined by the interface. Lastly, in phase 1, define the local gateway as follows:

```
config vpn ipsec phase1-interface
        edit <name of phase1 tunnel>
          set local-gw <ipv4 address of local terminating interface>
      next
end
```

The IPv4 address should be the FortiGate IPSec terminating interface. Even though there's a "set local-gw6" for IPv6 address, NP2 & NP4 do not support IPv6 hardware acceleration. Future releases of NPx ASIC will have IPv6 offloading capabilities.

FortiOS IPSec Phase 2 Tips
To ensure successful negotiation for phase 2 of building the IPSec tunnel, the following settings must match on both ends of the tunnel.

- Encryption (DES, 3DES, AES) and Authentication (MD5, SHA) cipher proposals.
- Anti-Replay Detection.
- PSF (Perfect Forward Secrecy) requires the DH Group level of choice (1,2,5, or 14).
- Keylife timers will use the lowest timer during the IKE negotiations.
- Quick Mode Selectors must, at minimum, match the local source and remote network. By default, it will allow all traffic through tunnel.

A phase 2 SA (Security Association) session will use the same phase 1 encryption and authentication ciphers as well as generated session keys. Therefore any rekeying that occurs when phase 1 keylife expires would create a new phase 2 SA. For additional security measures, PFS (Perfect Forwarding Secrecy) can be enabled to provide the unique encryption and authentication ciphers for the phase 2 SA by enforcing negotiations of Diffie-Hellman.

```
config vpn ipsec {phase2 | phase2-interface}
    edit <phase2_name>
       set pfs enable
    next
end
```

If PFS is used, then a separate DH keylife timer is used to negotiate a new set of keys. When the phase 2 keylife expires (with a 1800s default), rekeying will only occur if there is traffic in the tunnel at the time of expiration. To ensure that phase 2 rekeying occurs regardless of traffic usage, enable the Autokey Keep Alive:

```
config vpn ipsec {phase2 | phase2-interface}
   edit <phase2_name>
      set keepalive {enable | disable}
   next
end
```

To ensure tunnel availability, the auto-negotiate setting can be enabled within phase 2 such as:

```
config vpn ipsec {phase2 | phase2-interface}
   edit <phase2_name>
      set auto-negotiate enable
   next
end
```

As with the phase 1 auto-negotiate feature, if the phase 2 auto-negotiate setting is enabled, it will always attempt to re-establish the SA session regardless of traffic usage. By default, this setting is disabled, so if the tunnel is down, only traffic destined for the tunnel would trigger re-establishment. The re-establishment would inevitably cause delay and packet loss.

FortiOS IPSec 3rd party Interoperability Tips

- Multiple SAs are needed when interoperating with some third-party vendors (Cisco, Checkpoint, and Sonicwall). If you need to encrypt more than one network, then an SA is required for each. Thus, to create a phase2 tunnel definition for each network with quick mode selectors, you must match the local source and remote destination network of the remote third-party VPN concentrator network settings for the tunnel.
- If Dead Peer Detection (DPD) is not supported on the remote end, it should be disabled. When the remote peer does not support DPD, IPSec packet errors may be reported on the remote end. Generally, if you see these errors reported in periodic way, this could be an indication that the remote peer does not support DPD.
- Either Policy- or Interface-based IPSec will interoperate with that of any third party.
- If local and peer IDs are used, you may need to define specific IKE ID types for proper negotiation. FortiOS supports IKE ID types: Address, FQDN, User FQDN (email), and ASN.1 Distinguished Name. By default, the IKE ID is set to "auto", which automatically attempts to negotiate these IKE ID types.

However, in some cases, this may need to be explicitly defined. The following setting defines the IKE ID type:

```
config vpn ipsec {phase1|phase1-interface}
    edit <phase 1 vpn name>
        set localid-type {auto | fqdn | user-fqdn | keyid | address |
    asn1dn}
    next
end
```

There is often a need to make a FortiGate interoperate with existing Cisco IPSec clients. This is a commonly needed configuration set:

```
config vpn ipsec {phase1 | phase1-interface}
    edit <phase 1 vpn name>
            set type dynamic
            set ike 1
            set mode-cfg enable
            set unity-support enable
            set ipv4-start-ip <starting assign ipv4 address>
            set ipv4-end-ip <ending assign ipv4 address>
            // below are optional settings when 'mode-cfg' is enabled
            set ipv4-dns-server1 <ipv4 dns address>
            set ipv4-dns-server2 <ipv4 dns address>
            set ipv4-dns-server3 <ipv4 dns address>
            set ipv4-wins-server1 <ipv4 wins address>
            set ipv4-wins-server2 <ipv4 wins address>
            set ipv4-split-include <address object name>
    next
end
```

When using IPv6 with IPSec, phase 1 is a little bit different when mode-cfg is enabled.

```
set mode-cfg-ip-version 6
set ipv6-start-ip <starting assign ipv6 address>
set ipv6-end-ip <ending assign ipv6 address>
set ipv6-dns-server1 <ipv6 dns address>
set ipv6-dns-server2 <ipv6 dns address>
set ipv6-dns-server3 <ipv6 dns address>
set ipv6-wins-server1 <ipv6 wins address>
set ipv6-wins-server2 <ipv6 wins address>
```

You may wish to check other references for third-party IPSec interoperability:

- Fortinet Knowledge base site: http://kb.fortinet.com.
- ICSA Labs: https://www.icsalabs.com/product/fortigate-multi-threat-security-platforms.

SSL VPN

The SSL VPN provides a secure connection for remote users. This alternative to IPSec is often preferred for the following reasons:

Sometimes the user network has restrictions in place that block outbound IPSec traffic.

> UDP port 500 (IKE) and protocol ID types of 50 (ESP) and 51 (AH).
> UDP port 500 or 4500, if NAT-T is used.
> The SSL VPN uses standard HTTPS on TCP port 443, allowed most places.

Little to no installation needed on the end point.

The Web mode provides a secure through the end user's web browser to the FortiGate and, through it, to other resources. This, therefore, does not require any software installation on the remote end user machine. In Tunnel mode, however, a virtualized tunnel is provided to route IPv4 traffic from the remote end user machine. As this requires a client, there must be a one time installation.

Prior to configuring SSL VPN, it must be enabled. This can be done for individual VDOMs:

```
config vpn ssl settings
    set sslvpn-enable enable
end
```

Web Mode

When a remote user establishes an SSL VPN connection to the FortiGate via HTTPS, it is called Web mode. The primarily purpose of web mode is to provide secure access to network resources for the remote user. Only a few applications are supported through the web portal: HTTP, HTTPS, SSH, RDP, VNC, Telnet, SMB/CIFS, ICMP Ping, Citrix ICA, and FTP.

Configuration checklist for Web mode

1. Define SSL VPN portal. Either create a new one or use existing defaults.
   > // ssl vpn web portal settings under:
   > *config vpn ssl web portal*
2. Define user credentials. These credentials could be retrieved from a locally defined database, with FortiToken (see later in chapter) or via an external authentication server such as Radius, TACACS+, LDAP, or FortiAuthenticator.
   > // defining a local user credential:
   > *config user local*

// defining external authentication server:

config user {radius | tacacs+ | ldap}

3. Tie either the local user or external authentication server to a firewall authentication group and apply the SSL VPN portal to the group.

// defining authentication group:

config user group

// applying a authentication group to SSL VPN portal:

config user group

edit <group_example>

set sslvpn-portal <name of portal>

next

end

4. Define an SSL VPN firewall rule with the following attributes:

a. The source interface of the rule should match the incoming interface to which remote users connect.

b. The rule's destination interface is where the internal networks reside. The source and destination addresses for the rule can be further be tuned towards the actual allowed networks.

c. The rule's action must be set to 'ssl-vpn', to enable identity-based policing.

d. Define an ID rule for each authentication group as created in step 3.

// SSL VPN rule syntax:

config firewall policy

edit <id #>

// source interface to which remote users connect

set srcintf <interface name>

// destination interface to which remote users need access

set dstint <interface name>

// source addresses generally should be 'all' given remote user can come from any network or limit this with geographical address objects

set srcaddr <address name>

// destination address should be limited to networks allowed for the remote user

set dstaddr <address name>

set action ssl-vpn

// id based policy is enabled by default once action is set to ssl-vpn

set identity-based enable

// sub-section for id rules

edit <id #>

set schedule <schedule name>

set service <service name>

set group <ssl vpn group created in step3>

next

end

next

end

5. Ensure routes are in place to allow web portal application access. (See Chapter 4 for routing configuration.)

get router info routing-table all

From a high-level process diagram, Figure 5.8 provides this breakdown of what features and functions are involved with a SSL VPN session.

Accessing the FortiGate Web Portal

To access the FortiGate web portal, the remote user must first direct the browser to the FQDN or IP address of the FortiGate at the default port of 10443. E.g.: https://www.fortigateIP.com:10443.

Port 10443 is chosen to avoid conflicts with the FortGate administrative interface that runs, by default, on port 443. If you are not using the SSL VPN, you probably want this interface on 443. However, if you do need to use the SSL VPN, you should move the admin port:

```
config system global
     set admin-sport <port number>
end
```

The administrative HTTPS port is a global setting and will affect all the VDOMs that are configured. Once the administrative HTTPS port is changed, the SSL VPN port can be defined uniquely for each VDOM.

By default, the FortiOS will use a self-signed certificate. While perfectly secure, the drawback to this design is that users' browsers will present a security error

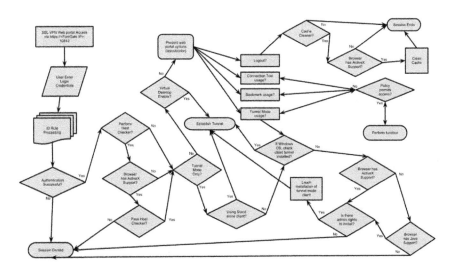

FIGURE 5.8 SSL VPN Usage Flow

indicating that the certificate is invalid or unknown. While the end user can bypass this error, it does train them to follow insecure practices. Avoiding this situation requires loading a CA certificate into the browser or installing a custom certificate into the FortiGate.

To allow the SSL VPN to use a custom certificate, the following settings are needed. Please refer to Fortinet Authentication documentation (http://docs.fortinet.com/fgt.html) for further details on creating and loading custom certificates into FortiOS.

```
config vpn ssl settings
    set reqclientcert enable
    set servercert <name of custom certificate loaded into FortiOS>
end
```

The SSL VPN web portal login page can be further customized. Customization of the SSL VPN login page can be done with the following syntax:

```
config system replacemsg-group
  edit default
    config sslvpn
      edit sslvpn-login
      set buffer <custom login page in HTML format>
      next
    end
  next
end
```

Once they connect, remote users must enter their credentials. The login credentials are checked against the resources defined by the SSL VPN authentication group setting. The SSL VPN can also be configured in additional ways:

```
config vpn ssl settings
  // define the session timeout value - default 28800 seconds / 8
  hours
  set auth-timeout <seconds>
  // define idle timer - default 300 seconds / 5 minutes
  set idle-timeout <seconds>
  // define whether certificates are required for remote user
  authentication
  set reqclientcert enable
  set servercert <name of cert to use>
end
```

Once the user provides their credentials, the pre-admission host checks begin.

Host checking requires ActiveX, so for it to work, the user must be connecting with Internet Explorer on Windows. The host check verifies that the user has antivirus and/or firewall running.

To enable host checking within the SSL VPN portal:

```
config vpn ssl web portal
            edit <name of portal>
            // av = antivirus, fw=firewall, av-fw=antivirus &
            firewall
                    set host-check {av | fw | av-fw | custom | none}
            // if 'custom' is used the below option is available
                    set host-check-policy <name of application,
                    multiple entries separated by space>
    end
end
```

Besides checking antivirus and firewall, host checks can be used to look for custom applications supported by FortiOS. This list is updated with the firmware. For a current list of which applications can be detected, perform a "*set host-check-policy ?*".

If the host checking fails after end user logins then an error message would be presented indicating the host checker failure had occurred and no further access is allowed. If the end user is coming from an OS and browser, that do not support ActiveX then by default, host checking would be bypassed and end user would be allowed to login. To disable this default behavior and make any failure of running host checking to implicitly not permit user access, then the following setting is needed to be defined at a per SSL web portal level:

```
config vpn ssl web portal
            edit <name of portal>
                ...
                    set skip-check-for-unsupported-browser disable
                    set skip-check-for-unsupported-os disable
                ...
    next
end
```

It is recommended to set both settings to disable in order to fully meet the implicit behavior of not allowing further access for the end user, if host checker is unable to be run. With these two settings disabled, if host checker fails to run after end user logins then the standard host checker failure error message would be presented and no further access would be allowed.

Functions within the FortiGate Web Portal:

Once a remote user logs into the SSL VPN web portal, the displayed features of the web portal functions can be further customized. The access widgets can be lain out and the color scheme can be changed:

```
config vpn ssl web portal
   edit <ssl vpn portal name>
      set heading "<custom heading message>"
      set theme {blue | crimson | darkgrey | gray | green | orange |
      steelblue}
      set page-layout {double-column | single-column}
   next
end
```

If widgets are enabled, four of them are displayed within the web portal:

* *Session Information*

This widget provides the current SSL VPN web session statistics based on the defined informational level:

  * The user logged in time
  * Inbound HTTP traffic statistics
  * Outbound HTTP traffic statistics

```
config vpn ssl web portal
   edit <ssl vpn portal name>
      config widget
         edit <id #>
            set type info
            set name "My Session Stats"
         next
      end
   next
end
```

* *Connection Tool*

This widget allows the end user to launch an application via the web portal. The widget can be enabled when the type is set to 'tool' and the 'allow-apps' are defined as follows:

```
config vpn ssl web portal
   edit <ssl vpn portal name>
      config widget
         edit <id #>
```

```
              set type tool
              set name "My Connection Tool"
              set allow-apps {web | ftp | smb | telnet | ssh | vnc | rdp
        | citrix | rdpnative | portforward}
           next
        end
     next
end
```

Access controls for the connection tool application are controlled by the SSL VPN firewall rule.

- *Bookmarks*

The bookmark widget provides predefined links to the supported web applications accessible via HTTP, HTTPS, SSH, RDP (windows terminal services), RDP Native (remote desktop access with native client), VNC, Citrix web server interface, Telnet, SMB/CIFS, and FTP. The syntax for enabling this requires the type to be set to 'bookmark' and subsequent bookmark are defined as follows:

```
config vpn ssl web portal
    edit <ssl vpn portal name>
       config widget
          edit <id #>
              set type bookmark
              set name "My bookmarks"
              config bookmarks
                 edit <name of bookmark>
                        set apptype <allow-apps types>
                        <further settings definable per allow-
              app types>…..
                 next
              end
          next
       end
    next
end
```

Access for the bookmarked applications is controlled by the SSL VPN firewall rule.

- *Tunnel Mode*

This widget provides the ability to launch an alternative SSL VPN mode that provides full layer 3 connectivity. The syntax for enabling this widget requires the type to be set to 'tunnel' as follows:

```
config vpn ssl web portal
    edit <ssl vpn portal name>
        config widget
            edit <id #>
                set type tunnel
                set name "Tunnel Mode"
            next
        end
    next
end
```

Tunnel Mode

SSL Tunnel mode operates similarly to an IPSec client. Once the SSL tunnel has been established, any IP-based data can be routed through a virtualized adapter/interface created on the remote user machine. There are two ways to run the tunnel:

1. Access through Web mode. Once authentication is successful, the Tunnel widget can be used to launch the adapter. Java or ActiveX is used to deliver the tunnel mode adapter (depending on browser support). The end user must have administrative rights on Microsoft Windows to install the tunnel mode adapter.
2. As a stand-alone client. The SSL VPN client can be installed and operate outside the web portal. This installation method can be used in scenarios where:

    a. The end user is not using a supported Microsoft OS, so the client installation files cannot be delivered.
    b. The end user lacks the administrative rights to install the adapter.
    c. The organization wishes to deploy clients company-wide.

Stand-alone versions of the SSL VPN client are available for Windows, MAC OS X, and Linux.

Configuration checklist for Tunnel mode
Tunnel mode is configured similarly to the steps outlined in the Web mode configuration.

1. Define the SSL VPN portal. In addition, add the 'Tunnel Mode' widget, as it is needed for the operation of tunnel mode, regardless of how the VPN is configured. Within the tunnel mode widget configuration, there are options to configure split tunneling or to direct all traffic through the tunnel. If choosing split tunneling, be aware that this creates a potential point of compromise if the

end point cannot be trusted. The syntax for the widget and its related optional settings are defined as follows:

```
config vpn ssl web portal
    edit <name of portal>
        config widget
            edit <id # for tunnel widget>
                set type tunnel
                set tunnel-status enable
// define 'ip-mode' on how IP address are assigned. 'usrgrp' will rely
on Radius group using attribute of framed-ip-address or 'range'
using locally defined IP range.
                set ip-mode {range | usrgrp}
// if 'ip-mode = range' the following setting define the IP assignment
range named object
                set ip-pools <name of IP range pool>
                // optional split-tunneling rules
                set split-tunneling enable
                set split-tunneling-routing-address <address_name>
                set split-tunneling disable
                // optional exclusive routing rules
                set exclusive-routing enable
```

1. Define the usage of user credentials.
2. Create the FortiOS user group and tie the SSL VPN portal to the user group.
3. Define the firewall rule for the SSL VPN as noted with Web mode. In addition, a rule must be defined for the tunnel mode communication. By default, the interface 'ssl.root', is needed for access controls with this interface. If VDOM is enabled, FortiOS will create this interface with a name linked to each VDOM on the system ('ssl.<vdom name>').

Here's an example of bi-directional "permit-any" policy for a tunnel mode interface:

```
config firewall policy
// tunnel mode interface name: ssl.root
// Internal network interface name: INTERNAL1
    edit 100
        set srcintf INTERNAL1
        set dstintf ssl.root
        set srcaddr all
        set dstaddr all
```

```
        set action accept
        set schedule always
        set service ANY
    next
    edit 101
        set srcintf ssl.root
        set dstintf INTERNAL1
        set srcaddr all
        set dstaddr all
        set action accept
        set schedule always
        set service ANY
    next
end
```

4. Define the route used by traffic through the SSL VPN:

```
config router static
// tunnel mode interface name: ssl.root
// SSL VPN IP address range is on the 192.168.1.0/24 network
    edit 1
        set device ssl.root
        set dst 192.168.1.0/24
    next
end
```

Port Forwarding Tunnel Mode

The port forwarding tunnel mode is used to communicate on specific ports without having to install or run a client.

Port Forwarding Tunnel Mode Highlights:

- This function only works when accessing the web portal via the web mode SSL VPN.
- This method may be configured in the Bookmark widget or dynamically launched via the Connection Tool widget.
- Upon launching the port forwarding mode, a java applet is downloaded to the end user's machine and generate a local listening port. Applications can then communicate on this port and the traffic can be proxied through the SSL VPN connection.
- Only supports static TCP ports.

Syntax for the port forwarding configuration in both Connection Tool and Bookmark widgets:

```
config vpn ssl web portal
    edit <ssl vpn portal name>
        config widget
            // enabling the ability within the Connection Tool widget
            edit 1
                set type tool
                set name "My Connection Tool"
                set allow-apps portforward
            next
            // predefining a bookmark within the bookmark widget
            edit 2
                set type bookmark
                set name "My bookmarks"
                edit <name of bookmark>
                set apptype portforward
                set host <host IP address to portward trafic to>
                set remote-port <host listening port>
                set listening-port <local ssl vpn user listening port>
            next
        next
        end
    next
    end
```

Virtual Desktop Mode

The Virtual desktop mode isolates the entire session from the end user's desktop environment. When the session is established, a virtual desktop is created, providing the complete isolation.

Virtual Desktop Mode Highlights:

- Supported only in Microsoft Windows XP, Vista, and 7.
- The virtual desktop client is automatically launched via Java when the user logs into the web portal and runs as a Java applet.
- All data is encrypted, including the cached user credentials, browser history, temporary files, cookies, and user files created during the session.
- Once the user logs out, all information is erased and the end user's desktop is restored.
- The cache may be cleaned on logout, but this must be explicitly enabled.
- If the session is abruptly disconnected, all data will remain on the end user's machine, but in an encrypted form. It will be purged once the user logs in again.

- Application controls can be applied during the virtual desktop session. This provides the ability to allow or deny specific applications.
- Two-factor authentication support with FortiToken.

```
config vpn ssl web portal
    edit <ssl vpn portal name>
        set virtual-desktop enable
        // specify the list of application controls
        set virtual-destop-app-list <app list name>
    next
end
// optional application control list. Applications match on MD5
    checksums, not names.
config vpn ssl web virtual-desktop-app-list
    edit <app list name>
        set action {allow | block}
        config apps
            edit <app name>
                set md5s <md5 string of application>
            next
        end
    next
end
```

Misc VPN

Additional VPN methods exist to assist with legacy implementations or to integrate with third-party solutions. In the next few sections we'll highlight the key configurations for these.

PPTP

FortiOS support of PPTP (Point-to-Point Tunneling Protocol) key points:

- Only FortiOS can act as a PPTP Server.
- Only IPv4 packets can be encapsulated within a PPTP VPN tunnel.
- PPTP is supported in layer 3 operational mode (NAT/Route) only.
- The feature is only configurable via CLI.
- Communicates on TCP port 1723.
- PAP, CHAP, and MSCHAPv2 authentication protocols are supported through the Auto mode and cannot be defined explicitly.
- User credentials can be referenced against a locally defined user database or external authentication server such as Radius, TACACS+, or LDAP.

- Up to 128 bit MPPE (Microsoft Point-to-Point Encryption) is supported. The encryption method is negotiated with the PPTP client, and cannot be explicitly defined. DNS and WINS server assignments to the PPTP client are not supported.

To successfully establish a remote client PPTP connection:

1. Use the CLI to define the PPTP settings. Due to the rarity of running in this mode, the WebUI does not support PPTP.

```
config vpn pptp
        set status enable
        set ip-mode {range | usergrp}
        // Define the IP address assignment range for the remote user
        set sip <starting IPv4 address assignment range>
        set eip <ending IPv4 address assignment range>
        // Define the user group used for authentication along with IP
address assignment from the group definition
        set usrgrp <FortiOS user group name>
        // If the ip-mode is set to 'usergrp', the following optional
setting defines the local address used when establishing PPTP with
another gateway for remote peering.
        set local-ip <IPv4 local address>
end
```

2. Define a firewall rule. Attributes of an PPTP rule are:

  a. The source interface of rule should be where remote PPTP users connect.
  b. The destination interface should be the internal networks to be accessed.
  c. The source address must match the PPTP address range defined.
  d. The destination address and services may be tuned to limit resources available to the remote PPTP users.
  e. Set action to 'accept'.
  f. Enable NAT if needed.

PPTP logging is not enabled by default. To enable it, and view it in the Event logs:

```
config log eventfilter
    set ppp enable
end
```

To display the real-time status of established PPTP session, use the following commands:

diagnose debug enable
diagnose vpn pptp status

Since "diagnose debug enable" enables the output, it will consume resources until it is disabled. It is best to enable it only when needed and to disable it when done with "diagnose debug disable". Further details on the diagnose command can be founded in Appendix B.

L2TP

FortiOS supports L2TP (Layer 2 Tunneling Protocol):

- Only the FortiGate can act as a LNS (L2TP Network Server).
- Only IPv4 packets can be encapsulated within a L2TP VPN tunnel.
- L2TP is supported in Layer 3 operational mode (NAT/Route) only.
- This feature is only configurable via CLI.
- Communicates on UDP port 1701.
- PAP, CHAP, and MSCHAPv2 authentication are supported only through auto-negotiation and cannot be defined explicitly.
- User credentials can reference either a locally defined user database or an external authentication server such as Radius, TACACS+, or LDAP.
- Up to 128 bit MPPE (Microsoft Point-to-Point Encryption) is supported, but in a negotiation mode only. It cannot be explicitly defined.
- DNS and WINS server assignments to L2TP clients are not supported.

To successfully establish a remote client L2TP connection:

1. Like PPTP, L2TP settings are definable only via the CLI.

```
config vpn l2tp
    set status enable
    set sip <starting IPv4 address assignment range>
    set eip <ending IPv4 address assignment range>
    set usrgrp <FortiOS user group name>
end
```

2. Define a firewall rule with the following attributes:
   a. Reference the incoming interface used by the remote users as the source
   b. The destination interface should reference the internal networks used by the remote user.
   c. The source address needs to match the L2TP address range defined.
   d. The destination address and services can be tuned to limit availability to remote PPTP users.
   e. Set action to 'accept'.
   f. Enable NAT if needed.

L2TP logging is not enabled, by default. To enable it, and view it in the Event logs:

```
config log eventfilter
    set ppp enable
end
```

To display real-time status of established L2TP session, use the following command:

diagnose debug enable
diagnose vpn l2tp status

Like PPTP, L2TP debugging should be disabled when not in use with the command "diagnose debug disable". Further details on the diagnose command can be founded in Appendix B.

L2TP over IPSec

The L2TP VPN provides encryption capabilities limited to 128 bit MPPE only. Given that IPSec is proven to be secure, encapsulating L2TP within IPSec is more secure. Most vendors (Microsoft, Apple, and Google) support this as a standard method used with L2TP VPN.

To use L2TP over IPSec, you must first configure it as described above. Then, IPSec must be configured.

When using L2TP over IPSec:

- IPSec must be policy-based
- The phase2 setting should set encapsulation to 'transport-mode'.

```
config vpn ipsec phase2
    edit <phase 2 vpn name for L2TP over IPSec>
        set encapsulation transport-mode
    next
end
```

- By default, the 'encapsulation' is set as 'tunnel-mode'. With transport-mode, only the payload data is encrypted. Since another L2TP will be handling the encapsulation, it cannot be encrypted. Microsoft operating systems older than (and including) Windows 2000 require certificates rather than pre-shared keys. To disable this behavior and force use of pre-shared key a registry setting must be changed (http://support.microsoft.com/kb/240262).
- If you wish to use Microsoft Windows 7 with L2TP over IPSec, it requires additional FortiOS IPSec tuning (http://kb.fortinet.com/kb/dynamickc.do?cmd =show&forward=nonthreadedKC&docType=kc&externalId=FD33431&slice Id=1).

GRE

GRE (Generic Routing Encapsulation) allows the tunneling of routing protocols across networks.

Key points of FortiOS GRE support:

- The feature is only configurable via CLI.
- Only IPv4 packets can be encapsulated within a GRE tunnel.

- GRE is a network layer protocol which uses an protocol ID type of 47.
- Supported in layer 3 operational mode (NAT/Route) only.

The GRE tunnel will be created as an interface and accessed like other FortiOS interfaces.

To successfully establish a GRE tunnel:

1. Define the GRE tunnel setting via CLI.

```
config system gre-tunnel
    edit <tunnel name>
        // define the GRE tunnel terminating interface
        set interface <interface name>
        // define the local GRE tunnel IP address
        set local-gw <IPv4 address>
        // define the remote GRE tunnel IP address
        set remote-gw <IPv4 address>
    next
end
```

2. Once the GRE tunnel has been created, it will appear as an interface within FortiOS. To encapsulate traffic through the GRE tunnel, routing decisions are needed. This can be accomplished by applying dynamic routing protocols or defining a simple static route.

```
config router static
    edit <entry #>
        set device <name of GRE tunnel>
        set dst <destinaton network> <netmask>
    next
end
```

3. Define access control for GRE tunneled traffic. Attributes of an GRE rule:

- **a.** Rules can be bi-directional and can be created with a source or destination interface of the GRE tunnel interface name. The corresponding interface for the rule would be the interface to which the GRE traffic should be routed.
- **b.** Definition of the network address and service objects.
- **c.** Set action to 'accept'.
- **d.** Enable NAT if needed.

GRE over IPSec

Like L2TP, GRE traffic can be encrypted with an IPSec tunnel.

1. When using GRE over IPSec, the tunnels will use the same addresses. By default, this would, be denied by FortiOS. To work around this, a VDOM level setting must be changed:

```
config system settings
    set allow-subnet-overlap enable
end
```

2. Create an IPSec tunnel before creating the GRE tunnel. When using IPSec with GRE:

    a. In Phase 1:
- Define the 'local interface' as the interface used to terminate the connection.
- Enable IPSec Interface Mode. Only interface-based IPSec works with GRE.

    b. In Phase 2:
- Use 'transport-mode' as the encapsulation method.

```
config vpn ipsec phase2
    edit <phase 2 vpn name>
        set encapsulation transport-mode
    next
end
```

- Unlike when using tunnel mode, transport-mode only encrypts the payload data. Since GRE will be handling the encapsulation, it cannot be encrypted. Define the Quick mode selectors to match the remote end. The Source Address should be the FortiGate 'local interface' IP address, the Destination address should be the Cisco remote end VPN terminating interface IP address, and the Protocol should be specified as '47' to represent GRE.

```
config vpn ipsec phase2
    edit <phase 2 vpn name>
        set encapsulation transport-mode
        set protocol 47
        set dst-start-ip <remote end gateway IPv4 address>
        set src-start-ip <local end gateway IPv4 address>
    next
end
```

1. The GRE tunnel should be tied to the IPSec interface name created in step 2. Define 'local-gw' with the IP address assigned to the FortiGate 'local interface' and 'remote-gw' as the IP address terminating the remote end of the VPN.

```
config system gre-tunnel
    edit <tunnel name>
        set interface <IPSec interface name from step 2>
        set local-gw <local end gateway IPv4 address>
        set remote-gw <remote end gateway IPv4 address>
```

```
   next
end
```

1. Two sets of policies are needed for communication. One is used to control access between the IPSec interface and GRE interface while the other set of rules control traffic between internal and GRE interfaces. The example below shows bi-directional rules in a "wide open" state. These would need to be further restricted in an actual deployment.

```
config firewall policy
// GRE interface name: GRE1
// IPSec interface name: IPSEC1
edit 1
    set srcintf INTERNAL1
    set dstintf GRE1
    set srcaddr all
    set dstaddr all
    set action accept
    set schedule always
    set service ANY
next
edit 2
    set srcintf GRE1
    set dstintf INTERNAL1
    set srcaddr all
    set dstaddr all
    set action accept
    set schedule always
    set service ANY
next
edit 3
    set srcintf IPSEC1
    set dstintf GRE1
    set srcaddr all
    set dstaddr all
    set action accept
    set schedule always
    set service ANY
next
edit 4
```

```
    set srcintf GRE1
    set dstintf IPSEC1
    set srcaddr all
    set dstaddr all
    set action accept
    set schedule always
    set service ANY
next
end
```

1. Define routing for GRE over IPSec. Either apply dynamic routing protocols or a simple static route entry for the GRE interface.

```
config router static
    edit <entry #>
        set device GRE1
        set dst <destinaton network> <netmask>
    next
end
```

Traffic Shaping

FortiOS can perform QoS (Quality of Service) on traffic traversing the FortiGate. There are three techniques available for QoS:

1. Traffic Policing: QoS based on bandwidth limiting at the physical interface level.
2. Traffic Shaping: QoS based on a guarantee and/or maximum bandwidth rates.
3. Traffic Priorities: QoS based on priorities queues such as High, Medium, and Low.

   a. TOS (type of service) priority and DiffServ (Differentiated Services) priorities are also considered.

FortiOS traffic shaping focuses on Layers 3–7. For more detailed technical information, please see the Fortinet documentation site (http://docs.fortinet.com/fgt.html).

Traffic shaping allows control of the traffic flow through the FortiGate. When a critical network application requires a guaranteed amount of bandwidth to function properly, traffic shaping can assist. For example, VOIP traffic is often prioritized by placing upper limits on non-critical traffic.

There are three traffic shaping methods available within FortiOS:

1. Shared policy shaping: bandwidth shaping by firewall rules.
2. Per-IP shaping: bandwidth shaping by user IP address.
3. Application control shaping: bandwidth shaping by application.

Both Shared Policy and Per-IP shaping is done on by individual rules, mainly by shaping traffic at Layers 3–4. Application control is applied at a per rule level but the actual shaping is configured per application. QoS extends the shaping to Layer 7. When processed by a firewall rule, priority is given as follows:

1. Application control shaping.
2. Shared Policy shaping.
3. Per-IP shaping.

Per-IP shaping requires that interfaces not be tied to NP2 ASICs (see Figure 5.9).

Shared Policy Shaping

Configuring a Shared Policy shaping function is a two step process.

1. Define the Shared Policy shaper profile:

```
config firewall shaper traffic-shaper
    edit <shaper profile name>
        // define shaper profile to use per-policy
        set per-policy enable
        // define the maximum amount of bandwidth
        set maximum-bandwidth <kilobits per second value>
```

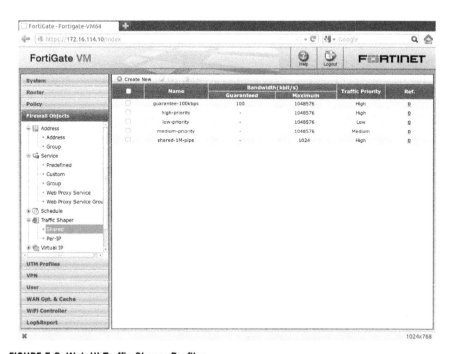

FIGURE 5.9 Web UI Traffic Shaper Profiles

```
    // define the minimum or guaranteed amount of bandwidth
    set guaranteed-bandwidth <kilobits per second value>
  next
end
```

2. Apply the Shared Policy shaper profile to a firewall rule.

```
config firewall policy
  edit <rule id#>

    ....

    set traffic-shaper <shaper profile name>
    set traffic-shaper-reverse <shaper profile name> // Optional, see
  below

    ....

  next
end
```

You may wish to define a different shaper profile for the reverse of network connection. If this is not defined, the forward-focused "traffic-shaper" will be used bidirectionally.

Per-IP Shaping

As with the Shared Policy shaper, the Per-IP shaper is also a two step process.

1. Define the Per-IP shaper profile.:

```
config firewall shaper per-ip-shaper
  edit <shaper profile name>
    set max-bandwidth <kilobits per second value>
    set max-concurrent-sessions <integer value>
  next
end
```

2. Apply the Per-IP shaper profile to a firewall rule.:

```
config firewall policy
  edit <rule id#>

    ....

    set per-ip-shaper <shaper profile name>

    ....

  next
end
```

Application Control Shaping

Application control shaping requires four steps:

1. Define the Application control list. This involves first creating an Application List then adding the application(s) to the list (further explored in Chapter 6).

Define the traffic shaper profile. This is similar to the creation of a Shared Policy shaper profile:

```
config firewall shaper traffic-shaper
    edit <shaper profile name>
    // Disable the use of this shaper profile as a Share Policy shaper.
    // By default this is already disabled
        set per-policy disable
        // define the maximum amount of bandwidth
        set maximum-bandwidth <kilobits per second value>
        // define the minimum or guaranteed amount of bandwidth
        set guaranteed-bandwidth <kilobits per second value>
    next
end
```

2. Apply the application control shaper profile to an individual application.

```
config application list
    edit <name of application list>
        config entries
            edit <id #>
                set category <id>
                set application <id>
                set action pass
                set shaper <name of shaper profile>
            next
        end
    next
end
```

3. Apply the application control list created in Step 1 to a firewall rule.

```
config firewall policy
    edit <rule id#>
        ....
        set utm-status enable
        set application-list <application list name>
        ....
    next
end
```

SSL Inspection

FortiGate models with the CP6 ASIC and higher have the ability to perform man-in-the-middle SSL inspection capabilities. At a high level, the FortiGate leverages transparent proxy-based engines to intercept the SSL session and inspect content. In a nutshell, the FortiGate proxy breaks a session in half, one between FortiGate and client and the other between FortiGate and server. This provides the ability to decrypt the communication for inspection and re-encrypt it to go back to the user. For further details on SSL interception, please refer to the FortiGate documentation (http://docs.fortinet.com/fgt.html).

With the ability to perform SSL content inspection, FortiOS can also leverage the CP6 & higher version ASIC to further offload the SSL processing from servers. SSL offloading primarily uses the load-balancing functionality of FortiOS. See the "Load Balancing" section of this chapter for more information.

FortiOS supports HTTPS, SMTPS, POP3S, IMAPS, and FTPS for various inspections.

- Antivirus, DLP, and DLP archiving for HTTPS, SMTPS, POP3S, and IMAPS.
- Web filtering for HTTPS.
- Anti-Spam for SMTPS, POP3S, IMAPS.

Antivirus SSL inspection
Enabling antivirus scanning within SSL inspection is done for each protocol.

```
config antivirus profile
    edit <name of profile>
        config { https | ftps | imaps | pop3s | smtps}
            set options scan
        end
    next
end
```

"set option scan" enables AV scanning for the supported protocols. Additionally, the quarantine option can be added to isolate detected files. Quarantining requires that a FortiAnalyzer be used in the environment. Once the AV profile is defined, it would then be applied to a firewall rule.

Web Filtering SSL inspection
Enabling SSL inspection with Web Filtering requires two configuration settings—one in the protocol option profile and one in the web filtering profile.

TIP

Invalid SSL certificate errors when using SSL offloading and inspection
Due to the way that SSL works with public/private keys, there is no way to present the user with the identical certificate used by the target server. Thus, the FortiGate defaults to present its own certificate. Since this is a self-signed certificate and is not on the list of CAs stored within the browser, the browser will generate an error. To address this, the certificate in the Fortinet should either be signed by an approved CA or the self-signed certificate should be whitelisted on each end point.

```
//First, enable HTTPS scanning in the protocol option profile.
config firewall profile-protocol-options
    edit <name of profile>
        config https
            set deep-scan enable
        end
    next
end
//Second, enable HTTPS scanning in the web filter profile
config webfilter profile
    edit <name of profile>
        set options https-scan

            …

    next
end
```

Once these two steps are done and the web filtering profile is applied to a rule, it is important to also apply the same protocol option profile for that rule.

DLP SSL Inspection

Like the web filtering HTTPS scanning, there is also a two step process in setting up the SSL scanning to use the DLP inspection feature.

```
//First, enable HTTPS scanning in the protocol option profile.
config firewall profile-protocol-options
    edit <name of profile>
        config https
            set deep-scan enable
        end
    next
end
//Second, define a DLP rule with the selected supported SSL protocol
config dlp rule
    edit <rule name>
    // if using HTTPS
        set protocol http
        set sub-protocol { https-get | https-port }
    // if using FTPS
        set protocol ftp
        set sub-protocol { ftps-get | ftps-put }
```

```
    // if using SMTPS, IMAPS, or POP3S
        set protocol email
        set sub-protocol { smtps | imaps | pop3s }
    ....
    next
end
```

Once the two steps are defined, the DLP rule would need to be added into a DLP sensor (see Chapter 6) then both the protocol option profile and the DLP sensor would be applied to a firewall rule.

Anti-spam SSL Inspection

```
config spamfilter profile
    edit <profile name>
       ...
       config { imaps | pop3s | smtps }
          set action {discard | tag | pass}
          ....
       End
    next
end
```

"set action" defines what is to be done with emails detected within SSL. If set to "discard", the system would not pass the detected spam, "tag" would tag the email with a customized message (using "tag-type" option to define the location), and "pass" would disable spam filtering for that message.

Two-Factor User Authentication

Two-factor authentication in FortiOS can be done in several ways.

- Hard- or Soft-Based Tokens with FortiToken
- Certificate-based User Authentication
- E-mail based
- SMS

These methods are supported for most FortiOS features that require authentication. These are typically administration, SSL VPN, IPSec VPN via Xauth, and firewall authentication for local, RADIUS, TACACS+, and LDAP users. Before any of these methods can be used, however, a hardware or software version of Fortinet's own two-factor solution, the FortiToken, must be registered to the FortiGate device. A FortiToken could be software- or hardware-based (a key fob) that randomly generates six digits at a short periodic interval. Tokens are generated, synchronized, and registered with FortiGuard center servers.

To add and activate a FortiToken, access the serial number on the back of the key fob or, if using a soft token, from the "support" account.

```
config user fortitoken
   edit <token serial number>
      set status activate
   next
end
```

Two-Factor Hard- or Soft-Based FortiToken

To configure a user account to use a token, you must define several parameters:

```
config user local
   edit <username>
      set type password
      set passwd <password>
      set two-factor fortitoken
      set fortioken <serialnumber>
      set status enable
   next
end
```

Two-Factor Certificate Based User Authentication

In addition to relying on a user certificate, a token can be added, so PKI users get two-factor protection. When two-factor is enabled, the user will be prompted to enter the token to login.

```
config user peer
   edit user1
      set ca <certificate name>
      // define either the 'subject' or 'ca' information of the
   certificate
      set subject <certificate subject info>
      set ca <certificate ca info>
      set two-factor enable
      set passwd <password>
   next
end
```

Email-based Two-Factor

The FortiGate can be configured so that specific user accounts generate and email a random six-digit code during the login process. Once the email is received, the user has 60 s to enter the code to successfully authenticate.

```
// define the email server settings
config system alertemail
   set server <email server FQDN or IP address>
   set port <email server port>
   set authenticate { disable | enable }
   set username <SMTP server login>
   set password <SMTP server password>
end
// define the email sender and recipient address
config alertemail setting
   set username <email address that would appear in the Form header>
end
// link the user account to the email token. This example uses a local
   account.
config user local
   edit <user name>
      set two-factor email
      set email-to <receiptent email>
      set two-factor email
      set type password
      set passwd <password>
   next
end
```

Two-Factor SMS

The FortiGate can also be configured to send an SMS text to the mobile phone associated with a user account. Once a user logs in, they are prompted for the SMS code and has 60 s to enter the code to successfully authenticate.

```
// first define the SMS provider profile
config user sms-provider
   edit <provider profile name>
      set mail-server <provider email server - FQDN or IP address>
   next
end
```

```
// link the user account to the email token. This example uses a local
   account.
config user local
   edit <username>
      set two-factor sms
      set sms-phone <mobile phone number - digits only>
      set sms-provider <provider profile name>
      set two-factor enable
      set type password
      set passwd <password>
   next
end
```

External Two-Factor Authentication with FortiToken

Fortinet offers an appliance-based solution called the FortiAuthenticator as an alternative option to an external authentication server. Key highlights are:

- Provides a built-in Radius and LDAP server to house and maintain login credentials.
- Optional Integration with existing LDAP or MS AD servers.
- Built-in Certificate Authority functionality.
- Two-factor authentication support with FortiToken leveraging the above features.

For further details of the product see: http://www.fortinet.com/products/fortiauthenticator/index.html

Load-Balancing Capabilities

FortiOS load-balancing leverages the Virtual IP feature configured in the firewall section of the FortiGate. There are two types of load-balancing capabilities: IP address & port range or server selection.

From an IP address & port ranged load-balancing feature, key highlights are:

- Uses the VIP type setting of "load-balance".
- Basic load balancing to a consecutive IP address and/or a consecutive destination port range definition.
- Load-balancing method is only based on a round-robin method.

Below, we'll highlight the minimal steps needed to configure this load-balancing feature.

1. Define the load-balancing address and/or port definitions similar to the VIP configuration noted earlier in this chapter. In addition, the VIP type will change to "load-balance" and the mapped IP and/or mapped port ranges would be defined.

```
config firewall vip
    edit <name of VIP>
        set type load-balance
        set extip <starting ip address range>-<ending ip address range>
        set extintf <inbound external interface name>
        set mappedip <starting ip address range>-<ending ip address
    range>
// The above provide only IP address load balancing to an IP address
    range. Below provides additional settings for port load balancing.
    Both
        set portforward enable
        set extport <starting port range>-<ending port range>
        set mappedport <starting port range>-<ending port range>
    next
end
```

2. Apply the virtual server to a firewall rule. As with a standard VIP configuration, once the VIP is defined, a firewall rule is needed to allow traffic to that VIP as a destination.

```
config firewall policy
    edit <rule number>
        ….
        set dstaddr <name of virtual server VIP>
        ….
    next
end
```

From a server selection load-balancing feature, key highlights are:

- Uses the VIP type setting of "server-load-balance"
- Specialty load-balancing capabilities for HTTP, HTTPS, and SSL session selection. In addition to generic Layer 4 TCP, UDP, and generic Layer 3 IP protocols.
- Session persistence based on injected HTTP/HTTPS cookies or SSL session ID.
- Ability to support up to eight real servers with one virtual server definition.
- Server monitoring to ensure load balancing is functioning.
- Several load-balancing algorithms to choose from:
  - first-alive
  - http-post

- least-rtt
- least-session
- round-robin
- static
- weighted

- FortiGate models with CP6 and higher ASICs can provide SSL offloading capabilities.

Below, we'll highlight the minimal steps needed to configure the load-balancing feature. Further in-depth information can be found in the Fortinet Load-Balancing guide (http://docs.fortinet.com/fgt.html).

1. Define the virtual servers by tying the external load-balancing IP address to the actual physical servers to which the traffic is being load balanced. This technology leverages the standard virtual IP configuration and extends it to operate with load balancing (see Figure 5.10).

```
config firewall vip
    edit <name of vserver>
        set type server-load-balance
```

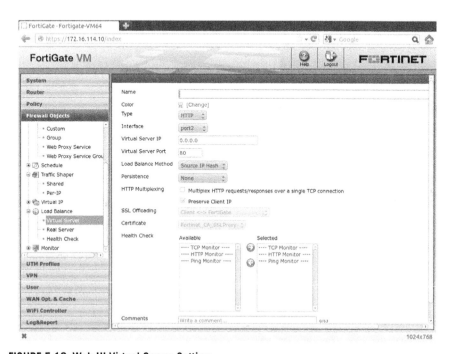

FIGURE 5.10 Web UI Virtual Server Setting

```
    set server-type { http | https | imaps | ip | pop3s | smtps | ssl
| tcp | udp }
    set extintf <external port name>
    set extip <external IP address>
    set ldb-method { first-alive | http-post | least-rtt | least-
session | round-robin | static | weighted }
    config realservers
        edit <id #>
            set ip <ip address of physical server x>
        next
        ....
    end
  next
end
```

2. Apply the virtual server to a firewall rule. As with a standard VIP configuration, once the VIP is defined, a firewall rule is needed to allow traffic to that VIP as a destination (see Figure 5.11).

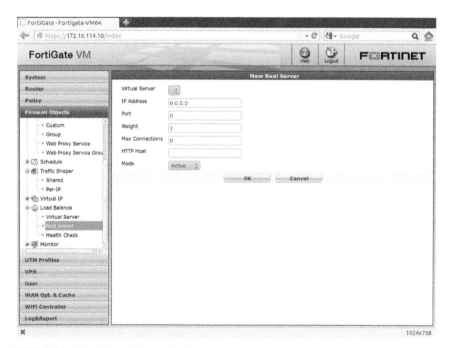

FIGURE 5.11 Web UI Real Server Setting

```
config firewall policy
edit <rule number>
    ….
    set dstaddr <name of virtual server VIP>
    ….
next
end
```

Application Security

- Before you Configure Network Antivirus (Sizing and Design steps)
- How Network Antivirus Works in the FortiGate
- Intrusion Protection (IPS)
  - Introduction
  - Before you Configure IPS (Sizing and Design steps)
  - How IPS Works in the FortiGate
- Web Filtering
  - Introduction
  - How Web Content Filtering Works in the FortiGate (Sizing and Design steps)
  - Configuring Web Content Filtering

As threats are constantly evolving, Network Security technologies and mechanisms are almost never static, especially when they aim to analyze content. To understand the importance of the topic, we must remember that many threats, such as Bots, Ransomware, Advanced Persistence Threats (APTs), Viruses or SPAM, have a heavy content component and are not purely focused on the network layer. In this case, "content" refers to the interpretation and analysis of the payload of packets and not the way they are being transported. In other words, we are talking about the layers four to seven of the OSI Model.

Content Inspection technologies such as Antivirus, IPS, DLP, or Application Control, have two main components: an *Inspection Engine* and a set of *Inspection Rules*.

The *Inspection Engine* is in charge of analyzing the traffic that it receives, and usually does this by extracting the content from the data flow, interpreting and applying the *Inspection Rules* that it obtains from a configuration. The strength of an inspection engine can be judged on how successfully it handles the changing threat environment particularly when considering the threat posed by mutant attacks such as polymorphic viruses. The configuration can be a file that lists a static set of rules, an automated source that provides dynamically updated rules or an inline configuration as performed by manual analysis. Each of these sources can include a time stamp component to address the rapid changes in content that must be assessed.

The engine analyzes the entire information flow and can be tuned to achieve better performance, gain a deeper understanding of the information context, or allow the Inspection Rules to become more precise and accurate. This tuning is not easy, but fortunately, does not need to be frequent either. The enhancements must be carefully designed and thoroughly tested. Otherwise, you face the risk of increasing failure, as the engine is usually more complex than the Inspection rules. The Inspection Engine must be rock solid, so it always behaves predictably.

The *Inspection Rules* are a different story. As new threats (viruses, bad applications, attacks, etc.) are discovered, inspection rules must be quickly released to address them. This can be in a specific way (describing a specific attack pattern) or more general (describing behavior related to the attack). Typically, a general defense is released and, as the attack it addresses is better understood, more specific rules are written that are less susceptible to false positives. If a highly focused attack is detected, local administrators may also write their own rules.

These rules have evolved in complexity, much as Inspection Engines have. These days, they are not merely a pattern or a sequence of characters that is recognized in traffic. It is now possible to derive information from both context and environment. This can include things such as the frequency of the events, the times the event has been seen from the same source or towards the same destination, or even to simulate behavior based on controlled execution.

Thus, to be effective with Content Scanning, you must have a very solid and robust Inspection Engine, but the security vendor behind the Content Scanning mechanism (i.e. behind the Inspection Engine) must also have a reliable, fast, and accurate way to deliver inspection rules. If both components are not in place and reliable, the protection will not be effective.

Fortinet has a team, named FortiGuard, dedicated to ensuring the Content Scanning technology is always updated, accurate, and robust. Every time you see this name, you know that there are a number of resources, technical and human, involved in maintaining the dynamic protections offered by all Fortinet products.

This chapter's examples assume that only one VDOM is being used in each scenario. If you are using multiple VDOMs, be aware that each configuration must be made within each of them.

FORTIGUARD
Introduction to FortiGuard

FortiGuard is important for all services that require updates. The FortiGuard Team consists of a large number of Security Analysts distributed in several countries that are dedicated to analyzing various areas necessary for complete security protection. These areas include Antivirus (AV), Web Content Filtering (WCF), Intrusion Prevention (IPS), AntiSpam, Application Security, Application Control, Vulnerability Control and Management (VCM), and Web Security. These researchers use automated tools to add updates to FortiGuard, so they only see action when something really new and complex is at hand, which happens more often than you would think.

This human FortiGuard team is focused on discovering ways to improve Fortinet's Inspection Engines. These engines are proprietary to Fortinet, which defines the roadmap and controls the future of the technology. When problems occur; the developers may assist with diagnosing, troubleshooting, and creating a fix. Finally, since the technology was developed in-house, Fortinet does not have to pay any royalties, keeping the price low. These same advantages apply to the creation of the signatures (Inspection Rules) that feed to the devices installed around the world.

The Fortinet Distribution Network (FDN) is how Fortinet effectively distributes content to all devices across the world. You can think of the FDN as a "repository in the cloud" for both Inspection Engines and Signatures. When Fortinet Devices (such as FortiGates, FortiWeb, or FortiCarrier) are configured for dynamic security inspection, they constantly query the FDN to determine which server is closest. Once determined, this server is queried for security updates which, once found, are downloaded and applied. However, this only occurs if the device is entitled. In other words, this occurs when the serial number is linked to a license contract which references the service that has been updated. If you wish to know the servers that feed your device, you may run the CLI command "diagnose debug rating."

Each mechanism (Antivirus, Web Content Filter, etc.) works differently, so the FortiGuard technology and processes differ from mechanism to mechanism, as explained later in this chapter. However, you must understand the general architecture:

1. FortiGuard Security Analysts scour the Internet for information. Information also is pulled from partnerships with companies like Adobe or Microsoft and is gleaned from independent research on new attacks and applications. Specialized groups also create information about specific fields of study. Analysts also approve updates generated via automated detection and classification tools.

2. Once a FortiGuard Security Analyst has identified a potential enhancement for an Inspection Engine or is able to create a signature, they commit the appropriate change. These changes are implemented through automated systems so errors can be reduced. Once done, the quality assurance process further vets the change.

3. The update is uploaded to the FDN, usually to a master server which handles propagation. Thus, sometimes, it can take several minutes before the server to which you are connected gets the update. There is some periodicity on the updates: Antivirus is updated four times a day, IPS twice a day, and AntiSpam and Web Content Filter updates are done in real time. Of course, the rise of an important threat could increase the frequency of updates.

4. The Fortinet device queries the FDN upon reboot (or upon network connectivity being established) and then determines the closest FDN server. This server is queried periodically, as configured, to determine if there are any relevant security updates. If there are, they are downloaded.

5. If a high-severity threat is discovered, updates may be pushed to the device outside of the normally scheduled update times. However, for this to occur, the device must be directly accessible from the Internet and configured to accept these emergency updates (see Figure 6.1).

The FortiGuard Portal and the Fortinet Blog

The FortiGuard team also maintains an online portal for information about the content inspection features and specific tools: http://www.fortiguard.com. As you work with your FortiGates, you will definitely want to become familiar with this portal. It is where Fortinet analysts publish papers and information about issues and behaviors for specific technologies. It is also where you may find the latest engines and signatures.

The FortiGuard portal also contains tools to submit new URLs for web filtering, virus samples, spam samples, tuning information for Application Control, and a tool to help you delist your systems if they are detected to be causing problems on the Internet. The FortiGuard portal also hosts a set of "Encyclopedias" that detail specific

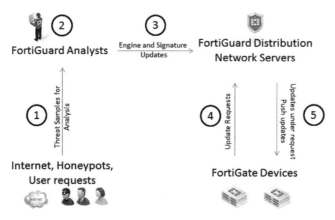

FIGURE 6.1 How FortiGuard Works?

> **TIP**
>
> **FortiManager as local FortiGuard Server**
> FortiGuard Distribution Network controls all security updates, effectively storing them "in the cloud". However, due to reasons of bandwidth or isolation, an organization may wish to store such updates within the local network. This is done with the FortiManager, a dedicated management device. Please verify the latest FortiManager datasheet from http://www.fortinet.com to review which FortiManager models support this feature.

---

viruses, attacks, and applications that have been built into the FortiGate. This can be useful when analyzing logs and alerts.

Another useful site is the Fortinet Blog: http://blog.fortinet.com. Most articles published here are written by the FortiGuard team and detail the current research being done to keep the systems up to date and protecting your environment. Occasionally, people from other departments submit articles to the blog. You probably want to review this site at least once a week.

FortiGuard Licensing

It can be challenging to hire a group of smart people capable of doing detailed security research and to maintain the infrastructure capable of distributing updates all over the world in a very short period of time. This is why most security firms charge for updates. Of course, Fortinet is no exception. FortiGate devices access these resources through appropriate licensing.

Fortinet offers licensing for updates on these features: Antivirus, IPS, AntiSpam, Web Content Filter, and Vulnerability Management. While many firms license such technologies in terms of total users, concurrent users, mailboxes, IP counts, or sessions, Fortinet simplifies the process and simply licenses according to the performance of the device. Basically, the bigger a box you have, the more you pay to keep it up-to-date.

Fortinet offers two options to license updates for the security services: As a Bundle and Individually (A la carte). Let's review each one.

Bundle Licensing

A "Bundle" or "Flat" license includes pretty much all the security features the FortiGate can support. However, a Bundle not only includes technical updates, but also additional services such as support. Since all possible services are packaged together, Bundle licensing often has a lower price tag than purchasing the updates and services individually.

Bundles typically include 8×5 Support, 8×5 Hardware Replacement (Return and Replace), Entitlement to Firmware Upgrades and new features, and licenses for Antivirus, IPS, Web Content Filter, and AntiSpam. However, depending on the FortiGate hardware model, some features might not be available to the bundle (such as Vulnerability Management). There are also advanced Bundle options that offer upgrades to 24×7 support or faster hardware replacement.

In general, you should expect that if you purchased a bundle, you have the license to download most security updates for your device. Bundles are convenient because all you have to worry about is configuring your device to obtain the maximum protection for your network, without the fear of missing a license.

It is also important to remember that you need more than one feature to provide maximum protection for your network. Since no security technology can ever protect against 100% of the threats, you need a combination to come close to this number. Web Content Filtering is a good example. If you do not also use Application Control to block proxies and anonymizers like Tor or Ultrasurf, your users may easily bypass your carefully crafted policies. If you don't leverage Antivirus, you run the risk of malware infecting your systems via the Web. This is why the Bundle model works: you can leverage all available protections.

Individual Licensing (per-feature or à la carte)

Despite the advantages of the Bundle model for most organizations, some may already have a good set of protections and are only interested in a single feature. If this is the case for you, you might find it more convenient to purchase only the license for the feature you need.

Fortinet offers separate licensing for each security feature: Vulnerability Management, Antivirus, IPS, Web Content Filter, and AntiSpam. It is also possible to purchase two or more separate licenses and apply them to the same device, even though this is often more expensive than going the Bundle route.

TIP

Application Control Licensing

You might have noticed that Application Control is not listed as a licensable feature. This is because Application Control leverages the IPS mechanism, so if you are entitled to IPS, you automatically get Application Control.

Configuring FortiGuard on the FortiGate
Concepts about FortiGuard Updates

Before getting into the configuration for FortiGuard, it is important to understand a few concepts. The first is that there are two methods for downloading security updates: scheduled and online.

Scheduled updates are used for Antivirus and IPS, and work by downloading incremental signature files for these features. This means the FortiGate only downloads the latest changes to the signature database, as opposed to the entire database. The Antivirus and IPS signature files are locally stored on the FortiGate and are updated only when scheduled. This way, the FortiGate may do faster inspection and be more resilient to network outages. In other words, even if the device cannot reach the FDN, it will still be able to perform Antivirus and IPS inspection. However, the tradeoff here is that a device could easily get out-of-date.

Consider that the longer the update cycle, the more data must be downloaded to bring the signature databases to current, but the shorter the update cycle, the more resources are spent updating rather than protecting. In general, updating every 3 h should be fine for most environments. However, in more sensitive environments, a higher frequency should be considered.

FortiGates also support Push Updates. These are used to ensure that important signature packages are automatically forced onto devices. This means that even if a signature package is released the minute after the FortiGate queried for updates, the FortiGate will get it immediately. This feature, however, must be configured locally by an administrator. By default, Push Updates are disabled.

Online updates are used for Web Content and E-mail filtering (AntiSpam). These features require the FortiGate device to be connected to the FortiGuard Network. In other words, every time the FortiGate needs to analyze content for AntiSpam or Web Content Filter, it submits information to the FDN and receives an analysis. Due to this, you must consider the ideal behavior in the case of a network outage or reliability issue. In most environments, loss of access to the FDN would match up to times when the organization would be receiving no email and no users would be browsing the web. However, if you are using FortiGate devices as internal barriers for scoping reasons or between security zones, you may still need protection. In these cases, you can effectively fake a constant Internet connection by placing an internal FortiManager device that caches the updates from the Internet. All internal FortiGates point to the FortiManager and pull updates from there. The FortiManager will update itself once the external network again becomes available.

TIP

FortiGuard Updates tunneling

It is generally assumed that there is direct connectivity between the FortiGate and the Internet. However, if this is not the case, and a proxy must be used, you must configure your devices to use "tunneling updates." This is activated with the command "config system autoupdate tunneling."

Configuring FortiGuard Updates

There are three things you need to verify before configuring any type of updates:

1. You are entitled to updates.

In order to be entitled to updates you must both (a) purchase your licensing as a "bundle" or have purchased the appropriate licenses for the specific features you need and (b) register your device on the support portal (https://support.fortinet.com). This is necessary because this step broadcasts your FortiGate's serial number to the FDN Servers to let them know it is entitled to the updates. Please bear in mind that the moment you register your FortiGate, your warranty begins. Also is important to remember that a FortiGate cannot be registered if it's been over one year since it was shipped by Fortinet to your distributor.

Once registered, a FortiGate unit should look similar to what is shown in Figure 6.2. What your device displays may differ depending on which licenses you purchased.

2. You have Connectivity.

Make sure the FortiGate you are configuring has connectivity to either the Internet or to the FortiManager that stores the updates. FortiManagers may be used both

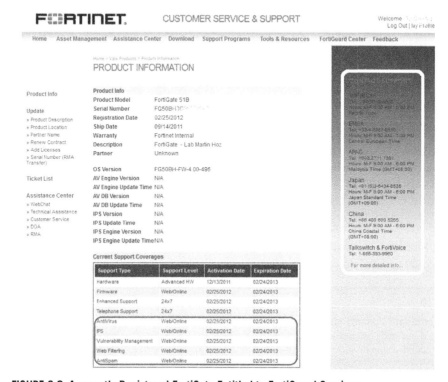

FIGURE 6.2 A recently Registered FortiGate Entitled to FortiGuard Services

to provide access in the event of a loss of Internet connectivity, but also to easily manage a large set of FortiGates. If you are configuring a FortiManager to store the FortiGuard updates, then you must configure it similar to the example below:

```
FGT # config system autoupdate override
FGT (override) # set address 192.168.1.1
FGT (override) # set status enable
FGT (override) # end
FGT # config system fortiguard
FGT (fortiguard) # set srv-ovrd enable
FGT (fortiguard) # config srv-ovrd-list
FGT (srv-ovrd-list) # edit 1
FGT (1) # set addr-type ipv4
FGT (1) # set ip 192.168.1.1
FGT (1) # end
FGT (fortiguard) # end
```

In this example, the address of "192.168.1.1" is that of the FortiManager. The first section configures the scheduled updates and the second configures the online updates. You must have access to UDP ports 53 and 8888 between the FortiGate and the real-time update source and on TCP ports 443, 8889, and 8890 to the scheduled update source.

3. You have DNS resolution working.

DNS is used for updates, as well as several FortiGuard functions, so it must be properly configured.

Configuring Scheduled Updates

In order to configure scheduled updates, you must first decide what period makes sense in your environment. Consider the following:

1. A higher frequency often results in greater security, as the window between an update becoming available and it being deployed will be minimized. However, it also means that more FortiGate resources will be spent (memory and CPU used for the task).
2. A lower frequency increases the risks from running outdated appliances, thereby reducing protection and increasing the chance of an incident.
3. Updates are particularly sensitive for Antivirus and IPS. The FortiGuard team generally releases Antivirus four times in a day and IPS twice a day. However, this is not necessarily at the same time each day. Thus, it is considered wise to update every 3 h. This means that, on average, you will connect twice and receive no update. Figure 6.3 shows the relationship between updates and query frequency. For high security scenarios, consider updating every hour.

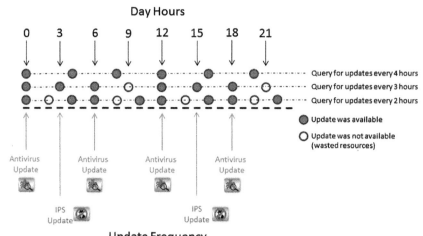

FIGURE 6.3 Finding the Right FortiGuard Update Frequency

Once you have determined the update schedule, you must follow the steps below. If you encounter difficulty, please refer to the troubleshooting section where each command is reviewed in greater detail.

Before you configure your unit, check which updates are already loaded. This way, you can check that, after configuration, you are receiving updates.

```
FGT # get system status
Version: Fortigate-51B v4.0,build0496,111108 (MR3 Patch 3)
Virus-DB: 14.00000(2011-08-24 17:17)
Extended DB: 14.00000(2011-08-24 17:09)
IPS-DB: 3.00097(2011-10-28 16:39)
FortiClient application signature package: 1.131(2011-11-08 20:53)
Serial-Number: FG50BH3GNNNNNNNN
BIOS version: 04000005
Log hard disk: Available
Hostname: FGT
Operation Mode: NAT
Current virtual domain: root
Max number of virtual domains: 10
Virtual domains status: 1 in NAT mode, 0 in TP mode
Virtual domain configuration: disable
FIPS-CC mode: disable
Current HA mode: standalone
```

```
Distribution: International
Branch point: 496
Release Version Information: MR3 Patch 3
System time: Sun Feb 26 21:27:41 2012
```

Notice that you can tell this system has not been updated for a while, due the difference between the System Time and the dates of the Antivirus and IPS Databases.

Now we must ensure updates occur at a given interval. Remember that Scheduled Updates are used for Antivirus and IPS updates. By default, the FortiGate is configured for daily updates. You can confirm this by the following command:

```
FGT # diagnose autoupdate status
FDN availability: available at Sun Feb 26 22:01:51 2012
Push update: disable
Scheduled update: enable
 Update daily: 1:56
Virus definitions update: enable
IPS definitions update: enable
Server override: disable
Push address override: disable
Web proxy tunneling: disable
```

This command tells you that the FDN is available and the FortiGate can reach the servers. It also tells you that Push Updates are disabled, so urgent updates created by Fortinet will NOT be pushed and instead will need to be downloaded on the next update period. It also says that Virus and IPS definitions will be updated (enable for both options), and that Updates are scheduled to happen daily at 1:56. The FortiGate uses a 24-h format, so that is really 1:56 in the morning.

Let's configure now the FortiGate to perform updates for Antivirus and IPS every 3 h, 30 min after the hour.

```
FGT # config system autoupdate schedule
FGT (schedule) # set frequency every
FGT (schedule) # set time 03:30
FGT (schedule) # set status enable
FGT (schedule) # end
```

The command above does NOT mean to update every 3 h and a half. Instead, the update will be done every 3 h, and the update will happen 30 min after the hour. Assuming updates began at a half hour after midnight, the next updates would happen at 3:30, 6:30, 9:30, etc.

Next, we may wish to enable push updates, so we don't miss updates to critical threats.

```
FGT # config system autoupdate push-update
```

```
FGT (push-update) # set status enable
FGT (push-update) # end
```

You can verify the changes using the "diagnose autoupdate status" command again.

```
FGT # diagnose autoupdate status
FDN availability: available at Sun Feb 26 22:20:56 2012
Push update:    enable
Push availability: unavailable
Scheduled update: enable
 Update every: 3 hours at 30 minutes after the hour
Virus definitions update: enable
IPS definitions update: enable
Server override: disable
Push address override: disable
Web proxy tunneling: disable
```

Finally, to ensure that the Antivirus and IPS updates are done immediately, use the command "execute update-now". Alternatively, you can issue "execute update-av" or "execute update-ips" commands to update Antivirus and IPS individually.

Configuring Online Updates

As mentioned earlier, online (real-time) updates are used for Web Content Filter and AntiSpam. This means every time a URL or a mail message is analyzed, the FortiGate queries the FDN in real time to determine the proper action.

To configure online updates, all you need to set is the port to use. By default, UDP port 53 is used. However, if you need to change it, you do so as follows:

```
FGT # config system fortiguard
FGT (fortiguard) # set port 8888
FGT (fortiguard) # end
```

Another thing you might want to modify is the cache for Web Content Filter and AntiSpam updates. Cache can improve the performance of the box, and by default is enabled to hold AntiSpam updates for 30 min (1800 s) and Web Content updates for 1 h (3600 s). You can specify also the amount of the FortiGate memory used to optimize the performance. The commands below show how to modify the default timeout for the AntiSpam and Web Content Filter cache entries, and leave it in 2 h for both. Additionally, we allocate four percent of the system memory for AntiSpam.

```
FGT # config system fortiguard
FGT (fortiguard) # set AntiSpam-cache enable
FGT (fortiguard) # set AntiSpam-cache-ttl 7200
```

```
FGT (fortiguard) # set AntiSpam-cache-mpercent 4
FGT (fortiguard) # set webfilter-cache enable
FGT (fortiguard) # set webfilter-cache-ttl 7200
FGT (fortiguard) # end
```

You can confirm that your FortiGate is ready to do Web Content Filtering and AntiSpam inspection when you get an output similar to that below.

```
FGT3 # diagnose debug rating
Locale: english
License: Contract
Expiration: Fri Mar 1 18:00:00 2013
Hostname:   service.fortiguard.net

_=_ Server List (Wed Feb 29 13:25:26 2012) _=_
```

IP	Weight	RTT Flags	TZ	Packets	Curr Lost	Total Lost
209.66.81.153	20	90 D	−8	2	0	0
209.222.147.36	10	113	−5	1	0	0
69.20.236.179	10	177	−5	1	0	0
208.91.112.198	20	91 DI	−8	5	0	0
208.91.112.194	20	98 D	−8	2	0	0
209.66.81.154	20	101	−8	1	0	0
80.85.69.37	60	220	0	1	0	0
116.58.208.39	140	341	8	1	0	0
121.111.236.180	150	227	9	1	0	0
121.111.236.179	150	236	9	1	0	0

You might also get a message similar to this:

```
FGT3 # diag debug rating
Locale: english
```

The service is not enabled.

If you get this error message, you either need to create a Web Content Filter profile and assign it to a Firewall policy or there are network communication issues. If you are seeing a shorter list of FDN servers, you definitely have network issues. Please review the troubleshooting section below for additional information.

Doing UTM Analysis: Concepts

UTM Inspection under the Hood

Thus far, all of the sample configuration steps were performed to ensure that the For-tiGate was going to receive updates from the FDN, allowing traffic to be inspected by

---

TIP

UTM Profiles and FortiGuard Updates

As of FortiOS 4.3, FortiGuard updates will NOT happen unless there is a UTM profile associated with a firewall policy. In other words, if no firewall policy has a UTM profile, FortiGate updates will NOT be performed.

---

the IPS, Antivirus, Application Control, Web Content Filtering, or AntiSpam mechanisms. We have told the FortiGate to be prepared to receive these updates and hold them ready. However, we have not told the FortiGate so far HOW these mechanisms should be put to work: what traffic should be inspected, when should be inspected, and what to do if a policy violation is found. There is a very important concept that applies to all the Content Inspection technologies... the Profile.

When the firewall policy allows traffic, the FortiGate may designate the content as needing further inspection. This behavior is dependent on whether the firewall policy has a UTM profile defined.

UTM profiles exist for each Content Inspection function, and it is their job to tell the FortiGate whether further inspection is needed, and how it will be performed. Specific Profile configuration will be discussed in each function's section. However, it is important to understand the concept and how it relates to a firewall policy.

Each Content Inspection function (IPS, Antivirus, etc.) has two internal components: a proxy and a daemon.

There are two methods to perform any of the UTM functions; one is by just looking into the traffic passing-by the FortiGate and performing a "string comparison". This is pretty much just looking for patterns in the traffic similarly to how you look for a given text string inside a document. This method is called "Flow-based" because it just analyzes the stream of traffic, searching for patterns and is usually limited to only analyzing small portions of the traffic. (As to do larger portions would cause traffic interruption.) This typically misses the context of the session.

The other method is to actually get into the middle of the traffic, effectively breaking the connection, and re-establishing it with the FortiGate in the middle, thereby ensuring that the entire session is inspected. This method is called proxy-based.

Both forms of inspection have their pros and cons. We can summarize the characteristics of each one in Table 6.1.

On FortiOS, the functions performed by Flow-Based Inspection regularly use the IPS Engine. The functions performed by Proxy-based Inspection regularly use a (you guessed it!) proxy process. This proxy process is responsible for understanding the connection (identifying e-mail attachments, HTTP downloads, etc.) and passing relevant information to other processes (sending PDF files to the DLP engine, executable files to the Antivirus engine, etc.).

Inside FortiOS, Inspection Engines like the Antivirus engine or the IPS Engine are run in the form of Daemon. Like a service in Windows or a Unix daemon, a FortiOS daemon is just a program that is always running and is responsible for specific tasks, such as scanning a file for viruses or deciding the category to which a URL belongs.

Table 6.1 Differences between Flow-based and Proxy-based Inspections

Type of Inspection	Flow-based	Proxy-based
Speed/Performance	Faster	Slower
Resources	Less resources (CPU, Memory)	More resources (CPU, Memory)
Security	Lower	Higher
Analysis method	Comparing information seen from a connection to a database of known bad situations	Understanding the session state and content, and conducted specific analysis on relevant information
TCP transparency	TCP flow is not broken. If necessary, only packet headers (at layer 4) are changed	TCP connection is broken, since a Man-in-the-middle operation occurs. This means that TCP sequence numbers are changed, for example
Protocol awareness	Doesn't really need to be protocol-aware. Flow-based inspection could recognize a virus on a flow, without actually knowing the file type. It would not unpack compressed files going on an e-mail attachment or FTP download for example	Understands the protocol being analyzed. For example, if a compressed file is detected as an e-mail attachment or while down-loading files from an FTP Server, it can be unpacked so the internal files are analyzed by an Antivirus. A proxy exists for HTTP, FTP, SMTP, POP3, IMAP, and IM protocols
File size limits	Does not have a file size limit when doing scanning, as it scans only a portion of the file at any time	Since it buffers the file for a complete analysis, it has a file size limit directly related to the amount of memory available in the FortiGate
FortiOS features Supported	Antivirus (Flow-based AV), IPS, Application Control, Web Content Filter (WCF)	Antivirus (Proxy-based AV), Data Leak Prevention (DLP), Web Content Filtering (WCF), AntiSpam

Connections that utilize Proxy inspection are stored in the Proxy Connections Table. This table is different from the firewall session table and helps to track all of the connections that are being inspected. A session is held in the Proxy Connections Table so long as it requires further inspection by a daemon, and is typically held for a shorter time than in the firewall session table.

FortiOS proactively assigns a percentage of the available RAM to host the Proxy Connections Table. This is always a fixed amount of memory that results on a given amount of connections available for Content Inspection operations done by the proxy. This number is different for every FortiGate model and can be obtained via a CLI command.

```
FGT# diagnose test application http 4 | grep Connections
Current Connections    26/3952
```

The command above will show how many HTTP connections are being proxied. The above says that from 3952 Proxy connections available on the table, only 26 are being used. We have to clarify that those are NOT all the HTTP sessions going through the system, but only those that are being analyzed using the Proxy-based inspection method.

You could also query the total amount of HTTP sessions going through the FortiGate.

```
FGT# diagnose test application http 4 | grep Connections //This command
    obtains the amount of concurrent proxy connections
Current Connections    18/3952
FGT# diagnose sys session filter clear
FGT# diagnose sys session filter dport 80
FGT# diagnose sys session list | grep "total session" // This command
    obtains the amount of concurrent firewall sessions that have port 80
    as destination port
total session 46
```

On this example, the system had recorded a total of 46 HTTP sessions at the same time that only 18 were being proxied. You can use the above commands to review the connections being inspected by the proxy of the several protocols: ftp, smtp, http, pop3, imap, nntp.

As of FortiOS 4.0 MR2, also known as 4.2, the number of proxy connections available is the same for all protocols that are subject to content inspection. FortiOS has a pool from which it assigns to each protocol that requests inspection. In older versions, each protocol had a different limit, but this resulted in wasted resources. The modern shared-pool method is more efficient.

You can, of course, use the above commands without the "| grep" part. This would display the entire output of the command, which can be useful for diagnostics. We are not reproducing that here because the output could get quite lengthy, but you can play with your FortiGate to see what other parameters exist. Some of them are interesting.

UTM Profiles

One of the biggest criticisms of Fortinet, when it launched the FortiGate, was that people could not believe that Fortinet could do in a single box what other vendors required many systems to accomplish. This is possible because the security adminis-trator can enable or disable inspections at will. Thus, it is possible to use a Fortigate for only Antivirus or IPS, both or more. This flexibility is done with the UTM Profile,

> **TIP**
>
> **Information Levels**
> What does the "4" mean in the "diagnose test application http 4" command?
> It means the level of information that the diagnose command will display. If you hit
> <ENTER> before putting a value there, the command will give you the options available,
> as you can see:
>
> ```
> FGT # diagnose test application ftp
> Proxy Worker 0 - ftpd
> [0:F]
> FTP Proxy Test Usage
> [0:F]
> [0:F] 2: Drop all connections
> [0:F] 4: Display connection stat
> [0:F] 44: Display info per connection
> [0:F] 444: Display connections per state
> [0:F] 4444: Display per vdom stats
> ```

a piece of configuration that tells the FortiGate exactly what inspection is to be done for particular traffic flows. However, the UTM profile alone is not sufficient. In order to be used, each profile must be connected to a firewall policy.

You can create several profiles for a single Content Inspection technology. Thus, you can have an Antivirus profile that inspects user-generated HTTP traffic and quarantines dangerous files. You can then have another profile that scans FTP traffic destined to a file server. This traffic should likely not be quarantined, as that could cause operations issues.

There are limits on the amount of UTM profiles you can create, the number dependent on the model of the FortiGate. You can find the exact number of UTM profiles allowed in the FortiGate Maximum Values document (available at http://docs.fortinet.com) available for each FortiOS release. Due to resource constraints, these may change between releases. An excerpt of the table is shown in Figure 6.4.

A UTM profile, however, has no limits to the number of rules that can use it. If it makes sense logically, you can use the same Antivirus profile for all the virus protection rules. Bear in mind, however, that this might not be optimal for either

> **TIP**
>
> **Profiles for each Content Inspection Technology**
> Older FortiOS releases had the concept of a Protection Profile. This was a single profile
> with settings for the different Content Inspection technologies. So, Antivirus settings, Web
> Content Filter settings, AntiSpam Settings, etc. were all configured within a single profile.
> Since FortiOS 4.0 MR2, there are separate profiles for each inspection technology. These
> are referred to as UTM Profiles.

FortiGate Model / Feature	110C, 111C, 100D	200A	224B	200B	300A	300C, 310B, 311B	400A	500A	600C, 620B	800, 800F
Static IP/Mac bindings					1000					
Traffic Shapers			32			500	32		500	
Per-IP traffic shaper			32			500	32		500	
UTM										
AntiVirus — Antivirus profiles			32			500	32		500	
File patterns for auto-submission to Fortinet					20					
File pattern lists			10			1000	10		1000	
File pattern list entries per VDOM			32000			50000	32000		50000	
Intrusion Protection — IPS sensors					32					
DoS sensors					32					
Custom IPS signatures					256					
Web Filter — Web Filter profiles			32			500	32		500	
Web content lists			10			1000	10		1000	
Web content list entries per VDOM			32000			50000	32000		50000	
URL filter lists			10			1000	10		1000	
URL filter list entries per VDOM	32000		20000		32000	50000	32000		50000	
Regex URL filter entries per VDOM			4000			10000	4000		10000	
FortiGuard local categories per VDOM					52					
FortiGuard local ratings per VDOM					12000					
FortiGuard admin overrides per VDOM			200			400	200		400	

FIGURE 6.4 Excerpt of the FortiGate Maximum Values Document, showing the Amount of UTM Profiles Available per Function and per FortiGate Model

performance or management of the device. The less tailored a UTM profile, the more likely you are to initiate inspection where you do not need to. It is wise to plan ahead.

Troubleshooting the FortiGuard Distribution Network (FDN) Connectivity

Troubleshooting Configuration and Connectivity Issues

When experiencing issues with updates, the first thing you should review is whether or not there is connectivity between the FortiGate and the external world. This specifically applies to the FDN Servers at service.fortiguard.net. You should be able to at least resolve a name, and if ICMP ping packets are not blocked, then you should be able to get replies. Here is a good test.

```
FGT # execute ping service.fortiguard.net
PING guard.fortinet.net (209.66.81.153): 56 data bytes
64 bytes from 209.66.81.153: icmp_seq=0 ttl=53 time=72.4 ms
64 bytes from 209.66.81.153: icmp_seq=1 ttl=53 time=70.8 ms
```

```
64 bytes from 209.66.81.153: icmp_seq=2 ttl=53 time=71.0 ms
64 bytes from 209.66.81.153: icmp_seq=3 ttl=53 time=71.5 ms
64 bytes from 209.66.81.153: icmp_seq=4 ttl=53 time=69.8 ms

--- guard.fortinet.net ping statistics ---
5 packets transmitted, 5 packets received, 0% packet loss
round-trip min/avg/max = 69.8/71.1/72.4 ms
```

The above result indicates that there is connectivity to both the Internet to one of the FDN servers. The name service.fortiguard.net has several IP addresses associated to it, so every time you query for the IP addresses associated to that name, you will always see more than one. You can try this by using the nslookup command (Windows) or dig command (Linux, OSX) to review the IP addresses associated to this name.

```
C:\>nslookup service.fortiguard.net
Server: google-public-dns-a.google.com
Address: 8.8.8.8

Non-authoritative answer:
Name: guard.fortinet.net
Addresses: 208.91.112.198
    209.66.81.153
    208.91.112.194
Aliases: service.fortiguard.net
```

At this point, if you are not resolving the names above, you should check your DNS for proper configuration. Remember that the FortiGate has some DNS servers preconfigured, and you may wish to change them. You can see what your DNS servers are with the following command:

```
FGT # show system dns
config system dns
    set primary 208.91.112.53
    set secondary 208.91.112.52
end
```

If you are resolving DNS names and the Internet connectivity is working, the next step is to review whether the Antivirus and IPS databases are being updated. Assuming, of course, your FortiGate is entitled to such updates.

```
FGT # diagnose autoupdate status
FDN availability: available at Sun Feb 26 22:20:56 2012
Push update: enable
Push availability: unavailable
```

```
Scheduled update: enable
   Update every: 3 hours at 30 minutes after the hour
Virus definitions update: enable
IPS definitions update: enable
Server override: disable
Push address override: disable
Web proxy tunneling: disable
```

This tells you that FDN is reachable and that scheduled updates are configured. Now you might need to take a look on how old your engines and definitions are by checking when the last update was done for each element.

```
FGT # diagnose autoupdate versions
AV Engine
---------
Version: 4.00382
Contract Expiry Date: Wed Feb 27 00:00:00 2013
Last Updated using manual update on Fri Oct 28 13:38:00 2011
Last Update Attempt: n/a
Result: Updates Installed
Virus Definitions
---------
Version: 14.00000
Contract Expiry Date: Wed Feb 27 00:00:00 2013
Last Updated using manual update on Wed Aug 24 17:17:00 2011
Last Update Attempt: n/a
Result: Updates Installed
.

.

.
Vulnerability Compliance and Management
---------
Version: 1.00251
Contract Expiry Date: Wed Feb 27 00:00:00 2013
Last Updated using manual update on Mon Feb 27 03:27:00 2012
Last Update Attempt: n/a
Result: Updates Installed
Modem List
---------
```

```
Version: 1.010
FDS Address
---------
208.91.112.75:443
```

This command has an extremely lengthy output, so the above is just an excerpt. However, you can see it gives you the time and date for each engine and definition update as well as when the last update attempt was performed. However, remember that, to save on resources, if an inspection module is not configured and linked to a firewall policy, it will not be updated.

To force the update of all configured signatures and engines that are licensed to you:

```
FGT3 # execute update-now
```

Alternatively, you could try to update only the signatures and engines for a given technology, using any of the following commands:

update-ase	update AS engine/rules
update-av	update AV engine/definitions
update-ips	update IPS engine/definitions

Another thing that also could hinder updates is not having clear communication on the necessary ports. You must ensure that the common ports used by FortiGuard updates are open: UDP/53, UDP/888, TCP/443, and TCP/8889. If you have configured Push Updates as part of the scheduled updates, then UDP Port 9443 needs to be open too.

For Online real-time updates (Web Content Filtering and AntiSpam), make sure that when you are issuing a "diagnose debug rating" or "get webfilter status" command, you get a list of several servers, as below:

```
FGT3 # get webfilter status
Locale:  english
License: Contract
Expiration: Fri Mar 1 18:00:00 2013
Hostname: service.fortiguard.net

-=- Server List (Wed Feb 29 13:34:54 2012) -=-
```

IP	Weight	RTT Flags	TZ	Packets	Curr Lost	Total Lost
209.66.81.153	20	75 D	−8	6	0	0
209.222.147.36	10	102	−5	5	0	0
69.20.236.180	10	130	−5	5	0	0
69.20.236.179	10	134	−5	5	0	0
208.91.112.198	20	190 DI	−8	9	0	0

IP	Weight	RTT Flags	TZ	Packets	Curr Lost	Total Lost
208.91.112.194	20	126 D	−8	6	0	0
80.85.69.40	60	226	0	5	0	0
62.209.40.72	70	261	1	5	0	0
116.58.208.44	140	332	8	5	0	0
121.111.236.180	150	243	9	5	0	0

A "healthy" status should show around 20 servers in the list above. Please bear in mind the IP addresses might be different between runs and that is ok, but the amount of IP addresses listed is important. If you are seeing only two or three, that's a common sign that there is something wrong. Usually that means port UDP 53 and UDP 8888 are both blocked. It can also mean that the reply packets coming from the FDN Servers are blocked. This sometimes occurs because the FortiGate uses a source port in the range 1024–1035 for communication to the FDN Servers. The FDN then replies using these numbers (1024–1035) as destination ports because that is where the communication was generated from. However, firewalls and IPS devices that are unaware of this communication might falsely block this as an attack. So, if you have difficulty and the FortiGate is not directly connected to the Internet, check your Firewall/IPS logs on the perimeter device. If you must change the source port range being used for this communication, use the commands below:

```
FGT2 # config system global
FGT2 (global) # set ip-src-port-range 2048-4096
FGT2 (global) # end
FGT2 #
```

This configuration tells the FortiGate to use UDP ports 2048–4096 as the source port of the FortiGuard queries for Online updates. The values you could use here are 1–25,000—If you are having issues with the default, which is 1024–25,000, then probably you should restrict the ports on chunks of 2048 ports (as the example above) and test. Unfortunately, you would likely have to do this by trial and error.

For a complete list of ports that are used by FortiGate, please refer the article in the Knowledge Center.[1] For a summary of FortiGuard update communication, see Figure 6.5.

Troubleshooting and Tuning Performance Issues

While we will discuss troubleshooting steps for each Content Inspection technology later on this chapter, there are some steps that are common to all.

---

[1] http://kb.fortinet.com/kb/microsites/search.do?cmd=displayKC&docType=kc&externalId=107 73&sliceId=1&docTypeID=DT_KCARTICLE_1_1&dialogID=29491108&stateId=0%200%20 29489670.

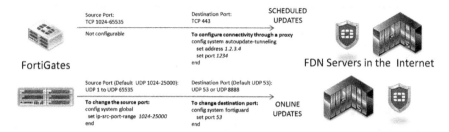

FIGURE 6.5 FortiGate to FortiGuard Communication Ports

1. Look at the number of Proxy Connections being used.

When people take a look at the FortiGate datasheets, it's not uncommon for people to think that the "Firewall Concurrent Sessions" number applies to all the functions, including Content Inspection. As we stated earlier, this is not true. Using the "diagnose test application" commands, we can monitor how many content inspection sessions are being used. Remember that each protocol will show its own numbers. You can display statistics for all protocols using the proxyworker statistics

```
FGT1 # diagnose test application proxyworker 4 | grep Connections
Current Connections                     4/3952
Max Concurrent Connections              54
Current Connections                     0/3952
Max Concurrent Connections              1
Current Connections                     0/3952
Current Connections                     2/3952
Max Concurrent Connections              5
Current Connections                     0/3952
Current Connections                     0/3952
```

Here you will get an idea on how close the Proxy Connections Table has been to exhaustion. You can run the "diagnose test application proxyworker 4" command, without the "grep," and it will give you detailed statistics on the usage of the general proxy for all protocols.

2. Configure a fast and reliable DNS.

Several Content Inspection functions require DNS. This is why the FortiGates shipped with DNS servers preconfigured. These preconfigured DNS servers are managed by Fortinet, and are often busy. The longer it takes to get an answer, the slower some FortiGate functions can become. Configuring an under-used and nearby DNS server will help ensure there are no delays.

3. Optimize UTM Profiles.

Use the minimum necessary UTM profiles. The idea is not to cut flexibility, but to avoid wasting resources, and potentially duplicating effort if you have many UTM profiles.

APPLICATION CONTROL
Introduction

Several years ago, when the Internet began, applications were better behaved. To begin with, there were no such things as "network-based applications". All applications ran on the local systems, and the Internet was used only as platform network, not as a platform. Back then, applications used well-defined ports, and you could establish a direct relationship for a network protocol (like POP3), to a port (TCP/110), to a program (Eudora or Microsoft Mail).

However, as the Web grew more popular, it was used to serve not only information but also taking feedback, information, and even code from users. Developers began changing first to a hybrid model where code ran both in the browser and on servers and then moved the servers to "the cloud". Cloud computing forced a change to the security paradigm. No longer could we rely on each protocol mapping to a single purpose. Now we had a single protocol (HTTP) being used for many purposes such as E-mail, Word Processing, File Transfer, Games, and, of course, malicious software. This paradigm change required network inspection to become smarter, so it could identify applications.

The Need of Application Control

Application control is in high demand for a number of reasons, but the two most important ones are (1) most traffic uses the port TCP/80 to exit the organization's network, and (2) we need more control over the information flowing through the network. Thus, we need the ability to detect, classify, and enforce a security policy for a given application, regardless of the method used to connect and transmit over the network.

Deciding when to use Application Control

Application Control is more often used for Outbound than for Inbound traffic. This is, you would normally need Application Control for connections being generated from your users to the Internet.

You would normally NOT need Application Control if:

- You are using your firewall to protect traffic between Internal Segments only, or between remote networks over which you have full administrative control that includes the servers and services throughout the entire network.

In this scenario, it is often better to enforce authentication in the application itself. The FortiGate would assist by controlling traffic based on source and destination IPs. If you know what applications are running on a given server, you can effectively white list the network traffic.

- You want to analyze data being sent over HTTP (Port TCP/80) to look for sensitive information. For this, you would use the FortiGate Data Leak Prevention (DLP) feature.
- You have the list of IP addresses or Fully Qualified Domain Names of the servers your users will access. If you can identify the server and trust that it will be running only known services (and you have means to periodically audit that), then you could use regular firewall rules.
- You are primarily concerned about the classification of web pages and are comfortable with Fortinet's categories ("Peer-to-peer file sharing", "social networking", "web-based e-mail", etc.) to block access. Or if you want to only allow access to categories such as "Child Education" or "Finance and Banking". Please note that in this case, you might still need Application Control to do a more granular analysis on the page content. This is particularly true, if you wish to be selective and strip content or shape traffic around applications that might be embedded on pages.

You might need Application Control if:

- For any reason you need to allow free access to the Internet for port HTTP/TCP/80, and you want to avoid applications that are typically used to abuse this access.
- You need to monitor and obtain reports on what web applications are being used by your people. It is possible to configure Application Control to just monitor applications without actually blocking anything.
- You need additional controls around web traffic to ensure that applications that could be embedded by authorized websites get proper treatment, such as blocking or Traffic Shaping.

You might also want to review the policies and regulations that affect you and your organization. Regulations are often why organizations enable Application Control on their FortiGates.

Before you Configure Application Control (Sizing and Design steps)

Application Control imposes load in the FortiGate. In general, since Application Control shares some internal mechanisms with IPS including the Inspection Engine, it would be fair to say that Application Control imposes around the same load that IPS would on the system. However, as it is a Flow-based inspection technology, the load is lighter than similar proxy-based technologies. Also, it does not use the Proxy Connection Table, so it does not add to the risk of running out of proxy connections.

You should use a Network Diagram to identify where the users are and how they are expected to generate HTTP traffic. This way, you can identify which flows carry traffic that would require deeper analysis than just source/destination. Pay special attention to the traffic that have little or no restriction on the destination addresses or ports, since the lack of restrictions can be used by potentially risky applications to transfer data. These are the traffic flows that should have Application Control applied to them. In general, be specific on what you are trying to achieve. For example: do you wish to reduce liability due to internal users running malicious applications or are you more interested in carving out the majority of your bandwidth for business-critical purposes? Having a statement on what you are trying to achieve will greatly help you create a configuration that will match that statement.

How Application Control works

Applications are constantly evolving, and in order to be effective, FortiGuard Analysts are constantly updating the list of supported Applications. We must remember that the only way the FortiGate can identify an Application is by analyzing the traffic it sees, correlating source and destination ports and IPs, as well as traffic patterns. However, the behavior can change over time as the developers creating these applications add features in real time. This is why it is important to keep the Application Control signature database up-to-date.

Remember that Fortinet keeps Encyclopedias online at http://www.fortiguard.com. By browsing to "Application Control Service" and then to "Application Control Encyclopedia", you can access detailed information about the applications recognized by the FortiGate. The same portal contains an Application Submission form that allows you to submit information to the FortiGuard analysts about an application that needs to be updated or added to the system. The submission form will return a ticket number via e-mail and Analysts will consider adding support for (or enhancing) the application mentioned. You don't need to own a FortiGate to submit, but existing customers will receive higher priority.

Just as with IPS, every modern FortiGate has an initial Application Control signature database. Since this database is stored locally, it is possible to start analyzing traffic at any time. This is good because it allows the immediate detection of known applications. However, once again it is important to remember that the efficiency and accuracy of detecting applications will largely depend on how up-to-date the database is. Due to this, you should first update the IPS database with the "exec update-ips" command, which includes the Application Control signatures.

Configuring Application Control
Creating an Application Control Profile

Before you may begin using Application Control, you must create an Application Control List and define the specific applications that you wish to either block or traffic-shape. In the example below, we will block Skype and Proxy Applications (UltraSurf, Tor, Hopster, etc.). This is where many Fortinet users start with Application Control.

```
FGT3 # config application list
// configure an application list
FGT3 (list) # edit My_AppCtrl_List
// My_AppCtrl_List is the name for this list
new entry 'My_AppCtrl_List' added
FGT3 (My_AppCtrl_List) # set comment "Block Skype and Proxies"
// A comment, so I can know what I'm trying to achieve here
FGT3 (My_AppCtrl_List) # config entries
// Config the entries for the list
FGT3 (entries) # edit 1
// First entry
new entry '1' added
FGT3 (1) # set application 10
// The application with ID 10…
FGT3 (1) # set action block
// will be blocked
FGT3 (1) # next
FGT3 (entries) # edit 2
new entry '2' added
FGT3 (2) # set category 6
// Applications that fall under category 6…
FGT3 (2) # set action block
// Will be blocked, which means the packets belonging to the
   application will be dropped. Other actions are pass, which will let
   the application through, and reset, which will generate a TCP RESET
   packet to the source of the connection.
FGT3 (2) # next
FGT3 (entries) # end
// We are done with entries on this list.
FGT3 (My_AppCtrl_List) # next
// We are done with the My_App_Ctrl_List configuration
FGT3 (list) # end
// We are done with all the Application List configuration
FGT3 #
```

As you can see, defining an Application list is simple, though the use of Application and Category IDs may be confusing. If you use the GUI, they are configured automatically when you select the names, but within the CLI, you might have difficulty determining the "magic numbers". To make this easier, you can use the "?" shortcut within the CLI. To get a list of all possible values, simply hit the question mark key when you need to enter an ID number and the system will provide you with a list.

```
FGT3 # config application list
FGT3 (list) # edit My_AppCtrl_List
FGT3 (My_AppCtrl_List) # config entries
FGT3 (entries) # edit 1
FGT3 (1) # set category ?
```

ID	Select Category ID
1	IM
2	P2P
3	VoIP
5	Media
6	Proxy
7	Remote.Access
8	Game
12	Web
15	Network.Service
16	Business
17	Update
19	Botnet
21	eMail
*	

```
FGT3 (1) # set application ?
```

ID	Select application ID
29025	1und1.Mail
17534	2ch
17535	2ch_Post
16284	3PC
16616	4shared
16534	6cn
17045	9PFS
18285	9PTV
26378	24im
16558	51.Com
28325	51.Com.BBS

.

.

.

```
FGT3 (1) # set application
```

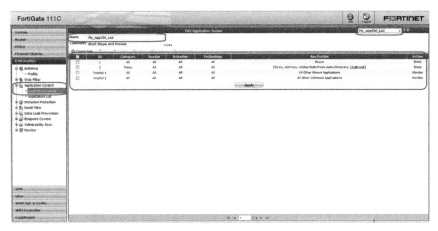

FIGURE 6.6 Application Control List as seen in the GUI

So, as you can see, applications can be referenced as directly and optionally chosen so that specific behaviors may be applied. However, applications are also grouped into Categories. If you use a category instead of an application, the selected action will be applied to each application in the category (see Figure 6.6).

Once you have defined an Application Control list, you can reference it from a firewall policy. In this example, we assume that the switch interface represents a network segment devoted to users and that WAN1 is the Internet interface. Thus, once applied, a computer on the switch interface will not be able to use Skype or any Proxy applications via the Internet.

```
FGT3 # config firewall policy
FGT3 (policy) # edit 99 // 99 is just a policy ID
new entry '99' added
FGT3 (99) # set srcintf switch // Source Interface is switch
FGT3 (99) # set srcaddr all // Source address is all, so any IP address
   will be accepted as source
FGT3 (99) # set dstintf wan1 // Destination Interface is WAN1
FGT3 (99) # set dstaddr all /// Source address is all, so any IP
   address
FGT3 (99) # set service ANY // Any IP service
FGT3 (99) # set action accept // Accept this traffic
FGT3 (99) # set schedule always // All the time
FGT3 (99) # set logtraffic enable // Log this traffic
FGT3 (99) # set nat enable // Enable NATting behing the FortiGate IP
   address of the outgoing interface. In this case, the IP address
   assigned to the WAN1 interface
FGT3 (99) # set utm-status enable // Enable UTM inspection
```

```
FGT3 (99) # set application-list My_AppCtrl_List // Use the Application
    List previously defined.
FGT3 (99) # next
FGT3 (policy) # end
FGT3 #
```

NETWORK ANTIVIRUS/ANTISPYWARE
The Need of Network Antivirus

Traditionally, Antivirus technology has existed on the endpoint, the specific worksta-tions, and servers where malware tends to run. However, as threats grew more com-plex, so did their protections. Thus, in addition to existing on the endpoint, Antivirus also moved to the perimeter.

Fortinet's technology provides protection against many types of malicious soft-ware. Being a network device, the FortiGate is better positioned than endpoint pro-tection to detect malicious network traffic, such as the communication channels that malware authors use to control the systems they infect. However, to properly protect against blended threats, nothing beats the combination of an edge technology like FortiGate combined with an endpoint Antivirus solution.

Basically, you don't want the Antivirus running on your system to be your last line of defense. This is especially true of reactive mechanisms, since the threat must first be detected before the protection be developed. Also, there are advanced threats that look for Antivirus software running locally on endpoints, and then shut them down or temporarily disable them to avoid detection. So, supplementing the endpoint protection systems with a network focused system makes a lot of sense. Not only do you have two potential catch points, but by filtering out malicious software before it reaches the endpoint, you are requiring less work of the endpoint, thereby saving resources for other uses.

Fortinet manages to save even more resources by implementing an offloading mechanism called the Content Pattern Recognition Language (CPRL) in the Content Processor (CP) ASIC. This chip is included in every FortiGate and has the ability to tie into the Antivirus and IPS functions, speeding them up drastically.

Deciding when Network Antivirus is a Good Idea

There are two network regions where you may wish to place network Antivirus: between a server and the rest of the network or between your users and the rest of the network.

For Servers, your goal would be to protect both the server itself and the data stored on the server. For example, if you have an FTP server, you may wish to pro-tect against attacks that compromise the server itself so it can then spread to other users that access FTP. This was a very common attack in the late 2000s and took

> **TIP**
>
> **Submitting Virus Samples to Fortinet**
> The FortiGuard team allows you to submit virus samples via the FortiGuard portal (http://www.fortiguard.com). If you suspect you have an infected file, you can scan it online and find out if it is detected as a currently recognized threat. If it was determined to not be a threat and you suspect this to be a false negative, you can go to the further step of submitting it to a FortiGuard Analyst. You will usually get a response before 48 hours.

over many webhosting companies. You may also want to protect email servers so your users, internally and externally, are not infected by malware that is delivered to their INBOX. Finally, you may wish to protect outbound traffic from web servers. Web servers are increasingly targeted by attackers and used to host multi-stage downloader malware.

Basically, it is wise to place Antivirus to look at bidirectional traffic to all servers on both IPv4 and IPv6 networks. When implementing Antivirus in this manner, be sure to check your firewall policies and make sure that each path to your servers has protection on it. It is common for FortiGate administrators to forget to protect a failover path or emergency access VPN. Any path without protection is a potential point of compromise.

When protecting users, it is important to remember that inspection is based on traffic flow. For example, when a user downloads a file, they initiate the connection to the file server, and the file is then downloaded across the established connection. Thus, even though the file is coming "in" to the network, it will be inspected based on the rules for traffic going "out", as that is the direction in which the session was established.

Secondly, bear in mind that, while the FortiGate is very efficient at scanning this traffic, it does take resources. If you have users communicating with systems that you know to be safe (text files coming from an FTP server, for example), you can turn off inspection on those pathways and reduce total load on the system. Note, however, that in some highly sensitive or regulated environments, you have to inspect all traffic regardless of expected content. In these situations, you may want to get a FortiGate one size larger than you would otherwise need, just to reduce the risk of load issues.

Before you Configure Network Antivirus (Sizing and Design steps)

Due to the amount of resources required to support it, Antivirus is often the most expensive feature on the FortiGate. Even though it is accelerated, not all of the processing is offloaded, so both CPU and RAM can be consumed quickly. This is especially true if you are using Antivirus in a Proxy-Based mode. Thus, you should be careful with WHAT you choose to scan.

- First, you should define which files will and will not be allowed. A typical configuration, for example, is to block executable files. This is done in the DLP configuration, but the choice made there will affect what will be scanned by Antivirus.

- Second, you should determine both your scanning size limit and whether files that exceed this limit will be allowed or denied. This only applies when you are doing Proxy-Based analysis, but if you are in this mode, you should know that the size of the file you allow determines how much RAM can be consumed by that part of the system. Generally speaking, since malware is becoming increasingly stealthy, larger files are safer, so many administrators choose to disable file scanning for files larger than 10 Mb (for example). While highly sensitive environments may wish to take a similar approach, files larger than the limit can be discarded, thereby providing greater security.

- Third, you will need to define the protocols, sources, and destinations to be scanned. Resist the temptation of scanning everything as that will likely waste resources on the FortiGate, causing you to purchase a larger device than you need, and cost you time and effort tracking down alerts.

Once you have defined the WHAT, you must determine the HOW:

- First, determine whether you need to use Proxy- or Flow-based scanning. Refer to Table 6.1 for a refresher on the differences. Basically, though, it's a decision between performance (flow-based) and security (proxy-based). Flow-based will catch a good amount of malicious software. However, it doesn't uncompress files, such as zip, rar, or arj. Proxy-based scans more deeply than flow-based scans do. Additionally, due to hardware limitations, not all FortiGate models support Flow-based Antivirus scanning.

- Second, you should determine which Antivirus database you wish to use. There are three different databases that can be used for proxy-scanning, though due to memory limitations, not all FortiGate models support all three.
  - Normal—Scans for "current" malware that's been seen on other networks within the last several months.
  - Extended—Scans for "recent" malware, that has been seen in the last year.
  - Extreme—Scans for all known malware, including both recent malware and "zoo" lists.

Zoo viruses are viruses that have not been active for more than a year.

As you can imagine, choosing "Extreme" will greatly reduce performance. This is a tradeoff and, in the interests of speed, many people choose to run as "Normal" or "Extended" and trust their endpoint AntiMalware system to catch older and custom malware. However, it is only a good idea to do this if you have an extremely trustworthy AntiMalware system running on the endpoints.

- Finally, you must determine the Antivirus priority. If performance is critical and the cost of downtime or slowness exceeds the cost of a security breach, you may set the device to favor throughput over scanning. You do this through the "optimize" command. If your device tells you that that command does not exist, your FortiGate does not have this capability. Once this mode is changed, your device will need to be rebooted.

```
FGT3 # config system global
FGT3 (global) # set optimize Antivirus // or "throughput"
FGT3 (global) # end
```

How Network Antivirus works in the FortiGate

Remember that FortiGates download updates from the FortiGuard team, so they reside locally. Thus, the more comprehensive your selected database, the more space it will take up on your device. You can choose the three databases defined in the previous section or "flow-based". You can also configure grayware protection which scans for attacks like adware, keyloggers, and spyware.

```
FGT2 # config Antivirus settings
FGT2 (settings) # set default-db extended
FGT2 (settings) # set grayware enable
FGT2 (settings) # end
FGT2 #
```

You should also give consideration to how the system will behave when resources are low. FortiGates automatically enable a protection mechanism called "conserve mode" when memory begins to run low. This is basically a series of memory recovery measures that include blocking new connections to avoid over-subscribing the system. Once there is enough RAM available, this mode is deactivated. If you choose to prioritize the system for Antivirus, you might want to define a fail-open state, so if the device becomes overloaded, Antivirus scanning ceases so memory can be recovered. However, be careful doing this, as it opens you up to a scenario whereby an attacker can launch a denial of service attack on your device to get their malware past your defenses. When using the "set av-failopen" mode, your options are "pass", so traffic is passed with no inspection until memory becomes available, "idledrop", which forces closure of unused connections, "off", which stops accepting new connections, or "one-shot" which turns off scanning completely.

```
FGT3 # config system global
FGT3 (global) # set av-failopen pass
FGT3 (global) # end
```

In addition to running out of RAM, you can also run out of proxy session table entries. This behavior is defined by the "set av-failopen-session" command. The parameters match those of "av-failopen" described above.

```
FGT3 # config system global
FGT3 (global) # set av-failopen-session enable
```

```
FGT3 (global) # end
FGT3 #
```

In addition to global options, there are also protocol-specific options. While these do apply to the way the UTM as a whole handles a protocol, they are technically not "global", because they do not apply to all protocols. Each protocol definition can affect one of: http, ftp, imap, pop3, smtp, nntp, and im. If you are running a FortiGate with SSL inspection capabilities, you can also define options for https, ftps, imaps, pop3s, and smtps. Each protocol also has its own specific options. In the HTTP example below, options include "clientcomfort", which avoids timeouts by sending the client packets every few seconds (as defined by the interval and bytecount), "no-content-summary", which masks the files from appearing in the GUI dashboard, and "oversize", which blocks files that exceed the size specified in the limit (in Mb). In the FTP example, the "splice" options keep a copy of the downloaded file as it streams it to the user. This way, if malware is found in the file, the connection can be aborted.

```
FGT3 # config firewall profile-protocol-options
FGT3 (profile-protoc~1) # edit My_Prot_Opts
new entry 'My_Prot_Opts' added
FGT3 (My_Prot_Opts) # config http
FGT3 (http) # set inspect-all enable // Inspect all ports, not just 80.
FGT3 (http) # set options clientcomfort no-content-summary oversize
FGT3 (http) # set oversize-limit 2 // Maximum threshold is 10% of
   systems RAM
FGT3 (http) # set comfort-interval 5
FGT3 (http) # set comfort-amount 5
FGT3 (http) # end
FGT3 (My_Prot_Opts) # config ftp
FGT3 (ftp) # set port 21
FGT3 (ftp) # set options oversize no-content-summary splice
FGT3 (ftp) # set oversize-limit 2
FGT3 (ftp) # end
FGT3 (My_Prot_Opts) # end
FGT3 #
```

Once the protocol options are determined, you can assign the profile to a firewall policy. In the example, you'll see that FTP-based malware is set to be quarantined on the FortiGate if found. This means that the administrator must be diligent at checking the quarantine and dealing with what is found. In contrast, HTTP-based scanning is set to drop any compressed files that have a password assigned. Since such files are encrypted and cannot be scanned, this is the safest approach.

```
FGT3 # config Antivirus profile
FGT3 (profile) # edit MyAVProfile
new entry 'MyAVProfile' added
FGT3 (MyAVProfile) # config ftp
FGT3 (ftp) # set options scan quarantine
FGT3 (ftp) # end
FGT3 (MyAVProfile) # config http
FGT3 (http) # set options scan
FGT3 (http) # set archive-block encrypted corrupted
FGT3 (http) # set avdb normal
FGT3 (http) # end
FGT3 (MyAVProfile) # end
FGT3 #
```

Finally, you must add an Antivirus policy to the firewall.

```
FGT3 # config firewall policy
FGT3 (policy) # edit 0
new entry '0' added
FGT3 (0) # set srcintf switch
FGT3 (0) # set srcaddr all
FGT3 (0) # set dstintf wan1
FGT3 (0) # set dstaddr all
FGT3 (0) # set service HTTP FTP
FGT3 (0) # set action accept
FGT3 (0) # set schedule always
FGT3 (0) # set utm-status enable
FGT3 (0) # set profile-protocol-options My_Prot_Opts
FGT3 (0) # set av-profile MyAVProfile
FGT3 (0) # end
```

INTRUSION PROTECTION (IPS)
Introduction

Network-Based attacks became quite common once it was demonstrated they were possible. As they grew more complex, it became important not only to detect them, but also to block them. Though the industry originally deployed Intrusion Detection Systems (IDS), which identified specific attack code targeting specific vulnerabilities and alerted people, it has since moved on to Intrusion Prevention Systems (IPS).

Though this change was originally viewed as risky because false positives could take a network offline, the technology has matured and is now very reliable.

The FortiGates leverage the CPRL and the Content Processor (CP) ASIC to implement IPS. When you configure your firewall to allow connections to your server, you increase the risk of attacks crossing trust boundaries. So, in general, if your network is connected to another network that is less trustworthy, you should consider running IPS.

While IPS has traditionally been used for edge-based protection as something of a firewall "backup", it is usually more effective to tie it into the network segmentation process. Thus, if you have servers that you isolate to a different network and dedicate a FortiGate interface to that traffic, you can activate IPS and protect against both internal and external attacks. This helps protect against attackers focusing on vulnerable operating systems and applications as well as simplifying various aspects of regulatory compliance.

Before you Configure IPS (Sizing and Design steps)

IPS is potentially resource intensive, so any deployment should be done with care. You must understand how IPS works: responsibility of the engine, and how signatures function.

The IPS engine is a "smart sniffer" that catches network traffic and compares it traffic against a signature database, where each signature represents a known attack. Properly written signatures tell the IPS engine what to look for without triggering false positives. Ideally, these signatures match against the behavior of an attack and are, over time, tuned to reduce false positives.

As seen in Figure 6.7, an IPS signature has several properties that:

- Name—Distinguishes the signature from others. By virtue of naming conventions, it usually references the product, service or protocol being affected, and the type of attack.

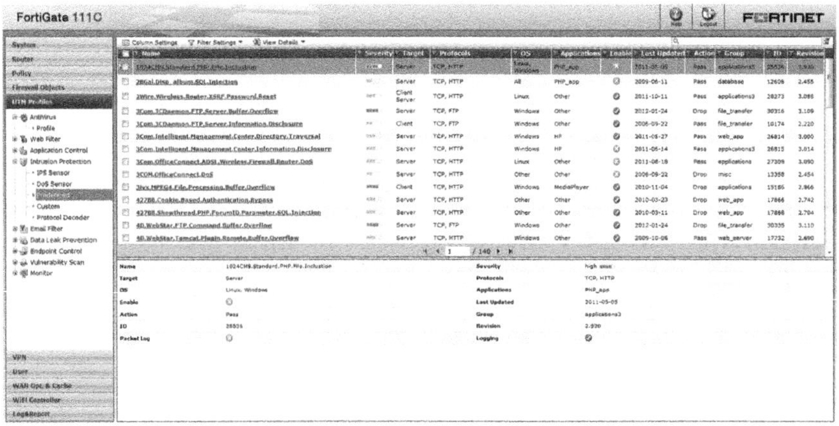

FIGURE 6.7 IPS Signature Properties

- Target—Specifies whether the attack attempts to exploit the client side of the connection, the server side of the connection, or both.
- OS (Operating System)—Identifies if this attack is specific to operating system. Values include Windows, Linux, BSD, Solaris, MacOS, Other, or all.
- Enable—Identifies whether this signature is enabled and being scanned for by the Engine.
- Action—Identifies whether the traffic should be passed or blocked if the rule is triggered.
- ID—Used for cross reference in reports and the FortiGuard Encyclopedia.
- Packet Log—Identifies whether packet log is enabled. This log records the traffic as it was seen by the IPS engine and can be used for further analysis. Logging can be done locally on the FortiGate (if the device has a hard disk) or sent to a FortiAnalyzer device.
- Severity—Indicates the criticality of the attack, according to the Common Vulnerability Scoring System (CVSS).
- Protocols—Identifies whether the attack is protocol specific. Applies to both specific protocols (HTTP, SSH, DNP3) and more general ones (TCP, UDP, ICMP).
- Applications—Identifies whether the attack is known to a specific application or group of applications such as Oracle, SCADA, P2P, or sendmail.
- Last updated—The date when the signature was updated by FortiGuard.
- Logging—Identifies whether this signature will generate a log entry when triggered.
- Revision—Helps track when the signature was released.
- Group—Organizes signatures based on type (applications, file_transfer, web_ app, etc.).

Before you configure your system, you must decide what will be scanned. You may wish to review network segments to identify which contain sensitive data, which operating systems are running or which applications are installed. This way, you won't have to enable all signatures.

There is always great temptation to enable more than what is needed, as this increases your visibility as to what is occurring within your network. Most people generally start by over-enabling to help get understanding about the network. However, this should be reduced over time, as each event that IPS triggers should be analyzed according to your incident management system.

Once you have decided which traffic will be scanned, you should consider logging. Some attacks might warrant no logging, if they are low risk. Others should be logged for future audit purposes and still others should have a pull packet capture run so that they may be analyzed by the forensics team at a later date. Also, keep in mind that as the attacks against the network are specific to operating systems and applications, and the FortiGate's checks are simplified versions of these, they will never be perfect. Thus, you will constantly be tuning your environment. You should also consider how you will address events that trigger on another system like server-side AntiMalware or Applicaton Whitelisting. Any true event that occurs there will likely have bypassed the FortiGate and are therefore false negatives.

FortiGates can leverage quarantines as an optional response to a triggered signature. While this is a very useful feature, you should think about it with care. A badly configured quarantine can lead to a self-inflicted Denial of Service (DoS) as, in the event of a false positive, the entire local network could be brought down. Thus, review any signatures that you wish to link to a quarantine for a long period of time (weeks, months, etc.). Basically, if your environment has processes that run once a week, testing for a week should be sufficient. However, if you have monthly processes, you may have to go longer.

You should also consider how you wish to respond to Denial of Service (DoS) attacks. To defend against these attacks, the only possible measure that can be implemented on the target side is measuring the frequency of the requests, and if they exceed what the infrastructure can support, break the flow. The FortiGate can do this, but you must perform your calculation carefully so you do not accidentally block legitimate requests. Trial and error testing works best.

Finally, you might want to verify that your Network Time Protocol (NTP) configuration is appropriate. Connect all servers and network equipment, including the FortiGate, to that NTP Server. While this is not required, it will greatly simplify any IPS analysis, as you could easily compare logs on many systems. This is essential if you must do forensic analysis on the attacks that you face. To review NTP on the FortiGate, you can use the following commands:

```
FGT3 # show system ntp
config system ntp
    config ntpserver
        edit 1
            set server "pool.ntp.org"
        next
    end
    set ntpsync enable
    set syncinterval 60
end
```

How IPS Works in the FortiGate

The first configuration step involves defining global IPS parameters for your environment. Possible values are explained after the comment (//) character.

```
FGT3 # show full-configuration ips global
config ips global
```

```
      set algorithm engine-pick // high, low and engine-pick
      set anomaly-mode continuous // continuous and periodical
      set engine-count 0 // process count: 0 to 999999999
      set fail-open enable// enable or disable
      set ignore-session-bytes 204800 // bytes: 1 to 999999999
      set session-limit-mode heuristic // accurate or heuristic
      set socket-size 8 // megabytes: 1 to 64
      set traffic-submit disable // enable or disable
end
```

The *algorithm* parameter tells the IPS engine how to do signature matching. *High* is faster but more memory, so it should be uses when performance is important. This mode is only used when IPS and Application Control are the only content inspection feature used. *Low* is slower but also uses less memory. *Engine-pick* is the default and bases its choice on the amount of memory available and the type of inspections being performed. In general it is safe to leave it that way.

anomaly-mode tells the engine how anomaly events (DoS-related events) will be caught: *continuous* blocks all the traffic once the threshold is exceeded, and traffic is allowed once the threshold is reached again. *periodical* blocks only the packets above the threshold, allowing all the packets below the threshold.

engine-count limits the number of IPS engine processes running on the FortiGate. If the value is changed from the default, you must ensure that you are not exceeding the capabilities of your CPU and memory. Tune this parameter only if IPS is the primary content inspection analysis performed. More IPS processes may result in better performance, but could also overload the system if they exceed your available hardware.

fail-open tells the IPS engine how to behave if, for some reason, the IPS engine becomes unresponsive. Leave it enabled on environments where availability takes precedence over security, but disable it if security matters more.

ignore-session-bytes identifies the number of bytes to be analyzed in a session. The larger the amount, the more memory will be used. The default is 204,800 bytes or around 200 kilobytes. The assumption is that if a session is malicious, the attack will be in the first 200 kb. If there is no indication of a problem, the rest of the session will be ok.

session-limit-mode tells the DoS sensors how to count sessions. By default, the FortiGate uses a heuristic formula to estimate the number of sessions. This is less CPU intensive but also less accurate. If, for example, you define a threshold of 100,000, you could trigger the limit with 99,500 or 101,000 connections. If you set it to *accurate*, more CPU will be used, but the count will be exact.

socket-size defines the amount of memory devoted to holding packets for the IPS engine. You usually do not need to change this, but if you require RAM for extra uses, you may wish to do so. You can also increase it if IPS plays an important role in your protection scheme.

traffic-submit tells the FortiGate whether or not key attack metrics will be submitted to FortiGuard for further analysis. Enable it to ensure Fortinet continues enhancing IPS engine and signatures.

Once the global parameters are properly tuned, you will need to create IPS profiles that cover two areas: Misuse detection (IPS Sensor) and Anomaly detection (DoS Sensor).

To create an IPS Sensor you must have first determined what you want to protect. Let's say that you have only Windows and Linux server and that they are running E-mail (SMTP, POP3), Web, and FTP. Further, you only wish to enable protection against "critical" and "high" severity threats. Finally, you want to enable all these signatures regardless of whether Fortinet disables them by default.

```
FGT3 # config ips sensor
FGT3 (sensor) # edit MyServerFarm
new entry 'MyServerFarm' added
FGT3 (MyServerFarm) # set comment "Protecting Server Farm: Windows/
    Linux"
FGT3 (MyServerFarm) # config entries
FGT3 (entries) # edit 1
new entry '1' added
FGT3 (1) # set location server //Only use signatures targeting servers.
    Another option is "client".
FGT3 (1) # set os Windows
FGT3 (1) # set protocol HTTP FTP SMTP POP3
FGT3 (1) # set severity high critical
FGT3 (1) # set status enable
FGT3 (1) # next
FGT3 (entries) # end
FGT3 (MyServerFarm) # end
```

Other properties of the signature filter that were not used in the example above include:

set application—Filters based on application, such as Apache or MySQL. Typing a "?" will give you a list of available options.

set log—When set to "enable", forces all signatures to be logged. When set to "disable", forces them to not be logged. Otherwise, the "default" setting allows each signature to log or not based on its own configuration.

set log-packet—Enables packet logging for the signatures that match the filter.

set quarantine—Blocks communication for a period of time upon triggering the signature. *attacker* blocks all communications from the IP address identified as source of the attack. *both* blocks only the traffic between the attacker and the victim, leaving the attacker free to send information to other systems behind the FortiGate.

interface will disable the interface itself, blocking all traffic, which can be dangerous depending on the interface that triggers. Be careful with this setting as it could cut your network completely off from others.

set quarantine-expiry—Only visible if quarantine is set to "attacker", "both", or "interface". Configures the amount of time (in minutes) to activate the quarantine block.

set quarantine-log—Configures whether or not a quarantining event will be logged.

Assigning an IPS Sensor to a firewall policy is similar to assigning any other Content Inspection:

```
FGT3 # config firewall policy
FGT3 (policy) # edit 0
new entry '0' added
FGT3 (0) # set srcintf wan1
FGT3 (0) # set srcaddr all
FGT3 (0) # set dstintf switch
FGT3 (0) # set dstaddr all
FGT3 (0) # set service HTTP FTP SMTP POP3
FGT3 (0) # set action accept
FGT3 (0) # set schedule always
FGT3 (0) # set utm-status enable
FGT3 (0) # set ips-sensor MyServerFarm
FGT3 (0) # end
```

IPS sensors detect misuse, but a completely different sensor is used to detect anomalies. These are caught with DoS Sensors. The DoS Sensors allow you to precisely define traffic patterns. The parameters below are groups based on the modes in which they are affected.

Anomaly Mode

tcp_syn_flood—TCP SYN packet rate (packets/second) to a single destination address.

udp_flood—UDP packet rate (packets/second) going to a single destination IP address.

udp_scan—UDP packet rate (packets/second) coming from a single IP address.

icmp_flood—ICMP packet rate (packets/second) going to a single IP address.

icmp_sweep—ICMP packet rate (packets/second) coming from a single IP address.

Session Limit Mode

tcp_src_session—Number of TCP sessions coming from a single IP address.

tcp_dst_session—Number of TCP sessions going to a single IP address.

udp_src_session—Number of UDP sessions coming from a single IP address.

udp_dst_session—Number of UDP sessions going to a single IP address.

icmp_src_session—Number of concurrent ICMP sessions coming from a single IP address.

icmp_dst_session—Number of concurrent ICMP sessions going to a single IP address.

If you wish to configure a DoS sensor to stop SYN flood at a rate of 10,000 packets per second from the Internet while simultaneously quarantining and logging more than 7000 connections for 10 min between a potential attacker and one of your servers, you could do as follows:

```
FGT3 # config ips DoS
FGT3 (DoS) # edit MyDoS_Sensor
new entry 'MyDoS_Sensor' added
FGT3 (MyDoS_Sensor) # set comment "DoS Sensor for the Internet"
FGT3 (MyDoS_Sensor) # config anomaly
FGT3 (anomaly) # edit tcp_syn_flood
FGT3 (tcp_syn_flood) # set status enable
FGT3 (tcp_syn_flood) # set threshold 10000
FGT3 (tcp_syn_flood) # set log enable
FGT3 (tcp_syn_flood) # set action block // If anomaly-mode is
   continuous, traffic to the IP address being attacked will be
   blocked. If it is set to periodical, packets below 10,000 per second
   will be allowed but packets above 10,000 per second will be blocked.
FGT3 (tcp_syn_flood) # next
FGT3 (anomaly) # edit tcp_src_session
FGT3 (tcp_src_session) # set status enable
FGT3 (tcp_src_session) # set log enable
FGT3 (tcp_src_session) # set threshold 7000
FGT3 (tcp_src_session) # set action block
FGT3 (tcp_src_session) # set quarantine attacker
FGT3 (tcp_src_session) # set quarantine-expiry 10
FGT3 (tcp_src_session) # set quarantine-log enable
FGT3 (tcp_src_session) # next
FGT3 (anomaly) # end
FGT3 (MyDoS_Sensor) # next
FGT3 (DoS) # end
FGT3 #
```

Next, you just assign this profile to a policy. In this example, we are applying to all source and destination addresses, but we could also specify a firewall object here. We could also restrict by protocol if we wished.

```
FGT3 # config firewall interface-policy
FGT3 (interface-policy) # edit 0
new entry '0' added
FGT3 (0) # set interface wan1
FGT3 (0) # set srcaddr all
FGT3 (0) # set dstaddr all
FGT3 (0) # set service ANY
FGT3 (0) # set ips-DoS-status enable //
FGT3 (0) # set ips-DoS MyDoS_Sensor FGT3 (0) # next
FGT3 (interface-policy) # end
FGT3 #
```

WEB FILTERING
Introduction

Web Content Filtering is a simple technology, but one with a tremendous impact. It basically analyzes two items for each URL requested: the category of the site and the content of the page. While similar to DLP in concept, it does not look for sensitive content and block based on what it finds. Instead, it identifies the category of the site and makes a determination based on that.

Reasons for using Web Content Filtering range from wanting to improve internal productivity, keep users off of dangerous and illegal sites or restrict sites based on the morals of those in charge of the organization. In general, the need to block content for whatever reason, can be met with Web Content Filtering.

How Web Content Filtering Works in the FortiGate (Sizing and Design steps)

As mentioned earlier in this chapter, the Web Content Filter (WCF) uses online, real-time updates. Thus, any website that you are browsing to is compared against the list maintained by FortiGuard and the decision is made in the moment.

Since the database is stored on the FDN and not locally, you get a more rapidly updating list at the cost of not being able to directly edit it yourself. Luckily, the FortiGuard team has tools in the FortiGuard portal (http://www.fortiguard.com) that allow you to both verify a URL's category and, if you disagree, suggest a change. Also, if the web page is not classified (which, while rare, does happen), you can submit the URL and a FortiGuard Analyst will classify it for you. Average response time is less than 48 h.

When a user browsing through a FortiGate requests a Web page that has not yet been classified, it is passed to a list of URLs that will be analyzed and pre-classified by automated mechanisms. Among other things, the number of times that the page has been requested is taken into account so popular but unclassified are reviewed first. If the automated mechanism can classify to an acceptable certainty level, then the classification is uploaded immediately. If, however, the automated mechanism is uncertain, a FortiGuard analyst will review it manually.

Configuring Web Content Filtering

There are two types of Web Content Filter: Regular and FortiGuard Web Content Filter.

For Regular Web Filter, you must decide on a list of words to detect on a web page and the score for each word. The score is a numerical value that is cumulatively added for each occurrence of a detected word, though each specific word only counts once. Our editors will not use actual profanity, so here is an example of blocking web pages that contain the names of planets.

```
FGT3 # config webfilter content
FGT3 (content) # edit 0
new entry '0' added
FGT3 (0) # set name "Planets"
FGT3 (0) # config entries
FGT3 (entries) # edit Earth
new entry 'Earth' added
FGT3 (Earth) # set status enable
FGT3 (Earth) # set action block
FGT3 (Earth) # set lang western
FGT3 (Earth) # set pattern-type wildcard // Could be regexp for regular
    expression, or wildcard
FGT3 (Earth) # set score 5
FGT3 (Earth) # next
FGT3 (entries) # edit Mars
new entry 'Mars' added
FGT3 (Mars) # set status enable
FGT3 (Mars) # set action block
FGT3 (Mars) # set lang western
FGT3 (Mars) # set pattern-type wildcard
FGT3 (Mars) # set score 5
FGT3 (Mars) # next
FGT3 (entries) # end
FGT3 (0) # next
FGT3 (content) # end
```

To activate it, we must first assign this configuration to a Web Content Filter profile. The threshold is set to 10, so both words must be present to trigger the action.

```
FGT3 # config webfilter profile
FGT3 (profile) # edit My_WebFilter
new entry 'My_WebFilter' added
FGT3 (My_WebFilter) # config web
FGT3 (web) # set bword-threshold 10
FGT3 (web) # set bword-table 1 // reference to the WebFilter list
    by its index. 1 means the first (and assuming this is a new
    configuration, the only) we have.
FGT3 (web) # end
FGT3 (My_WebFilter) # next
FGT3 (profile) # end
FGT3 #
```

Finally, we must assign this list to a firewall policy. However, before we do that, let's configure a profile with FortiGuard Web Filtering. Suppose, we want to block security risks or the categories, Malicious Websites, Phishing, and Spam URLs. Everything else will be allowed.

```
FGT3 # config webfilter profile
FGT3 (profile) # edit My_FGD_WCF_Profile
new entry 'My_FGD_WCF_Profile' added
FGT3 (My_FGD_WCF_Pro~i) # config ftgd-wf
FGT3 (ftgd-wf) # set options log-all-url
FGT3 (ftgd-wf) # config filters
FGT3 (filters) # edit 26 // An ID
new entry '26' added
FGT3 (26) # set action block
FGT3 (26) # set category ? // here after hitting the question mark, the
    list of categories appears
<id> category ID
0 Unrated
1 Drug Abuse
...
25 Streaming Media and Download
26 Malicious Websites
28 Entertainment
...
59 Proxy Avoidance
61 Phishing
62 Plagiarism
...
```

```
86 Spam URLs
87 Personal Privacy
FGT3 (26) # set category 26 // we want to block category 26, which is
   Malicious Websites
FGT3 (26) # next
FGT3 (filters) # edit 61
new entry '61' added
FGT3 (61) # set category 61 // we want to block category 61, which is
   Phishing
FGT3 (61) # set action block
FGT3 (61) # next
FGT3 (filters) # edit 86
new entry '86' added
FGT3 (86) # set category 86 // we want to block category 61, which is
   Spam URLS
FGT3 (86) # set action block
FGT3 (86) # next
FGT3 (filters) # end
FGT3 (ftgd-wf) # end
FGT3 (My_FGD_WCF_Pro~i) # next
FGT3 (profile) # end
FGT3 #
```

Once the WCF Profile has been defined, it can be assigned to the firewall policy.

```
FGT3 # config firewall policy
FGT3 (policy) # edit 0
new entry '0' added
FGT3 (0) # set srcintf switch
FGT3 (0) # set srcaddr all
FGT3 (0) # set dstintf wan1
FGT3 (0) # set dstaddr all
FGT3 (0) # set service HTTP DNS
FGT3 (0) # set action accept
FGT3 (0) # set schedule always
FGT3 (0) # set utm-status enable
FGT3 (0) # set profile-protocol-options default
FGT3 (0) # set webfilter-profile My_FGD_WCF_Profile
FGT3 (0) # end
```

Once this is configured, the system will block categories not allowed by the Profile.

Bear in mind, the above example was to restrict users based on the IP address they belong to. In this case, all devices behind the interface *switch,* regardless of their IP address, will be filtered. We can also use authentication to apply Web Content Filtering to only a group of users, based on what user group they belong to. It is also possible to apply more (and different) Content Inspection mechanisms to several groups of users, so guests are more restricted in the type of Web Pages they can access via the corporate Internet connection and get applied stricter Application Control and Antivirus configurations, for example. But discussing user authentication is beyond the scope of this chapter. In general, once the FortiGate authenticates a user and identifies it as part of a group, it can use that information to apply to the user a set of controls by using UTM profiles, adequate to the type of user being identified.

Extended UTM Functionality

INTRODUCTION

This chapter explains some of the additional UTM functionality of FortiOS and certain FortiGate hardware platforms. These are either extensions of the base UTM functions explained earlier in this book or functionality that complements the core security of FortiGate appliances. In this chapter, we will cover:

- Wan Optimization (WanOPT).
- Web Caching.
- Endpoint Control.

- Data Leak Protection (DLP).
- Vulnerability Management.

WAN OPTIMIZATION
Introduction

WAN optimization (WanOPT) should be a familiar concept to anyone who has set their Internet browser to use a caching proxy when "surfing the web." This web caching proxy would typically also cache frequently used web page objects and other files, thereby saving bandwidth and appearing to speed up loading when a user visits a page that a previous user has also viewed.

WanOPT also connotes "getting more out of that Internet pipe," allowing the same bandwidth saving and increased efficiency of caching with two additional benefits: LAN-like behavior over WAN and justification for server consolidation. WanOPT delivers these benefits by employing one or more of the following techniques:

- Duplication reduction.
- Bandwidth management.
- Caching.

While the technical details of these techniques is beyond the scope of this book, this chapter will focus on implementation and usage of the FortiGate WanOPT technologies.

Duplication reduction attempts to avoid resending the same data over a connection by sending reference tags that represent data block patterns. This allows one end of a WAN connection to reconstruct the original packet. This process requires a "data dictionary" to be compiled, which can require significant training time and numerous data streams. Although similar to caching, duplication reduction works at the byte level and is application independent.

Bandwidth management directly improves the efficiency and usage of a path. A few commonly used methods are:

- Compression: For certain known data types, data compression can be applied to greatly reduce the size of a data block. However, be aware that compression algorithms can be processor intensive and will incur latency at both ends of the WanOPT path.
- Latency optimization: For certain protocols, the overhead of traffic passing over the WanOPT can be reduced by modifying aspects like window size and selective acknowledgements, or by combining multiple individual requests into a single message. This functions largely as client-side protocol spoofing or server-side reply buffering.
- Forward error correction: Reduce retransmission across a link through error correcting codes.
- Traffic shaping: Prioritize packets latency-sensitive applications and apply bandwidth limiting to large data transfers.

Caching, particularly for web traffic, simply means answering client-side requests using local versions of webpage objects such as images, icons, and style page items. These items are stored from previous requests so WAN bandwidth does not need to be consumed sending data that the FortiGate has already received. These items are usually set to expire automatically and to be prefetched when the caching system predicts that a user will need them.

FortiOS and FortiGate Support

Fortinet's WanOPT only works between FortiGate devices running compatible firmware (FortiOS 4.0 and later) or between a FortiGate device and a Windows system running FortiClient 4.2 Premium. The FortiOS firmware release notes from the Fortinet Support site (https://support.fortinet.com) will provide a list of FortiGate models and FortiClient versions that support WanOPT. The Fortinet Documentation site (http://docs.fortinet.com) also provides an excellent guide explaining the various options for configuring WanOPT.

WanOPT can be enabled on a FortiGate running in either NAT/Route or Transparent mode. However, if you wish to filter WanOPT traffic using UTM features, the implementation must separate the functions into different VDOMs.

Hardware Requirements

WanOPT requires some form of storage. This can be built-in internal HDD or SDD, add-in AMC (ASM) or FSM storage modules, or even sufficiently sized flash memory as found on some of the SOHO models (see Table 7.1). Additionally, to support the WanOPT secure-tunnel feature, the FortiGate appliance model must have a FortiASIC CP6 or newer. An exception is the FortiGate-VM, which implements the functionality in software but incurs a performance penalty. Finally, bear in mind that WanOPT is CPU and I/O intensive and can significantly increase the system load on a FortiGate. Therefore it is recommended that 100-class models and higher be considered if WanOPT is necessary.

Table 7.1 provides a sample list of the FortiGate models supporting WanOPT.

Table 7.1 WanOPT Supporting FortiGate Models (2011–2012)

Model	FortiASIC	Storage (minimum/default)
FG-51B	CP6	Internal 32 GB SSD
FG/FW-60C	CP7 (FortiSoC)	8 GB nand Flash
FG/FW-80C(M)	CP7	8 GB nand Flash
FG-111C	CP6	FSM 64 GB SSD
FG-100D	CP8	Internal 16 GB
FG-200B	CP6	FSM 64 GB SSD (add-in)
FG-310B	CP6	ASM-08 80 GB HDD (add-in)
FG-311B	CP6	Internal 64 GB SSD

Table 7.1 WanOPT Supporting FortiGate Models (2011–2012) (*continued*)

Model	FortiASIC	Storage (minimum/default)
FG-300C	CP6	Internal 32 GB
FG-620B	CP6	ASM-08 80 GB HDD (add-in)
FG-621B	CP6	Internal 64 GB SSD
FG-600C	CP8	Internal 64 GB SSD
FG-1000C	CP8	Internal 128 GB SSD
FG-1240B	CP6	Internal 64 GB SSD
FG-3016B	CP6	ASM-08 80 GB HDD (add-in)
FG-3040B	CP7	rev1 FSM 64 GB SSD
		rev2 Internal 256 GB SSD
FG-3140B	CP7	FSM 64 GB SSD
FG-3240C	CP8	Internal 64 GB SSD
FG-3600A	CP6	ASM-08 80 GB HDD (add-in)
FG-3810A	CP6	ASM-08[a] 80 GB HDD (add-in)
FG-3950B	CP6	FSM-064 64 GB SSD (add-in)
FG-VM (32/64-bit)	N/A	30 GB (min.) [virtual disk]

[a] *Newer ASM-08 units are 500 GB capacity.*

WanOPT Deployment Basics

Detailed explanations of the WanOPT GUI and CLI configuration can be found in the official Fortinet documentation for WAN Optimization [1] as well as the CLI reference guide [2] (see http://docs.fortinet.com). Instead of duplicating this information, this section explains some WanOPT concepts and provides guidelines for specific scenarios.

WanOPT is implemented between two "WanOPT peers" which establish a tunnel, optionally encrypted, through which the optimized traffic will flow. WanOPT peering can be between two FortiGate units or between a FortiGate unit and a FortiClient PC. Specific WanOPT rules determine which traffic flows will be selected for optimization and how the optimization will be applied. If a NAT/Route VDOM is used, then the traffic must also be routable. When a WanOPT rule is applied to a new traffic flow, the peer "A" which initiates the WanOPT tunnel is called the "client-side," while the other peer "B" is termed "server-side." This "client-side" and "server-side" labeling is applicable in the context of a single WanOPT rule and the associated WanOPT tunnel. Another WanOPT rule may flip orientation with peer "B" as the client-side and peer "A" the server-side.

UTM inspection enabled in a firewall policy will override the WanOPT rule and cause the WanOPT rule to be ignored in a given VDOM. Thus, if you wish both UTM inspection and WanOPT, you must cause the traffic to cascade between VDOMs. The first VDOM will perform the UTM inspection and the second will do WanOPT. The ordering is important and the traffic must first be inspected and then optimized. This is because, once optimized, the traffic can be substantially altered by the data compression and byte-caching techniques, so the UTM inspection proxies or flow detection will not see original files or data objects. When cascading VDOMs, it is common for the WanOPT VDOM to be in NAT/Route mode while the UTM VDOM is in Transparent. It is certainly feasible to switch this mode arrangement or even set them both to the same mode, if it makes sense in your network environment.

The WanOPT VDOM must have associated firewall rules that allow the incoming traffic, but without any UTM inspection profiles enabled.

The WanOPT rules are evaluated and processed in a top-down fashion and applying the first matching rule. However, if there are no matching WanOPT rules for a particularly traffic flow, no optimization is applied and the flow is processed normally using the firewall security rules.

WanOPT Deployment Strategies

Before configuring the devices, you should consider your network environment and the constraints or overall plan for the WanOPT deployment. Some questions that can be useful in choosing which WanOPT functions or options to use are listed below:

- How many sites will require WanOPT?
- Will only a handful of sites peer with one another or with a main central location?
- Will the sites be statically addressed or use dynamic addressing (DHCP or PPPoE)?
- Is this for road warriors equipped with PCs running FortiClient Host Security software?
- Will there be a VPN between the sites where the peers are located?
- Do you already have a PKI for use with the WanOPT peer authentication?
- What type of application traffic or protocols will be used?

WanOPT with Peer-to-Peer Rules

When there are only a few WAN links where WanOPT is required, the simplest set-up is with "peer-to-peer" rules. The peer FortiGate units that are to be allowed to initiate or receive WanOPT tunnels are predefined by a unique short identification name and IP address. WanOPT peer authentication is optional, but should be used in most cases as it improves security with minimal overhead. With a peer-to-peer rule configuration, only the site (client-side peer) which initiates the request for the WanOPT tunnel has the rule explicitly specifying the other peer device (server-side peer). On the server-side peer, we need only to define the requesting client-side IP address in the WanOPT peers list.

The peer-to-peer WanOPT rules need to specify, at minimum, the source and destination addresses, destination TCP port, optimization protocol type, and the server-side peer-ID. By default, byte caching and transparent options are enabled. The variations and peculiarities of the individual protocol-typed flows selected by a WanOPT rule for optimization can cause the optimization to vary and be unpredictable. There can be at least some link efficiency improvement from the TCP-generic byte caching even if the protocol optimization techniques provide marginal effect for a given packet flow.

The transparent setting in the WanOPT rule controls how the server-side peer will populate the source address field of the packets sent to the destination. When WanOPT transparency is enabled, the actual requesting client IP address is used; otherwise when transparency is disabled, the server-side FortiGate will use its nearest interface IP address to the destination. Transparency is enabled by default since it is expected that for applications using HTTP, CIFS, and MAPI, visibility of the originating source IP address is preferred or even required. However, there are certain scenarios where disabling this can simplify routing or access control. The WanOPT transparent setting can be treated as a "WanOPT NAT" and should not be confused with VDOM transparent mode operation.

The ordering of the WanOPT rules is significant. First, the traffic must be accepted by a standard firewall security policy and, so long as UTM inspection is not enabled, the WanOPT rules are evaluated and processed in a top-down fashion. The first WanOPT rule that matches will be applied and subsequent rules will be ignored. The matching of a WanOPT rule is based upon a triplet of source address, destination address, and destination port. This then causes the creation of a separate WanOPT tunnel for each rule to WanOPT peer specified by the particular rule. When there are only a few WanOPT rules, the separate tunnels are not much of an issue. When there are many WanOPT rules for different traffic flows, the additional overhead may become noticeable. There is an option to allow sharing a WanOPT tunnel between rules but this is only recommended for traffic types with similar behavior and latency tolerances. So-called aggressive protocols which will tend to use as much available bandwidth as possible, such as HTTP and FTP, should remain in their own "private" WanOPT tunnels. However, a TCP protocol for an interactive and delay-sensitive application like Telnet could use "express sharing" for the WanOPT tunnel.

Whether the WanOPT transparent setting is enabled or not depends on two factors:

- Does the destination server or application need the client-side IP address?
- Does the destination server have a routable path for the client-side IP address?

If "yes" can be answered for each of these questions, then WanOPT transparent mode should be enabled. If you do not know for sure if WanOPT transparency is required by the destination server or application, you may need to experiment. The optimized traffic can be NAT'ed on a path between the client-side and server-side FortiGate units by a firewall security policy, but at the server-side, the packets to the destination server will use the IP address as determined by the WanOPT transparency setting. If you encounter downstream routing or access issues, consider this.

Finally, if the path between the two peers is not already through a private dedicated connection or a VPN tunnel, you may need to use encryption. A WanOPT tunnel can be secured with AES 128-bit CBC SSL encryption over port 7810 (same TCP port as nonencrypted WanOPT tunnels). If there is only WanOPT traffic between the two sites, it is feasible to just use a secure WanOPT tunnel and to dispense with configuration of a separate VPN tunnel between the peers. Of course the reverse argument could also be made if there is a VPN tunnel already established between the peers. This avoids unnecessary system load from double-encryption.

A secured WanOPT tunnel between the client- and server-side FortiGate units requires an authentication group ("auth-group") be set up with the same name and PSK or certificate on both client- and server-sides. The WanOPT auth-group can also serve to distinguish between different groupings of WanOPT peers. A WanOPT rule can specify an auth-group and the name must be present on both peers and contain the same authentication method and parameters (pre-shared key or certificate reference).

Example of Peer-to-Peer with WanOPT Secure Tunnel

The following is an example configuration for two FortiGate units in NAT/Route operation with a peer-to-peer WanOPT secure tunnel. Client-side host "T123" will construct a secured WanOPT tunnel to Server-side "A777" for web, file transfer, and Microsoft Exchange traffic as well as for generic TCP traffic as well.

Client-Side FortiGate Peer-to-Peer WanOPT Set-up

1. Define local host-ID, WanOPT traffic logging, and secure-tunnel strength.

```
config wanopt settings
  set host-id "T123"
  set log-traffic http mapi cifs ftp tcp
  set tunnel-ssl-algorithm medium
end
```

2. Define server-side FortiGate unit ID and IP address. (The server-side IP address can be that of any interface on the server-peer running in NAT/Route VDOM mode or, if running in Transparent mode, the management IP address.)

```
config wanopt peer
  edit "A777"
    set ip 192.168.11.138
  next
end
```

3. WanOPT authentication group for secure-tunnel operation.

The name of the authentication group must be the same on both peers. For simplicity, only the pre-shared key authentication limited to the specific server-side host-id is shown. For X.509 certificate authentication, refer to the FortiOS CLI guide.

```
config wanopt auth-group
    edit "wauth01"
        set auth-method psk
        set peer-accept one
        set psk "some-good-preshared-secret-for-wanopt-tunnel"
        set peer "A777"
    next
end
```

4. Add the WanOPT rules.

In this example, we want to optimize and secure the traffic from two web servers. WanOPT transparency is enabled in rule #1 for most traffic. It is then disabled in rule #2 for FTP traffic. If permitted by the the firewall security policy, other client-side addresses outside the specified source range in rule #1 can still access the web servers but will lack protocol or data optimization. Note the explicit setting of the server-side peer ID in the WanOPT rules. Rules for other server-side peers can be distinguished with the "set peer" parameter setting.

```
config wanopt rule
    edit 1
        set src-ip 10.168.10.11-10.168.10.20
        set dst-ip 172.17.97.118-172.17.97.119
        set auto-detect off
        set transparent enable
        set port 80
        set proto http
        set peer "A777"
        set secure-tunnel enable
        set auth-group "wauth01"
    next
    edit 2
        set dst-ip 172.17.97.117
        set auto-detect off
        set transparent disable
        set port 21
        set proto ftp
        set peer "A777"
        set secure-tunnel enable
        set auth-group "wauth01"
    next
end
```

5. Routing to destination server.

Just as if WanOPT is not being used, the valid route to the destination server is required. In this example, we use a static route but dynamic routing could also be used. Technically, the destination route needs only to point to a path that includes the server-side FortiGate unit, but in practice specifying the destination route is considered better as it allows a connection to be made in case there is an issue with WanOPT.

```
config router static
  edit 10
    set dst 172.17.97.0 255.255.255.0
    set device wan1
    set gateway 192.168.11.254
  next
end
```

6. Firewall security policies.

To allow the traffic the client-side must have a matching firewall policy. NAT is needed only if routing requires it. WanOPT takes priority over traffic shaping, so any traffic shaping in the matching firewell policy will be ignored. As mentioned previously, UTM must not be enabled.

```
config firewall policy
  edit 2
    set srcintf "internal"
    set dstintf "wan1"
      set srcaddr "all"
      set dstaddr "net-172-17-97-0"
    set action accept
    set schedule "always"
      set service "HTTP" FTP"
  next
end
```

This completes the client-side WanOPT peer configuration. Next we will step through the server-side peer configuration.

Server-Side FortiGate Peer-to-Peer WanOPT Set-up

1. Define local host-ID and WanOPT traffic logging.

The host-id must be unique for all WanOPT peers connecting to this unit.

```
config wanopt settings
  set host-id "A777"
  set log-traffic http mapi cifs ftp tcp
end
```

2. Set up peer list.

The client-side peer name must match its WanOPT host-id and IP address of the interface to be used to connect to the server-side peer.

```
config wanopt peer
  edit "T123"
    set ip 192.168.11.128
  next
end
```

3. WanOPT authentication for secure tunnel.

The authentication group name and method must be the same as the client-side but the "peer-accept" may differ. In this case, for convenience when managing the server-side, all the defined peers are members of this auth-group. It would likely be the case that all the WanOPT peers will have need to access the server-side site.

```
config wanopt auth-group
  edit "wauth01"
    set auth-method psk
    set peer-accept defined
    set psk "some-good-preshared-secret-for-wanopt-tunnel"
  next
end
```

4. WanOPT Rules.

The server-side of a peer-to-peer WanOPT tunnel does not need any explicit WanOPT rules to accept and process the optimization request from the client-side. In fact, the client-side WanOPT rule provides the directives for the server-side so in a peer-to-peer WanOPT configuration, both the client- and server-side behave as a coordinated WanOPT device pair.

5. Routing to destination server.

Because the server-side receives the rules from the client-side, the only requirement is a valid route to the destination server. Depending on the client-side WanOPT transparency setting, the packet sent will have the original client IP address ("set transparent enable") or use the server-side FortiGate IP address ("set transparent disable").

```
config router static
  edit 20
    set dst 172.17.97.0 255.255.255.0
    set device dmz
    set gateway 192.168.21.254
  next
end
```

SECURING WANOPT USING IPSEC VPN TUNNEL

To secure the WanOPT traffic, there is an alternative to SSL encryption. A WanOPT tunnel can be carried by an IPSec VPN interface-mode tunnel. The only configuration needed is to add a route that uses an IPSec interface. Basically, in this configuration, there will be an IPSec VPN tunnel between the two WanOPT peers for carrying other generic traffic. You can take advantage of the IPSec tunnel's encryption to secure the WanOPT traffic. In the client-side WanOPT rules shown above, add "set secure-tunnel disable" to turn off the WanOPT tunnel SSL encryption feature.

6. Firewall security policies.

No explicit firewall security policy is required on the server-side FortiGate for the peer-to-peer WanOPT tunnel. So long as a valid route is available from the server-side FortiGate, the requests to and responses from the destination server are allowed for the WanOPT tunnel traffic.

If it is desired to control access for the WanOPT tunnel, then just as the case for applying UTM inspection, a second Vdom is required: one Vdom for WanOPT, one for access control.

Example of Active-Passive WanOPT Rule Deployment

This example shows WanOPT using Active-Passive rules. Here, we will disable the WanOPT secure-tunnel function and rely on an already configured IPSec VPN interface-mode tunnel between the client-side FortiGate unit and the server-side FortiGate location. WanOPT peer definitions are not required for the Active-Passive set-up, but if you need to distinguish between the multiple allowed endpoints, a WanOPT authentication group would be used. If you need to further distinguish or separate WanOPT endpoint groups, add additional WanOPT authentication groups with unique names.

Client-side FortiGate Active-Passive WanOPT Set-up

1. Local WanOPT settings: Host-ID.

The WanOPT local host-id must be unique across all the other WanOPT peers that could form a connection. This short-name can be different from the FortiGate's assigned hostname. The settings for the WanOPT secure-tunnel encryption strength and WanOPT traffic logging are also set here.

```
config wanopt settings
   set host-id "T123"
   set log-traffic http mapi cifs ftp tcp
   set tunnel-ssl-algorithm medium
end
```

2. WanOPT authentication group.

Although the WanOPT secure-tunnel will not be used in this example, authentication groups can be used to distinguish between different groups of WanOPT client-side peers connecting to the same server-side peer. Since we are not explicitly configuring the WanOPT peers, the auth-group setting is for "any" peer and will match as long as the same auth-group name and parameters are present when attempting to establish the WanOPT tunnel.

```
config wanopt auth-group
  edit "wauth02"
    set auth-method psk
    set peer-accept any
    set psk "another-good-psk-string"
      next
end
```

3. Add WanOPT rules.

The rules shown here are the equivalent Active-Passive rules as shown in the previous peer-to-peer example. To indicate an active rule, "auto-detect" is set to active and there is no "set peer" setting. WanOPT rule #1 is specific for source addresses in a range between 10.168.10.11 and 10.168.10.20 to destination servers in the range 172.17.97.118 to 172.17.97.119 for HTTP traffic on the well-known TCP port 80 with the server-side WanOPT peer presenting the actual source address to the destination server. Rule #2 allows any source address to the specific destination server at 172.17.97.117 for FTP traffic on the well-known TCP port 21.

These WanOPT rules are the triggers for the WanOPT tunnels that will cause the client-side FortiGate to attempt to establish an optimization connection with a server-side FortiGate. Since there are no explicitly defined WanOPT peers in the Active-Passive rule set-up, the client-side FortiGate adds data in the TCP option area. When this is detected by an upstream server-side FortiGate, it opens a proprietary WanOPT tunnel communication on TCP port 7810 between the peers to negotiate the WanOPT parameters and complete the WanOPT authentication.

```
config wanopt rule
  edit 1
    set src-ip 10.168.10.11-10.168.10.20
    set dst-ip 172.17.97.118-172.17.97.119
    set auto-detect active
    set transparent enable
    set port 80
    set proto http
    set auth-group "wauth02"
  next
```

```
    edit 2
      set dst-ip 172.17.97.117
      set auto-detect active
      set transparent disable
      set port 21
      set proto ftp
      set auth-group "wauth02"
    next
end
```

4. Routing to destination server.

There needs to be a valid route, static or dynamic, to the destination server. Since a matching firewall security policy must exist before any WanOPT rules are checked, a destination route is mandatory.

```
config router static
  edit 10
    set dst 172.17.97.0 255.255.255.0
    set device wan1
    set gateway 192.168.11.254
  next
end
```

5. Firewall security policies.

A destination server matching firewall security policy will use an outgoing IPSec VPN interface to the server-side FortiGate, so no NAT will be required to traverse the VPN tunnel. UTM inspection must not be enabled.

```
config firewall policy
  edit 2
    set srcintf "internal"
    set dstintf "To-server-side-VPN"
      set srcaddr "net-10-168-11-0"
      set dstaddr "net-172-17-97-0"
    set action accept
    set schedule "always"
      set service "HTTP" "FTP"
  next
end
```

This completes the client-side WanOPT peer configuration. Next, we will step through the server-side peer configuration.

Server-side FortiGate Active-Passive WanOPT Set-up

1. Define local host-ID and WanOPT traffic logging.

The host-id must be a unique name and different from that of any other WanOPT peer connecting to this unit.

```
config wanopt settings
  set host-id "A777"
  set log-traffic http mapi cifs ftp tcp
end
```

2. WanOPT authentication.

This authentication group name and method must be the same as the client-side. In this example the authentication group allows a coarse distinction between groups of clients that access a particular destination server using one WanOPT rule or another. There is only a loose authentication grouping used here since as long as the auth-group name and pre-shared keys match between a pair of peers, the WanOPT authentication will succeed.

```
config wanopt auth-group
  edit "wauth02"
    set auth-method psk
    set peer-accept any
    set psk "another-good-psk-string"
  next
end
```

3. WanOPT Rules.

The active to passive rule list does not have to be one-to-one between Client and Server-side. It is typical to have several active rules on one side and a single (or fewer) "receiving" passive rule on the other side of the WanOPT connection.

```
config wanopt rule
  edit 1
    set src-ip 10.168.10.1-10.168.10.254
    set dst-ip 172.17.97.1-172.17.97.120
    set port 21-80
    set auto-detect passive
  set auth-group "wauth02"
  next
end
```

The server-side has "auto-detect" set to passive and specifies only the target destination ports along with the source and destination address ranges for the optimized traffic. Notice that the scope of the addresses and ports in the server-side passive rule can be wider than the corresponding client-side rule to simplify the server-side configuration. This is useful when there are other client-side peers that may be using slightly different but nearby addresses for their WanOPT traffic.

4. Routing to destination server.

The server-side of a WanOPT tunnel gets the rule information from the client-side FortiGate and the only set-up requirement is a valid route to the destination server. Depending on the client-side WanOPT transparency setting, the packet sent will have the original client IP address (set transparent enable) or use the server-side FortiGate IP address (set transparent disable).

```
config router static
   edit 20
      set dst 172.17.97.0 255.255.255.0
      set device dmz
      set gateway 192.168.21.254
   next
end
```

5. Firewall security policies.

The server-side firewall security policy must match or encompass the request traffic stream just as if WanOPT were not being used. Once again, for the WanOPT functionality to work, UTM functions must not be enabled in this VDOM firewall policy.

```
config firewall policy
   edit 2
      set srcintf "Server-side-VPN"
      set dstintf "dmz"
        set srcaddr "net-10-168-11-0"
        set dstaddr "net-172-17-97-0"
      set action accept
      set schedule "always"
        set service "HTTP" "FTP"
   next
end
```

The above server-side example firewall policy does not have NAT enabled, so it is the *client-side* WanOPT rule transparency setting that determines whether the server sees the actual client PC address that of the server-side FortiGate. Referring back to the client-side WanOPT rule, "set transparent enable" will mean that the server will see requests from the 10.168.11.0 subnet. Now the server-side firewall policy can override the WanOPT transparency with enabling NAT.

The interaction between the WanOPT rule transparency and firewall policy NAT can lead to some misconfiguration that will prevent the WanOPT traffic from passing

Table 7.2 WanOPT Rule and Firewall Policy Combinations

Client-side			Server-side
WanOPT Rule	**Firewall Policy**	**Rcv'd Src-IP**	**Sent Src-IP[a]**
set transparent enable	set nat disable	PC-addr	PC-addr
set transparent disable	set nat disable	PC-addr	Server-FG
set transparent enable	set nat enable	Client-FG	PC-addr
set transparent disable	set nat enable	Client-FG	Server-FG
[a] *Subject to Server-side firewall policy NAT setting.*			

through as expected. To help avoid the firewall policy issues, Table 7.2 shows the net outcome for the possible combinations of WanOPT transparency and firewall policy NAT.

Depending on the overall network topology and routing restrictions, there may be a need for any of these combinations. One must just understand which client-side settings are being used and then, which corresponding settings may be required in the server-side firewall policy to allow the WanOPT traffic to reach the destination server.

Peer-to-Peer and Active-Passive WanOPT Comparison

This section presented two simple but different methods for configuring WanOPT in FortiOS. The first section listed some questions to consider and now after seeing the Peer-to-Peer and Active-Passive methods some generalities can be drawn.

The simplest or easiest set-up is Peer-to-Peer when:

- A small number of sites exist between which WanOPT is desired.
- IP addresses are static.

With Peer-to-Peer, the WanOPT rules and firewall security policies are on the client-side. The server-side need only have routes to the destination server. If the server-side is required to have its own firewall security policies to further control access to the destination server, these must be put in another VDOM or FortiGate unit placed between the server-side WanOPT VDOM and the destination server. This second server-side VDOM would also be the location where any further UTM inspection could be applied.

In a scenario where the client-side peers use dynamic addressing such as DHCP-connected FortiGate units or when there may be many tens or even hundreds of potential peers in the form of FortiClient equipped PCs, it is impractical to set-up individual WanOPT peer entries. Instead, authentication is based on a pre-shared key (or X.509 certificates) that can be used along with Active-Passive WanOPT rules that do not require explicitly specified peers.

WEB CACHING

As mentioned, web caching can be considered an form of Wan Optimization in that you are saving bandwidth by avoiding repeated fetching image or other webpage objects across a WAN link. Instead, it saves local copies that can be substituted and supplied to the requesting client over the local LAN at speeds one or two orders of magnitude faster. Web caching is automatically applied for HTTP WanOPT rules. Web caching can also be implemented separately by using an Explicit Web Proxy configured on an interface, or by enabling within a firewall security policy in which case a Transparent Web Proxy is used. For technical details, please refer to the Web Caching section of the FortiOS Handbook at http://docs.fortinet.com. Here, we will highlight only the foundational concepts and provide practical caveats for the set-up and use of Web Caching in firewall policies.

Firewall Policy Caching

Firewall security policies that use web caching will apply caching only to unencrypted HTTP traffic. If HTTPS caching is desired, you must use a WanOPT policy. Also, if you wish to cache HTTP traffic on ports other than 80, you must modify the "protocol-options" configuration.

Firewall policy web caching will take place before WanOPT caching. UTM inspection is also supported for the HTTP cached traffic, so some files or objects may be blocked or replaced according to the UTM profiles applied to this firewall policy.

The example below shows the relevant CLI commands for web caching and UTM inspection for web traffic on the well-known TCP port and for web proxy traffic on TCP port 8080.

```
config firewall profile-protocol-options
    edit custom-HTTP-proto
        config http
            set port 80 8080
        end
    next
end
configure firewall policy
    edit 1
        ...
        set webcache enable
        set utm-status enable
        set profile-protocol-options custom-HTTP-proto
        ...
    next
end
```

Web Cache Exemption

It may be necessary for certain Websites to be exempted from web caching for performance or legal reasons. The URL or IP address of sites not to be cached can be listed in "config wanopt webcache." Any pattern in the URL string can be specified, so objects from URLs containing the string will not be cached.

```
config wanopt webcache
  set cache-exemption enable
    config cache-exemption-list
      set url-pattern www.example.com
      set status enable
      end
  ...
end
```

The "config wanopt webcache" configuration also contains other settings for adjusting the web caching behavior. These usually do not require modification from the default settings. Detailed descriptions of these other options can be found in the FortiOS CLI Reference.

ENDPOINT CONTROL

Endpoint Control is a subset of Network Access Control (NAC), which ensures that workstation computers meet security requirements or they are not permitted. Endpoint Control can be thought of as the set of methods enforcing compliance of client software running on the client computer. Fortinet's implementation of Endpoint Control combines FortiGate functionality with FortiClient software installed on the client PC. At the time of writing, FortiClient is available for several versions of the Microsoft Windows operating system in both 32bit or 64bit versions. There are no per-seat licensing costs for FortiClient when used with the Endpoint-Control feature, only a one time cost for a FortiClient license key use, which would vary based on FortiGate platforms used with the Endpoint-Control feature. Use of Endpoint Control means enforcing the use of the FortiClient software, the presence of specific applications, and the absence or blocking of other specific applications. Any non-compliant computers are either quarantined or issued a warning with a link for downloading the FortiClient installation package. Optionally, they may be provided with a method to access the network in a non-compliant state.

Requirements

Full Endpoint Control functionality requires the installation of FortiClient Host Security software (version 4.2 or later) on the client PC. Most current FortiGate units have at least the minimum 128 MB flash storage and are able to act as a distribution server for the FortiClient installation package. Even if the FortiGate model does not support native storage of the FortiClient installer, you may specify a URL as an alternate download location.

Prior to enabling Endpoint Control, you must determine the version and specific FortiClient feature configuration for the intended network environment. Although you can set up Endpoint Control with the factory-default settings, a typical FortiClient deployment usually includes some organization-specific configuration settings. A customized FortiClient installer is beyond the scope of this chapter, so we shall assume that a suitable FortiClient installer package has already been prepared by the administrator. This package would be uploaded to FortiGate or provided as a URL download link in the Endpoint-Control Warning message.

Currently, the FortiClient only installs on Microsoft Windows 2000 or later. When Endpoint Control is enabled, other computers will be blocked by a firewall security policy and the FortiGate will be unable to gather statistics and environmental information about these devices.

FortiClient and FortiGate Communication

Endpoint Control involves communication between FortiClient and an upstream FortiGate unit. Depending on the version of FortiClient installed on the client PC, there are slight variations in the discovery, keepalive, and message passing. The process is described for FortiClient 4.3.1 and later:

1. Upon startup FortiClient sends a specially formatted HTTP-GET request message containing some basic status information about its Antivirus, Web Filtering, and Firewall settings to a FortiGuard Distribution Server (FDS) network address. The FortiClient PC sends this HTTP message not knowing where or even if there is a FortiGate in its network environment.
2. If there is a FortiGate in the path, it intercepts this HTTP message and compares the FortiClient status with the endpoint-control compliance settings of the profile for the firewall policy which received the FortiClient's transmission. If found compliant, the FortiGate returns a message to the FortiClient asking for more information about the endpoint (such as installed and running applications), as well as the IP of a FortiGate interface which is reachable from FortiClient host. Otherwise, a "blocking" message is sent back and further traffic from the FortiClient IP address is blocked.
3. The FortiClient PC then responds to the FortiGate request with information of the installed and running applications in a series of messages to the FortiGate IP address specified in the FortiGate's initial request message.
4. The FortiGate then determines if the FortiClient endpoint is compliant based upon the application list of the firewall policy endpoint-control profile and creates an authenticated policy session that effectively whitelists all subsequent traffic from that endpoint. The endpoint traffic is not checked until a period of idle time occurs that is longer than the `"compliance-timeout"` setting.

5. The FortiClient PC will periodically send keep-alive messages with AV, firewall, and web filtering status and application list information to the FortiGate IP address.

6. The FortiGate updates the compliancy status of the endpoint based on the keep-alive messages and sends the result back to the FortiClient PC, as well as resetting the "compliance-timeout" countdown timer for that endpoint.

7. If the FortiClient keep-alive message is not received when it is expected by the FortiGate, such as when the endpoint was shut down or put into a sleep mode, the endpoint information is stored for the duration of the compliance-timeout idle time, after which its authentication entry is removed and any subsequent traffic from that endpoint IP address is blocked until a new endpoint compliancy check can be performed.

FortiClient 4.2.x behaves somewhat differently since it lacks the keep-alive mechanism. Once the FortiGate has an authenticated entry for a specific client, that status is not re-checked. In practice, this means that compliance is only re-checked for that client should all sessions terminate and the compliance-timeout is reached. If you are using this version of FortiClient, you can moderate your risk somewhat by adjusting the "compliance-timeout" value via the CLI.

If you make a change to the Endpoint policy and want it to take effect immediately, working on both new connections and existing connected clients, you must first remove the existing authentication sessions, thus re-enforcing the Endpoint verification.

Endpoint Configuration

Endpoint Control has three components that must be configured to provide endpoint security:

1. Define the minimal endpoint client characteristics.

2. Define certain applications for software detection (running and/or installed).

3. Enable Endpoint Control in the desired firewall traffic policy.

Endpoint Minimum Settings

The download location and minimum accepted version of FortiClient is set in "config endpoint-control settings." An inactivity timer for compliant endpoints is also set here so endpoints may be queried regularly.

```
# Factory-default settings
config endpoint-control settings
    set compliance-timeout 5
    set download-location fortiguard
    set enforce-minimum-version disable
end
```

GLOBAL SETTINGS

There are two Endpoint-Control settings under "config system global" that determine if non-compliant endpoints have access to FortiGuard Services and to specify the TCP port used for the Endpoint-Control portal. This applies for any and all Vdoms so it is not possible to have Vdom-specific settings for these two Endpoint-Control paramters.

```
config system global
  set endpoint-control-fds-access enable
  set endpoint-control-portal-port 8009
end
```

```
#Example customized settings
config endpoint-control settings
    set compliance-timeout 15
    set download-location custom
    set enforce-minimum-version enable
    set version 4.2.5
set download-custom-link "http://get.example.com/forticlient/"
end
```

Application Detection List

Application detection lists define which applications should be running or at least installed on the client computer. When an application is detected, it is matched with the defined action: allowed, denied, or monitored. As of this writing, there are over 7500 applications assigned to one of 37 categories to simplify management. Once an application detection list is defined, it can be used in an Endpoint-Control profile.

Configuration of an application list in the CLI is a challenging and time-consuming activity since an integer ID must be specified for the specific application or category group or vendor. The factory-default configuration provides some sample lists that show the structure as shown below:

```
config endpoint-control app-detect rule-list
    edit "Block_P2P_application"
        config entries
            edit 1
                set category 15
                set status running
            next
        end
    set comment "deny access from endpoints running P2P applications"
```

```
        set other-application-action allow
    next
    edit "Monitor_Microsoft_Office"
        config entries
            edit 1
                set category 31
                set vendor 53
                set action monitor
            next
        end
        set comment "monitor installed Microsoft Office applications"
        set other-application-action allow
    next
    edit "Monitor_game"
        config entries
            edit 1
                set category 20
                set action monitor
            set status running
            next
        end
        set comment "monitor running games"
        set other-application-action allow
    next
    edit "Monitor_Internet_browser"
        config entries
            edit 1
                set category 12
                set action monitor
            next
        end
        set comment "monitor installed Internet browsers"
        set other-application-action allow
    next
end
```

Endpoint Control is likely to be configured using the FortiGate GUI and the set-up should be intuitive, but if needed detailed instructions are available in the FortiOS UTM Handbook. When using the GUI, the application detection list is part of the

Endpoint-Control profile screen and there is no separate menu item for the application detection list set-up. Here, we will show a CLI approach to setting up Endpoint Control.

Viewing the corresponding application, category or vendor from the ID number in the CLI configuration is possible with the "get" command when in the context of a specific entry.

```
FG111C-TEST (rule-list) # edit Block_P2P_application
FG111C-TEST (Block_P2P_appl~c) # config entries
FG111C-TEST (entries) # edit 1
FG111C-TEST (1) # get
id              : 1
application : any
category     : P2P File Sharing
vendor        : any
tags:
action        : deny
status        : running
```

Each application detection list has a unique name and, if enclosed with quotes, can include whitespace. The list name will be referenced in an Endpoint profile so a best practice is to use an obvious name to indicate the association. The application detection list specifies applications as separate entries. An entry can be either a single application or a group reference (category or vendor). Typically, you would specify at least one of these selection parameters, though if unset, they will default to "all." Each application entry has an associated "status" and "action" setting:

status: what condition is satisfied by the application matching this entry rule; *action*: how should the FortiGate will treat the endpoint traffic. This is not application-specific, but applies to all traffic from the particular endpoint.

The list is processed from top to bottom and when the first matching application condition is found, that entry's action is invoked by the FortiGate. Specific application entries should be entered before entries for a vendor or a category. A "move" command can be use to reorder application entries to achieve the desired ordering.

Application detection lists are created in the CLI in "config endpoint app-detect rule-list" under the sub-section "config entries." Each application entry has an index number. Traditionally, they begin with "1," but any positive integer number can be used. Just as with other indexed configuration objects, index "0" is special and means "take the next lowest available". When configuring an application detection list from the CLI start by selecting the category. This list is only 37 items long and can easily be displayed by entering "set category?". Once a category is selected, the displayable applications from "set application ?" becomes more manageable since the category setting pre-filters the output. However, there still may be many items shown. The "set vendor ?" output is, unfortunately, not pre-filtered

> When capturing a long output, it may be convenient to turn off the "more" paging of your CLI session and instead allow the CLI output to continue until completion with "standard" console output mode. This mode is convenient when you are capturing the output of your CLI session to a log file on your management PC.
>
> ```
> config system global ### If Vdoms are enabled ###
> config system console
>   set output standard
> end
> ```

and as there are over 3000 entries attempting to display and choose from the list is impractical. If you are determined to configure the application lists from the CLI, it would be advisable to first prepare by capturing a log file of the output from selected combinations of category and the `set application?"` command.

This example application detection list shows how to block the `"hacking"` category and a specific game application while allowing Microsoft Office applications and warning when two specific P2P applications are running.

```
config endpoint-control app-detect rule-list
    edit "test-ec1"
      config entries
        edit 1
            set application 2306
            set vendor 268
            set action warn
            set status running
        next
        edit 2
            set application 9697
            set category 14
            set action warn
            set status running
        next
        edit 3
            set category 31
            set vendor 211
            set action allow
        next
        edit 4
            set application 5306
```

```
                set category 20
                set status running
            next
            edit 5
                set category 5
            next
        end
    next
end
```

We will use this list in a profile described in the next section.

Endpoint-Control Profile

An Endpoint-Control profile applies an application detection list. Additionally, each Endpoint-Control profile has mandatory non-deletable entries for the FortiClient Host Security software application. If this is unwanted, they can be set to a benign state and effectively ignored. These entries for FortiClient allow you to define the minimum version of FortiClient, whether the FortiClient AntiVirus is running or up-to-date, or if FortiClient Firewall or Web Filtering is running.

An example profile using the application detection list from the previous section is given below. While the profile name and application list have the same name, this is just for convenience. There is no technical requirement that the names be the same.

```
config endpoint-control profile
    edit "test-ec1"
        set application-detection enable
        set application-detection-rule-list "test-ec1"
        set feature-enforcement enable
        set recommendation-disclaimer disable
        set require-av enable
        set require-av-uptodate enable
        set require-firewall enable
        set require-license enable
        set require-webfilter enable
    next
end
```

The resulting application compliance check for this profile is most easily understood through the GUI and is shown in Figure 7.1.

Recall that the Endpoint Check works from the top down. The first application checked is FortiClient, and indeed, if FortiClient is not installed or not running, then there will no further information available about the subsequent applications in the list.

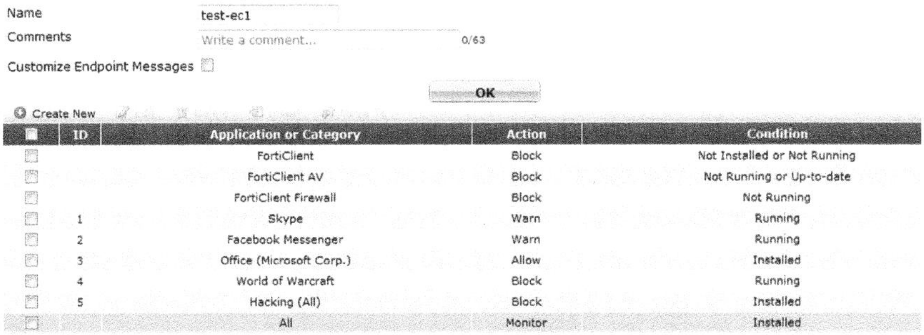

Name   test-ec1

Comments   Write a comment...   0/63

Customize Endpoint Messages ☐

OK

○ Create New

☐	ID	Application or Category	Action	Condition
☐		FortiClient	Block	Not Installed or Not Running
☐		FortiClient AV	Block	Not Running or Up-to-date
☐		FortiClient Firewall	Block	Not Running
☐	1	Skype	Warn	Running
☐	2	Facebook Messenger	Warn	Running
☐	3	Office (Microsoft Corp.)	Allow	Installed
☐	4	World of Warcraft	Block	Running
☐	5	Hacking (All)	Block	Installed
☐		All	Monitor	Installed

FIGURE 7.1 A Sceenshot of the GUI for an Endpoint Profile Using example "test-ec1" Application Detection List

In the above example, it is important to avoid situations where a banned application (in this example, a game called "World of Warcraft") would be allowed as long as there was a Microsoft Office application installed. The Microsoft Office application rule check occurs prior to the check for running game. This shows the importance of the application list ordering and also points to the importance of testing a particular Endpoint-Profile application to ensure that the desired outcome is met. A simple fix is to put the blocking application rules above the other application rules to ensure the desired behavior; in this example, entries #4 and #5 should be before entry #1 for Skype.

```
FG111C-TEST # conf endpoint-control app-detect rule-list
FG111C-TEST (rule-list) # ed test-ec1
FG111C-TEST (test-ec1) # conf entries
FG111C-TEST (entries) # move 4 before 1
FG111C-TEST (entries) # move 5 before 1
FG111C-TEST (entries) # show
config entries
  edit 4
    set application 5306
    set category 20
      set status running
  next
  edit 5
    set category 5
  next
  edit 1
    set application 2306
```

```
      set vendor 268
      set action warn
      set status running
    next
    edit 2
      set application 9697
      set category 14
      set action warn
      set status running
    next
    edit 3
      set category 31
      set vendor 211
      set action allow
    next
  end
FG111C-TEST (entries) # end
```

There is a workflow difference when using the CLI versus the GUI for Endpoint Control set-up. When configuring through the GUI, the Endpoint profile and associated application list are created from the same screens and appear to just be part of the profile set-up. However, when using the CLI, the application detection list is first defined and then the list is referenced in the Endpoint profile. The application detection list will have the same name as the profile appended with ".list" suffix. For example, if the GUI was used to create a profile called "ec-test1" with the application compliance rules as shown earlier, the CLI configuration would have an application rule list called "ec-test1.list." This is just as a matter of convenience since through the CLI you can assign any pre-defined application rule list to a profile using `"set application-detection-rule-list"` command.

Endpoint-Control Firewall Security Policy

The final step in the configuration is to apply the Endpoint Control profile in a firewall security policy. The addition of the Endpoint Control has the effect of "pass or deny" for any traffic from the client computer so it can be viewed as an access-control-list function. It would be expected that UTM inspection would be enabled to further control this traffic.

```
config firewall policy
  edit 4
    set srcintf "port1"
    set dstintf "wan1"
      set srcaddr "all"
```

```
        set dstaddr "all"
      set action accept
      set schedule "always"
        set service "ANY"
      set utm-status enable
      set comments "test EC"
      set endpoint-check enable
      set av-profile "default"
      set webfilter-profile "default"
      set profile-protocol-options "default"
      set nat enable
      set endpoint-profile "test-ec1"
    next
end
```

One caveat is that Endpoint Control is not compatible with the User setting for redirecting HTTP authentication to HTTPS. This is sometimes enabled on FortiGate systems when identity-based policies are used with non-FSSO type user groups, that is, with explicit firewall policy user authentication.

```
config user setting
  set auth-secure-http disable
...
```

Monitoring Endpoints

A list of compliant or non-compliant computers can be viewed in the Endpoint Monitor GUI (UTM Profiles > Monitor > Endpoint Monitor). A computer is added to the list when it accesses a Firewall policy that has Endpoint-Control enabled. Once a computer is added to the list, it remains there until the FortiGate is restarted or rebooted. Figure 7.2 provides an overall graphical representation of compliant vs. non-compliant endpoints.

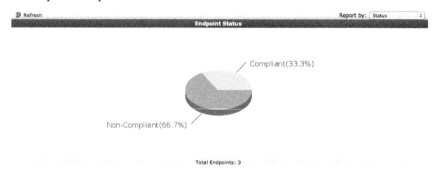

FIGURE 7.2 Endpoint Status GUI Summary

Every time an endpoint computer attempts to access network services through the FortiGate, the entry for the endpoint is updated. This list can provide an inventory of endpoints.

For example:

1. Those systems not running the FortiClient application will be displayed as only an IP address, last update time, and traffic volume/attempts as shown in Figure 7.3.

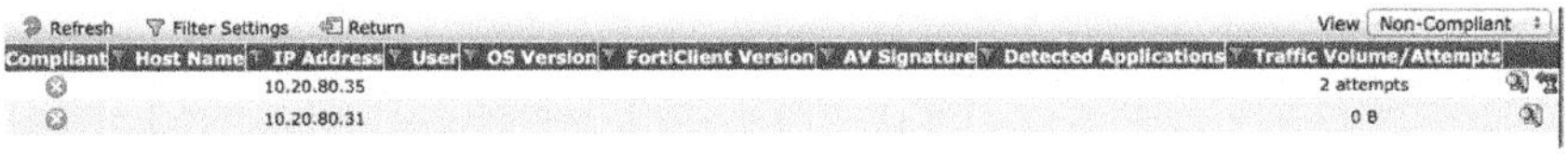

FIGURE 7.3 Non-Compliant Computer List

2. Those running the FortiClient application will show much more information including endpoint hardware and the software running on those computers as shown in Figure 7.4.

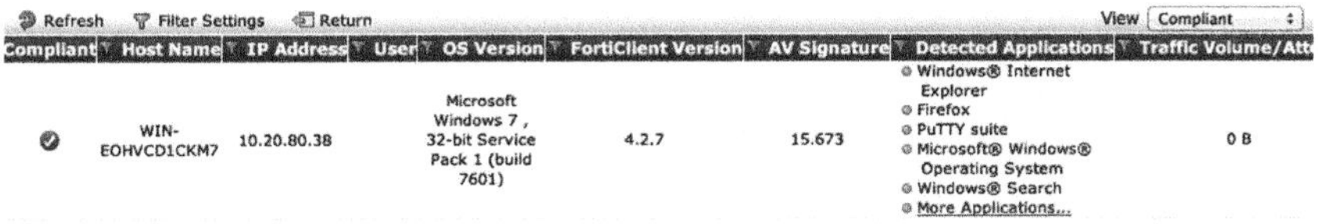

FIGURE 7.4 Compliant Computer List

3. From the endpoint list you can temporarily exempt blocked endpoints and restore exempted endpoints to their blocked state.

The CLI only provides the ability to list the client computer and Endpoint Control information using the following commands:

```
FG111C-TEST (root) # diag endpoint compliant/non-compliant record-list
Record #1:
        IP_Address = 10.20.80.35
        Status: non-compliant, exempted by recommendation disclaimer
        Timeout: 60 seconds
        Last_check_failed: 0
        Con_lic_status: 0
        Con_lic_handle: 0
        Con_lic_granted: 1339353547
        FortiClient version: 0.0.0
        AVDB version: 0.0
        Endpoint Sent Capability Info: no
```

```
            Capability_Not_Support Flag: 0
            Host_Name:
            OS_Version:
            Host_Description:
            Domain:
            Last_Login_User:
            Host_Model:
            Host_Manufacturer:
            CPU_Model:
            Traffic_Amount: 0
            Memory_Size: 0
            Features: 0
            System Uptime: 0
            Installed_Software: 0
            App_List(0):
            Unknown_App_List(0):
            Block_App_List(0:0):
            Monitor_App_List(0:0):
            Traffic_Statistics(0):
    Record #2:
            IP_Address = 10.20.80.31
            Status: non-compliant, exempted by recommendation disclaimer
            Timeout: 254 seconds
            Last_check_failed: 0
            Con_lic_status: 0
            Con_lic_handle: 0
            Con_lic_granted: 1339353547
            FortiClient version: 0.0.0

    .. .
    Record #3:
            IP_Address = 10.20.80.38
            Status: compliant
            Timeout: 163 seconds
            Last_check_failed: 0
            Con_lic_status: 0
            Con_lic_handle: 0
            Con_lic_granted: 1339353812
            FortiClient version: 4.2.7
```

```
AVDB version: 11.901
Endpoint Sent Capability Info: yes
Capability_Not_Support Flag: 4294967040
Host_Name: WIN-EOHVCD1CKM7
OS_Version: Microsoft Windows 7 , 32-bit Service Pack 1 (build
    7601)
Host_Description: AT/AT COMPATIBLE
Domain:
Last_Login_User:
Host_Model: VMware Virtual Platform
Host_Manufacturer: VMware, Inc.
CPU_Model: Intel(R) Core(TM) i5-2415M CPU @ 2.30GHz
Traffic_Amount: 0
Memory_Size: 768
Features: 15
System Uptime: 5813
Installed_Software: 0
App_List(6): 85(R); 2281(R); 2887(R); 777(I); 2222(I);
    2285(I);
Unknown_App_List(20): cmd.exe(R); conhost.exe(R); explorer.
exe(R); fcappdb.exe(R); fcdblog.exe(R);
        firefox.exe(R); fmon.exe(R); fortifw.exe(R); fortiproxy.
exe(R); fortiscand.exe(R);
        fortitray.exe(R); fortiwf.exe(R); iexplore.exe(R); lsm.
exe(R); msdtc.exe(R);
        msiexec.exe(R); scheduler.exe(R); spoolsv.exe(R); taskhost.
exe(R); tpautoconnect.exe(R);
Block_App_List(0:0):
Monitor_App_List(6:20): 85(-1); 2281(-1); 2887(-1); 777(-1);
2222(-1);
        2285(-1);
        cmd.exe(-1); conhost.exe(-1); explorer.exe(-1); fcappdb.
exe(-1); fcdblog.exe(-1);
        firefox.exe(-1); fmon.exe(2560); fortifw.exe(0);
fortiproxy.exe(0); fortiscand.exe(1);
        fortitray.exe(-1073760740); fortiwf.exe(0); iexplore.
exe(0); lsm.exe(0); msdtc.exe(0);
        msiexec.exe(0); scheduler.exe(0); spoolsv.exe(0); taskhost.
exe(0); tpautoconnect.exe(0);
Traffic_Statistics(0):
```

```
Compliant list(1):
      #1: 10.20.80.38
Installed but non-compliant list(0):
Uninstalled list(2):
      #1: 10.20.80.35
      #2: 10.20.80.31
Top 10 endpoints by sent traffic:
Top 10 applications by sent traffic:
```

DATA LEAK PREVENTION (DLP)

Data Leak Prevention in FortiOS is applicable when data is being transported and is typically used to protect the content of email, web pages, or file transfers. With DLP, the transport of certain data patterns and files using one of the supported scannable protocols can be detected by a FortiGate: HTTP, FTP, SMTP, POP3, IMAP, and the IM protocols for Yahoo Messenger, MSN Messenger, AOL, and ICQ. However, be aware that the same limitations that affect AntiVirus scanning also affect DLP: namely maximum file size, data (but not necessarily packet) fragmentation, and encryption can limit the effectiveness of detection.

DLP is applied in a firewall security policy by assigning a DLP Sensor, which is an administrator-defined set of DLP Filters, which in turn are made up of component DLP Rules, File Pattern Filters, and Fingerprinting. When a data pattern is detected, the data can be blocked and archived and the offending user or IP address quarantined. Archiving of either summary or detailed content of the monitored protocols by the enabled DLP sensors is also possible.

DLP Sensors, Filters and Rules

DLP configuration is a hierarchical construction of a sensor made up of a list filters that prescribe particular actions to take when a rule is triggered. The sensor configuration determines whether the DLP detection is performed via a man-in-the-middle, "transparent" proxy or a flow-based IPS engine.

```
config dlp sensor
  edit "default"
     set comment "summary archive email and web traffics"
        config filter
```

> In older versions of FortiOS (4.0 and earlier), the archiving of session meta-data and files of supported proxy-scanned protocols was called Content Logging and Content Archiving.

```
...  <commands hidden>
            end
        set dlp-log enable
        set nac-quar-log disable
        set flow-based disable
        unset options
    next
end
```

In the CLI snippet above, the "default" DLP sensor settings for general logging, quarantine logging, proxy detection, and options are shown. For reasons of simplicity, the "config filter" section is hidden. The DLP detection method defaults to "proxy mode," providing full support of all DLP features. As implied by the "set flow-based" command, an alternate method using the IPS engine for DLP is available, but this has limitations of the types of detection that can be used (see Table 7.3).

Table 7.3 DLP Functionality by Inspection Type

DLP Rule Functionality	Proxy-based	Flow-based
File size	Yes	Mail, NNTP only
File name	Yes	No
File type	Yes	Yes (except NNTP)
Fingerprinting	Yes	No
Regex	Yes	Yes
Field rules	Yes	Yes (except NNTP)
Archiving	Yes	No

As with the AntiVirus scanning described in an earlier chapter, both methods have their advantages and disadvantages. Proxy-based methods buffer and analyze the entire file, including archive types (up to a maximum configurable file size). This is, however, at the cost of higher latency and system memory usage. However, flow-based methods analyze smaller segments of files and messages so overall latency and memory utilization is lower. A trade-off decision between proxy and flow-based is "slower-but-more-thorough" against "speedier-but-limited."

In a DLP Sensor, the collection of search filters functions as a logical-OR so a DLP sensor is matched if any one of its filters is satisfied. Each filter sets an action to be executed when the rule specified by the filter is matched. The action can be one of:

- log-only
- block
- ban
- quarantine-ip
- exempt
- ban-sender
- quarantine-port

The log-only and exempt actions will allow passing of the file or message, while any of the other actions will prevent the file or message from reaching its destination and also display or insert a replacement message. The DLP Filter will attempt to execute the action for each matching filter rule, but to reduce management and troubleshooting it will prevent duplicate actions.

Care must also be exercised with DLP rule actions which may overlap: DLP does not prevent the setting of opposing actions such as when a block rule is matching that will prevent subsequent actions of quarantining and archiving. And a matching rule with an exempt action will override any other matching rule actions. Further details of the actions can be found in the FortiOS Handbook section on Data Leak Prevention.

When a DLP Filter Rule with a block or quarantine action is matched, a replacement message will be substituted for the file or message matching the particular rule. The DLP replacement messages can be found in the CLI organized by the transport protocol:

```
config system replacemsg mail "email-dlp"
config system replacemsg mail "email-dlp-subject"
config system replacemsg mail "email-dlp-ban"
config system replacemsg mail "email-dlp-ban-sender"
config system replacemsg http "http-dlp"
config system replacemsg http "http-dlp-ban"
config system replacemsg ftp "ftp-dl-dlp"
config system replacemsg ftp "ftp-dl-dlp-ban"
config system replacemsg nntp "nntp-dlp"
config system replacemsg nntp "nntp-dlp-subject"
config system replacemsg nntp "nntp-dlp-ban"
config system replacemsg im "im-dlp"
config system replacemsg im "im-dlp-ban"
config system replacemsg nac-quar "nac-quar-dlp"
```

In addition, the DLP filter rule can be set to archive either the complete or metadata summary of the files, email messages, or IM messages matching the rule with the "set archive <disable | enable | summary-only>" command. Archiving requires a FortiAnalyzer and can present a noticeable system load due to increased traffic to the FortiAnalyzer since the FortiGate will send two copies of the file or data. One copy will go to the originally intended recipient and another to the FortiAnalyzer. Archiving of files is also limited to a file maximums. These maximums are model-specific and cannot be changed. The archive file size limit is controlled by the firewall protocol-options profile as the example CLI snippet below shows for a FortiGate-111C model with built-in hard-disk storage and other models with add-in or built-in storage will be similar.

```
FG111C-test (root) # conf firewall profile-protocol-options
FG111C-test (profile-protoc~1) # ed default
```

```
FG111C-test (default) # conf http
FG111C-test (http) # set oversize-limit ?
<value> maximum scannable filesize (min: 1MB, max: 139MB)
```

Each filter of a DLP sensor can specify one pattern-matching rule. There are a few different types of rules that can be specified by a filter type.

```
FG111C-test (example) # config filter
FG111C-test (filter) # edit test
FG111C-test (test) # set filter-type
advanced-rule           use an already defined DLP rule
advanced-compound-rule  use an already defined DLP compound rule
file-type               match a dlp filepattern list
file-size        match any file over with a size over the threshold
regexp                      match the transfer to a regular
    expresion
fingerprint          match against a fingerprint sensitivity
```

The filter-type determines the kind of rule and these can be grouped into three building blocks:

- File Pattern Filter rule (file-type, file-size).
- Pattern rules (regex, advanced-rule, advanced-compound-rule).
- Fingerprinting rule (fingerprint).

To help explain the parts that go into the definition of a DLP filter, we'll build a simple sensor starting with a File Pattern Filter.

File Pattern Filter

A File Pattern Filter defines a list of file name search patterns and file types. The file name search pattern is case insensitive and uses a simple wildcard notation to specify partial names using "?" for single character wildcard match and "*" for multiple character wildcard matching. A File Pattern Filter is made up of individual entries and an entry can only look for either a file name patter or a file type, not both. Two sample File Pattern Filters are provided in the FortiOS factory-default configuration: one for blocking some common file name extensions ("builtin-patterns;" another for blocking executable files ("all-executables"). Partial excerpts of these default File Filters (called "filepattern" in the CLI) is shown below.

```
config dlp filepattern
    edit 1
      set comment"
          config entries
              edit "*.bat"
```

```
                        set filter-type pattern
                        unset active
                        set action block
                  next
                  edit "*.com"
                        set filter-type pattern
                        unset active
                        set action block
                  next
                  edit "*.dll"
                        set filter-type pattern
                        unset active
                        set action block
                  next
   ...
         end
      set name "builtin-patterns"
   next
   edit 2
      set comment"
         config entries
            edit "bat"
                  set filter-type type
                  set file-type bat
                  set active imap smtp pop3 http ftp im nntp
                  set action block
            next
            edit "exe"
                  set filter-type type
                  set file-type exe
                  set active imap smtp pop3 http ftp im nntp
                  set action block
         next
   ...
         end
      set name "all_executables"
   next
end
```

The index numbers in the "edit 1" and "edit 2" above are used to reference a particular file pattern in the DLP filter. There is also a CLI command ("set active") that limits the File Filter to only specific traffic protocol types. In other words, the "set active" command sets whether a FortiOS protocol proxy will search for a particular "file pattern" entry. A caveat of file pattern detection rules is that the name search and file typing is actually completed by analyzing the meta-data of the particular transport protocol before the file itself has reached or passed through the FortiGate. These file patterns are also used by the AntiVirus module and, when used for DLP, the "set action" command is ignored in the file pattern. Instead, the DLP Filter action is run. So when the DLP filter action is set to "block," archiving will not be possible.

To use a file pattern in a sensor, the file pattern index number must be referenced in the DLP filter rule. Also the content of archives is not scanned unless this is enabled in the CLI. If you create a file pattern filter rule using the GUI, you will still need to use the CLI to add this setting. The supported archive file formats are the same as for AntiVirus, namely: zip, zipx, jar, rar, 7z, bz2, cab, tar, gzip, arj, lzh, msc, sis, swf, nsis. A DLP sensor rule match the index number for that file pattern and "set file-scan" could be used to determine whether archived files would be checked.

```
config dlp sensor
    edit "example"
        config filter
            edit "check-executables"
                set filter-type file-type
                set file-type 2
                set file-scan archive-content
                set action block
            next
        end
    next
end
```

The example filter rule action "block" is required to prevent the transport of executable files specified by the file pattern even if the "config dlp filepattern" entry has "set action block." This is a carry over from a legacy implementation in older versions of FortiOS.

One more point to keep in mind is that a File Pattern Filter is intended to detect and block unintentional disclosure of a particular file or file type rather than function as a robust file blocking mechanism. A File Pattern Filter is unlikely to foil a determined individual intent on sneaking a file out of an organization's network.

File-Size Rule

Another filter rule that is available is that of the size of file. When this size exceeds a certain threshold, actions can be taken. Using this rule on it's own would clearly be simplistic, but you can grow highly complex and flexible rules when you combine this with other rule types. This example shows two file-size filters, one blocking the transfer of a CD ISO image, and the other logging file transfers larger than 5 MB. It is important to note that the file size detected is not the actual file size that will have passed through the FortiGate, but rather that declared by or detected from the transport protocol. This is because truncating or aborting a file transfer at the file-size threshold value is wasteful of the link bandwidth, so a decision is made prior to the actual file transfer whether to allow or block the file.

```
config dlp sensor
    edit "dlp-test"
        config filter
            edit "filesize-CD-iso"
                set filter-type file-size
                set file-size 681984
        set action block
            next
            edit "filesize-5MB"
                set filter-type file-size
                set file-size 5120
                set action log-only
            next
        end
    next
end
```

A few caveats about file-size filters is that contradictory settings are not checked and a setting may simply be ignored. For example, enabling archive will have no effect when the filter action is set to block when the filter action is log-only and the file-size is larger that the maximum. Similarly, the file-size filter may be ignored if the DLP method is set to flow-based instead of proxy-based.

DLP Rules

DLP Rules can include regular expression search strings as well as some protocol-specific directives and selected data fields. There are three types of DLP rules that can be configured: regex, advanced, and compound. A basic regex rule takes a wild-card or standard regular expression for searching ASCII strings (set regex-wildcard). Multilingual searches are possible by enabling UTF-8 mode (set regex-utf8). An advanced rule combines regex search strings with a protocol-specific field or file attribute search parameter. To compose a rule with multiple regex searches or field parameters, a compound rule can be used with previously defined advanced rules in a logical-AND combination.

> When only using the GUI, only the basic regex search type rule can be added as a Filter to a DLP sensor. The CLI allows you to add your own advanced and compound DLP rules under config dlp rule and config dlp compound.

A basic regex rule can be entered directly as a filter entry of an individual sensor, but if done in this way, only this sensor can use that regex rule. This is fine for a very specific or unique search pattern, but if there is the possibility of a regex rule being reused by another sensor, a more efficient method is to use an "advanced rule." This type of rule can be referenced by other DLP sensor filters or by compound rules. This is shown in the simple examples below:

1. A regex rule for the pattern "FortiClientSetup" is directly entered as a filter entry.
2. An advanced rule "FCT" is defined as a regex search for "FortiClientSetup" and then referenced by name in a sensor's filter entry.

For regex scanning of archive type files, Microsoft Word and Adobe PDF files, there are two CLI directives that must be included. Otherwise these file types will be ignored by the regex search. If you create a regex filter rule using the GUI, you will still need to add the "set field regex" and "set file-scan archive-content" settings through the CLI.

```
FG111C-test (FCT-search) # set field ?
always       match all transfers
encrypted      match encrypted files
file-size    file size
file-type    file type
fingerprint match a DLP fingerprint sensitivity
regexp       regular expression match on all fields
transfer-size  transfer size
user         authenticated user
user-group  authenticated user group
FG111C-test (FCT-search) # set field regex
FG111C-test (FCT-search) # set file-scan ?
archive-content scan archived files
archive-whole   scan archived files as a whole
ms-word-content scan ms word file text
ms-word-whole   scan ms word file as a whole
pdf-content scan pdf text
pdf-whole          scan pdf whole
FG111C-test (FCT-search) # set file-scan archive-content
```

Additional options for Microsoft Word ".doc" and Adobe Acrobat ".pdf" files are available when employing a regex search rules to scan the extracted text. While one may use "ms-word-whole" and "pdf-whole," using "ms-word-content" and "pdf-content" can allow for more accurate searches against extracted text. Note that "set field" defaults to "body" when creating a new rule and in this case "set file-scan" will be hidden.

```
## Basic regex rule defined in a DLP sensor
config dlp sensor
    edit "dlp-test"
        config filter
            edit "Find-FCT"
                set filter-type regexp
                set regexp "FortiClientSetup"
                set file-scan archive-content
            next
        end
    next
end
## Basic regex rule defined as a Advanced Rule and referenced in a DLP
    sensor
config dlp rule
    edit "FCT-search"
        set protocol all
        set field regexp
        set regexp "FortiClientSetup"
        set file-scan archive-content
    next
end
config dlp sensor
    edit "dlp-test2"
        config filter
            edit "Find-FCT-2"
                set filter-type advanced-rule
                set rule-name "FCT-search"
            next
        end
    next
end
```

The factory-default configuration provides a number of "advanced rules" for searching for common items such as credit card numbers in HTTP and email, or identifying large file attachments. Advanced rules can be applied to specific protocols and or sub-protocols. The credit card rule shown below applies to the HTTP-POST sub-protocol. Although you can configure a regex search in an advanced rule, they are more effective for providing comparison or equality searching for certain fields based on the specified protocol. For example, the "Large-Attachment" rule shown below is a search applying to IMAP, POP3, and SMTP mail protocols for a file attachment size threshold greater or equal to 5 MB. Compare this to the previous example for the "filesize-5MB" filter which would produce a similar result but would apply to every supported protocol, increasing system load unnecessarily.

```
config dlp rule
    edit "HTTP-Visa-Mastercard"
        set protocol http
        set sub-protocol http-post
        set regexp "(\\W|\\b)(4\\d|5[1-5])\\d{2}([ \\-]?)\\d{4}
            (\\3\\d{4}){2}(\\W|\\b)"
    next
...
    edit "Large-Attachment"
        set protocol email
        set sub-protocol smtp pop3 imap
        set field attachment-size
        set value 5120
        set operator greater-equal
    next
...
```

When adding a new rule via the GUI, only the regular expression string entry is available. The CLI "config dlp rule" permits more advanced parameters. There are numerous DLP rule options that will not be listed here, but can be found in the FortiOS Handbook UTM section and FortiOS CLI Reference on the Fortinet Documentation website.

The construction of an individual DLP rule specifies a single regex search pattern or a set of protocol-specific data field search parameters. A compound DLP rule combines individual rules in a logical-AND, so each member rule must be satisfied in order to satisfy the overall compound DLP rule. A constraint of the compound rule is that only advanced rules with the same protocol and sub-protocol can be included. This necessitates pre-defining protocol-specific advanced rules. In the factory-default supplied DLP compound rule below, the separate rules for detecting the Canadian Social Insurance Number pattern and not the "Webex" string in email protocols are put together as member sub-rules.

```
config dlp compound
   edit "Email-SIN"
      set comment "Emails containing Canadian SIN but are not WebEx
   invites"
      set protocol email
      set sub-protocol smtp pop3 imap
         set member "Email-Canada-SIN" "Email-Not-Webex"
   next
...
```

Unfortunately, up to and including FortiOS 4.3.7 firmware, advanced rules using protocol "any" cannot be included in a compound rule. The member rules must have both protocol and sub-protocol specified.

This particular compound rule is not very rigorous. A determined person could subvert the rule detection by simply including the "WebEx" string anywhere in the body of the email. The purpose of DLP is to catch and alert on accidental leakage of sensitive information. It works well as an auditing tool, but is not intended to be a robust blocking technology.

Fingerprinting

Fingerprint rules in a DLP filter specify a sensitivity level to which documents have been pre-assigned and have had a checksum generated. Fingerprinting requires internal storage so the CLI commands are displayed only on models which have suitable storage.

On devices that have sufficient storage, either internal or via an additional hardware module, you may define the behavior of a system when the fingerprinting database becomes full. The CLI snippet below is from a FortiGate-111C with built-in internal hard-disk storage. The minimum size is 16 MB and the storage-device name shown is model dependent.

```
FG111C-test (global) # conf dlp settings
FG111C-test (settings) # set db-mode ?
remove-modified-then-oldest    Remove modified chunks first, then
   oldest file entries
remove-oldest                          Remove the oldest files first
stop-adding                  Stop adding entries
FG111C-test (settings) # set size ?
<integer>      please input integer value
FG111C-test (settings) # set storage-device ?
<string> please input string value
```

```
HDD1  storage
FG111C-test (settings) # show
config dlp settings
    set db-mode stop-adding
    set size 100
    set storage-device "HDD1"
end
```

The document file checksums stored in the Fingerprint Database are only 32-bytes each and are based on small data chunks. There will be a few dozen to hundreds of checksums depending on the size of the file. Even the minimum Fingerprint Database size of 16 MB can hold the fingerprints of several thousand files.

Although called Document Fingerprinting, any file type can be fingerprinted by either manually uploading via the GUI (UTM Profiles > Data Leak Prevention > Document Fingerprint) or scanning a Windows Share folder on a server computer via password authenticated access.

The fingerprinted file is processed by the FortiGate to produce a series of checksums stored in the internal DLP Fingerprint Database along with an administratively set sensitivity level. There are three pre-defined sensitivity levels (Private, Critical, Warning) which are simply labels. Additional levels can be added. Later, when checking for a fingerprint match, the checksums for a specified sensitivity level are compared to the contents of the device's Fingerprint Database and must match exactly. Since fingerprinting uses a checksum calculated over the bytes of a data chunk, any modified bits will cause a different checksum value. This is true even if there is no visible change when viewing the file on an endpoint. In an "advanced-rule," it is possible to use a match percentage, allowing a relaxed matching. For example, document files which contain revision meta-data but with largely unchanged body text could have a match-percentage set below 100% to account for the meta-data changes while still providing an overall fingerprint match.

```
### Windows shared folder Document Source example
config dlp fp-doc-source
    edit "server01"
        set file-path "/Sales/upload/"
        set file-pattern "*-pricelist.xls"
        set password ENC x86ZXDvejg73vhRoBp...
        set period weekly
        set sensitivity "Critical"
        set server "172.16.20.144"
        set username "fingerprint"
    next
end
```

```
## Fingerprint sensitivity default labels
config dlp fp-sensitivity
    edit "Private"
    next
    edit "Critical"
    next
    edit "Warning"
    next
end
## Fingerprint Filter rule example
config dlp sensor
    edit "dlp-test"
        config filter
            edit "pricelist-fp"
                        set fp-sensitivity "Critical"
                set action quarantine-ip
            next
        end
    next
end
## Fingerprint rule example
config dlp rule
    edit "private-fp-files"
        set protocol all
        set field fingerprint
            set sensitivity "Private"
        set match-percentage 80
    next
end
config dlp sensor
    edit "example"
        config filter
            edit "private-fp"
                set filter-type advanced-rule
                set rule-name "private-fp-files"
                set action block
            next
        end
```

```
      next
end
```

A DLP filter rule simply specifies a Fingerprint sensitivity level and all files tagged with that level are included. To allow for more granularity when organizing the files for fingerprinting, you can add more sensitivity labels to use where required.

```
## Fingerprint Sensitivity label example
FG111C-test (root) # conf dlp fp-sensitivity
FG111C-test (fp-sensitivity) # edit "HR files"
new entry 'HR-files' added
FG111C-test (HR-files) # next
FG111C-test (fp-sensitivity) # edit 'pricelists'
new entry 'pricelists' added
FG111C-test (pricelists) # next
FG111C-test (fp-sensitivity) # ed contracts
new entry 'contracts' added
FG111C-test (contracts) # next
FG111C-test (fp-sensitivity) # show
config dlp fp-sensitivity
    edit "Private"
    next
    edit "Critical"
    next
    edit "Warning"
    next
    edit "public"
    next
    edit "HR files"
    next
    edit "pricelists"
    next
    edit "contracts"
    next
end
```

When creating the checksum library from a Windows Share folder, files are processed one at a time and with a low process priority. This avoids interfering with other latency-sensitive FortiGate functions. For a folder with many or large files, a fingerprint scan may take a significant amount of time, so it is wise to schedule this activity for a low network activity period.

Finally, individual file fingerprinting is available, but only through the GUI. Navigate to UTM Profiles>Data Leak Prevention>Document Fingerprinting, and in the Manual Document Fingerprints section you can manually upload a file to the FortiGate for fingerprinting. The file is buffered in the FortiGate system memory, fingerprint checksums calculated, and the file is deleted. If the file is an unencrypted archive, you may generate fingerprints for files internal to the archive as well as for the archive container file.

DLP Log Settings

The logging of DLP events and messages is controlled per destination (local disk, FortiAnalyzer, FAMS, etc.). The default settings of DLP events and archiving are enabled under the log filter.

```
config log fortianalyzer filter
   set dlp enable
   set dlp-archive enable
   set dlp-all enable
end
```

To view DLP log messages from the CLI, you need to set up the appropriate log filters:

```
FG111C-TEST # exec log filter device
Available devices:
0: memory
1: disk
2: faz
3: fds
FG111C-TEST # exec log filter category
Available categories:
16: netscan
10: application control
9: dlp
6: content
5: spam
4: ids
3: webfilter
2: virus
1: even
0: traffic
FG111C-TEST # exec log filter device 1
```

```
FG111C-TEST # exec log filter category 9
FG111C-TEST # exec log filter dump
category: dlp
device: disk
start-line: 1
view-lines: 10
max-checklines: 10000
```

Remember that basic DLP requires local disk, FortiAnalyzer or FAMS support, so the device must be either "1," "2," or "3" in order to specify DLP category "9." Some examples of DLP log messages for a file pattern rule blocking jpeg files over HTTP and for a regex rule are shown below.

```
FG111C-TEST(example1) # show
config dlp sensor
    edit "example1"
        config filter
            edit "mallard"
                set filter-type regexp
                set regexp "mallard"
                set archive summary-only
                set action block
            next
            edit "image-type"
                set filter-type file-type
                set file-type 3
            next
        end
    set nac-quar-log enable
    next
end
FG111C-TEST # exec log display
149 logs found.
10 logs returned.
1: 2012-06-02 12:44:36 log_id=0954024576 type=dlp subtype=dlp
   pri=warning vd="root" policyid=4 identidx=0 serial=5002174
   user="N/A" group="N/A" src=192.168.11.160 sport=44272 src_
   port=44272 src_int="port11" dst=76.12.35.222 dport=80 dst_port=80
   dst_int="wan1" service=http status=detected filefilter="file
   pattern" filetype="png" sent=1620 rcvd=1556 mail_size=0 att_size=0
   att_count=0 hostname="www.polarcruises.com" url="/antarctica/
```

```
    articles/wildlife_4/images/info_blip_right.png" from="N/A" to="N/A"
    subject="N/A" msg="data leak detected(Data Leak Prevention Rule
    matched)" rulename="N/A" compoundname="N/A" filtername="block-pics"
    file="info_blip_right.png" action=block severity=1
2: 2012-06-02 12:44:36 log_id=0954024576 type=dlp subtype=dlp
    pri=warning vd="root" policyid=4 identidx=0 serial=5002177
    user="N/A" group="N/A" src=192.168.11.160 sport=44275 src_
    port=44275 src_int="port11" dst=76.12.35.222 dport=80 dst_port=80
    dst_int="wan1" service=http status=detected filefilter="file
    pattern" filetype="png" sent=1616 rcvd=1155 mail_size=0
...
10: 2012-06-02 13:33:42 log_id=0954024576 type=dlp subtype=dlp
    pri=warning vd="root" policyid=4 identidx=0 serial=5032963
    user="N/A" group="N/A" src=192.168.11.160 sport=60513 src_
    port=60513 src_int="port11" dst=173.194.79.94 dport=80
    dst_port=80 dst_int="wan1" service=http status=detected
    filefilter="none" filetype="html" sent=985 rcvd=58684 mail_
    size=0 att_size=0 att_count=0 hostname="www.google.ca" url="/
    search?hl=en&gbv=2&sclient=psy-ab&q=duck&oq=duck&aq=f&aqi=g4&aql=
    &gs_l=serp.3..014.5293.5660.0.6928.4.4.0.0.0.0.175.593.0j4.4.0...0.
    0.uLrHfFaEAQ8&pbx=1&bav=on.2,or.r_gc.r_pw.r_qf.,cf.osb&biw=1384&bi
    h=873&ech=1&psi=nXjKT5_zNILu2gWD8eHaCw.1338669218341.3&emsg=NCSR&n
    oj=1&ei=nXjKT5_zNILu2gWD8eHaCw" from="N/A" to="N/A" subject="N/A"
    msg="data leak detected(Data Leak Prevention Rule matched)"
    rulename="N/A" compoundname="N/A" filtername="mallard" file="N/A"
    action=block severity=1
```

Some DLP Usage Guidelines

Applying DLP to firewall security polices is done by selecting a DLP sensor to include in the policy configuration. Recapping a statement made earlier, the DLP sensor is made up of an logical-ORed list of filters; each of which specifies a DLP rule and an action to take if the rule is triggered. If more than one matching parameter or character pattern is needed to detect a particular data leak item, a compound rule should be used. Since compound rules must specify a particular protocol, you may need to replicate similar advanced-rules for each transport protocol to be monitored.

It is worth pointing out again that DLP is only effective for certain protocols and will only scan those protocols even when the associated firewall security policy includes many other service (traffic) types. DLP requires CPU processing, either by the FortiGate's main CPU or, if so equipped, an SP ASIC. It can add significant load to your FortiGate system. The main CPU supports both proxy- and flow-based DLP inspection, while the SP can only handle flow-based.

It is recommended that proxy-based inspection be used for best DLP inspection, but if performance and latency issues arise then switching to the flow-based method may provide some relief.

VULNERABILITY SCAN

FortiGates can perform network vulnerability scans to detect flaws in software or faulty configurations based upon a list of known vulnerabilities from the FortiGuard Vulnerability and Compliance Management (VCM) Service hosted on the Fortinet Distribution System (FDS) network. The results are viewable on the FortiGate unit or from an attached FortiAnalyzer unit.

Vulnerability Scan Requirements

Vulnerability scans are supported on most FortiGate models, though not on the SOHO/ROBO modules (40C, 30B, 20C). While models equipped with storage provide a limited reporting capability, it is best to use a FortiAnalyzer or FAMS to get full reporting capability. Minimally, all FortiGate models capable of Vulnerability Scanning with the results of the network scan being available as summary graphs or log entries. A valid FortiGuard license is required to be able to download updates as new vulnerabilities are discovered, so the network can be scanned for the most current security risks. A FortiGate with a valid license will download the latest VCM package from the FDN. To check the current VCM package version installed on a particular FortiGate unit, the log messages "plugin=" field or the CLI command shown below can be used.

```
(global) # diag autoupdate versions
...
Vulnerability Compliance and Management
---------
Version: 1.00264
Contract Expiry Date: Wed Mar 6 00:00:00 2013
Last Updated using manual update on Thu Jun 7 06:11:00 2012
Last Update Attempt: n/a
Result: Updates Installed
```

The Vulnerability Scan involves making connections to various network ports on the target client computer so firewalls or ACL-equipped routers may interfere with the scan. To scan accurately, there should be a "clear" network connection between the FortiGate and client computers.

Some of the vulnerability tests require user authentication. If they are not supplied, these checks will be skipped. However, when accurate credentials are supplied, the system can log into the system and scan beyond the open ports that a basic network scan involves. To provide nonrepudiation, care should be taken that the credentials used do not match those that a user regularly uses. This will result in the most accurate scan. To prevent privileges creep, please review the FortiOS UTM Handbook chapter on Vulnerability Scan.

One additional consideration that it takes time for the Vulnerability Scan to complete. Depending on the configuration, number of target client computers, and network traffic conditions, it may take several minutes to a dozen hours or more to complete a Vulnerability Scan.

Vulnerability Scan Process and Configuration
Asset and Discovery Scan

The Vulnerability Scan first requires the list of client computers by IP address to be entered in so-called asset entries. This can be as either a list of individual client computers or a range of IP addresses. The difference between the types of asset entries is that to specify authentication credentials then the individual or "ip" asset entry is to be used in the scan; a "range" asset entry is used when unauthenticated scans are planned and when you may not know the exact IP addresses of the client computers in a particular subnet.

```
config netscan assets
   edit 1
      set addr-type range
      set name "wf-hosts"
      set scheduled disable
      set start-ip 10.20.80.30
      set end-ip 10.20.80.38
   next
   edit 2
      set addr-type range
      set name "LAN-hosts"
      set scheduled disable
      set start-ip 192.168.10.1
      set end-ip 192.168.10.254
   next
   edit 3
      set addr-type ip
      set auth-unix disable
      set auth-windows disable
      set name "LAN-host-222"
      set scheduled disable
      set start-ip 192.168.10.222
   next
   edit 4
```

```
        set addr-type ip
        set auth-unix enable
        set auth-windows disable
        set name ''
        set scheduled disable
        set start-ip 192.168.11.160
        set unix-password ENC uWc/
      Ay4IIomPLwcCHcxijDZb3jdB5MjRvrmod4JT4sqTx9xnrjzEcVcBbADOsOn3Z6LEGIbK
      fkmLE+lyDvxv17DcXNwBdMBcyryxhMRfinjjlkzk
        set unix-username "vcm-test"
    next
end
```

In the CLI, the Vulnerability Scan is referred to as "netscan" and the asset configuration is under "config netscan asset." The example CLI configuration shows
a mix of individual "ip" entries with and without user authentication and "range"
type entries. Note that "start-ip" is re-used in the individual client computer case to
specify the IP address. If user authentication is enabled, the password is stored in an
encrypted format. There is also a schedule option to enable periodic scans.

Before any actual tests are run, the FortiGate uses a Discovery Scan to compile
a list of on-line and reachable client computers of a particular asset entry. To start a
Discovery Scan from the CLI, use the "execute netscan start discovery" command
plus the asset entry ID number. If the ID number is left blank, it will perform a Discovery Scan on all defined asset entries. If there is an connected FortiGate interface
in the same subnet as the asset entry, an ARP query is sent. Otherwise, an ICMP echo
request (ping) is attempted. If there is no response, TCP and UDP probes are sent to
a short list of well-known ports in sequence until a response is received. A probe is
only sent once and as soon as the client computer responds to that probe, the Discovery scan is concluded for that particular IP address. The Discovery Scan progress can
be observed from the Vulnerability Scan log or queried with "get netscan scan host
asset" (see Tables 7.4 and 7.5).

```
FG111C-TEST (root) # exec netscan start discover 4
FG111C-TEST (root) # exec log display
34 logs found.
10 logs returned.
...
2: 2012-06-08 11:01:44 log_id=1600004097 type=netscan
   subtype=discovery pri=notice vd="root" action=scan status=complete
   engine=N/A plugin=N/A
3: 2012-06-08 11:01:41 log_id=1600004104 type=netscan
   subtype=discovery pri=notice vd="root" action=host-detection
   ip=192.168.1.160 method=ARP asset_id=4 asset_name="N/A"
```

Table 7.4 Discovery Scan Ports—TCP

TCP Ports	Well-known Protocol Name
21	FTP
22	SSH
23	TELNET
25	SMTP
53	DNS
80, 88	HTTP
110	POP3
111, 135	RPC
139	NETBIOS
443	HTTPS
445	SAMBA

Table 7.5 Discovery Scan Ports—UDP

UDP Ports	Well-known Protocol Name
53	DNS
111,135	RPC
137	NETBIOS
161	SNMP
500	IKE

```
4: 2012-06-08 11:01:41 log_id=1600004097 type=netscan
   subtype=discovery pri=notice vd="root" action=scan status=start
   engine=1.264 plugin=1.264
...
FG111C-TEST (root) # get netscan scan host asset
Summary of scan started at 2012-06-08 11:01:41
Scan completed at 2012-06-08 11:01:44
Total number of hosts found: 1
1 hosts found for asset"(4)
ip            192.168.11.160
method        ARP
FG111C-TEST (root) # exec netscan start discover
FG111C-TEST (root) # get netscan scan host asset
Summary of scan started at 2012-06-08 11:02:45
   Scan completed at 2012-06-08 11:02:48
   Total number of hosts found: 1
```

```
1 hosts found for asset" (10)
ip              66.171.121.34
method          ICMP
```

In the CLI snippet shown above, a Discovery Scan for asset entry #4 was performed and the subsequent log message display shows the start and end of the scan along with the method used to confirm the client computer. In this case, the device was directly connected to one of the FortiGate interfaces. The next Discovery Scan shown is for a device on a different network than any of the FortiGate interfaces and which was confirmed using a simple ping.

Based on the results from a Discovery Scan, you may choose to create additional asset entries to group a certain IP address range or create individual IP address asset entries for running an authenticated Vulnerability Scan. As shown by the log messages and CLI output, the time to complete a Discovery Scan may range from a few seconds for to a several minutes depending on the number of addresses in the range of an asset entry.

Vulnerability Scan Settings and Running

Once a Discovery Scan is complete for the asset entry, the "real" Vulnerability Scan using the VCM database can be run with "execute netscan start scan <asset-id>." Pausing, resuming, and stopping a current scan is also possible with "pause," "resume," or "stop" in place of the "start" parameter. The progress of the current scan is available with "execute netscan status."

The type or characteristics of the Vulnerability Scan to be run is set by "config netscan settings" where there is a choice of Quick, Standard, and Full scans ("set scan-type"). This defines the TCP or UDP port ranges and applications used as part of the scan. By default, the Vulnerability Scan will also try to determine which service is running on a particular port as well as attempt to match the client computer responses to known operating system signatures. Consequently, the time taken to perform a Standard or Full scan could take up to 24 h, especially if authenticated scan is enabled. The scans may also be modified to only scan the TCP ports ("set tcp-ports") or the UDP ports ("set udp-ports"). In addition, to check only that a port is open and not verify the service running it, you can use "set service-detection." Finally, you can turn off port response checks looking to determine an operating system signature with "set os-detection" and greatly speed up the scanning process.

Service and OS detection require both TCP and UDP ports, so disabling either TCP or UDP port scans will also force service and OS detection to be disabled. The candidate list of TCP and UDP ports for current Vulnerability Scan settings can be displayed with "get netscan settings" or using the "get" command when within the "config netscan settings" context.

```
FG111C-TEST (root) # conf netscan settings
FG111C-TEST (settings) # show full
config netscan settings
```

```
    set day-of-week sunday
    set os-detection default
    set recurrence weekly
    set scan-mode quick
    set scheduled-pause disable
    set service-detection default
    set tcp-scan default
    set time 00:00
    set udp-scan default
end
FG111C-TEST (settings) # get
day-of-week : sunday
os-detection    : default
recurrence      : weekly
scan-mode       : quick
scheduled-pause: disable
service-detection     : default
tcp-ports       : 11,13,15,17,19-23,25,37,42,53,66,69-70,79-81,88,98,
   109-111,113,118-119,123,135,139,143,220,256-259,264,371,389,411,443,
   445,464-465,512-515,523-524,540,548,554,563,580,593,636,749-751,873,
   900-901,990,992-993,995,1080,1114,1214,1234,1352,1433,1494,1508,
   1521,1720,1723,1755,1801,2000-2001,2003,2049,2301,2401,2447,2690,
   2766,3128,3268-3269,3306,3372,3389,4100,4443-4444,4661-4662,5000,
   5432,5555-5556,5631-5632,5634,5800-5802,5900-5901,6000,6112,6346,
   6387,6666-6667,6699,7007,7100,7161,7777-7778,8000-8001,8010,
   8080-8081,8100,8888,8910,9100,10000,12345-12346,20034,21554,32000,
   32768-32790
tcp-scan    : default
time        : 00:00
udp-ports   : 7,13,17,19,37,53,67-69,111,123,135,137,161,177,407,464,
   500,517-518,520,1434,1645,1701,1812,2049,3527,4569,4665,5036,5060,
   5632,6502,7778,15345
udp-scan    : default
FG111C-TEST (settings) # set scan-mode full
FG111C-TEST (settings) # end
FG111C-TEST (root) # get netscan settings
day-of-week : sunday
os-detection    : default
recurrence  : weekly
scan-mode       : full
```

```
scheduled-pause: disable
service-detection    : default
tcp-ports        : 1-65535
tcp-scan     : default
time         : 00:00
udp-ports        : 1-65535
udp-scan     : default
```

Setting a particular Vulnerability Scan to run periodically is possible using the recurrence, day-of-week, and time parameters. It is also possible to define a period during which the scan would be temporarily halted. This can be useful when there is a regular batch job on one or more client computers with which a scan might interfere. If you want to disable the next scheduled scan, simply enable "schedule-pause" and set the "pause-from" and "pause-to" to the same time (hh:mm) value. The time and date settings are relative to the FortiGate unit's clock setting.

The FortiGate model also has limits to the number of scanned addresses or assets, as smaller devices may not be able to handle the load of larger scans. This is, however, not limited to the total number of IP addresses in a range, but to the number of computers that are on-line and respond to the Discovery Scan. While you should consult the latest datasheet and FortiOS Release notes for the firm limits, Table 7.6 should serve as a rough guide.

Only a one scan at a time can be run on a FortiGate unit and the time required for the scan to complete depends on the number of assets to be scanned and the scan parameters. A new scan always includes a discovery scan of the assets so you do not have to run a discovery scan separately. Vulnerabillity Scan runs as a low priority process and the number of concurrent connections is kept low so as to not adversely affect the performance of other UTM functions which may also be running on the same FortiGate unit.

```
FG111C-TEST # exec netscan start scan 6
FG111C-TEST # exec netscan status
Scan completed at 2012-06-08 15:17:47
-----------------------------------------
Completed Hosts 15/15 Tasks 146715/146715
-----------------------------------------
```

Table 7.6 Vulnerabillity Scan Maximum Client Computers

Model Level	Max Scannable Assets
100-series and lower	200
200–300 series	1000
400–800 series	2000
1000-series and higher	65535

```
Progress      |   100% complete
Elapsed Time  |      00:18 (hh:mm)
------------------------------------------
```

Vulnerability Scan Results

When a Vulnerability Scan is completed, the results are presented in a tabular format in the GUI (UTM Profiles > Vulnerability Scan > Vulnerability Result). If you do not have GUI access and only have a CLI session, the results are also available using "get netscan scan host" commands:

- *get netscan scan host list* :display the summary of scanned client computers
- *get netscan scan host vuln <ip-address>* :display specific Vulnerability Scan results

```
FG111C-TEST # get netscan scan host list
Summary of scan started at 2012-06-08 14:59:25
    Scan completed at 2012-06-08 15:17:47
    Total number of hosts found: 15
Host vulnerability summary
    asset_name   mantis-subnet2
    ip                    192.168.1.190
    os           Linux 2.6.15 - 2.6.26
    vuln_level   critical
    n_vuln       21
    asset_name            mantis-subnet2
    ip           192.168.1.191
    os           Linux 2.6.15 - 2.6.26
    vuln_level   critical
    n_vuln       20
    asset_name   mantis-subnet2
    ip    192.168.1.192
    os           Linux 2.6.15 - 2.6.26
    vuln_level   critical
    n_vuln       48
...
FG111C-TEST # get netscan scan host vuln 192.168.1.191
Summary of scan started at 2012-06-08 14:59:25
    Scan completed at 2012-06-08 15:17:47
    Total number of hosts found: 15
    Vulnerabilities for host 192.168.1.191
```

```
vuln        Sun.MySQL.Database.Select.Subquery.DoS
vuln_id     18084
vuln_ref    http://www.fortinet.com/ids/VID18084
vuln_cat    database
severity    medium
port        3306
vuln        MySQL.Server.Version
vuln_id           18984
vuln_ref    http://www.fortinet.com/ids/VID18984
vuln_cat    database
severity    low
port        3306
vuln        MYSQL.MyISAM.Table.Security.Bypass.Vulnerability
vuln_id     19651
vuln_ref    http://www.fortinet.com/ids/VID19651
vuln_cat    database
severity    high
port        3306
..(and 17 more)..
```

The Vulnerability Scan results available on the FortiGate are only intended for quick viewing. In conjunction with a FortiAnalzyer Log and Reporting system or the FAMS subscription service, the Vulnerability Scan on the FortiGate can be part of your overall environment. The logs can then be incorporated into customizable reports and previous scan result reports compared over time to get a more comprehensive view of the client computers in your networks.

REFERENCES

[1] FortiOS™ Handbook WAN Optimization, Web Cache, Explicit Proxy, and WCCP, v3. Doc. no. 01–433-96996-20120113.
[2] FortiOS CLI Reference, FortiOS 4.0 MR3 Doc. no. 01–433-99686-20120217.

Analyzing your Security Information with FortiAnalyzer

While current FortiGate with local storage devices provides integrated log viewing and reporting, this only allows the administrator visibility into events that occur on that device. To provide this level of awareness to an entire enterprise, it is helpful to combine all events, often via a syslog server. Once this is done, it becomes possible to generate reports for the entire organization. Within the Fortinet product family, this need is filled with the FortiAnalyzer.

The FortiAnalyzer, in addition to serving as a log target, provides a location for long-term storage. This can be used for packets tagged by the IPS engine, payload data detected by AV, or transactions captured by the DLP system. This data is important as without it, it becomes difficult to trace an incident or tune your system.

However, there are two issues that people commonly encounter with a straight syslog implementation. The first is the amount of data. Syslog maxes out at 1024 bytes per call, but some packets are larger than this. The second issue is that many sensors have an IP address that is assigned via DHCP and is therefore changeable. To address these problems, Fortinet has developed a proprietary secure transfer protocol with a higher size limit and that uses serial numbers to encode data, breaking the reliance on source IPs for identification. This is what the FortiAnalyzer uses. Once on the FortiAnalyzer, the native interface can be used to decode the packet data and display it in a human readable format.

The FortiAnalyzer is also capable of continuous monitoring and reporting, which can augment your existing security and compliance teams. Your audit teams can get automated reports detailing which DLP triggers have been activated on all FortiGates in your enterprise. Your incident managers can be alerted as events without having to configure individual units. Also, your operations people can leverage the vulnerability assessment tools to keep all systems fully patched.

CONFIGURING THE FORTIANALYZER

Much like other Fortinet products, the FortiAnalyzer supports virtualization. Referred to as ADOMs (Administrative Domains), these virtual domains are used to isolate devices and user accounts. A regular user account only has visibility into the data for the devices in their ADOM.

Network Interface Configuration

All FortiAnalyzers have multiple Ethernet interfaces. These interfaces exist to allow the separation of log delivery from administrative access from other services such as log aggregation and the interface to Web Services. If each interface is configured, the device will act as a multi-homed host. It will not route between the interfaces in either static or dynamic mode.

Smaller organizations may wish to avail themselves of the Fortinet Discovery Protocol. This allows the security devices (FortiGate, FortiClient, and FortiMail) to automatically discover any FortiAnalyzers on the network. This capability does require the systems to share a Layer 2 network connection.

The interfaces are configured similarly to those on a FortiGate. From the WebUI, navigate to System → Network → Interface. Then select the interface you wish to edit, either by double-clicking the row or selecting the checkbox and clicking "edit" in the menu bar. This is also where you would enable the Fortinet Discovery Protocol, control the network access allowed and whether to enable the Web Services or log aggregation capabilities.

File System Configuration

All FortiAnalyzers larger than the 100 series support multiple disk drives. These may be configured to various levels of redundancy via RAID. In accordance to the limitations of RAID, devices with a limited number of disks are also limited to the type of RAID that they support. For example, in a dual-disk device like a 400B, the types of redundancy would be limited to simple striping (RAID-0) or mirroring (RAID-1). These two raid levels are implemented in software. For reasons of speed, more complex RAID levels are implemented in hardware. So long as a sufficient number of drives are installed, all RAID options are supported.

Data Storage Options

When first introduced, the primary requirement of the FortiAnalyzer was to store log messages quickly and efficiently. Thus, logs were simply files to which the system continuously appended. Then, when reporting was required, a custom binary indexing process was developed, so the reporting engine would quickly locate the relevant data.

However, as the number of logs received began to climb and the reports became more complex, it became necessary to move from log files to a full-fledged database. Today, this design allows for users to create their own reports and, if they wish, store data in an external MySQL database. By making this change, total storage capacity is no longer linked to the size of local storage. Additionally, data backups are simplified and the CPU impact from generating long and complex reports is drastically reduced.

However, when moving to a database design, there is a latency issue where, when the system is under load, packets may come in more quickly than they can be logged. This is why, even when a database is configured, the FortiAnalyzer stores to local disk in the form of raw text files and then periodically inserts data from those files into the database.

Configuring Data Storage

While it is possible to switch between using local text files and a database (local or remote), it is not always possible to migrate the stored data. Thus, if you decide to switch from text to SQL, you will likely lose historical information and reports will need to be regenerated. To do this, use the WebUI to navigate to System → Storage and select the option that you need. However, you can migrate a certain amount of data from text to SQL. Thus, when you switch to one of the SQL options, you will be prompted to supply a start data and time. If you plan to insert a very large number of log messages into the database, you should begin the process at a time when the number of logs being received is low (after hours) and also temporarily disable report generations. This will reserve more system resources to the log migration.

Adding Devices

The default FortiAnalyzer configuration allows it to receive and process log messages from any device. This, however, may not be preferred. This is particularly true if the

FortiAnalyzer has an interface that is publicly reachable. As an alternative, you can configure the FortiAnalyzer so it only accepts logs from specific devices. This is enabled in Devices → Unregistered Options → Known Device Types. Then, select the radio button for "Ignore connection and log data". If using the CLI, you can set the handling option under "config log unregistered" to "drop-all".

```
FAZ # config system unregistered
(unregistered) # set handling drop-all
(unregistered) # end
FAZ #
```

Obviously, using this feature requires the administrator to manually add the devices to the FortiAnalyzer before it may save their log messages. If a FortiAnalyzer is configured to ignore unregistered devices and it receives an unauthorized log message, this device will appear in the "Blocked Devices" list. They can be activated by simply selecting them and clicking "Unblock" from the menu bar. If the administrator manually adds a device to the FortiAnalyzer prior to it sending logs, it will immediately be activated and all logs will be stored.

The administrator has device-level control over what types of log data will be processed by the FortiAnalyzer. While the default behavior is to accept all log messages, including enhanced logging (IPS packet captures, AV quarantined files, DLP detections, etc.), this can be changed in the WebUI from Devices → Allowed → Device. Simply select the checkboxes from the list of "Device Privileges" (see Figure 8.1).

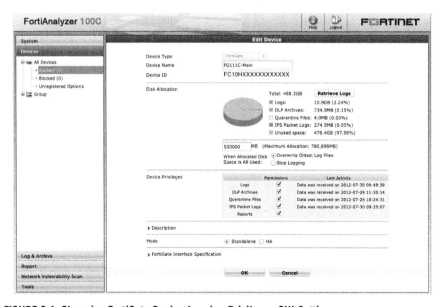

FIGURE 8.1 Changing FortiGate Device Logging Privileges GUI Setting

High Availability Devices Configurations

Multiple FortiGate units operating in a HA cluster generate their own log messages, each containing that device's Serial Number. By default, these will appear on the FortiAnalyzer as independent devices. After all, no information is passed in the log message to indicate that the unit is part of a cluster. To change this behavior, the administrator must logically combine the individual units in the FortiAnalyzer's configuration. This simplifies the use of other features such as alerts and reports, as the cluster can be incorporated by reference and used as if it were a single device.

To convert a standalone device to an HA configuration, select one of the devices from the cluster, then select the edit option. From there, set the Mode radio button to HA. At this point an additional dialog will open and the administrator can select unallocated devices to the HA cluster, select the desired units from the List of Devices, and move them to the Membership side using the right arrow icon (see Figure 8.2).

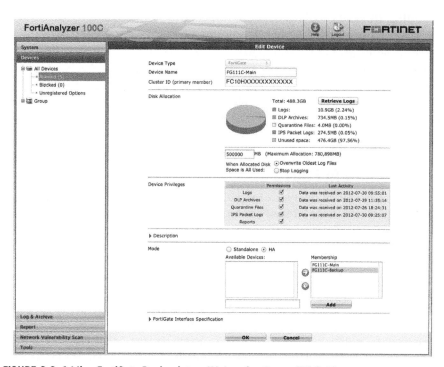

FIGURE 8.2 Adding FortiGate Device into a HA Logging Group GUI Setting

Controlling Storage Utilization

When a FortiGate is configured for extensive logging, you run the risk of a particularly busy FortiGate using an excessive amount of storage, reducing the amount available to the other devices. This may prevent you from storing logs for as long a duration as you wish off of devices that do not generate as much data. This will, of course, also affect the age from which you can generate reports.

If you do have a device that generates abnormally large amounts of data, it is possible to configure per-device disk quotas to ensure that sufficient storage remains available. To assign this in the WebUI, navigate to the desired device and select the "edit" option. The next dialog allows you to specify the amount of storage allocated to that device. When a device reaches its configured quota, the FortiAnalyzer will automatically begin deleting the oldest data until the device is once again under the quota "low-water" mark.

It is possible to oversubscribe the total storage capacity when doing this. If this occurs and the oversubscribed unit runs out of storage space, it begins to delete data from all the devices until the oversubscription is solved.

Grouping Devices

Most organizations find it desirable to generate a report for a common set of Security Enforcement Points (all Internet firewalls, all remote offices, etc.). While you may individually select the devices when creating a report definition, that can lead to a lack of consistency. To avoid this, the FortiAnalyzer allows the administrator to create a group of FortiGate devices (or VDOMs). This group is then used in all report definitions.

CONFIGURING REPORTS

To give you an idea of the type of reporting available, there are a number of pre-defined reports available on the FortiAnalyzer. In addition to the Cover Page, the typical report consists of a set of graphical elements, a data table, and an optional textual description. The graphical element for each report is chosen to best represent the type of data in the set. For example, a protocol breakdown uses a pie chart, while a report that compares values over time will typically use a stacked bar chart.

The textual elements are useful for customizing the report to the target audience. You may choose different textual contents if the recipient is a C-level executive, an auditor, or the IT staff. For example, the executive may not be interested in the details, but information about the amount of non-HTTP(S) traffic or changes in the amount of total traffic could be useful as that indicates overall trends. In contrast, the IT staff would be interested in specific protocol and application data.

It is also possible to have the reports automatically generated and distributed. Reports can be emailed to a recipient list or uploaded to a remote system via (S)FTP. This can be used to integrate the reports into an already existing portal. Each report can be uploaded to a unique destination directory as necessary.

Traditional Flat File Reports

Flat file reports are being rapidly deprecated in favor of the far more flexible SQL-backed reporting. This allows for increased scalability by moving the SQL Database engine to an external system.

It is still possible to use the flat file-reporting engine in the 4.3 version of the FortiAnalyzer firmware. However, this was primarily intended for backwards compatibility during the upgrade process from earlier releases. In environments where this is in use, the administrator should plan to migrate to the SQL-based reporting system before applying the 5.0 release. In this release, the flat file report system is being completely removed.

SQL-backed Reports

A SQL database engine for reporting was first introduced in the 4.2 FortiAnalyzer firmware. Over time, the capabilities and report creation/configuration tools have matured to where there is no longer any reason to continue with the flat-file backed reporting. You can choose to use either the built-in SQL database server or you can configure the FortiAnalyzer to act as a SQL client to a database server. At this time, only MySQL is supported for external access. Configuration for SQL logging options is located under System → Config: SQL Database as shown in Figure 8.3.

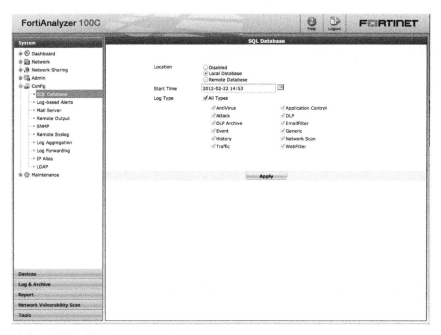

FIGURE 8.3 SQL Database Configuration Options

There are many predefined reports that are likely sufficient for most users' reporting needs. Each report is comprised of a number of both graphical and textual elements. These basic components are referred to as charts. They display the output of a SQL query. The actual query itself is referred to as a dataset. The dataset determines the data to be returned while the chart configuration determines the number of rows returned and allows for more friendly names to be used for the returned data.

Report Server

In addition to the delivery methods provided when defining reports, it is also possible to provide the reports via either SMB/CIFS or NFS. Since this can expose the FortiAnalyzer to additional load, these options do not appear in the WebUI by default. To make the options visible, navigate to System → Admin → Settings and then select the "Show Network Sharing" option. Once the configuration pages are visible, you can configure these file sharing protocols by navigating to the Network Sharing option under "System" and then selecting the desired protocol.

SMB/CIFS Configuration

The FortiAnalyzer can act as a standalone SMB/CIFS workgroup server. It will use the NetBIOS protocol suite, but cannot join an existing domain. Think of the FortiAnalyzer as if it's an older pre-AD windows server.

To activate this, navigate to System → Network Sharing → Windows Share and specify a windows workgroup name. Then select the "Create New" option. This will allow the creation of share names that represent a specific subdirectory branch point. For example, a share called "Reports" allows access to the FortiAnalyzer directory/Storage/Reports, which is where the reports are stored.

NFS Configuration

The FortiAnalyzer can also act as a NFS server. Providing read-only or read-write access to the existing device logging & reporting directories or a custom shared folder can be created. Access is based on the NFS client source IP, FQDN, or network.

To activate this, navigate to System → Network Sharing → NFS Export then checkbox "Enable NFS exports". Once the NFS service is enabled, define the NFS shared directory by selecting the "Create New" option. Specify the "local path" then add the remote NFS client access rights one at a time under "Remote Client" for read-only or read-write access to the specified Local Path.

When mounting to a FortiAnalyzer NFS shared, it is recommended to use the reserved socket port number "resvport" as part of the NFS client option settings.

FORTIANALYZER GENERATED ALERTS

The FortiAnalyzer can operate as a lightweight event correlation engine and send alerts for correlated events to remote syslog servers, SNMP Trap Receivers, and a list of SMTP destinations. Multiple destinations of each type are supported, allowing for multiple event correlation configurations, each with a different list of alert targets.

The alert destinations are configured globally, under System → Config, Remote Syslog, Mail Server, and SNMP respectively. These destinations are then available when you configure alerts. This way, when an incoming log message is received, it is evaluated against the list and any counters are incremented as necessary.

An alert can be configured to match log messages from a single device, multiple devices, groups of devices (shown in blue in the WebUI), or any combination thereof. To trigger an alert, a combination of message type and severity is required. Multiple combinations are possible. Internally, these combinations are logically OR'd together so any match will trigger. In addition to type and severity, you may optionally add a text matching rule. This filter is AND'd with the type/severity filters so that alerts may be matched more precisely.

One risk you face is that a poorly defined alert could result in a flood of alert messages, so an attack against your Fortinet infrastructure could inadvertently result in a denial of service. To avoid this, it is wise that you also configure threshold conditions. This way, an alert will only be generated when a level is exceeded.

LOG AGGREGATION

When a FortiGate is configured to log aggressively, the volume of messages can be surprisingly high. For example, a single packet flow could generate traffic, web filtering, application control, and IPS log messages. To avoid the impact that this can create on a WAN, FortiAnalyzers can be distributed throughout the environment. By placing a FortiAnalyzer on a local network segment, logs are not natively passed across the small WAN links. Instead, they are stored locally and forwarded in compressed batches to the central collection point. This is more efficient than transferring each individual log entry.

A single FortiAnalyzer may be configured to operate either as a collector or an aggregator. A collector will send logs to an upstream aggregator on a password-protected connection (TCP/3000). However, as there is only level of aggregation available, you cannot have one aggregator forward to another.

To configure a FortiAnalyzer for either mode or to disable a previously configured FortiAnalyzer, navigate to System → Config → Log Aggregation, and select the desired option. The password that you enter must be identical between the collector and aggregator. Thus, all collectors that report to the same aggregator must use the same password. This is also where you define the timing for log forwarding. To avoid overwhelming the aggregator, it is recommended that you stagger the upload times.

As of FortiAnalyzer 4.3 you can configure this more simply by setting the "operating mode". From the WebUI dashboard, select the "Change" option in "operation mode" in the System Information widget. Then select with mode it will run in: standalone, collector, or analyzer. The term "analyzer" is the same as "aggregator". In this mode, all menu options are available. However, if you select the "collector" mode, you will no longer have the ability to create and run reports on that device. After all, the device will no longer be storing logs, so creating reports wouldn't make much sense.

If you do change modes, be sure to back up your configuration, as when the menu options are disabled, any previous configuration will be removed.

When configuring a collector, you must specify the IP address of the FortiAnalyzer acting as an analyzer/aggregator. At this point, you will also have the opportunity to define the timing, as mentioned above, or to set the forwarding to take place in real time… based on severity. This allows significant events to be acted upon more quickly. If you do this, it must also match the configuration on the analyzer. This way, an administrator may enable or disable real-time log processing without having to change it on each and every collector in the environment. You can also tell the analyzer to run a de-duplication process, purging all duplicate log entries. This will save space, at the cost of increased CPU usage when the updates are processed.

LOG FORWARDING

As an organization grows, it becomes ever more important to send all log information to a single central source. This way, information may be gathered from FortiGates, routers, switches, and host-based security products and processed in once place. These are often centralized on third party SEIM (Security Event Information Management) products like Arcsight, Netforensics, LogRhythm, and Security Onion. These products typically work by receiving syslog messages.

If you desire, you can send syslog messages from each FortiGate directly to your SEIM. However, this approach does not scale well for widely dispersed networks. Bandwidth can fill up rapidly and the amount of log storage can grow beyond what the infrastructure can support. To avoid these issues, it is often best to configure a FortiAnalyzer to receive all log entries, de-duplicate them, and then pass them along to the SEIM. Not only is this more efficient in terms of network capacity, but as many SEIMs are licensed based on total amount of data processed, this can reduce licensing costs as well.

To configure Log Forwarding, navigate to System → Config → Log Forwarding and select the option to "Enable log forwarding to remote log server". Once this is enabled, you must enter the IP address of the remote system and the severity of the messages to forward. You may also forward all logs or only specifically the "authorized" logs coming from those devices in the "Allowed category" in the Device configuration section. The "authorized" logs can be further tuned to a minimum severity level of log forwarding. The severity levels are Debugging, Information, Notification, Warning, Error, Critical, Alert, and Emergency. Based on the provided order of severity, the Debugging level provides the most verbose level of logging then as the severity level increases the amount of potential events is lowered. By default, severity level is set to "Information". For a breakdown on the various logs generated per severity, Fortinet has this publicly documented under their "Log Message Reference" for each FortiOS release.

LOG MIGRATION

At some point it may become a requirement to upgrade your FortiAnalyzer to a model with greater capacity (disk or CPU/RAM). To help transition existing log data to the replacement FortiAnalyzer, the log migration feature can be configured for this task.

By default, the GUI configuration for log migration is disabled. To enable the option to configure log migration, go to Admin → Settings and select & apply "Show System Migration".

For log migration to work, the following criteria are needed:

1. Both FortiAnalyzers are recommended to have the same firmware version. At minimum for migration to work both FortiAnalyzers need to be at version 4.0 MR1 or higher.
2. There is a two-migration mode role a FortiAnalyzer can be configured for. The FortiAnalyzer that contains the logs to migrate from is considered the "source" role and the FortiAnalyzer where the logs are being migrated to is considered to be the "destination" role.
3. The "source" FortiAnalyzer would be required to reboot into migration mode. Once the source FortiAnalyzer is in migration mode, it could not accept any further log entries until the migration is completed and the unit is rebooted back into a non-migration mode. During the migration, the "destination" Forti-Analyzer can be configured to accept new log entries.

To enable log migration mode on the "source" FortiAnalyzer, go to Maintenance → Migration; select role as "source" then define the FortiAnalyzer IP address under Peer IP where the logs would be copied to then click "apply". Before starting the migration, the destination FortiAnalyzer would need to be configured. On the destination FortiAnalyzer, make sure the migration feature is enabled to be configurable under Admin → Settings then under Maintenance → Migration; select role as "destination", define the source FortiAnalyzer IP address under Peer IP then define the Password which would be the administrator password used on the source FortiAnalyzer. To allow the destination FortiAnalyzer to accept new logs while per-forming the migration, select "Accept Logs & Data". To restrict certain content from being migrated, the setting under "All Categories" can be deselected to not migrate the particular category.

Once the source and destination migration settings are completed, there is an optional setting to test the migration connectivity before actually running the migra-tion. As shown in Figure 8.4, clicking on the "test migration" would perform this function, which would be done on the destination FortiAnalyzer.

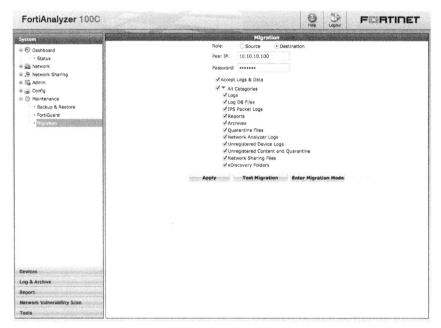

FIGURE 8.4 Log Migration Destination FortiAnalyzer with Test Connectivity

Once the connectivity is confirmed to start the migration, select "Enter Migration Mode". Monitoring of the migration status and progress can be done on the destination FortiAnalyzer.

CONFIGURING FORTIGATES

A single FortiGate can be configured to send data to up to three separate FortiAnalyzers. Each of these is configured separately, though only the first may be configured via the WebUI. To configure the other two devices (for redundancy), you must use the CLI. Each defined FortiAnalyzer can also be configured to receive only specific log messages, as defined by log-type filters. These filter rules are also only available via the CLI.

Direct Logging from Cluster Units

Clusters can create a very large number of log messages. This can negatively affect user traffic, especially since log messages may only be forwarded out the primary unit, as it is the only one with an active IP address.

For these high volume log scenarios, you may use a dedicated interface to send the log messages. This interface would not be managed by the FGCP configuration sync process. This process uses its own IP addresses via hidden system VDOMs which prevents routing or MAC table overlap issues. Once an interface is dedicated to log forwarding, it is effectively isolated from the system and cannot be used for any other purpose. Due to the special nature of this configuration, it is only available from within the CLI.

```
FGT # config system ha
FGT (ha) # set mode <HA Mode>
FGT (ha) # set ha-mgmt-status enable
FGT (ha) # set ha-mgmt-interface <interface name>
FGT (ha) # set ha-mgmt-interface-gateway <ip address>
FGT (ha) # end
FGT # config system interface
FGT (interface) # edit <interface name>
FGT (<interface name>) # set ip <ip address> <subnet mask>
FGT (<interface name>) # end
FGT #
```

There are similar configuration options for the non-FGCP clusters, but those are not commonly deployed and have configuration requirements that are beyond the scope of this book. If you have this need, please discuss the requirements with a Fortinet product specialist.

Testing Configuration

When troubleshooting configuration, it can be very useful to have the ability to test configurations. From within the WebUI of a FortiGate, you may navigate to Log & Report → Log Config → Log Setting → Upload Logs Remotely. In this area, you will see a "Test Connectivity" link. However, this will only test the validity of the TCP connection. So, it can determine device capability and reachability, but cannot verify that the log messages will actually be processed. To do this, you must use a CLI command.

```
FGT # diag log test
generating a system event message with level - warning
generating an infected virus message with level - warning
generating a blocked virus message with level - warning
generating a URL block message with level - warning
generating a DLP message with level - warning
generating an attack detection message with level - warning
generating an application control IM message with level - information
generating an antispam message with level - notification
```

```
generating an allowed traffic message with level - notice
generating a wanopt traffic log message with level - notification
generating a HA event message with level - warning
generating netscan log messages with level - notice
generating a VOIP event message with level - information
generating authentication event messages
```

The "diag log test" command would generate several fake log types from the FortiGate to the log destination configured such as a FortiAnalyzer and/or a Syslog server. The fake logs are usually denoted with a source or destination of a "1.1.1.1" address.

ADDITIONAL FORTIANALYZER FEATURES

In this section we'll cover the remaining FortiAnalyzer features that are included with most FortiAnalyzer hardware and VM versions. FortiAnalyzer Hardware and VM platforms supporting 4.0 MR3 (as of this writing) will support these discussed features. Older FortiAnalyzer hardware models that are limited up to 4.0 MR2 or below may not. It is best to consultant Fortinet FortiAnalyzer product and release note documentation to cover hardware model support for various firmware versions.

eDiscovery Filtered Log Views

eDiscovery or Electronic Discovery is a term used in legal litigations that deals with the exchange of information stored in electronic format. The FortiAnalyzer includes a section to specifically sort archived email message for eDiscovery usage. Archiving of email messages is accomplished via the FortiGate DLP feature covered in Chapter 7.

Besides providing a filtered sort, view, and download of filtered content, the FortiAnalyzer also generates a MD5 and SHA1 digest calculated on the downloaded file. Having a corresponding MD5 or SHA1 hash can confirm the exact copy of data extracted from the FortiAnalyzer device.

eDiscovery can be configured under Log&Archive → eDiscovery. The general steps are highlighted in the following order to help create a eDiscovery output:

1. Create a folder to store the eDisovery sorted log data under Log&Archive → e Discovery:Folders
2. Run the search function base on the filtered criteria needs to extract email messages needed in addition define the "save to folder" option of the folder created in step 1 to save the output to.
3. Go back to the created folder in step 1 to view and download the email messages that were logged based on the search filter functions performed in step 2.

Restriction on disk space set aside to store the filtered eDiscovery logs can be defined under Log&Archive → eDiscovery: Config.

Network Vulnerability Scanner

FortiAnalyzer includes a network-based scanner that provides the ability to conduct scheduled or on-demand TCP/UDP port, OS detection, and network application-service vulnerabilities scans. These scans can be conducted toward a single to a subnet range of hosts. Depending on FortiAnalyzer platform, the maximum number of hosts and number of concurrent scans could vary. Consult Fortinet FortiAnalyzer Administrator guide for an updated list of platform and respective max values.

The operation of the network vulnerability scanner is included with the cost of the FortiAnalyzer solution. For an updated list of network application-service vulnerabilities, a FortiGuard subscription service is required.

To launch a network vulnerability scan, follow the following steps in order:

1. Define an asset to be scanned under Network Vulnerability Scan->Assets Definition. This could be a single or range of hosts' definition. In addition, Microsoft Windows or Unix authentication can be defined to provide more granular host level access to conduct further system level logging and vulnerability assessments.
2. Define when and how to perform the scan for the defined asset created in the above step. This is created under Network Vulnerability Scan->Scan Schedule. Select "create new" to start the Scan Schedule definition which would involve selecting the asset(s) to scan as defined in step 1, choosing the vulnerability scan mode of Quick, Standard, or Full then defining whether to schedule the scan or run it on-demand.

The scan progress can be seen for each scan scheduled under Network Vulnerability Scan → Scan Schedule. Once the scan is completed, the report is produced under Network Vulnerability Scan → Vulnerability Results.

The vulnerability reports can provide a high-level executive summary and a breakdown of service ports discovered, the operating system detected, and any vulnerabilities discovered. Detail of the discovered vulnerability within the report would provide the individual vulnerability URL link to the FortiGuard website outlining the vulnerability severity, impact, description, recommend actions to remediate the vulnerability, and any third-party references such as BugTraq, CVE, or MS Bulletins.

Network Analyzer

The network analyzer feature is a network sniffer that can be used to assist with network diagnostics and troubleshooting. This feature requires the configured network analyzer port on the FortiAnalyzer to be connected to a switch SPAN port to assist with the preferred network segment captures. The captured packets can be displayed historically or in real time via the FortiAnalyzer web GUI console. In addition, the capture raw traces can be downloaded into text or CSV format. Rolling over of the capture traces can be uploaded via FTP, SFTP, or SCP to an external server for storage.

By default, this feature is hidden. To enable network analyzer feature, go to System → Admin: Settings and select & apply "Show Network Analyzer". Once enabled, the feature would be located under the left menu "Tools" section.

To launch a network capture, the following steps are performed:

1. Set up a SPAN port on switch for the network segments needed to be monitor. The FortiAnalyzer would need to have physical Ethernet connectivity to the switch SPAN port for the network analyzer to function.
2. On the FortiAnalyzer, go to Tools → Network Analyzer: Config and checkbox "Enable network Analyzer on" then select the FortiAnalyzer port where the SPAN port is connected.
3. Optional settings could involve defining the allocated disk space for storage of the network capture traces, defining the log roll over settings based on size along with time frame, then option for uploading the logs once it's rolled over to an external site via FTP, SFTP, or SCP.

To view the captured traces, go to Tools → Network Analyzer: Historical. To view the logs in real time, click on the icon with the clock on the document. There are options to add additional column views, sort each column by clicking on the funnel icons next to the column names, and ability to print the filtered historical views.

To browse historically collected captures and also to download the captures, go to Tools → Network Analyzer: Browse.

Managing Your Security Configurations with FortiManager

INFORMATION IN THIS CHAPTER:

- System Settings Console
- Administrative Domains
  - Top Down vs. Bottom Up Management
  - Creating Administrative Domains
- Device Manager
  - "Add Device" Wizard
  - Adding Multiple Devices
  - Device Groups
- Device Level Management & Configuration
- Policy & Objects
  - Policy Package Management
  - Managing Security Objects
  - Installing Policy and Device Configurations
  - Global Policy & Objects
- Managing Site-to-Site Distributed IPSec VPNs
  - Policy and Device VPNs
  - Central VPN Console

FortiManager is the centralized management console for maintaining Fortinet device deployments, which can be deployed in an appliance form factor or as a Virtual Machine (VM). This technology scales to potentially thousands of devices depending on the size of the FortiManager console deployed. The centralized console aids an organization by allowing granular controls and administrative privileges. It allows for template-based configurations of large deployments with configuration revision control capabilities and the ability to host the signature updates and web database queries as an extension of the FortiGuard Distribution Network for the managed devices among other features all through a single Web UI.

Upon first logging into the FortiManager an administrator will find multiple console tabs across the top of the web interface. The "System Settings" console is where the FortiManager device itself will be configured along with settings that affect options available in the other tabs. The "Device Manager" console is the location where you will maintain all managed devices and where device-specific configuration will occur. The "Policy & Objects" tab is the primary security console where all policies are managed and the object database is stored. The last tab presented is the "Real-Time Monitor" console where basic device monitoring can be configured and one can observe the status of the devices under management.

Later in this chapter we will also explore the "Administrative Domain" and the "Global Policy & Objects" tabs.

Being that the FortiManager could realistically be a stand-alone topic for its own book, we will provide an overview of each console while providing additional detail on points that will help an administrator begin using a FortiManager to maintain a large Fortinet deployment.

SYSTEM SETTINGS CONSOLE

The System Settings console contains four main sections, "General," "Admin," "FortiGuard Center," and "Advanced."

The first screen the administrator sees is the System Settings → General → Dashboard. Like the dashboard seen in the FortiOS device Web UI, this dashboard is also made up of multiple Widgets. The Widgets can be opened, closed, and positioned for each administrator logging into the platform. Like FortiOS, there are the System Resource and CLI widgets, but for the FortiManager arguably the two most important widgets are the System Information and License Information widgets.

The System Information widget provides your serial number, HA Status, and other basic information, but it is also the widget that allows us to verify and upgrade the FortiManager firmware, back up and restore the system configuration, as well as enable advanced features such as the use of Administrative Domains and the Forti-Console Software.

The License Information widget allows us to add to the features of the FortiManager by adding the license data to increase the number of administrative domains supported by the system, enabling the use of Global Policy & Objects and the Web Portal.

The System Settings → General → Network section gives you the ability to maintain the IP configurations for the interfaces on the system, modify the routing table, and apply the appropriate DNS server information to ensure you can communicate with the managed devices and the FortiGuard Distribution Network (FDN). In addition to the basic IP information applied to each interface, the administrator will also choose the interfaces on which to enable FortiGate and FortiClient updates to be served.

The System Settings Certificate and Local Log sections are exactly what one would expect. You can view and maintain the Local and CA Certificates in the Certificate section while in the Local Log section you can view the local event logs. The Diagnostic Tools section provides the user access to the ping and trace route utilities in the GUI without needing to navigate to the CLI.

The HA section allows you to configure the High-Availability (HA) Cluster Settings. FortiManager High Availability differs from the FortiGate implementation. With FortiManager you configure one primary and up to four secondary or backup units. So long as all units have IP connectivity, units in the HA cluster do not have geographic limitations. While all configuration and database information is automatically replicated between HA members, in the event of a loss to the master unit, you must manually promote one of the backup units to the role of master.

The Admin subsection of the System Settings tab allows you to create administrators and authenticate them locally or remotely via Radius, LDAP, or TACACS+. Regular user accounts, or non-"Super_User" accounts, can be restricted to specific Administrative Domains.

The administrator accounts are assigned a "Profile" which outlines the privileges allowed to that user. Privileges are allowed in a Read-Only or Read-Write mode and are provisioned based on the "Scope" of the Profile, either "Global" or "ADOM" (see Figure 9.1).

Many of the features you will want to leverage when managing devices throughout the rest of the web interface are enabled in "Admin Settings." Features such as IPv6 administration and the enabling of the Central NAT table will become useable throughout the web interface by selecting them here and applying changes. If you enable the use of administrative domains via the Dashboard Systems Information widget, you will also be able to enable the Global Policy & Objects features.

In some environments you will prefer that your Fortinet devices do not connect directly through the Internet to access the FortiGuard Distribution Network for updates. In this case, FortiManager can be configured to act as an extension of the FDN. The FortiManager will directly pull signatures and update the URL and SPAM databases in order to allow the security devices within the environment to then get their updates directly from the FortiManager.

FIGURE 9.1 Admin Profile

By choosing your configuration options within the "FortiGuard Center" section, you can have the FortiManager download the update services for any FortiGate, FortiClient, FortiMail, and FortiAnalyzer that have the appropriate subscription services enabled. Understand, though, that the FortiManager will enforce the same limitations on downloads to devices without subscription services, as would the FortiGuard Distribution Network. In addition to service updates, the FortiManager can be configured to download the firmware for the managed devices to be used when scheduling firmware upgrades.

The "Advanced" section also supports "Meta Fields." These data fields can be created to allow and/or require administrators to add additional information when manipulating system and security objects. By default, there are many optional Meta Fields, such as the Company/Organization, Country, Province/State, City, and Contact fields that are available when you create a new device. As an example, it is common to use a mandatory meta field when creating a firewall policy object where the field requires the administrator to include as a value, a reference number to a change order. This allows the auditing of rules created based on who created the change and under what authority the change was made and simplifies the change control process.

ADMINISTRATIVE DOMAINS

A FortiManager Administrative Domain (ADOM) is analogous to the Virtual Domain concept within the FortiGate. The use of ADOMs allows us to create separate logical environments in which we can maintain separate sets of devices. These devices may be physical (i.e. FortiGate appliances), virtual (i.e. FortiGate-VM), and/or logical (FortiGate Virtual Domains). Each administrative domain provides a separation of management based on geographic responsibilities, business unit partitioning, or any other reason one might need to maintain separate zones of responsibility. The number of ADOMs you can create is dependent on the FortiManager platform you have deployed, however, at the time of this writing, even the smallest FortiManager supports 10 ADOMs and larger units can support hundreds.

Top Down vs. Bottom Up Management

When creating an Administrative Domain you define one of the two modes in which you wish the ADOM to operate: "Normal" or "Backup."

An ADOM in "Normal" mode operates, as most would expect when using most centralized management solution, with a "Top Down" structure enforced. In a Top Down management architecture, all device configurations are centrally maintained and then provisioned to the managed devices.

When a FortiGate is managed in a "Normal" mode ADOM, direct access to the devices is still supported. However, making changes at the device can cause synchronization conflicts with the FortiManager, which would need to be remedied as described later. If the managed devices are running FortiOS 4.3 or later, you will be warned when logging in that the device is centrally managed and that changes should be done via the FortiManager. The warning banner also provides you with the option to login into the system in a read-only mode, in a privileged (read and write) mode or to logout.

One of the advantages of a FortiManager over many other solutions is the ability to additionally support the "Backup" mode. This allows for a "Bottom Up" deployment where all configuration is performed at a device level, but the FortiManager Administrative Domain allowing for a "Bottom Up" deployment architecture. When managing device within a "Backup" mode ADOM, the administrators are able to continue operating in an environment where all configuration management is maintained at the device level. While no configuration provisioning is centrally maintained, the FortiManager can still be leveraged for revision control as a configuration repository, for script deployment, centralized firmware upgrades, FortiGuard service updates, and device monitoring.

Creating Administrative Domains

Before you can create multiple ADOMs to suit their deployment requirements, you must first enable Administrative Domains.

To enable ADOMs through the Web UI, simply go to the "System Settings" tab and navigate to the "System Settings → General → Dashboard." Once at the dashboard, locate the "System Information" widget and select the "Enable" link on the row for "Administrative Domain." After confirming that you want to enable ADOMs, you will be required to log back into the FortiManager.

Upon re-authenticating, the administrator will encounter a slightly different tab layout. Gone will be the "Device Manager" and "Policy & Objects" tabs and instead we will now see the "Administrator Domain" tab. In this new tab, we are able to create, edit, and delete administrative domains for our administrative needs.

From the ADOM tab we are able to view the ADOMs created on the Forti-Manager as well as the device statuses within each ADOM. If this is the first time accessing the ADOM tab, only the default "root" ADOM will be visible. In order to create additional ADOMs, we simply select the "Create New" button or right click and select the option "New." Upon doing so we will be presented with the ADOM creation screen (see Figure 9.2).

Start by giving the new ADOM a name and "Version." The Version selected must correlate to the firmware revision of the devices to be managed. As of this writing, the supported versions are 4.0 MR2 and 4.0 MR3. The "Mode" of operation will either be left as "Normal" or changed to "Backup."

If you choose to continue to create the ADOM in Normal mode, you will also need to select the "VPN Management" options. The choices are "Central VPN Console" and "Policy & Device," both covered in some detail later. Last, you will have the option to select from devices already being managed and include them into the ADOM. You can select none, one, or many devices depending on the requirements. However, bear in mind that any devices moved into this new ADOM will no longer be accessible in their previous.

FIGURE 9.2 ADOM Creation

After ADOM creation, you can always use the right click option to "Edit" the ADOM and change any of the configuration options. To enter an ADOM and manage your device, you can right click over the desired ADOM and select "Enter ADOM." Then hover your mouse over your intended ADOM and select the "Enter" button that appears or use the drop down menu in the top right of the Web UI.

Once in the ADOM, you will find your "Device Manager" and "Policy & Objects" tabs unique to the ADOM. Each ADOM maintains its own device, policy, and objects databases, allowing for unique configurations of the devices within each ADOM.

DEVICE MANAGER

Within each Administrative Domain you will find the "Device Manager." The Device Manager is the tool used to add devices to be managed and to maintain all of the device-specific configurations.

"Add Device" Wizard

There are multiple approaches for importing devices into the FortiManager. The first of the two approaches we will cover is the "Add Device" wizard. This wizard will walk you through discovering your device settings, importing policies and objects, and exporting them to the security console "Policy and Object" tab. It will also walk you through the process of mapping the device interfaces to the security console's Zones.

Selecting the "Add Device" button toward the top of the window will launch the import wizard and walk you through the steps to import your device.

The first screen is where we input the IP Address, User Name, and Password information for the device we want to add to the manager. The User Name and Password must be that of a privileged administrator on the device we intend to import. FortiManager will use this account to read and write directly to the managed device when we deploy configurations, execute CLI scripts as well as manage firmware upgrades. If there is a concern about the level of privilege for the specific administrative account, that account can be locked down to the IP addresses of the FortiManager system using the trusted host option on the device.

You also have the option to add a modeled device if you want to prepare to manage a system that is not yet in production. When adding the modeled device, you will provide the IP Address, User Name, and Password for the device to be managed. However, unlike when adding a live device, the wizard will not walk you through the importation of objects and policy configuration as those settings would not yet exist.

By selecting "next," the FortiManager will attempt to login and query the device using the account provided. Assuming good IP connectivity exists, allowing TCP port 514 access to the device, the account has the correct access right to the device and the device is configured to allow FortiManager administration on the interface to which you are attempting to connect, the device will be discovered and you will be provided a summary. This summary will include the IP Address, Admin User, Device Model, Firmware Version, Serial Number, and the High Availability Mode of the device. If all the information is what as expected, you can select "next" to move forward. If there was an error, you can go "Back" and correct your mistakes.

The next step allows you to choose a name and description for the device. The default value will be what is configured on the device, though if that is not unique enterprise-wide, you may wish to change it. During this step, you can also choose to include this device into one of the defined groups. You will also be able to add other administrative information such as the location and a primary contact.

As you move to the next step in the wizard, the FortiManager will retrieve all the device's configuration settings and load them into the FortiManager device database. Once added, the FortiManager will walk you through mapping the device's interfaces to Zones, importing the security objects into the ADOM's Object Database, and copying the policies into a Policy Package. If the device being imported is configured with multiple VDOMs, the wizard will walk you through these processes for each individual VDOM.

During the Zone mapping of the device's physical interfaces, the FortiManager will present you with those interfaces that have policies applied and offer to create Zones with names that match the interface names. At this point, you can choose to accept the new Zone names, to map the interfaces to a new Zone, or map them to Zones that have already been created in the Policy and Object console. If you wish to select an existing Zone, you can begin typing the name of that Zone. If you are not positive of the Zone name you wish to select, character match-based suggestions will be presented. However, be aware that these suggestions are case sensitive.

The last option to select is whether or not you want the FortiManager to automatically map all of the interfaces to Zones with names matching those of the interfaces themselves, but without policies applied. This is often useful for devices with many interfaces.

The next steps walk through the process of importing the policy configuration from the device into a New Policy Package where you can select the name of the package as well as the package folder in which to store it. You also have the option to import all of the device's policies or choose to select specific rules to be imported. Understand though that everything set in the Policy Package, the next time you push to the device, will be the policy set on the device. If you do choose to leave policies out of the import process, expect those policies to vanish from the device when the package is modified and redeployed to the platform.

During the import process, you will be able to review the object being imported, view any duplicates that will not be imported, and be presented the option to choose which object to keep to resolve conflicts with an already-existing object of the same name in the database. Once this process is complete, you will see a summary created as well as the option download and view the "Import Report." The import report provides us a more detailed summary of the zones, policies, and object imported.

Adding Multiple Devices

The second method to discuss is only available if you have enabled the "Show Add Multiple Button" in System Settings → Admin Settings. This provides the ability to add multiple devices to an administrative domain in a single action. By navigating to the "All FortiGate" folder within the Device Manager tab, you can select the "Add Multiple" button and be presented with a new screen. By providing the Name, Device Type, IP Address, Admin User, and Password for each device you intend to add, the FortiManager will query each and import the configuration into the database (see Figure 9.3).

This process does not include an automatic walk through to assist with importing the objects and policies into the FortiManager's Policy & Objects database. This can be helpful when adding multiple devices to be managed by the same policy package.

If you must install the objects and policies from any of the devices, the process is pretty straightforward. After you select the "All FortiGate" folder, right click on the device you wish to import and select "Import Policy." This will walk you through the Zone Map, Object, and Policy portion of the Add Device wizard and, following the same process outlined earlier, will import the information into the Policy & Objects database. For each additional device to import, you will repeat this process (see Figure 9.4).

FIGURE 9.3 Adding Multiple Devices

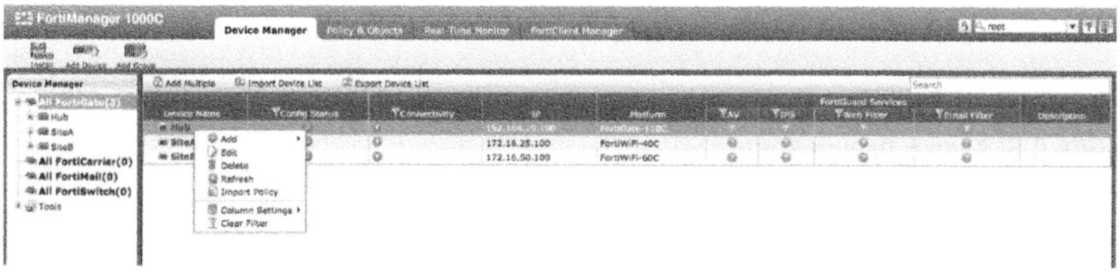

FIGURE 9.4 Policy Importing

Device Groups

With many devices to manage, the creation of Device Groups will help to organize and manage the environment. Groups not only allow us a way to view our device-based organization relationships, but also allow us to execute actions such as configuration and firmware deployments at the group level, thereby reducing the operational step to managing the environment. It is also possible to nest group to provide a potential hierarchy of management.

Select the "Add Group" button to create your Device Group. The "Add Device Group" window will appear, allowing you to name the group, select the group OS type, and the device and/or groups to be included in the new group.

Once your groups are created, they will allow you to monitor those devices in the group as well as allow you to deploy scripts and firmware to the devices in the group without requiring you to perform those tasks on a device-by-device basis (see Figure 9.5).

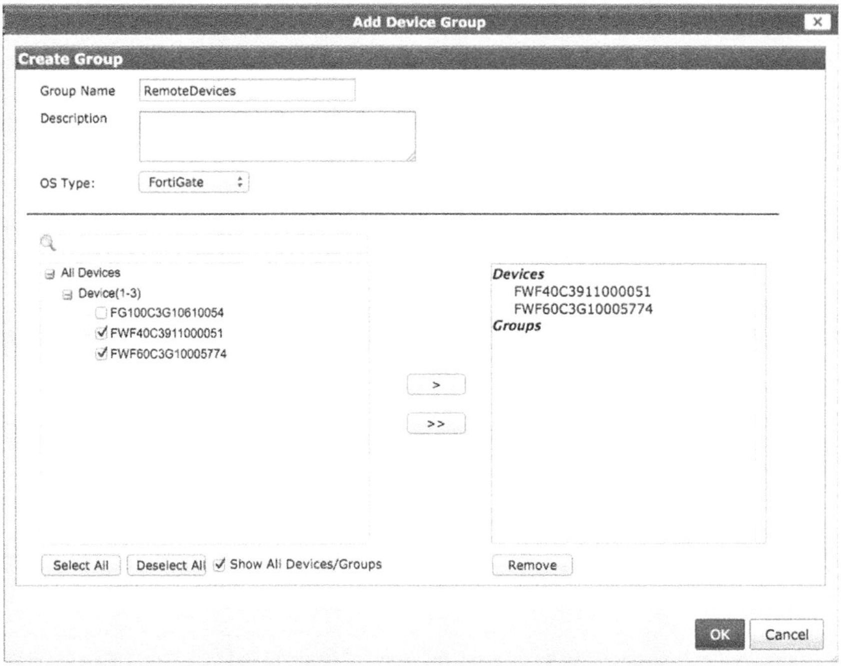

FIGURE 9.5 Adding Device Group

DEVICE LEVEL MANAGEMENT & CONFIGURATION

The Device Manager allows us to monitor licensing, firmware revision, and configuration status of each device on the system. You can also manage the configuration revisions of each device, view the changes deployed or planned to be deployed and, if required, revert to a previous revision.

With your devices are added and your device groups are created, you can maintain all of the system-level configurations required to manage your environment. Selecting a device to manage will offer a layout for the configuration workflow similar to that seen in the FortiOS Web UI. One difference to remember is that any changes made are not performed immediately. Instead, they are staged and installed at a later time using the "Install" wizard (see Figure 9.6).

While the majority of the device configuration is nearly identical to that of the native devices, there are some additional configurations to be maintained with FortiManager. The first is the "Zone Map." The Zone Map associates each device's physical interfaces with the logical representation of source and destination zones used in the Policy & Objects section. If you have used the "Install" wizard, the FortiManager will have a mapping for each interface. If, however, you did not use the wizard or desire to change the mapping, navigate to the device "Network" → "Zone

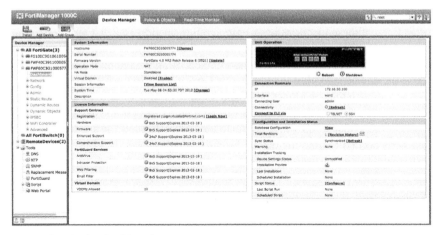

FIGURE 9.6 A Device Dashboard

Map" section and right click on a row. You will be able to add to or edit the existing interface mapped to that zone. If you must map an interface to a new, not displayed, zone, select "Show Unmapped Zones" in the upper left portion of the right pane and all available zones will be displayed. Then, as before, you may right click on the row containing the zone to add an association (see Figure 9.7).

The other main area that differs from the FortiOS-based workflow is the "Dynamic Objects" configuration. Security objects used during policy creation are maintained in the object database in the Policy & Objects section. There are times when an object may use a global name, but must have locally unique value. A simple example would be an environment with a thousand distributed locations where each device

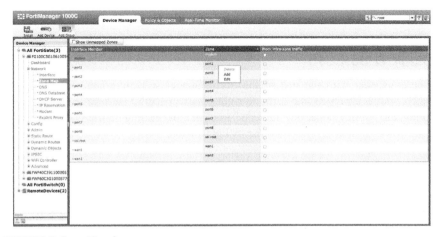

FIGURE 9.7 Zone Mapping

is managed by the same policy set… an ability of the FortiManager to be explored shortly. Each of these locations has a unique range of addresses that require the same policy applied. Instead of needing to maintain one thousand unique objects in the policy set, you can create a single address in your database and map that to its unique value at the device level through "Dynamic Object" → "Address."

To accomplish this, an object is defined in the object database. Once that object is created, the administrator will create a new dynamic object at the device level, mapping the unique value to the object name in the object database. While there are additional steps needed to map the device level dynamic objects, it will save significant time to maintain the security posture of potentially thousands of devices. During the import of a device using the "Add Device" wizard, if an object exists on the device with the identical name of an existing object in the object database that local object will automatically be mapped to a dynamic object on the FortiManager.

The types of Dynamic Objects supported as of this writing are addresses, virtual IPs, IP Pools, Local Certificates, and policy-based VPN Tunnels.

If the administrator has selected "Show Device Manager Tools" in the administrator area, you will also have access to advanced tools such as the Script and Web Portal Managers. While we will not be able to cover these topics in detail, these tools can be powerful.

The scripting tools allow an administrator to create CLI and/or TCL-based scripts to be deployed to the devices being managed. A simple example of this could be the need to change the "admin" password on all devices at once. More information on this topic can be found in the "FortiManager Administrator's Guide" found at http://docs.fortinet.com/fmgr40.html.

The Web Portal allows an administrator to create unique web portal access to sub-administrators, potential users, with configuration capabilities limited to very specific object types. This way, you could delegate the responsibility of managing URL filtering to someone in HR without needing to worry about them causing problems with firewall or routing.

POLICY & OBJECTS

To be consistent with the rest of the FortiManager web interface, the "Policy & Objects" tab is arranged into left and right panes of focus. Starting in the left pane you find the "Policy" tree, the "Objects" tree, and, depending on the system configuration, you may also be presented the "VPN Console."

Policy Package Management

The "Policy" tree is where you will maintain and organize the policy packages used to define the firewall security configurations that are to be installed down to the managed devices. Policy packages can be assigned to a single or multiple devices based on the administrator's requirements. This allows for a significant reduction in the workload required to maintain the security posture of potentially thousands of devices.

The first time entering the "Policy & Objects" tab, the administrator will find the policy package named "default." If the administrator has already used the "Device Manager," there may also be additional policy packages available. Use of the installation wizard was covered in detail during the "Device Manager" section above.

To create a new policy package, simply right click on "Policy" in the left pane and select "New," "Policy Package." This selection will present the administrator with the "Create New Policy Package" pop-up. When creating a new policy package, you are required to provide a unique name for the new package. When creating it, you also have the option to clone an existing policy package and/or select the installation target or targets to which the package will be applied (see Figure 9.8).

The cloning option allows you to create a new package based off of an existing template, to create a copy or backup of an existing package that you plan to manipulate, or for any other reason to duplicate an existing package. Once you select "Clone Policy Package," a list of the available packages is displayed. Simply select the presented package you intend to clone.

The last decision to be made when creating a new policy package is to determine the installation target or targets for the new package. Targets can include a single managed device, multiple managed devices, one or more device groups, or any combination of devices and groups, including none. Selecting "apply" to complete package creation without selecting at least one device to install the package on will result in a warning that no targets have been selected. If you did not select a target in error, simply select cancel when warned and choose your targets and reapply. It is, however, perfectly acceptable to create a package that does not contain any active targets. Installation targets can always be selected after package creation by right clicking on the package name and selecting "Edit." A screen similar to the package creation screen will be presented, allowing the administrator to select additional devices and/or remove existing targets.

While a single policy package can be assigned to multiple devices, deploying multiple policy packages to a single device may not have the desired or expected results. While it is possible to have more than one package configured for the same target, the intent is not to have multiple packages applied to the device at the same time. During the deployment process, each package overwrites the previous. So, installing multiple policy packages to a device in sequence will have the result of only the last package taking effect. If an administrator was to install multiple policy packages to a device or group of devices in sequence, the last policy package applied will define the rule set on the device or devices overwriting the rule sets applied in the previous installations. Without the understanding that applying multiple packages does not have a cumulative effect on the security posture will create a situation where you do not have the setting you want on the device and potentially cause a degraded security posture.

If there is a requirement to have a layered rule set, a simple example being a corporate security policy that needs to be applied to all Firewalls regardless of the

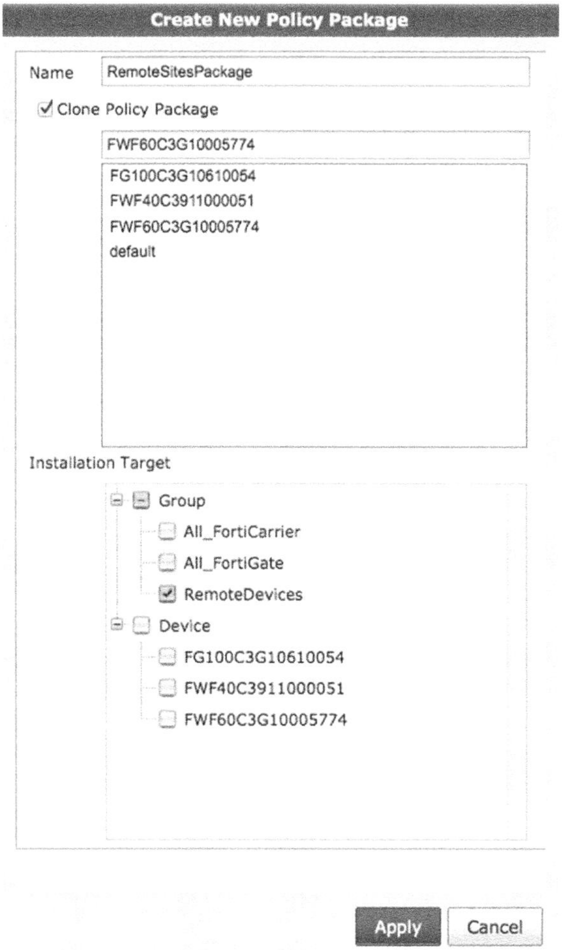

FIGURE 9.8 Creating New Policy Package

local administrators rule base, this is possible with FortiManager. We will cover this topic by describing the use "Global Policy Packages" later in this chapter.

If an administrator finds they need to manage many policy packages, it may be convenient to organize the packages into folders. Similar to creating a new package, one would again right click on "Policy" in the left pane and then select "New" → "Folder," provide a name for the new folder, and select "OK." In order to organize the policy packages into folders, simply left click on the package and drag that package into the folder desired. If the complexity is warranted, folders can be created and organized hierarchically.

As packages are intended to maintain the security policies to be deployed to the devices, individual policies are created similarly to how policies are created within the FortiGate Web UI. However, the Web UI of the FortiManager is much more flexible, as it allows you to copy, cut, and paste polices, as well as drag and drop policies for reordering. You are provided much more flexible search and "where used" capabilities and a context-sensitive right click function that will present different functions, based on the policy package you intend to manipulate (see Figure 9.9).

Unlike a policy set on a device that references the interfaces and security objects of that device, policy packages can apply to a single device or many devices. To accomplish this, the packages will reference values from the domain's Object database.

Managing Security Objects

Each Administrative Domain has a database for administrators to create the security objects needed to maintain their environment while avoiding name and value conflicts, as different ADOMs have their own database space.

As mentioned previously, the administrative workflow is nearly identical to that seen in the FortiOS Web UI. The key difference is that these objects will be applied across policy packages that affect the security posture of potentially thousands of devices. This greatly reduces the work required to tune the environment's security.

Installing Policy and Device Configurations

When an administrator must deploy configuration changes to the managed device, they will want to verify them prior to deployment. First, an administrator may wish to leverage the "Policy Check" feature. This is only available if you have enabled it in the "Admin Setting" section. Policy Check runs a validation process against all the Policy Packages in the domain and will indicate conflicts, shadowed policies, duplicate objects, and candidates for optimizations (see Figure 9.10).

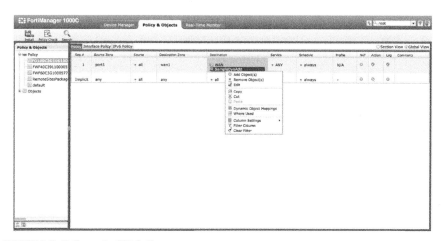

FIGURE 9.9 Policy rule GUI Options

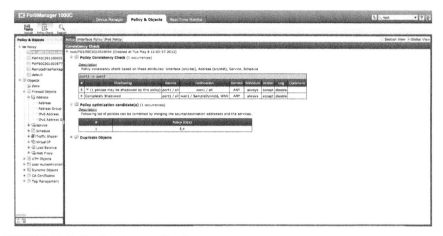

FIGURE 9.10 Policy Consistency Checks

After you are comfortable with your packages and are ready to deploy them, the "Install" wizard will walk you through the process. You will be prompted to install all pending changes including the Policy Package data or to just install the device level configurations. If you choose to deploy all pending changes, the wizard will allow the selection of which Policy Packages are to be deployed and to which of the targeted devices. During the wizard execution process, the interface to zone mappings will be validated, giving you an opportunity to preview the changes. After successful deployment, the FortiManager will save a new revision in the device's revision history, assisting with future auditing (see Figure 9.11).

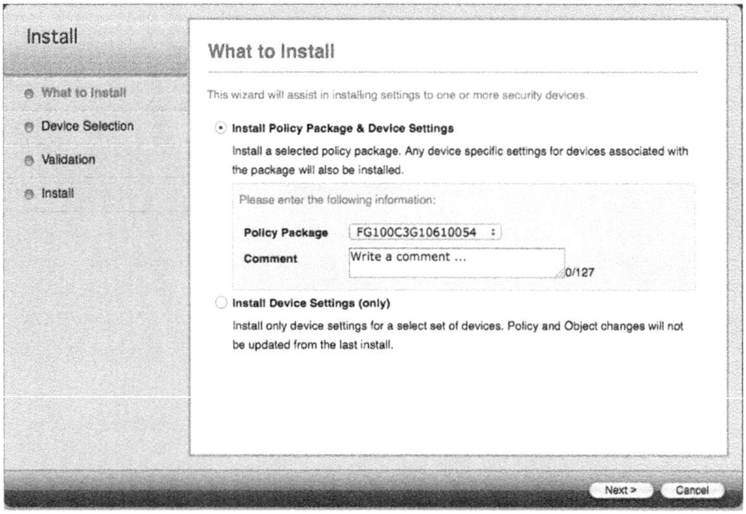

FIGURE 9.11 Installation Wizard

Global Policy & Objects

In some environments, there will be a need to have individual administrators responsible for their respective devices while still allowing a more senior administrator to override policies. The FortiManager allows this hierarchical approach to deploying policy through the use of "Global Policy & Objects."

Like the other features on the device, Global Policy & Objects is a licensed feature that is enabled in Admin Settings. This workflow and configuration tasks are nearly identical to the workflow of tasks in the Policy & Objects section. The few differences between the workflows are detailed below.

First, the Global Packages consist of "Header" and "Footer" policies. While the policies are created and managed like those in a normal packager, in a Global Package, the Header Policies will be prepended to any Policy Package at the ADOM level. However, the Global Package is also assigned as the Footer Policies will be appended to the policy set in the local ADOM packages. This provides the ability to override the ADOM Packages with Header Policies and to use Footer Packages to add trailing rules prior to the implicit deny (see Figure 9.12).

Like the ADOM "Install" wizard used to deploy changes to the managed devices, Global Policy & Objects are deployed to the Policy Packages in the ADOM using the "Assignment" wizard. When launching the Assignment Wizard you select the Global Package to be deployed and the ADOMs and/or Policy Packages within the ADOMs to which you will assign the Header and Footer Policies. New Header and Footer Policies are not deployed to the managed devices until you select to use the Install wizard in the appropriate ADOM (see Figure 9.13).

Finally, understand that to use Global Zones their names must match those of the ADOM zones to which they will be applied. If there are no matches, the assignment will fail. As of this writing, zone names do not "inherit," so preplanning zone naming is important.

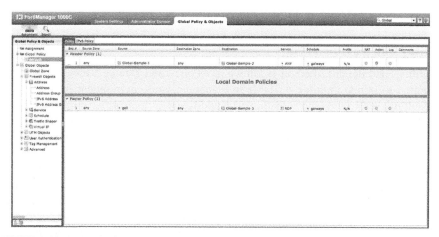

FIGURE 9.12 Global Policy

FIGURE 9.13 Global Policy Assignments

MANAGING SITE-TO-SITE DISTRIBUTED IPSEC VPNS

Most people choose to use a centralized management console when they must maintain a large distributed IPSec VPN network. There are many complexities involved and these challenges tend to increase faster than the network does. To provide service at scale as these networks grow, the FortiManager provides two different methods for managing IPSec VPNs.

Policy and Device VPNs

The first, and default, method is known as "Policy and Device VPNs." If you are required to utilize multiple ADOMs in managing your environment, it is also the default mode selected when creating each additional administrative domain.

With this approach, IPSec configuration is managed in the "Device Manager" tab. The Phase I and Phase II configurations are constructed and maintained on a device-by-device basis with a configuration workflow effectively identical to that seen in FortiOS. Because the IPSec configurations are maintained on an individual device basis, this mode of operation does not provide much economy of scale during the tunnel creation process. However, there are still many advantages in using the FortiManager to maintain devices security postures. You can leverage the common object database and policy packages to simplify the workflow required once the tunnels are established.

Preparing to Create the VPN

Once a network plan is in place, you will need to determine how you want to apply policy to the devices and tunnels. The decision process will include whether to leverage the simplicity of using a single policy package across multiple devices to reduce administrative overhead or if each device will require a unique policy package. In addition to determining how to best apply the policy packages, you must determine how to treat a device with multiple tunnels defined. Will each of the tunnels have a unique set of policies or will they share a common policy structure? If the tunnels will share the same security requirements, you can group them together, again reducing the maintenance overhead.

It is reasonable to see environments with many devices, each possibly with multiple tunnels defined, all managed with a single policy package and little forethought. This approach can be used to allow a simple network design to scale. However, be aware that the "heavy lifting" is required initially in the creation of the actual IPSec tunnels, accomplished device by device through the device manager.

To illustrate how a FortiManager assists with VPN management in the Policy and Device VPN mode, below is a simple Hub and spoke VPN network. We will now walk through the creation of both a Policy Mode VPN network as well as an Interface Mode VPN network. As you will see shortly, how you define the tunnels will determine how they are treated within by FortiManager (see Figure 9.14).

Creating and Managing a Policy Mode VPN

In the simple case, the security posture for the Hub location will be maintained with a unique policy package. The package will allow traffic sourced from the internal protected segment (the 192.168.10.0/24 subnet) will access the remote protected segments of Sites A and B through the appropriate IPSec tunnel.

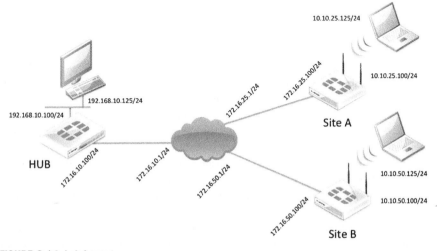

FIGURE 9.14 Lab Layout

Both Sites A and B will have identical security requirements, allowing traffic sourced from their local segments (10.10.25.0/24 and 10.10.50.0/24 respectively) back to the Hub's internal protected segment and will be able to share a common policy package. Sharing the same package helps us reduce the management overhead of this type of distributed network and could allow us to grow far beyond the two remote sites in our example.

To create this VPN we will need to do six steps:

- Define the VPN Tunnel Dynamic Objects.
- Create the Firewall Address objects representing the protected segments.
- Configure the appropriate Policies in the Policy Packages.
- Construct the IPSec Tunnels.
- Define VPN Tunnel and Address Dynamic Objects for each device.
- Install the configuration to production devices.

When creating the tunnels in Policy Mode, you are required to define VPN Tunnel Dynamic Objects to use when building Policy Packages. Within the Policy Packages, these dynamic objects allow you to select the appropriate tunnels for IPSec policies.

For each tunnel defined on a device you will need a unique Dynamic Object. In this example we have created three of these objects. "Tunnel-To-SiteA" and "Tunnel-To-SiteB" will be associated with tunnels on the Hub to the appropriate remote location. The object "Tunnel-To-Hub" will be associated at both Site A and B devices, representing the corresponding tunnels from each site back to the Hub. By using this one dynamic object for each remote location, we can create a single policy package across multiple remote sites. This approach can be applied across hundreds of sites. You will see how to apply these dynamic objects shortly (see Figure 9.15).

The next objects we must prepare are the Firewall Address objects used to define the protected subnets. We will use these to identify the traffic that must be secured. With the same workflow we covered earlier in this chapter, we create the Firewall Address objects "Hub-Internal" (192.168.10.0/24), "SiteA-Internal" (10.10.25.0/24), and "SiteB-Internal" (10.10.50.0/24) to be applied in our Policy Packages. While most networks require a more complex use of address objects to restrict or allow access more granularly, our example is kept straightforward to focus on the steps required to get the VPN up and operational (see Figure 9.16).

Now that our objects are defined, we can define the policies needed to define which traffic will be selected for transport over the VPN. In the Policy Package to be installed onto the Hub device, we must create policies that define the traffic associated with each tunnel on the device. The greater the number of tunnels, the more complex the Policy Package will need to become. In this package, we create one policy identifying traffic sourced from the Hub's internal segment destined to Site A's internal segment. This will transport through the tunnel between Hub and Site A. Similarly, we will create a second policy for traffic destined to Site B using the tunnel between it and the Hub (see Figure 9.17).

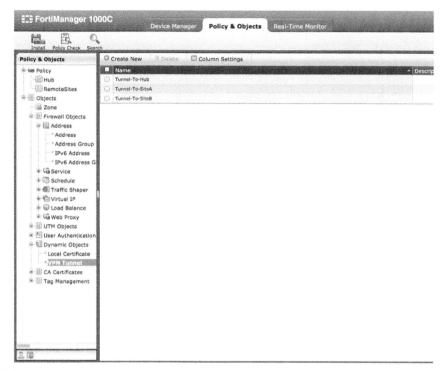

FIGURE 9.15 Policy Mode IPSec Dynamic Tunnel Objects

For the remote locations, we will leverage a single policy package across multiple devices and use them to define the traffic to be encrypted back to the Hub site. To accomplish this goal, we will use a very broad policy allowing "all" traffic destined

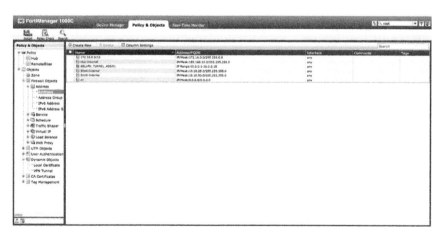

FIGURE 9.16 Policy Mode IPSec Address Objects

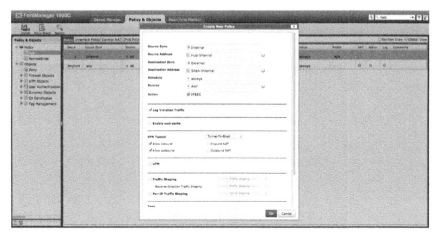

FIGURE 9.17 Policy Mode IPSec Local Device Encryption Policy

to the protected segment of the Hub, "Hub-Internal," sourced from the Internal zone of the remote locations to be sent to the "Tunnel-To-Hub" VPN Tunnel Dynamic Object (see Figure 9.18).

At this point in the configuration, VPN Tunnel Dynamic Objects are used to define the tunnels in our policies. What may not be clear, though, is how these objects are associated with the actual tunnels, yet to be constructed.

As mentioned earlier, the actual creation of the tunnels is accomplished by navigating to the IPSec configuration section. At each device we will apply the appropriate Phase I and Phase II configuration parameters for the tunnels with the same

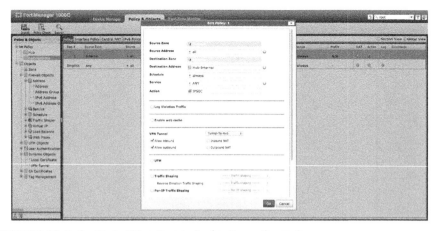

FIGURE 9.18 Policy Mode IPSec Remote Device Encryption Policy

workflow seen within FortiOS. As we are utilizing Policy Mode VPNs, it is important to NOT select "IPSec Interface Mode" during the Phase I creation (see Figure 9.19).

An additional item to verify is that our routing configurations contain the appropriate routes for the remote segments. Being Policy Mode, the routes will identify the interface to which we have bound the tunnels. In most networks the tunnels will be bound to the "External" interface of the firewall and we will see the default 0.0.0.0/0 route satisfy this requirement most of the time. Keep in mind that this will not be the case when for Interface Mode VPNs.

The last configuration requirement for deploying our configurations will be to bind the VPN Tunnel Dynamic Objects to the appropriate tunnels. To bind the tunnels, we simply navigate to the "Dynamic Objects → VPN Tunnel" configuration section for each device. Here we will select "Create New" for each Dynamic VPN Tunnel binding to be created. On the Hub site, we will need to select a binding for both the Site A and B tunnels. The configuration is extremely straightforward in that it provides two drop down menus. One will select the Dynamic VPN Tunnel object created in the previous steps and one will identify the VPN Tunnel to which we will bind it. For this example, we will bind "Tunnel-To-SiteA" to the tunnel created for Site A and "Tunnel-To-SiteB" for the tunnel created for Site B.

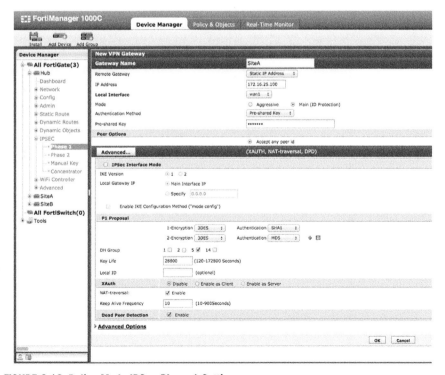

FIGURE 9.19 Policy Mode IPSec Phase 1 Settings

On the remote site devices, we will bind our Dynamic Tunnel objects to the configured tunnels at each device. In each configuration, we will tie the same dynamic object, "Tunnel-To-Hub," to the appropriate tunnel at each device. This allows the FortiManager to translate the configuration of a single policy package created for all the remote site to a proper working configuration at the device level. While in the package our IPSec policy points to the dynamic object, that dynamic object is bound to many different tunnels based on the device's binding (see Figure 9.20).

Now that we have completed our configuration, we must deploy our configurations to our devices using the Installation Wizard. Once the Policy Packages and Device Settings are pushed to the Hub and remote sites, the network can be tested and used.

Creating and Managing an Interface Mode VPN

Our second example will use Interface Mode IPSec tunnels. While the workflow is similar to building a Policy Mode IPSec VPN, there are some distinct differences. The first is that we will not be utilizing VPN Tunnel Dynamic Objects. As we wish our new tunnels to be treated as interfaces, we will map our new interfaces to Zones. These zones will then be used during policy creation, just as if they were physical interfaces. The second major difference is that we will not use the action "IPSec"

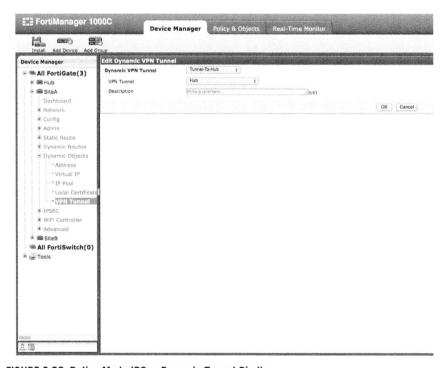

FIGURE 9.20 Policy Mode IPSec Dynamic Tunnel Binding

when creating our policies. As our policies will reference the zones bound to the IPSec tunnel interface, we will be using policies with the "Accept" action, allowing traffic both to and from our tunnels.

As we are using the same network layout as earlier, we will not walk through creating the Interface Mode IPSec VPN. The same requirements exist: traffic sourced from the internal protected segment (192.168.10.0/24) must reach Sites A and B through the appropriate IPSec tunnels. Sites A and B will again have the same requirements and allow traffic sourced from their protected segments (10.10.25.0/24 and 10.10.50.0/24), to reach the Hub's internal protected segment via a common policy package.

The steps will be:

- Create our Zones.
- Define Firewall Address Object for the protected subnets.
- Configure our Policy Packages.
- Map Dynamic Address Objects where required.
- Create the IPSec Tunnels.
- Map our Tunnel Interfaces to Zones.
- Create the required routing.
- Install the configuration to the production devices.

The tunnels will be seen by the devices as interfaces and will be configured as such. To apply policies to devices, the device interfaces must be mapped to Zones. Because we are creating a simple Hub and spoke VPN, we must only create two Zones. One Zone will be used for our tunnel(s) and one will define our internal protected interface (see Figure 9.21).

We will create two Zones, the first called "Internal" and a second called "IPSEC_VPN_ZONE." Internal will refer to the protected interface at each device.

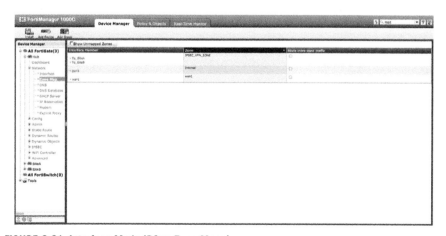

FIGURE 9.21 Interface Mode IPSec Zone Mappings

IPSEC_VPN_ZONE, of course, will refer to our IPSec VPN tunnel. However, not only will it refer to the tunnel at each remote location pointing back to the Hub, but will also refer to any and all tunnels providing secure connections to the remote sites.

In addition to our Zones, we must also create the appropriate Firewall Address objects to define which traffic will be allowed through our tunnel interfaces. We will again keep it simple by creating only two address objects, one defining the protected subnet of the Hub, 192.168.10.0/24, and one summary address that encompasses all remote protected subnets. We have chosen to use a simple byte-boundary bound summary of 10.10.0.0/16.

Depending on how well thought-out your IP scheme is, you can keep the creation of your objects and policies very simple, but understand that if you must create multiple addresses and groups, the management of your Policy Packages is no different than as if you were controlling traffic between any other interface types. Thus, there is no reason to be concerned about needing to readdress your environment. You may just need to have a more robust policy package (see Figure 9.22).

Once the Zone and Address objects are created we may create our Policy Packages. With this method of VPN creation, our Policy Packages can remain fairly basic. Because we are using a Zone to represent the tunnel at our Hub location, we are not required to create an IPSec policy for each individual tunnel as in the previous example. Instead, we will bind each tunnel interface to IPSEC_VPN_ZONE. Another difference is that we will create "Accept" policies for both in and outbound traffic flow, just as we would for any interface pair. This is also the case for the Remote Sites Policy Package, however each remote site will share the same package. For this to be work, we must map each Zone to its respective Tunnels and Interfaces (see Figure 9.23).

When we created our Address object for the Remote Site protected segments, we did it using the 10.10.0.0/16 summary. We could choose to use it as is, but we have also chosen to map the Address object at each remote device to a Dynamic Object Address. As described earlier, the Dynamic Address Object allows us to redefine the value of the Address object from the Object Database for a specific device. By defining the object value to that of 10.10.25.0/24 for Site A and 10.10.50.0/24 at

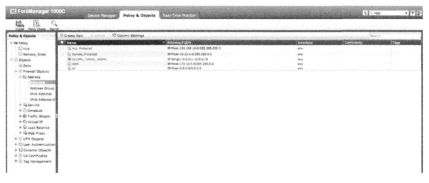

FIGURE 9.22 Interface Mode IPSec Address Objects

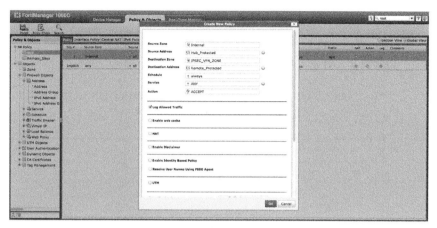

FIGURE 9.23 Interface Mode IPSec Policy

Site B, the associated Policy Package, simple as it is, can manage all remote devices and now has very specific device-level meaning, allowing us to granularly control what is and is not allowed for each location. We are not mapping any Dynamic Address Objects at the Hub device, as we will accept the object database values (see Figure 9.24).

Like before, the tunnel creation is accomplished by navigating to the IPSec configuration for each device requiring tunnels. At each device, we will apply the appropriate Phase I and Phase II configuration tunnel parameters with the same workflow seen within FortiOS, but for this exercise we are utilizing Interface Mode VPNs and we WILL select "IPSec Interface Mode" during the Phase I creation (see Figure 9.25).

Now that our interfaces are created, we can map them to the appropriate Zones. We will map each Interface Mode Tunnel at the Hub device to the IPSEC_VPN_Zone and map its protected interface, port1, to the Zone Internal. This will allow our Policy Package to be properly translated to the device and provide the security we

FIGURE 9.24 Interface Mode IPSec Dynamic Addresss

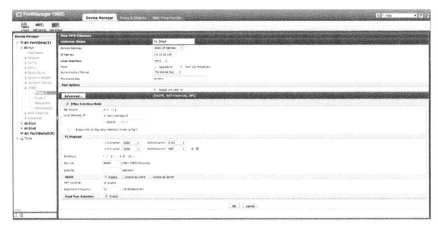

FIGURE 9.25 Interface Mode IPSec Phase 1 Settings

desire. Similarly, we will map the Interface Tunnel at each Remote Site to the tunnel built back to the Hub and map the protected interfaces to the Internal Zones, again letting our Policy Package be applied at each device.

The last thing we must do before deploying our configurations is to add the required route. Unlike our Policy Mode configuration, where the default route was sufficient, we will need to have more specific routes defining the path our traffic will take. When a device determines which path specific traffic will take, it consults the routing table. Unlike Policy Mode configuration, where the "External" interface was our egress interface, in Interface Mode the tunnel is our egress interface.

At each remote location, a simple static route pointing toward 192.168.10.0/24 via the tunnel back to the Hub is all that is required. However, at the Hub we will need to be more detailed and ensure we have a route to each remote protected segment that traverses the appropriate tunnel. Our routing will determine which tunnel to send traffic while our policy package will determine if that traffic will be allowed to traverse the tunnel (see Figure 9.26).

We again find ourselves having completed our configuration can deploy our configurations to our devices using the Installation Wizard described earlier. Once both the Policy Packages and Device Settings are pushed to the Hub and remote sites, you may start testing and using your centrally managed Policy Mode VPN.

Central VPN Console

As you can see, using FortiManager with to maintain a distributed VPN environment has advantages over accessing each device individually. What may also be evident is that, for every device we want to add to the VPN, there are many steps for creating the objects, polices, tunnels, and routing required. The more steps involved with any process, the greater chance for errors to occur causing unwanted results.

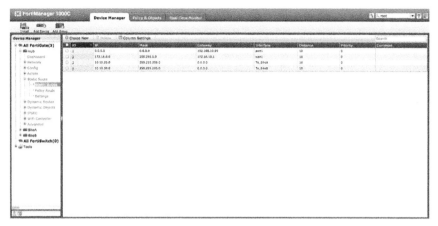

FIGURE 9.26 Interface Mode IPSec Static Routing Definition

To help us reduce the number of steps required to build a VPN network, Forti-Manager provides a second mode of VPN management. The "Central VPN Console" helps automatically provision IPSec VPN tunnels and routing requirements when creating a large-scale distributed Hub and Spoke or Fully Meshed VPN.

The Central VPN Console is configured on a per ADOM basis, but before an administrator can use this function, they must globally enable the option. To do this, simply navigate to the Admin → Admin Setting section within the System Settings tab, check the option for "Show VPN Console" and select apply. Once this option is selected, the VPN console will show up within those ADOMs where we will change the VPN management mode from "Policy and Device VPNs" to "Central VPN Console" (see Figure 9.27).

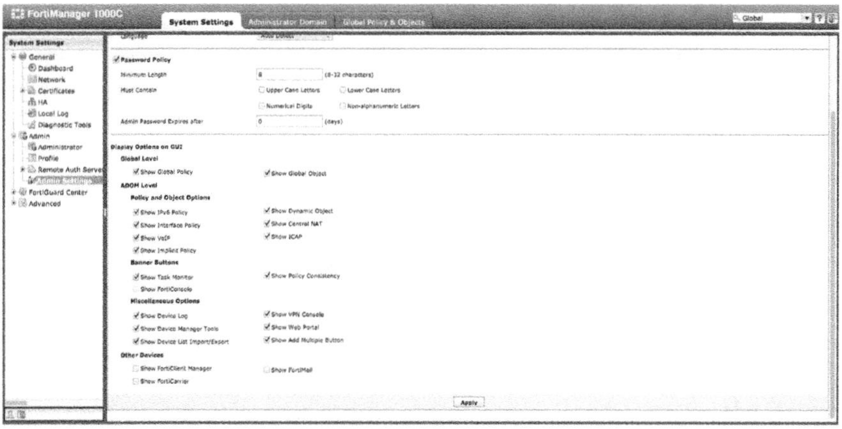

FIGURE 9.27 Enabling GUI option for VPN Console

If you are not using multiple ADOMs, you will enable the Central VPN Console in the System Information widget of the General → Dashboard within the System Settings tab. If the FortiManager is configured to use multiple ADOMs, enabling the Central VPN Console on a per ADOM basis is accomplished by right clicking and selecting "Edit" for the ADOM to be modified. Once the edit screen for the ADOM appears, change the VPN Management option to "Central VPN Console" and then "OK" (see Figure 9.28).

Now that we have enabled the Central VPN Console, we may reenter the ADOM and generate our VPN. To punctuate the advantages of using this mode, we reference the same VPN layout as earlier. Assuming your devices are already installed to the FortiManager and your Zones for firewalls are mapped, there are just a few steps to prepare before creating your VPN. There are then a mere handful of actions to define and deploy your VPN.

- Define Firewall Address objects for the protected subnets.
- Create the "VPN."
- Define the gateways participating in the VPN.
- Modify the Policy Packages.
- Deploy the configurations.

First, we must define a Firewall Address object for each protected subnet. These address objects will be used in our policy creation as before but they will be also used when defining each managed gateway device in our VPN configuration.

Once our address objects are defined, we may construct our VPN. The Central VPN Console is capable of maintaining multiple Star, Mesh, or Dialup VPNs. If we navigate to the Policy & Objects tab, we find the VPN Console nested at the bottom of the left window pane. With our focus on the VPN Console, we select "Create New" and then select a Star configuration for our example. We must then define our

FIGURE 9.28 ADOM setting for VPN console

Phase I and Phase II configuration. These settings will be used by the VPN Console to create the tunnel configurations on each of the devices which we will add as managed VPN gateways. This allows us to define these settings once for each device in the VPN, eliminating the risk of misconfiguration that occurs when we configure tunnels on a device-by-device basis (see Figure 9.29).

After committing our changes by selecting "OK," our focus will shift to the main screen and require us to select the VPN we just created. To select this, click on the VPN name you wish to manage. Once in the VPN you can select "Create New" to define either a "Managed" or "External" gateway. As each device you create is part of the VPN, and managed by the FortiManager, we will create all of our devices as Managed Gateways.

The first VPN member to be created is the "HUB" in our Hub and Spoke/Star configuration. While there are only a few items to define, there are a few things that will make your first installation go smoothly. Set the "Node Type" to "HUB," and select the Device named Hub. Then select the Zone name mapped to the outside interface where the IPSec tunnel is created with the value "Default VPN Interface." At the time of this writing, the name of this value is misleading. The options in the drop down list are Zone names, not physical interfaces. It is likely that this will be renamed in a subsequent software release so it will more appropriately describe the value needing to be selected.

The value "Hub-to-Hub Interface" could also be a Zone name. While supported, in our example we are not creating a dual hub star configuration and will not need to define a Hub-to-Hub connection. If we were to create a dual hub solution, this value would help create an IPSec tunnel between the two hubs for routing of VPN traffic.

Another task we had to perform in the earlier examples was the creation of the appropriate routes to ensure traffic would traverse the correct tunnel when accessing the protected segments. With the VPN console, you can have the FortiManager

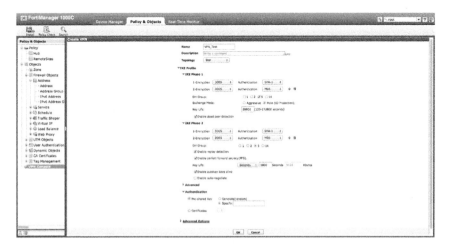

FIGURE 9.29 VPN Console

automatically create the routes. By selecting "Automatic" as the routing value, the FortiManager will take the "Summary Network(s)" and "Protected Subnet" values and propagate them to the remote devices so they can use the tunnels for the correct subnets.

The two values "Summary Network(s)" and "Protected Subnet" are populated with the firewall address objects created earlier. You can use either "Protected Subnet" for individual routes desired to be seen on the remote devices. "Summary Network(s)" can also be used, assuming the summary route is not overly general. This avoids routing confusion at the remote locations (see Figure 9.30).

Once we commit the configuration for our Hub, we will follow the same process for adding the remote locations as spokes in our VPN. The one difference in the configuration is selecting the "Node Type" as "Spoke."

Once the VPN is configured, we simply configure our Policy packages to allow the appropriate traffic in and out of the new tunnels. The VPN Console creates the VPN with Interface Mode tunnels, so we will create our policies as "Accept" policies. Another advantage of using the VPN Console is to not have to create Zones and map them to the interfaces at each individual device.

When using the VPN Console, FortiManager automatically creates three different Zones to be automatically mapped to the appropriate interface based on our configurations when adding devices into the VPN Console. These special Zones appear as options for the source and destination Zones when creating policies in our policy packages. Each Zone name will be created with three values separated by the "_" character. The first value is "vpnmgr" to identify that the Zone was created by the VPN Console. The second value will be the VPN name used when the VPN was created, allowing you to select to correct Zone when multiple VPNs are defined.

The third is one of the three values. The first of these, "hub2spoke," is used to identify the source and/or destination Zone when defining the policy for the Hub.

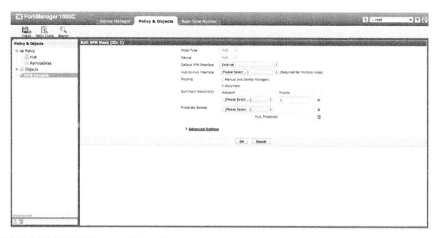

FIGURE 9.30 VPN Console Hub Setting

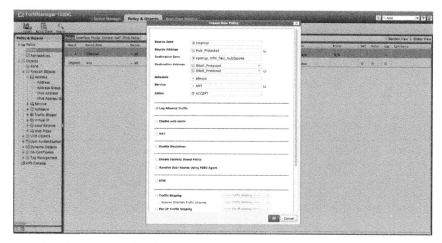

FIGURE 9.31 VPN Console Hub Policy

The second of these values, "spoke2hub," is used to identify the source and/or destination Zone when defining policy for the spokes. The last of these values, "mesh," is used to identify the source and/or destination Zone by all locations in a full mesh VPN.

In our example we find the Zones vpnmgr_VPN_Test_hub2spoke, vpnmgr_VPN_Test_spoke2hub, and vpnmgr_VPN_Test_mesh. For those paying attention, you may have noticed a third "_" between the words "VPN" and "Test." This underscore is actually part of the name "VPN_Test" used when we initially created our VPN. All spaces in VPN names will be converted to underscores when accessed in this manner (see Figure 9.31).

We once again find ourselves having completed our configuration and may deploy our device and policy package configurations. Like before, once both the Policy Packages and Device Settings are pushed to the Hub and remote sites, you may begin testing and using your centrally managed Policy Mode VPN.

CONCLUSION

While we have just scratched the surface on FortiManager, we hope this overview gives you a good understanding of its capabilities and a head start for deploying FortiManager into your environment.

In the absence of a FortiManager-specific publication, please refer to the following link for the FortiManager public documentation. Fortinet continues to deploy new features, so please keep current on both the documentation and your licenses, so your device continues to meet your needs.

http://docs.fortinet.com/fmgr.html.

Implementing a Security (UTM) Project III

Designing a Security Solution

INFORMATION IN THIS CHAPTER:

- Security as a Project
  - Understanding you are Working in a Project
  - Finding the Organizational Driver(s) for the Project
  - Dealing with Personal Motivations
  - Project Management
  - Viability and Feasibility of the Project
- Establishing a Network Security Architecture
  - Against what are we Protecting?
  - How are we Protecting?
- Gathering Information for Sizing and Configuring a UTM Solution
  - Network Information
  - Application Information
  - Environment Information
- Considerations for Planning a UTM Deployment
  - Using FortiGate from Scratch
  - Migrating from Another Vendor Using a Point Technology
  - Consolidating Services

INTRODUCTION

This is not a purely technical chapter. Designing a security solution requires "business" thinking. While we do cover some technical content here, we must start with the business, and identify what needs to be protected before we can leverage Fortinet solutions to do so. We must understand the ramifications of preventing accessing to different individuals and systems and the impact with regard to confidentiality, integrity, and availability of the network as a whole.

Different entities that have to work together to complete a Network Security project often have issues communicating with one another. The knowledge, vision, and, language needed for success is often not taught in schools or courses. This chapter is an attempt to bridge this knowledge gap.

However, this chapter is not a crash course on project management or how to relate IT to business objectives. Rather, it is a series of suggestions and ideas that you can put to use when working as part of a design or implementation team on a Network Security project with Fortinet products. If you lead the design and/or implementation teams, this information will help you understand the other teams with which you may be working. It will also provide tips on how to achieve ideal results. If you are not in this role, this information can still help you to understand the other parties involved and to provide additional value during the project.

It is understandable that most readers purchased this book for its technical nature, however, the authors have seen many times tons of time and effort being spent unnecessarily, and that can change by just taking into account the points raised on this chapter. This is why we feel this material needs to be here. Many (if not all) the lessons and issues discussed here are not commonly taught, but given the amount of pain and frustration entailed in learning them, we decided to place them here.

SECURITY AS A PROJECT

The product with which you are working, be it a FortiGate, FortiAnalyzer, or FortiManager, is part of a larger objective. It may help your organization to be more efficient, bring in more money, or avoid liability. Understanding the bigger picture will help you deliver more value to other individuals on your organization. And value is something everybody appreciates. Value is perceived when you say something that helps to enhance the chances of success on whatever you are doing, but you put in words that make it an appealing statement to the people that are listening to you. In other words, value is perceived if you appeal to someone's interests or motivations.

Understanding you are Working in a Project

Plainly put, if someone spent money on systems for you to configure and on your services, the organization is expecting a return. To ensure the objective is met, it helps to have a project. A project can be defined in many ways. For the computer security, a good definition is the organized alignment of resources (people, money, hardware, and software) working to achieve an objective within a given timeframe.

Organizations run projects because they have needs that must be solved. Whether such projects are formal and whether a project is visible, the project exists. There is always some method to control the amount of money being spent and there always is someone monitoring the efforts being undertaken to reach an objective. We must remember that security and technology are used to help the organization, not for their own sake.

All organizations have common needs, such as improving efficiency, refining their markets, or cutting costs. However, the one thing that all organizations must never forget is their mission: why that organization exists. All commercial organizations exist because they must make money. Everything else expressed as a need must relate to that mission. For example, being more efficient, attracting new markets, or cutting costs all relate to making more money. Being more efficient reduces the money spent. Refining the market helps bring in more money. Cutting costs reduces the money spent, thereby resulting in higher profits.

Of course, different organizations have different goals as not all organizations are profit-driven. However, when you work on a Security project, you must at least have an idea as to the project's objective and how it helps to the overall mission. So, if you are a non-profit organization that helps vulnerable groups from society, how will this project help those people? How can you use the mission to more effectively communicate with your counterparts? If you can answer those questions, it will help you more effectively communicate with people outside of your team, including people at managerial levels that might not have the technical level you possess.

Finding the Organizational Driver(s) for the Project

Knowing the objective of the project will help you gauge the *importance* of the project within the organization: if this project is strategic (directly impacts the organization's ability to achieve its key objectives) it is more likely that you will garner more attention when you have requests. This is because you communicate *value* when you relate your comments to the organization's goals.

If the project is viewed less strategically and more as a necessary evil, it is more likely you will experience resistance. This is sadly common in the Security industry where external factors like compliance drive projects. Knowing how important the project is directly affects how people will listen to you and your ability to obtain resources. Projects are driven by many factors. Some of the common ones are:

- Reduce Costs—Reducing costs requires first measuring how much is spent and finding ways to achieve similar results with less expense. Regardless of the environment, money is never an abundant resource and it must be well spent. Sometimes when equipment reaches end of life, or it is time to renew maintenance contracts, organizations decide to evaluate alternatives. Organizations also face operations' challenges and are driven to reduce the number of devices needed to be managed. UTM technology can help to reduce cost, and, if positioned that way can help you communicate your suggestions to the decision makers.
- Compliance—Many industries are heavily regulated. Governments have laws that have to be obeyed. Financial institutions must securely store information and track transactions. Health care organizations must also secure and store their patients information, though the specifics will vary country by country. Retail establishments must also guarantee the security of financial data. In all these cases, regulations exist to address these common concerns. Regulations ensure minimal certainty in a given environment by mandating controls on

critical systems, thereby reducing risk. If data must remain unmodified and protected in transit, a control must be in place to ensure that. One example of such a control would be an IPSec VPN. If a limited group of people must access data, reasonable controls could include Client-to-Site VPNs or, in simpler environments, regular firewalls with simple authentication.

- Enabling New Products or Services—Internet access has evolved from a rarity to an essential need. Today, companies are often looking for new customers and creativity plays an important role when a company decides to offer a new service or product, or reshape an existing one. When these activities are driven by the constant need for increasing revenue, there is a tendency to rely on creativity and let procedure lapse. When in this situation, there is a chance that any efforts you take to improve the security of the project could be viewed as counter to the revenue goals. Thus, to protect yourself and advance the project, you must ensure that you understand the purpose of the project itself at a business level. Things to consider include:
  - Understanding whether the new project replaces an existing revenue source. If this is the case, it likely indicates that the current revenue source is failing and failure of your project risks the health of the company AND that success of your project may place the jobs of other people in your organization at risk.
  - If, however, this project has the potential of adding incremental revenue, your environment is likely more relaxed.

In these situations, understanding how security can assist with meeting revenue objectives is critical. It may exist to enhance customer loyalty by demonstrating the safety of your organization's services. It may exist to improve customer experience by reducing application response times. It may just be compliance focused to meet arbitrary requirements on the part of external entities. If you keep these in mind as you progress, you will gain more attention within the organization.

The above is for sure not an exhaustive list of motivations for security projects, but are commonly encountered. It is vital to remember that people responsible for computer security are often just links in a chain. We are part of a project whose goal is not mere computing, but is more focused on real concerns such as aiding the needy, keeping our communities safe, ensuring the availability of critical services, or helping to bring in more revenue. We must understand the goal so as to be more effective when making suggestions, comments, or requests of others.

Dealing with Personal Motivations

While every organization has a mission, every person in an organization also has their own goals. While these would ideally align, that is not always the case. When a person has an agenda, personal motivations and interests can seriously derail projects.

Typical projects are sponsored by a high-level executive. Unlike lower-level workers, the executives are most likely to see strong alignment between their goals and those of the business. Thus, you should make sure you identify this sponsor and understand the motivations behind the approval. Does this person see this project as critical? If so, why? Is the project being done to benefit the organization as a whole, a particular department, or to gain the sponsor specific advantage over others?

Also, make sure you identify the project leaders that may lack the political power to approve a project, but are responsible for bringing the project to a good conclusion. Understand why they are involved and how project success or failure affects them personally. Verify with them what your role in the project is to be. Don't be afraid to ask things like "How do you think I could contribute to the success of the project?" or "What would help make my participation in the project successful?". Listen to their response and be ready to use it as a guideline when discussing the project.

Project Management

Thus far, we have reviewed items focused on human behavior, or perception. Now let's look at technical project management. While this is not a book on project management, we will briefly explore basic project management concepts so we can discuss how Security projects are different from others you may have worked on.

Objective or Scope

Every project must have a clear objective or scope. This is, the project must consist of accomplished tasks that move toward a goal. Everybody involved should agree that goal was either achieved (project success) or not (project failure). One of the best ways to ensure this is to have an objective that is clear and precise. This can be done by ensuring that the project is SMART... Specific, Measurable, Achievable, Realistic, and Time-bound.

- Specific—A project must be clear and unambiguous. It could be specific in terms of time, money, location, geography, percentages, or any other factor. But it must, at minimum, answer the W questions: What, Who, Where, When, Which, Why. If two or more people are asked about the objective, they have the same answer. Good examples of Specific goals include: "decrease application response times by 20%" and "ensure that infrastructure can process a 10 Gbps link to the Internet for 2000 internal users".
- Measurable—A project must have mechanisms to answer the "how much have we done and how much is it left?" question. Someone should be able to determine the progress of the project in terms of time, percentage, or money. For example, if our goal is to improve response time, we may have a current metric of 10 ms and a goal of 8, so when we have improved to 9 ms, we are half way to the goal.
- Achievable—Some times this "A" is also used for "Attainable". The idea behind this is to ensure the objective can be reached by the entity in charge of the objective. This usually implies that the entity in charge has the necessary tools and capabilities to complete their tasks. Let's remember an "entity" could be an individual or a team. The question "Can this entity perform this task

with the resources, knowledge, and abilities it possesses?" able to be answered affirmatively. A team in charge of reducing response times by 20% should have everyone required to make changes to the application, including OS, server, network, and security. Also, everybody must agree that the goal of a 20% reduction can be done by the team.

- Realistic—Some times this "R" is also used for "Relevant". This is similar to the "A", in the sense that it must be within the context and constraints posed by the environment. For example, attempting to do a full conversion from another network technology to Fortinet in two days might be possible if we are only considering a simple firewall with less than 10 routes. However, if the configuration includes thousands of rules, many user groups, and complex routing, a goal of two days is not sufficient. Similar failures of realism can occur if the network team has no visibility of knowledge as to how the previous solution worked.
- Time-bound—This item answers the questions "when does this end?" and "what is the deadline?". It can be a specific date like December 31st 2014, or it can be a relative date like 4 weeks from yesterday. However, there must be agreement on when the objective is expected to be finished.

Schedule or Timing

Once the objective has been defined, it must be clearly planned out. These steps must follow an order to ensure every activity has a clear relationship with its predecessor and successor. Each activity has to have an associated time (duration) to be performed.

This is probably one of the most difficult tasks for network and security engineers. How many times have you been asked to estimate the amount of time it would take to configure something and you ended up spending a lot more time than expected? This is very common, especially with engineers. Engineers are trained to think efficiently, so we tend to assume the best case scenario and often underestimate the amount of effort and time required to accomplish a task. When you are considering the amount of time required to accomplish a task, it is important to consider not only the net/effective time to do the task, but also the amount of time that it will require to coordinate with people, teams, departments, suppliers, vendors. This should also include the time it will take to gather all the necessary information: configurations, diagrams, finding out the whys (why is this rule/route here? why was this configuration done this way and not in this other way? why was this configuration done here and not somewhere else?) that could add time to the activity.

Tasks, activities, or steps of a project often have other properties, such as an "owner" who is responsible for bringing the task to completion, "resources" like budgets and personnel, and "requirements", items that must be ready for the task to be performed. Finally, tasks also have "expected outcomes"—but we will talk about those later. Currently, we are focusing on the time aspects, as this often determines the feasibility of the project.

To accurately estimate time, it is important to ensure that all the primary activities are considered. For example, if the objective is to reduce the response time of an important application by 20%, it is important to consider everything from measuring current response times, to analyzing alternatives or tuning options. Then, determine which changes are needed and how to apply and verify them. Here you can be as detailed as you wish, but generally, you should at least list the activities where many people will be involved and those that directly affect the project.

Once the different tasks, activities, or steps have been determined, it may be wise to put them in a GANTT chart, or in some other format that can help illustrate the dependencies to everyone. This is also a good way to identify which tasks may be done in parallel. It will also be important to determine the "critical path" of the project, the sequence of activities that begins with the earliest activity and ends with the latest activity, without altering the project duration in any way. This critical path can be used to estimate the duration of the project.

Project Deliverables

One of the most important things to be considered is the project outcome. This is commonly defined as deliverables:

- Documentation is important to track how the project functioned, what decisions were made, why particular choices were made, and how pieces were configured. Ideally, the documentation will be "living", so it may be kept up to date as the environment grows and changes. From a FortiGate-specific perspective, you would want to document the architectural decisions (Gateway vs Transparent, single vs Multiple VDOMs, which inspection modules are enabled), how the device was configured, and any modifications needed by the infrastructure to accommodate the FortiGate (VLANs, routes, port speed/duplex, or connections added or modified).
- Methods or Processes: The project sometimes requires changes in how common tasks are done or who does them. If this is the case, it must be clear to everyone involved as to how and why things are changing. As an example, if users had been provisioned locally and are now provisioned in Active Directory, the operators in charge of provisioning must understand the change. Similarly, if the FortiGate raises Network Management alerts, the escalation support path must be clear to the people monitoring the network.

In general, any environmental change produced by the project should be inserted into the organizational's day-to-day activities to ensure a smooth transition.

Budget or Cost

All projects must have an associated budget. Budget needs to consider both Capital Expenditure (CAPEX) or money spent up front on purchasing goods or services and Operational Expenditure (OPEX) or money spent on utilities (like electricity) or services for maintenance. These are especially true if the organization has a formal process around budget scheduling.

While it is not common for technical people to be part of budget planning, it is important to remember that there may be budget constraints on the projects you work on. So asking for resources after the budget has been set can be difficult. Commonly missed resources include software, hardware, and services, such as a VDOM license for our FortiGate, a transceiver, a 24×7 support contract, and consultant services. So, to avoid issues you should communicate with project managers and/or sponsors as to resources that may be required.

Human Resources or Personnel

The project planning process should consider the people that may be involved, both from within the organization and any external resources that might be required. Each of the project tasks should list the people required to complete it, and define everyone's role. The task owner probably plays the more important role, since this person has the authority to stop an activity or make immediate decisions. The owner is the person responsible for making sure the task is completed successfully.

During FortiGate implementations it is common for people from the network and security departments to work together. However, this can cause conflict. It is important to create a mechanism to resolve this conflict before everyone gets involved. Techniques that work include voting or naming a decision maker. Conflict resolution can also be determined by the nature of the conflict: if it relates to data transport, the network department wins. If, however, it is related to data inspection or attack detection, the security department wins. Whatever mechanism is used, everyone should agree to work together and avoid delays and other issues.

Viability and Feasibility of the Project

Once everything has been decided, each point should be analyzed against constraints (time, budget, knowledge, personnel, etc.) to ensure everything will be possible. At this point, everyone should agree that the project scope is clear, resources can be obtained, the team is identified, and all foreseeable risks evaluated and found acceptable. While this document must be formal (i.e. issued by proper authority through proper channels) it needn't be long, complex, or boring. The idea is to document that due diligence was performed especially for long or difficult decisions, so it can be referenced in the future.

ESTABLISHING A NETWORK SECURITY ARCHITECTURE

As mentioned previously, FortiGate installation projects often need to be managed. Typically this means the installation must integrate with both Security and Network architectures.

Reasonably mature organizations have likely already conducted a Business Impact Analysis or at least a Risk Assessment before placing a control like a FortiGate onto the network. If your organization uses formal processes for these steps, the rest of this section will likely not apply to you. However, as many organizations do not do this there are a few things you should consider before selecting a security device so you can protect your assets and help your organization achieve its goals.

Each point below should be documented and included as a deliverable in the project. After all, at some point in the future, someone may need to audit the FortiGate or alter the environment. Understanding why things were done as they were is critical to success.

As a word of caution, this is not a book on security engineering. Issues like Service Level Agreements, Multi-tenancy, and High Availability at the business level are out of the scope here. The rest of this section is very focused on specific practical issues and applications.

What is Being Protected?

If you are installing a FortiGate, you are undoubtedly trying to protect something, but it must be clear which assets are to be protected. For example, if you place a FortiGate in front of a server farm, you may think that you are "protecting the servers", but to protect them properly, you must look a bit closer:

- What data assets and services on the servers need to be protected? This can include files containing social security numbers or services that can access them like FTP or HTTP.
- Is remote access to the servers allowed? If so, how are those services being protected?
- Which traffic flows will be protected? Are you protecting traffic originating from a single network or a group of them? Do all zones require the same levels of protection?

Against what are we Protecting?

This is another important question for which we need a clear answer. It also has a few sub-points:

- Who—Are the expected users of the service also potential attackers? Is it possible to identify individual users or is the service anonymous by nature?
- How—Are you defending against automated attacks (bots, worms, ...) or are more targeted attacks likely?
- What—Are we protecting against Denial of Service, Misuse, or any other type of attacks?
- When—Are there any service windows when protection levels need to be lessened or strengthened? Is there any need to maintain availability as compared to a specific metric?

These risks should be identified, understood, and weighed according to likelihood.

How are we Protecting?

Every mechanism used in a network to protect an asset is a security control. When you install a FortiGate, you must understand what are your control types so you may use them effectively:

- Preventive/Deterrent: Will the FortiGate be used to prevent attacks or make them less likely?
- Detective: Will it be used to identify attacks and notify other people or systems so they can be handled?
- Corrective/Compensating: Will it be used to recover from an attack or keep it from spreading?

The above control types relate closely to the asset types being protected and to the risks being protected against. For example, if you must protect against a Denial of Service attack and your asset must have an availability of 99.999% on 5.25 min of outage per year, you may decide to use three FortiGates in parallel working in an active-passive configuration to meet the target. You may also choose to use the FortiGate as a preventative control by using the SSL Offloading capability to reduce server load (assuming the FortiGates have sufficient resources to accept the traffic, of course). You could also use it as a detective control by using SNMP and SMTP to monitor and alert on issues.

Once you decide how you will use each control, you will be able to use it more effectively and blend it into your organization's operations.

GATHERING INFORMATION FOR SIZING AND CONFIGURING A UTM SOLUTION

We discussed Sizing in Chapter 2. We will not duplicate that information here, but instead will focus the process and human perspective. If you have the chance to deploy as part of a demo or a Proof of Concept (PoC) run, you can directly measure how the device works in your environment. However, resource constrains may prevent this approach, so you'll have to gather sizing information differently.

Network Information

If your organization is sufficiently large, you likely want to talk to network administrators and collect metrics. They should be able to provide information about average throughput/bandwidth used, typical concurrent connections numbers, protocol distribution, and other useful statistics.

If that is not the case, either because the network administration function is not formalized or because the information is simply not available, you will need to gather it yourself. This will likely involve running data gathering/manipulation applications. Many of these applications are available for free in GNU/Linux repositories, so having an updated Linux system on hand would be useful.

> **TIP**
>
> **Your network analysis toolkit**
> Three free-software tools that are vital for your toolbox are:
>
> - Wireshark—http://www.wireshark.org/—A network sniffer that will help you capture traffic samples. Able to identify average packet sizes, packets/second, and throughput.
> - TCPtrace—http://www.tcptrace.org/—An analysis tool for pcap files (packets saved to disk). Able to provide statistics graphically.
> - NTOP—http://www.ntop.org/—A web-based network sniffer that can identify and report on the protocols/applications being used in the network.
>
> These programs will be useful not only for acquiring sizing data, but also for troubleshooting network issues. Keep them handy.

If you install FortiGates for a living, or work on an organization where they are installed frequently, make a procedure focused on acquiring necessary data. Even if you are using it just to validate the environment, it is always good to avoid surprises. This is doubly true in high-traffic environments.

There are three items that are important to consider:

- Bandwidth—The most common mistake is to believe that the only important bandwidth considerations involve the speed of the links directly attached to the FortiGate. This is only true if you will use the FortiGate internally. If, however, you are going to use the technology to protect the link to and from the Internet, you must consider the size of the link. If you are going to protect a group of links (such as a series of MPLS connections), you must consider the sum of all the bandwidths of all the links. When considering your FortiGate's maximum bandwidth, you must ensure you are right.
- Concurrent Connections—This will be probably one of the most difficult values to obtain. If you already have a network device that you plan to swap out for the FortiGate, you can likely gather statistics from that device. If not, your next best option is to SPAN a port or insert a network tap in that area and run Wireshark to gather statistics. If that is not an option, you will have to estimate by determining the average bandwidth per connection used by typical network applications. You can then divide the bandwidth available by the amount required for each connection. If your application administrators cannot provide this information to you, you may get useful data by running the *netstat* command on the busiest servers and workstations.
- Traffic mix—Without a doubt, the best way to obtain this is to place a sniffer in the network. This must be done in the same spot where the FortiGate will be installed. If that is not possible, at least place a sniffer on a typical machine (a typical server and a couple of typical users) and obtain statistics there to extrapolate later. Here the goal is to understand the percentages of traffic being used for protocols that will be deeply inspected by the FortiGate, such as HTTP, FTP, SMTP, or POP3.

Application Information

When identifying applications it is important to remember that the more granular information we can get about an application, the better we can protect it. For example, if we are protecting port TCP/80, we will do a much better job if we know that it is connecting to Facebook than if we just knew it was running HTTP.

A sniffer can be quite useful here. Tools like wireshark or ntop can provide statistics on network protocols. Another option is to audit applications with a network scanner to match actual installed applications against the FortiGate configuration. This is especially useful on servers…, however, be aware that network scanners are very complex and often updated to correct security concerns. If you install a scanner or a sniffer on a server to profile the system, be sure to remove it when you're done. That way, you do not have to maintain it, and it's not sitting there waiting for an attacker to exploit it.

Environment Information

Some information is dependent on the organization's structure and how different business processes work.

User Groups

All users are not the same, and every organization has a unique way to classify them. Classifying users is necessary to establish an effective access control policy, where users only have rights based on the group to which they belong. Groups can be formed based on:

- Role—You can establish group membership based on the activity the user must perform. One group represents a role (administrative, engineering, etc.) and could access different assets (different servers or applications). Typically the roles are associated to user type, such as information owner, data custodian, or user. It is likely a user will belong to different groups if they must perform different task types.
- Discretional access to an asset—Groups can be formed based on the asset they will access. This way each asset would have an associated group and one group would be used for Application A, another group for Application or System B, and so on.
- Based on data classification—If the organization has classified the systems or data in some way (such as public, semi-public, and internal only) group membership would be granted based on the type of clearance or level of authorization of the user. This way, members of group A would have access to public information only, users of group B to systems, applications, or data classified as internal only.

Having a systematic and deterministic way to classify users will avoid issues when new users are added to the system (and have rights granted), and will also simplify the way you will build access control rules for the Firewall, Web Content Filter,

VPN, or any other security mechanism on the FortiGate. This will also ease future operations since it will define a path for when new groups must be created.

Identify if the organization has a preferred method of assigning groups. They probably already exist somewhere, often in Active Directory, and they probably are already aligned with the organizational structure. If this is the case, you need to only import the existing groups. If, however, the users are not organized within another system, you will need to recommend something. Ask the people in charge of the security policy if they already know what they'd like to do. Then, check their plan against the criteria above. You will need to warn them if they seem to want to use more than one option, as that will increase the level of complexity and make it more difficult to manage.

Business Cycles

Organizations have business cycles. People arrive to work at some point (8 AM is popular), they take breaks, go to lunch, come back to the office, and go home in the afternoon. Some organizations have processes that occur with a much lower frequency: payroll might be processed every week or every month. Certain administrative processes might run every 3 months or once a year. These cycles must be understood.

The FortiGate can link expiration or validity to firewall rules based on timeframes. You can use this to correlate business cycles to firewall configuration. If a process must run at the end of every month, why grant access where there is no need to have it? This is leaving a door open all the time, not just when you're walking through it.

Make sure you talk to the data owners, custodians, and users of the application and data that is being protected. Try to clearly define business cycles. This is especially true for internal applications as these typically have a well-defined time window in which services must be active. Once you understand the business cycles that affect protected assets, use this information to establish the validity of your FortiGate rules.

CONSIDERATIONS FOR PLANNING A UTM DEPLOYMENT

You know the project you are working involves a FortiGate deployment. You know the tasks associated to your function, and when, how, and with whom you are supposed to do them. You also understand how the FortiGate fits on your network and

---

TIP

Document the Business cycle on the rule

If you are going to use a schedule for a firewall policy on the FortiGate, you likely want to document it in the comment field. The comment field is short, and in some organizations it is reserved for specific purposes. However, if you can, documenting the business process and cycle will help you understand why the rule is there when you revisit the configuration in the future.

how it complements the Security Architecture. You know which FortiGate model is right for you, as you gathered and processed all the information that allowed you to make an informed decision.

Now, this is the part where we give you a bit of advice on three scenarios that are commonly encountered when you deploy a FortiGate. The sections on Migrating Services and Consolidating Services assume you are replacing existing technology with a FortiGate. The section on Using FortiGate From Scratch assumes the Forti-Gate will be your first security device.

Using FortiGate From Scratch

The simplest use case is when you are building a brand new IT infrastructure and have decided to base it around a FortiGate. As no one has yet experienced the service, there is no expectation to deal with, so the challenge is mostly technical. However, things are a bit different when you have a pre-existing infrastructure and are adding security to it using Fortinet technology. In this case, you must educate your users on the advantages they will experience with the secured environment.

However, since in neither case have your users experienced a security environment before, you are starting with a blank slate.

Set Proper Expectations

One of the most important things to do when working on a potentially disruptive project is to set expectations, especially to the users.

The first thing that must be communicated is how normal operations look like and what can potentially go wrong, so users can report anomalies. The idea is to be proactive and avoid unnecessary phone calls or technical support when things are running normally.

This must be done with a focus on the processes and activities that will be affected by the installation of the FortiGate. If Internet browsing will show an authentication message when a user visits a webpage, this change must be communicated. If accessing internal servers requires additional steps to establish an encryption channel to protect information and provide non-repudiation, it must be communicated. If services might experience a performance impact, that must be noted as well. Abnormal situations (or a threshold on what should be considered as normal) also need to be defined and communicated. For example, if no authentication message is seen or if the auth message pops up every minute, then something is probably wrong. Also, if performance is affected such that a process now takes 20 s when it used to take only 10, something is wrong and someone should be informed. Of course, those to whom these issues are reported should have a process in place, so the proper actions are taken.

Expectations should also be set for positive changes. The idea is to communicate the advantages of the security solution, not only for the organization as a whole but also to users as individuals. Yes, the organization will be protected against "bad things" and will be compliant. Yes, the organization will avoid potential liabilities.

It also must be communicated that individual users will be less likely to lose their work because of a computer security issue, are less likely to experience degraded performance due to a locally running malware sample, and is less likely they will be subject to any kind of investigation due to bad behavior on their systems from malware. Organization-specific benefits should also be considered.

Finally, you must define expectations around risk and what might go awry. These likely should be addressed at project owners and sponsors than users. However, remember that if the project made it this far, it is because the project was assessed and determined to be viable. Some risks are mitigated with proper controls during the project deployment and are thereby minimized. Other risks may be discovered and some remain the same. If any of these risks have a high probability of occurrence, the chances and recovery plans should be communicated to the stakeholders.

Run a Quality Assurance (QA) Environment

Since you will be establishing a new service, you need to be able to ensure quality. One way to do this is by creating a Quality Assurance (QA) environment that mimics your real environment as best you can. This way, you can test changes and new firmware versions before deploying them to production. Thus, if issues arise, you can troubleshoot them without also having to worry about stress and potential lost revenue. QA environments are also useful for testing restores from backup, so you can gain high assurance that the restore won't cause serious problems when applied to production.

There are several ways to create a FortiOS-based QA environment. The most common way is to purchase an identical system to use in QA. However, you can use the second unit in a HA cluster. Of course, while you're testing, you will lose availability. You can also use a smaller FortiGate unit, but be aware that you may lack the ability to test hardware-specific features if you use a smaller model.

Remember that FortiOS is designed to take advantage of the custom hardware found in FortiGates, especially the ASICs. Due to this, when FortiOS is running on older FortiGates, it might miss some features that are only available on more recent hardware. When choosing a FortiGate model for QA, be sure it can run all the features you will be using in production.

There are many ways to get a QA environment:

- You can use a completely separate and isolated environment (network, servers) that serves as a lab to test duplicating everything you have in production. Organizations that can afford this type of environment should include duplicate FortiGates, or a virtual (VM) equivalent.
- If you cannot create a separate identical environment, you can probably use a separate network segment. It is not unusual to find IT departments that isolate themselves and function as a QA environment. You can also select a segment of users that are relatively isolated due to job function and have little impact on the overall organization. You can use a FortiGate to protect this segment and use it to test new configurations, features, or software versions.

- If you have a QA FortiGate that is an identical model of production, you use it as an emergency backup for your production FortiGate. This idea, of course, only works well if you have proper change control and can flip between devices quickly.

While these are the biggest considerations for a new deployment, there are a few others. However, as they are more likely to apply to changing existing installations, they will be discussed in later sections.

Migrating from Another Vendor Using a Point Technology

The other potential deployment for a FortiGate is to replace an existing point-technology product. This is, you can replace your existing firewall product with a FortiGate using just the firewall features. You can substitute your current IPS with a FortiGate that is only by running the IPS module. You could also replace your VPN or Web Content Filter product, with the FortiGate by just doing that.

However, even though you are substituting a single technology, and both technologies do the same job, they do not necessarily do it in the same way. It's much like replacing a Brand A videogame system with Brand B, or changing from a domestic to foreign-made car. Both technologies perform the same function and are familiar, but due to implementation differences are just different enough to be operated differently.

Set Proper Expectations

The first thing to recognize is that when you replace one technology with another, expectations are formed by the technology being replaced. This means that users will be accustomed to specific message styles, performance metrics, and ways to use the system. This means that you must be aware of how the user experience will change so you may prepare your users. However, not all changes are user-focused. Change may also occur at the administrator level and affect how your devices are provisioned and operated.

Make sure that everyone in the organization understands the reason behind the change. This may include future growth, increased performance or efficiency, decreased cost, or decreased complexity. Remember that people take time to adjust to change, so work towards acceptance and stabilization.

Build a Baseline

Ideally you should create a baseline of the environment before you implement change. Many IT organizations document metrics like average throughput, concurrent connections, protocol distribution, number of users, and other technical parameters. It is also important to gather non-obvious metrics: mean time between failures, frequency between changes and response times. Also identify the systems and applications that are affected by the technology being replaced, and the processes around them.

Once you make the change, it is likely that someone in your organization will complain, so it is important to have these metrics so you can prove that the new system is not causing the problem or easily troubleshoot if it is.

In general, you should gather and document as many operating metrics as you can before you make the change. You should then re-measure once the change is complete, especially those more relevant to your type of organization as the amount of tolerance to differences largely depends on the organization. For example, financial organizations are often less tolerant of system delays than marketing firms.

Perform the Configuration Conversion

Migrating complex systems can be overwhelming. This is particularly true when converting firewalls and IPSec VPNs. Fortunately, Fortinet has a tool called the FortiConverter that simplifies this process. FortiConverter can be found at https://convert.fortinet.com/forticonverter/. However, these are the stable versions. Less stable versions are released internally often with enhancements that are not available in the public version. If you must convert a system that is not supported by the public version, contact your Fortinet representative for assistance. There are, of course, third-party tools available for doing other conversions.

Conversion tools reduce the time and effort required to enter the configuration from the scratch, reducing the likelihood of typos. However, keep in mind that automated tools do fail. The more sensitive the environment, the more care you should take during configuration. So, if you use a tool, be sure to spend some time reviewing the generated configuration.

Run a Quality Assurance (QA) Environment

Details about QA environments were discussed in the "Using FortiGate From Scratch" section, and will not be revisited here. Instead, we will just discuss the differences that apply when you are replacing technology.

QA environments within a replacement project are very important as they allow you to test equivalencies and differences between the legacy technology and the new FortiGate. You can also run identical tests to ensure that the FortiGate will behave properly once it is replaced. This also allows you to tune the FortiGates to best leverage the ASICs. For example, if you are displacing a Web filter, you may wish to explore using Application Control to filter even better than what you are replacing.

Perform (and test) a Full Backup

If despite your planning and testing, something still goes wrong, you need to be able to rollback the change. This requires, among other things, that you have a fresh backup of your configuration and the equipment available to undo your change.

However, never take a backup for granted. There have been many cases where a backup existed, but was not tested and failed when it needed… effectively compounding the initial failure. So, before you make your change, test your backups. This of course, implies either the use of a QA environment or using a maintenance window to test the restore on production systems. (This is unwise and is not recommended.) Remember, if you test in production and the backup doesn't work, you risk leaving the service inoperational for a period of time, until you can restore the original configuration.

Once you have backed up and tested your configuration, you can follow one of these approaches to ensure the backup remains fresh.

- Configuration Freeze: You can declare a configuration freeze period, meaning no one may change the configuration until the replacement has been done and tested. This avoids two issues: (1) getting an outdated backup, (2) getting an outdated converted configuration.
- Maintain a log of changes: This can be done if the organization cannot tolerate a period of configuration freeze. Here you must remember that it is better to have a fresh backup (possibly incremental) of the changes done after the full backup. Also, it is likely that the converted configuration will no longer be accurate, and it will require similar updates to provide similar functionality.

Build your Change Control Plan

Once everything is ready, it's show time. Here are some points that you might want to consider:

- Keeping the old system: Parallel or Hot-Standby?
  Until the change has been performed successfully and tested over time, you might wish to keep your old box handy. It may be active on the network, run in parallel with the FortiGate or in a Hot-Standby mode. In this mode, the box is turned on and configured, but network cables are not plugged in. If the time it would take to move cables is considered excessive in your environment, then it is best to use a parallel installation. However, bear in mind that this option is more complex and more error-prone, so it should be avoided whenever possible.
- Test plans.
  All user groups and applications that route through the box should have a test defined for them as part of the test plan. This way, you can quickly ascertain whether the appropriate services are up and running within acceptable parameters after the change is complete.
  Make sure you run all the tests before the change is declared to be complete, and that you have documented the output. There are many instances where a test is not tested prior to the change and fails later. This can cost significant time, as it directs troubleshooting activities toward the wrong system. To avoid this, it is best to work with system-specific experts to create and test the tests before the change.
- Support contacts (From your reseller or Fortinet).
  Security devices are often considered to be critical assets. Because of this, it is wise to gather the support information of all vendors potentially affected by a change before the change is implemented. In the case of proactive organizations like Fortinet, you can even open a change ticket ahead of time, so if you need help, you get priority. Bear in mind that Fortinet Technical Support scope does not include installation assistance (this is provided by Fortinet Professional

Services). However, they may be able to help when problems do arise with your system, whether it is during an installation or later.

- Verify the details of your installation plan.

  The installation plan should be detailed as much as possible, but not to the point of falling into an "analysis paralysis" situation. Make sure the order of the steps makes sense and conduct a test run to imagine activity flow. Think of who should be present and help the project manager identify the critical people and inform them as to what is expected of them so they may prepare.

  One thing that may be forgotten is how to deal with things that go wrong. For example what happens if users can't authenticate, the IPSec VPN tunnel doesn't go up or the IPS is not catching an attack launched as part of the tests. Yes, rolling back is always an option, but sometimes the issues will not be easily reproduced outside the environment where the FortiGate has been installed. So, one must be able to gather troubleshooting information as the problem exhibits itself. Being able to gather basic information would be wise: a traffic sample, memory information, CPU, resource-intensive processes, connections, and network utilization. The commands needed to gather this information should be included in the troubleshooting portion of the plan. More information about diagnostics can be found in Appendix B.

- Roll back plan (including restoring old technology).

  If things don't go well and enough tests fail, you must decide when to revert changes and when to leave the FortiGate in a partial configuration state (such as passing traffic without inspection, or with minimal Firewall and IPSec VPN rules). Whatever is decided, the roll-back plan should include more than enough time in the maintenance window to go through the entire test plan. This is to recover from failed tests.

  When things go poorly, it is common for engineers to believe they are close to resolving the problem. However, when critical services depend on infrastructure availability, there could be a major organizational impact. Due to this, it is important to define a "point of no return", or a limit that clearly defines a threshold on time and effort to be spent identifying the root cause(s). If such a threshold is reached, the rollback procedure should be performed. This should be defined clearly such as "1 hour before the maintenance window closes". Otherwise, it may be subject to interpretation and, therefore, likely misinterpreted in times of high stress.

After the Change

Assuming the change was completed and everything went fine, what is next? It is important to consider a monitoring period and associated technology.

- It is useful to have a monitoring program that gathers important system health statistics (CPU, Memory, Disk, Concurrent connections, etc.) at a predefined frequency. Every 5 or 10 min should be fine. This information might be used later if an issue arises.

- Constant status calls with a given frequency (such as hourly) to users with the more demanding business processes. They should be able to tell you whether everything is OK.

There should also be a defined limit for how long monitoring is performed. Many environments find 24 h are acceptable. Some require even less. Some more sensitive environments might require additional monitoring, such as until a full business cycle is finished.

Consolidating Services

Once you have a working FortiGate in your environment, you have a chance to reduce administrative load, simplify your network and perhaps add additional security. However, do not attempt to implement everything at once. This increases complexity and therefore the likelihood of widespread system failure. This will be much more difficult to troubleshoot. Instead, migrate service by service. Always begin with the features related to connectivity. Thus, if you are going to migrate a firewall, that should be the first service transferred to the FortiGate. Then, IPSec and SSL VPNs should be migrated, and then WAN Optimization. Once connectivity is fully migrated, there should be fewer issues with pure inspection features like IPS, DLP, or Web Content Filtering.

Once you have migrated the first service, wait for a reasonable time and only migrate the second service after a reasonable monitoring period. Once these two are stable, add the third. While this may seem to be obvious, many organizations take the big leap and face the consequences later. The first impression is that the product is failing, but after analysis (which can be very complex) it often becomes apparent that the root cause is a typo or a misunderstood configuration switch. So, it is best to migrate service by service. Even though it seems that this will take more time, in the end, it is often actually less.

Security with Distributed Enterprise and Retail

The purpose of this chapter is to provide insight into the needs and security challenges of an enterprise or retail environment that has a distributed network infrastructure. The network consists of a corporate core with remote branch offices and mobile users. A branch network can range from a handful of remote employees to a large satellite office consisting of up to a thousand employees. These remote locations require communication back to the company data centers and/or between other remote locations. Distributed communication between remote physical locations would require a secure infrastructure. This chapter will outline a real-world example of a distributed network based on FortiGate technology.

SECURITY NEEDS AND CHALLENGES

It is critical to secure and protect network infrastructure, regardless of how extended it may be. To begin, you must outline the purpose of each network zone along with its associated security requirements.

What are the general needs for the distributed network?

- They could consist of both physically remote office locations and mobile users.
- It is important to be able to access company-provided network resources, such as intranet servers and company email.

DISCLAIMER

Compliance examples

The scenarios and designs are discussed here to make the reader aware of certain compliance requirements. They are based on the authors' field experiences. As every network environment varies, so do the ways to meet compliance requirements within them. Please consult a qualified PCI-certified consultant or firm to validate your specific infrastructure.

What are the security challenges surrounding these needs?

- The communication entering and exiting the company's infrastructure must be secured. By default, most network communication is unencrypted and could expose sensitive company data. To address this, a high-level form of encryption is needed to secure communication. It is recommended that this be at least 128-bit level encryption, but higher is generally better.
- All levels of communication require access control rules to be specified. This can include restricting access to business-related information and blocking access between specific nodes.
- An authentication policy should provide identification for all user-related functions. This can include enforcing good passwords and tracking activity.
- Threats should be monitored and prevented proactively. Since malicious activity can occur between any network entities, all zones must be appropriately hardened. For example, company employees could attack network resources intentionally or through malware infection. In retail or service environments, networks are often made available to the public and could therefore easily be attacked from within.

The above requirements are typical in business and retail environments. However, there are other drivers for network segmentation. One common example is compliance. Some compliance is mandated by law, such as HIPAA (Health Insurance Portability and Accountability Act), GLBA (Gramm-Leach-Bliley Act), and SOX (Sarbanes-Oxley). Others are enforced contractually, such as PCI-DSS (Payment Card Industry Data Security Standard). As PCI applies to the most industries, we will use that regulation in this example, but we will be focusing on the FortiGate solutions. For additional details on how Fortinet's other products can address non-network aspects of PCI-DSS compliance, please refer to the latest FortiOS Certification and Compliance guide (http://docs.fortinet.com/fgt/handbook/40mr3/fortigate-compliance-40-mr3.pdf).

EXAMPLE DISTRIBUTED ENTERPRISE AND RETAIL ENVIRONMENT TOPOLOGIES

For the deployment example, we'll highlight the network topology requirements and the common UTM security configuration used to secure the environment for both distributed and core locations.

Network Layout

A distributed environment with the following infrastructure and communication requirements:

1. A remote FortiGate would be deployed in a layer 3 route/NAT mode, which would have two network segments: a private LAN (RFC1918 IP numbering) called Remote_LAN and the Internet.
2. Remote User access would include individual home office workstations, laptops, and mobile devices via the Internet.
3. All remote offices and users must communicate to their company headquarters securely via an IPSec VPN (named Remote_VPN) to access critical resources. In a retail environment, the credit card data leaving the point of sale (POS) system would also be routed securely to the processing server. To meet PCI compliance, the POS data must be separated from other traffic. Therefore, it is essential to have a separated IPSec VPN tunnel (Remote_POS_VPN) to isolate the POS traffic from other traffic heading to the company's headquarters.
4. Internet access to remote offices would be restricted for web and ftp.
5. Remote access to the Intranet web site is to be limited to only GET and POST requires. Uploading of files and web server "write" access is prohibited.
6. Corporate email is using FortiMail to provide dedicated Anti-spam/Anti-virus for company email.
7. To limit data leaks, the headquarters (HQ) is prohibited from originating communication to remote users.
8. The HQ FortiGate will be deployed in a layer 3 route/NAT mode, which would have three network segments: a private LAN (HQ_LAN), a private DMZ (HQ_DMZ), and an Internet segment with high-speed connectivity. End-user workstations will reside on the HQ_LAN and company servers will be on the HQ_DMZ segment. Communication must take place securely between all HQ network segments.
9. Remote and HQ FortiGates will be centrally managed by a FortiManager at HQ.
10. All FortiGates will log to a FortiAnalyzer at HQ to provide a centralized log repository and reporting on all devices.

Common UTM Deployment Configuration

Continuing with the topology depicted in Figure 11.1, the data and security requirements are:

- Remote sites:
  - To secure communication between a remote location and HQ, a gateway-to-gateway IPSec VPN is required. For retail environments, there

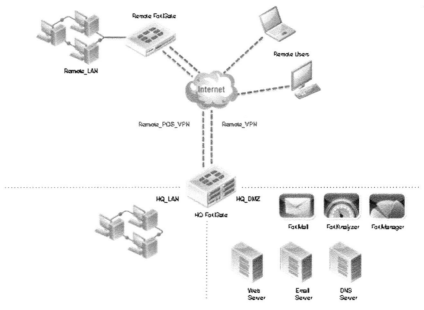

FIGURE 11.1 Distributed Network Topology

TIP

Policy for using FortiGate as a DNS server

There's no need to add DNS service to a rule if end users are pointing their system's DNS server settings to the FortiGate for processing.

---

would be two separated IPSec VPN tunnel configurations: Remote_POS_VPN and Remote_VPN.

- VPN traffic would operate in a split tunnel configuration, where corporate traffic would route through the VPN and all other traffic would be routed to that location's Internet Service Provider.
- It is recommended that IPSec be deployed in an interface-based configuration. With an IPSec interface-based configuration, VPN routing between route locations and HQ can be easily implemented using a dynamic routing protocol (OSPF, BGP, RIPv1/v2, ISIS) or static routes.
- All DNS queries would be resolved at the FortiGate local to that network. Thus, FortiOS would be used to handle split DNS, forwarding company-specific domain queries though the VPN and all other queries would be sent to the ISP-defined DNS server.

- To further protect infrastructure from network threats, access controls and UTM features are defined for all communication paths. The following security access control policies are needed on each Remote FortiGate:
  - Policy from Remote_LAN to Remote_VPN:
    - Firewall or Application Controls: Access controls will be implemented up to layer 4 and/or 7 on permitted traffic to HQ to control access to corporate email and intranet web servers. This would permit only the services SMTPS, POP3S, IMAPS, HTTP, and HTTPS services. All other services will fall under an implicit deny rule.
    - IDS/IPS profile: This profile will be tuned to the allowed services and the applications to which they connect.
  - In remote retail environments, the policy dictating traffic between Remote_LAN and Remote_POS_VPN will be controlled as follows:
    - As the primary purpose of the Remote_POS_VPN is for POS credit card transactions, access control will be implemented up to layer 4.
    - The IDS/IPS profile will be tuned to allowed services & application threats.
  - The traffic between the Remote_LAN and the Internet will be controlled as follows:
    - NAT will provide translation between the private network and the Internet.
    - Firewall or Application Controls will be defined to only allow HTTP, HTTPS, and FTP.
    - The network Anti-virus profile will be applied to web and FTP.
    - The IDS/IPS profile will be tuned to allowed services & application threats.
    - The Web Filtering profile will be tuned to allow only specified web categories.
  - The implicit deny policy will be used to restrict the following packet flows:
    - Internet to Remote_LAN.
    - HQ_VPN to LAN.
- Remote users:
  - The IPSec VPN tunnel will terminate at the HQ. The VPN will be in a split tunnel mode, so corporate-related traffic will route through the VPN and all other traffic to the Internet local to that location.
  - To further secure and protect the end-user's workstation, it is recommended that each endpoint run client software that provides the following:
    - Local "endpoint" firewall.
    - Anti-virus.
    - Web Filtering—this is not necessarily to restrict the end-user from limited web browsing which is an additional layer to filter out malicious web sites.

- HQ:
  - Must have the ability to terminate the IPSec VPNs and process traffic through from remote locations and users.
  - Interface-based IPSec configuration is recommended. With this configuration, routing decisions can be easily implemented using dynamic routing protocol (OSPF, BGP, RIPv1/v2, ISIS) or static routes.
  - To further secure and protect the infrastructure from network threats, access controls and UTM features will be defined on all communication pathways. The following security access control policies are needed:
    - Traffic from Remote_VPN to HQ_LAN is to be permitted. Since the remote FortiGates have access controls defined along with UTM-enabled inspection capabilities on the VPN tunnel, there is no need to double system resources. However, to ensure that this does not create a weakness, the configuration of the remote devices must be monitored.
    - Retail traffic, from the Remote_POS_VPN to the HQ_LAN will be permitted with up to layer 4 controls on the source to protect credit card data. Additionally, the IDS/IPS profile will be tuned to protect the allowed services and applications.
    - The policies between the HQ_LAN and the Internet and the HQ_DMZ and the Internet will be controlled as follows:
      - NAT will be used to provide translation between the private network and the Internet.
      - Firewall or Application Controls would be defined to allow only HTTP, HTTPS, DNS, and FTP. Since the users at HQ are not using the FortiGate as a DNS server then DNS must be explicitly allowed on both TCP and UDP DNS ports. Network Anti-virus must be enabled for web and FTP.
      - IDS/IPS profile is to be tuned to allowed services and application threats.
      - Web Filtering profile is to be used to restrict access to only allowed web categories.
    - Traffic from Internet to the HQ_DMZ must use a Virtual IP (VIP) or one-to-one static port forwarding to allow email traffic to the Anti-spam gateway relay and the IDS/IPS must be tuned to mail-related threats.
    - Traffic from the HQ_LAN to the HQ_DMZ will be controlled with either the Firewall or Application Controls to allow only DNS, SMTPS, POP3S, IMAPS, HTTP, and HTTPS. The IDS/IPS profile will be tuned to protecting these services.
    - The implicit deny policy will be used to restrict traffic between the Internet and the HQ_LAN, the HQ_DMZ and Remote_VPN, the HQ_DMZ and the HQ_LAN and the HQ_LAN and the Remote_VPN. The latter couples with the fact that the policy is defined to only allow inbound traffic to the HQ_LAN, so this zone should have no reason to connect outwards.

Best Practices

There are some standard practices for a distributed environment with remote locations and users.

Routing Decisions

Network connectivity from remote sites to HQ_LAN will rely on an IPSec gateway-to-gateway tunnel. You should use an Interface-based IPSec VPN for this as they provide a robust way to scale VPN configuration, access control, and routing capabilities. See Chapter 5 for more information on Interface vs. Policy-based IPSec VPN.

An interface-based IPSec VPN can make routing decisions for both static and dynamic protocols. Generally speaking, unless static routes are unmanageable in your environment (usually due to sheer number of routes), the administrative simplicity of static routing is preferable.

Whether static or dynamic routes are used, you should review the maximum values of your model of FortiGate. As smaller devices support fewer routes, the number of potential remote devices and networks will identify the devices you require. This type of an assessment is part of the sizing requirements covered in Chapter 3. Consider the following:

When using static routing, determine the number of routes needed between the remote sites and HQ. Also consider the likely number needed in the future.
If using dynamic routing instead, count the maximum number of routes likely to be needed and check that the existing FortiGate can handle both the number of routes and the number of neighbors to the HQ location.
Also, check the IPSec phase1 and phase2 capacity on all FortiGates, especially the HQ. When using interface-based IPSec VPNs, also check the supported interface count.

Access Controls

Tuning the firewall rules requires an understanding of both the network communication and the organization's security policy. In an enterprise environment, it is common to tune firewalls at layers 3 and 4, but complexity could arise at other layers. A common problem involves the use of application controls, as many network administrators are not application experts. If you are in this situation, it may help to apply the access control discovery process to application control. Typically, you can leave open access but enable logging so applications can be discovered. This is best done by using FortiOS to define rules up to layer 4, so everything can be locked down to the application layer and then tightened as the discovery process allows. Leveraging the FortiAnalyzer to provide historical logging and data mining capabilities, application reports can be generated to help identify which applications are and are not required.

In our example environment, distributed retail processing involves credit card information being transmitted over the network. It is critical to control traffic into and from these cardholder data environments. Firewall rules affecting this traffic require explicit definition of the allowed source, destination, and service. All unspecified traffic would be blocked. Isolating the cardholder data onto its own network segment can help reduce the PCI scope, but is not technically required. For example, if all POS systems are connected to a dedicated subnet and do not mix with other systems, they can be isolated onto their own VLAN or physical connection.

Since FortiOS can define firewall rules based on the direction of VLAN communication, it can be used to manage critical compliance requirements. Since, in this example, there is a need for POS credit card information and data network communication to occur between remote FortiGates and corporate headquarters, the POS traffic must be segregated from other traffic via dedicated IPSec VPN tunnels. When used with interface-based IPSec tunnels, the routing decisions and access controls can be easily configured and controlled based on the direction of flow between tunnel interfaces.

In addition to our example, other types of network segmentation are seen in enterprise and retail environments. These vary from multiple network paths to the use of non-conventional devices with built-in IP stacks. The network communication flows, however, some network access and security protection will be required. Figure 11.2 shows various network devices that can be segmented onto dedicated physical, logical (VLAN or wireless), or VDOMs for further access controls and UTM security protection.

Examples of segmentation access control includes:

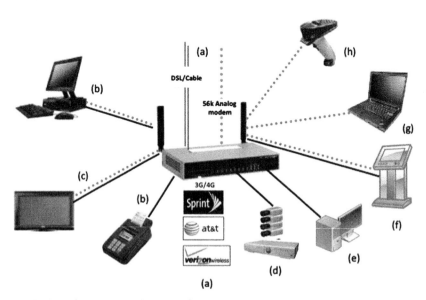

FIGURE 11.2 Various Network Segmentations

a. Route traffic destined to the Internet through an alternate access method. These often include analog modems, 3G or 4G mobile connections, or dedicated DSL or Cable lines. These connectivity options can be configured for redundancy. Based on layer 2-link status or layer 3-connectivity integrating with the Ping Server feature, failure within these layers can be detected. The FortiGate can be used to leverage static- or dynamic-routing and restrict access to specific paths with firewall rules. Basic load balancing with Equal Cost Multiple Path can be used to take advantage of multiple ISPs (see Chapter 4 for further details).

b. Dedicated POS machines used for credit card processing.

c. Isolated digital signage used for advertisement, menus, or informational purposes.

d. Security cameras used to monitor employee activities and customer use of counter applications.

e. Dedicated classes of Workstations to be used by employees, guests, or customers.

f. Kiosks used for advertisement, in-store online ordering, or for informational purposes.

g. Mobile network/internet access used by employees, guest, or customers.

h. Handheld devices used for inventory tracking purposes.

The examples provided are not complete, as technology evolves, segmentation access controls will also continue to evolve.

Authentication

Authentication can be considered as another layer defense. In the example environment, remote VPN user authentication would provide an excellent additional protection. This way, if an employee were to leave the company, their login credentials could be easily removed from the supported authentication servers (local database, TACACS+, RADIUS, LDAP, and FortiToken) used for the remote VPN authentication. Without a VPN authentication infrastructure, maintaining users' VPN access could be unmanageably complex.

Implementation of remote IPSec VPN users' authentication can be accomplished with the XAuth (Extended Authentication) feature covered in Chapter 5. For remote

---

NOTE

Multiple Wireless segments

As highlighted briefly in Chapter 2, Fortinet wireless solutions offer multiple SSIDs, each with its own network fully isolated from each other segments using UTM controls. A location could have one SSID wireless for customer/guest usage and another SSID for employee usage.However, if this is done to provide access on the wired side for credit card transactions, be aware that the PCI-DSS wireless rules will still apply, as the FortiGate device itself would be considered in scope.

users using the SSL VPN, the authentication mechanism is built into the web browser or the standalone tunnel application.

For the retail distributed environment that must conform to PCI-DSS, two-factor authentication is required for remote VPN users to access the data network. Two-factor authentication is possible with IPSec VPN using XAuth and the FortiToken solution.

Additionally, PCI requires that administrators follow specific password requirements to access the FortiGate. These include a minimum password length of at least seven characters, passwords that contain both numeric and alphabetic characters, and a password change enforced every 90 days (http://docs.fortinet.com/fgt/handbook/40mr3/fortigate-compliance-40-mr3.pdf).

Splash screen and web page redirects are optional and can be applied during authentication. A splash screen could consist of a list of terms and conditions with acceptance as shown in Figure 11.3. If an end-user does not accept the disclaimer then they will be denied access to the network.

FIGURE 11.3 Splash Screen Disclaimer Web Page

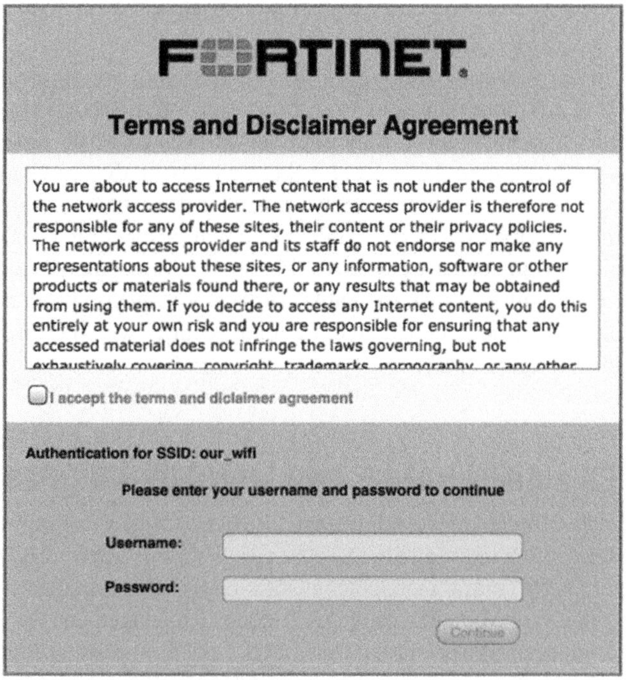

FIGURE 11.4 Wireless Captive Portal Disclaimer and Login Web Page

When the wireless feature is used with the FortiGate, a captive portal can be enabled for each SSID, which can provide both terms and conditions and enforce authentication. Figure 11.4 displays an example of a captive portal session.

Web page redirects can be configured so users' browsers default to the company website instead of the locally defined home page. Web page redirects can be configured without authentication, after accepting disclaimer, or after authentication.

Applying UTM Security Profiles

Consider the differences between the UTM profiles defined in the remote site policy definitions for Remote_LAN to HQ_VPN vs. Remote_LAN to Internet. There is no web filtering profile defined on the rule "to HQ_VPN". The reason there is no need for a web filtering profile on the "to HQ_VPN" rule is, when Remote_LAN accesses only a handful of company web servers, there is no need to perform this function. Having the web filtering profile on the Remote_LAN to Internet policy makes more sense since there are many web site accesses that need to be controlled and monitored.

Also, consider Anti-virus profiles. Anti-virus inspection is supported for web, email, ftp, nntp, and some IM protocols. Therefore, there is no reason to inspect traffic that does not include these protocols. Additionally, if the Anti-virus services are used in the policy, there are times when virus inspection is not necessary, such as the Remote_LAN to HQ_VPN route.

As noted in the Network Topology infrastructure and communication requirements, Remote_LAN communicates to intranet web servers but only via HTTP/S GETs and POSTs. Now, when the intranet site is used as a file repository, using an Anti-virus profile would be wise. Furthermore, with this same policy, email traffic is expected, but since the company is using a dedicated solution (FortiMail) for Anti-spam/Anti-virus of their email, additional inspection on the FortiGate would be redundant. In scenarios where a third-party Anti-spam solution is used at headquarters, it may make sense to enable Anti-virus inspection and Anti-spam on email protocols to provide a second layer of email security which leverages different Anti-virus and Anti-spam databases.

SUGGESTED MAINTENANCE AND MONITORING OPERATIONS

When there's a distributed network infrastructure consisting of five or more deployed devices, managing them individually could be cumbersome. Therefore, it is generally recommended to use a central management solution like FortiManager. As discussed in Chapter 9, the FortiManager provides a central management interface for all devices. More importantly for our example, PCI-DSS requires that logs be retained for a specific period of time. A FortiAnalyzer (Chapter 8) can be used for reporting and data mining. An alternative option to log from the FortiGate devices would be syslog. Configuration for logging to a syslog server from FortiGate can work in parallel with the FortiAnalyzer. Redundant servers can also be defined.

As the distributed environment grows, it is always important to monitor system resources used by the overall security infrastructure. Examples of system resources include CPU, memory, and local storage on the FortiGate. The variables that affect CPU and memory are related to static and run-time features. Static features include an increase in the number of IPSec tunnels, concurrent sessions, static routes, learned dynamic routes, firewall rules and objects, and other variables outlined in the FortiOS Maximum system value guide (http://docs.fortinet.com/fgt/handbook/40mr3/fortigate-max-values-40-mr3.pdf). Run-time features include things like the increased amount of traffic needed for UTM processing. A common example would include using proxy-based Anti-virus scanning where a compressed file must be loaded into memory, uncompressed, then scanned from beginning to end. This can take an unpredictable amount of memory along with ASIC & CPU processing. When the overall system CPU and/or memory hits critical metrics, such as consistent 90–100% CPU or 80%+ memory usage, it is generally a good indication that you have outgrown that particular FortiGate's ability to handle the load.

Before upgrading the solution to a higher-end FortiGate model, it is highly recommended to first contact Fortinet TAC to assess whether any sort of known issue is causing the high system resources. During this assessment, the TAC would generally provide advice on tuning the system reduce resource usage. FortiGate system resource tuning tips can also be found in the Fortinet Knowledge Base (http://kb.fortinet.com), search for 'conserved mode'.

If one needs to lower system resource utilization and there is some budget available, you may wish to consider an Active/Active High Availability deployment. As described in Chapter 4, Active/Active HA leverages the FortiGate Clustering Protocol (FGCP) to load balance TCP traffic to other FortiGate devices in the cluster. The ability to offload TCP traffic can decrease system utilization on the primary FortiGate. Given that the majority of the UTM inspection is based on TCP-related traffic such as web and email, offloading these services provides room for growth. For optimal performance, it is recommended that an HA FortiOS FGCP cluster be limited to up to five devices.

In a retail distributed environment where PCI-DSS compliance is required, wireless monitoring is essential. Whether the remote sites or HQ have wireless deployed, you must monitor for rogue wireless access points. This can be done with either the FortiGate models with built-in 802.11 AP (access point) functions or the standalone FortiAP. FortiAP can be implemented to work with most FortiOS devices, so they can act as a wireless controller to manage the FortiAP. A FortiAP can dedicate a radio for monitoring for unauthorized devices (see Chapter 3—FortiAP). Rogue device detection can be logged and optionally configured to be suppressed/blocked from company's network.

Security on Financial Services

INFORMATION IN THIS CHAPTER:

- Electronic Trading
- Market Data Networks
- The Industry Trends
    - Latency
    - Financial Service Providers
    - Direct Market Access
- The Challenge
- Market Data Multicast Distribution
    - Inter-domain Multicast
    - Address Group Collisions
- Protocol-Independent Multicast-Source-Specific Multicast (PIM-SSM)
    - PIM-SM Operation Overview
    - PIM-SSM Operation Overview
    - Configuration Steps to Enable PIM-SSM
    - Monitoring IP Multicast

Large financial services companies face many of the security challenges seen by all large distributed companies. They must protect key internal assets while still providing enough access to them for their users. However, since Financial Services is required to process data in near real time, the industry experiences some unique challenges.

ELECTRONIC TRADING

For many years trading systems have been evolving. Today, computers are used to execute trades with little or no human involvement and, as a result, high-frequency and algorithmic trading has increased significantly in the past decade. By many estimates, these trades account for greater than 60% of the daily market volumes.

The Financial Information eXchange ("FIX") protocol is a de facto-standard designed to enable electronic transmission of trading information on the Financial Services market. It has experienced wide and rapid adoption as a straightforward, non-proprietary way to communicate between hundreds of brokerage firms, exchanges, and financial service providers. FIX is a real-time, bi-directional session-based communication mechanism that runs over TCP and has been a key driver in the use of computers to generate and execute orders as the system continues to grow at an incredible rate.

MARKET DATA NETWORKS

Knowledge is power and, in the financial services industry, Market Data services are the primary means of providing information. Market Data feeds consist of flows of information distributed to and analyzed by the financial institutions and include pricing information, market news, and other time-sensitive information used to help develop trading strategies. While identical information is provided to each institution, individual firms apply different analytics to the data to create the competitive advantages that allows these firms to succeed.

The Market Data environment is made up of a few basic components. The first is the source of the information, i.e. the content providers. The primary content providers are the exchanges for stocks, futures and options, and news agencies. The data streams generated by these providers are distributed to the financial trading firms or brokerage houses. These firms then use the information to help determine the strategies to stay competitive in today's quickly evolving financial markets.

Market Data is primarily distributed as a uni-directional, one-to-many application and as such is ideally suited to and implemented using IP Multicast over UDP.

THE INDUSTRY TRENDS

The increasing commoditization of high-frequency trading has many organizations looking for competitive advantages. With electronic trading's increasing bandwidth requirements and demands for a continuous effort to minimize latency, one good advantage is to simply use the fastest network possible. Many firms have shown a direct correlation between meeting these network demands and revenue growth.

Latency

When dealing with latency in most environments, users in other industries think first about voice and video applications over the network and ensuring an appropriate level of latency in order to avoid quality issues such as echo or an uncomfortable lag when trying to communicate between multiple parties. While latency is important to these applications, the acceptable delays are measured in milliseconds. The reality is that with VoIP applications, a delay of 150 ms would be hardly noticeable to the human ear.

When looking at latency concerns in the Financial Service space, however, voice and video concerns are much easier to manage and maintain when compared to the requirements for supporting applications that include the high-speed, ultra-low latency algorithmic trading platforms and the market data platforms that support them where Firewall latency measured in microseconds.

Financial Service Providers

Exchanges and financial trading institutions are dealing with ever-increasing volumes of information and many firms are moving away from traditional self-maintained data centers and leveraging Financial Service Providers' (FSP) data centers. With latency varying greatly, depending on the speed of the provisioned links and the number of hops along the path, firms are seeing an opportunity to access thousands of new endpoints while increasing throughput, improving latency and the in-house infrastructure maintenance costs.

These providers compete to offer interconnects for critical applications and to protect intellectual properties, helping to provide competitive advantages for the trading firms while increasing network performance and reducing latency to microseconds where possible.

Direct Market Access

As the firms strive to get to the data as quickly as possible, many are looking closer to the source by selecting feeds directly from the exchanges. By directly accessing markets, stock traders interact directly with the exchanges rather than being forced to execute through intermediary stockbrokers. These firms are establishing these Direct Market Access (DMA) feeds and driving competition among the exchanges for the fastest processing times.

THE CHALLENGE

With ever-increasing volumes of information needing to be disseminated and the competitive pressures of the industry, all entities are being pressured to interconnect their environments while increasing network performance. With business-critical applications and key intellectual properties defining competitive advantages, securing these connections while trying to reduce the latency is imperative.

The idea of compromising network performance for the sake of security was, at one time, seen as nearly impossible to accept. However, the days when you could get by without a firewall are long gone... as is the thought that a basic firewall is sufficient. In the Financial Services sector, network security is critical to effective data management, business continuity and compliance. With electronic trading and market applications driving an ever more interconnected ecosystem, new challenges arise in ensuring only appropriate communications are occurring.

Network security has become business-critical, but in many cases, network latency is caused by traditional firewalls. Many traditional firewalls typically account for up to 20% of latency in the network. Fortinet's FortiGate firewalls' ASIC approach embed purpose-built Network Processors deliver the low-latency, zero packet-loss firewalling, required in these environments with documented latencies averaging 5–7 µs at line rate of 64 byte packets for IPv4 traffic and similar performance metrics from the Security Processors and for hardware acceleration of not only IPv4 traffic, but also IPv6 and multicast acceleration.

While these acceleration capabilities have been discussed earlier in the book, we will not go over this topic again. But there is another key component of the application deployments we just outlined that has not been discussed in detail when it comes to deploying a secured Market Data solution.

MARKET DATA MULTICAST DISTRIBUTION

As discussed, Market Data is a one-to-many application with content providers distributing streams of information using IP Multicast so as to not replicate every data packet for each and every user. While many environments solely use Protocol-Independent Multicast-Sparse Mode (PIM-SM), this is suited to Any Source Multicast (ASM) [1, 2]. By this, we mean that the requesters of the data streams receive information by joining a "group" (G) based on the multicast address. These requesters, or applications, are not concerned with the "source" (S) or sources of the stream so long as the network can forward the correct stream to that requestor.

This model can represent some specific challenges for content providers, transmission providers, and the recipient networks of these multicast streams.

Inter-domain Multicast

One challenge when deploying a multicast environment, such as one that would support a market data distribution network, is dealing with the concerns around supporting a multi-domain architecture. While most of today's environments support a PIM-SM deployment, this works best within a single domain. Where the source or sources for a particular multicast stream may not be well known, a new set of concerns must be addressed when expanding multicast coverage across multiple dispersed networks.

PIM-SM uses a "shared tree" to distribute the multicast stream to the requestors of the multicast group. This tree is represented as a (*, G) tree routed at a "Rendezvous Point" (RP). While we will go into more detail on this process shortly, it is important to understand that the use of an RP is required with PIM-SM.

Needing to statically coordinate the Rendezvous Point deployments in support of PIM-SM between domains can be difficult to support and prone to errors.

These errors can cause issues in the neighboring domains. Statically maintaining multicast routes or deploying additional protocols such as Multicast Source Discovery Protocol (MSDP) and Multiprotocol Border Gateway Protocol (MBGP) can help discover multiple sources between domains and propagate multicast routes between domains. This will also provide more opportunities for error and unneeded complexity to be injected into the environment.

These options can clearly lead to an increase in the administrative overhead and the difficulty of coordinating between domains would be exacerbated for the content providers and distribution network maintainers as end users attempt to all get closer to the data. This will, over time, lead to an increase in configuration error. Inter-domain deployment often adds extra complexity to the tasks of maintaining and troubleshooting statically defined networks.

Address Group Collisions

Another concern in an Any Source Multicast environment is address space collision. With the IPv4 address space limited and the limited or experimental designation of actual address assignments within the multicast space, it is very likely that administrators from multiple domains will attempt to use the same address groups for different applications. While this is most likely unintentional, address collision can occur and could consume more bandwidth than expected or send unexpected data to applications, resulting in unexpected behavior.

PROTOCOL-INDEPENDENT MULTICAST-SOURCE-SPECIFIC MULTICAST (PIM-SSM)

PIM-SSM is effectively an extension to PIM-SM [3]. While dependent on PIM messaging between routers to create multicast distribution trees, we will review some of the advantages to using PIM-SSM in environments common to Market Data Providers which distribute feeds to many self-maintained network domains.

PIM-SM Operation Overview

In a traditional ASM environment supported by PIM-SM, requesters use IGMPv1, 2, or 3 to request membership into a group. These requests do not include information as to the source requesting the data. If a request is made in a properly configured PIM-SM environment a (*, G) entry will be created on the Rendezvous Point (RP) for the requested address group. Using the administratively scoped address group of 239.10.10.100 as an example, the PIM-SM routers along the path would each create an entry for (*, 239.10.10.100) toward the RP.

The routers closest to the multicast sources are responsible for tunneling the data streams to the RP so those streams can be forwarded by the RP via the shared (*, G) tree when requested to the router ultimately responsible for the receiving host.

Once the final router receives a stream for a given multicast group, it can choose to create a more optimal distribution tree, perhaps by using the actual source as opposed to continuing to use the share distribution tree. This more optimal source-specific path is identified by an (S, G) entry in the router's multicast routing table. The (S, G) path is determined by routers using the normal routing table to do a "Reverse Path Forward" lookup toward the source and determine the best route back.

Using our 239.10.10.100 example, if we were to receive multicast packets for this group from a source example of 10.10.50.125, we would see a table entry for (10.10.50.125, 239.10.10.100) requesting the stream to be received on the interface perceived as "closest" to the source based on the RPF check of the routing table.

The (*, 239.10.10.100) entry would still exist for any potential new sources for them to forward down the shared tree, again potentially a less optimal path from the new source. The final router receiving the stream on behalf of the requesting host can send another more specific path request toward the new source using another (S, G) entry.

Aside from the complexity of troubleshooting potential problems and the likely less than optimal forwarding for multicast streams via the shared tree, there also exists the chance that we would receive data associated from one or more unwanted sources.

PIM-SSM Operation Overview

When deploying a PIM-SSM environment, hosts use IGMPv3 [4] to request not only group membership but also to define the source or sources from which to receive the groups. This "source, group" paring can be thought of as a "channel." Channels are discussed and addressed at the application level, but this mechanism helps us to ensure that the application is only receiving multicast packets from the sources specified and that our routers avoid having to maintain a less than optimal shared distribution tree. With PIM-SSM, the routers know the source when the host makes its request allowing the router to create an (S, G) entry from the onset of the communication request. This way there is granular control of our sources, avoiding address collision concerns. There is no need for an RP to support a shared tree and the most efficient route from the onset handles forwarding of multicast packets.

Channel Redundancy

Many applications that tie to financial operations require redundant infrastructure. Market Data solutions are no exception. By supporting the ability to define the source and multicast channels, it is fairly straightforward to deploy content sources in multiple locations and to stream both primary and backup sources for the subscribers' required channels.

Channel Control

An advantage an application like Market Data has is knowing the source addresses of the channels ahead of time. This allows the ability to ensure, or secure, which channels are to be allowed into a subscriber's network either by the subscriber themselves or by the content provider.

This also allows for the content providers to plan for appropriate network address translation of the source and/or the destination to be defined per channel.

Configuration Steps to Enable PIM-SSM

To configure our FortiOS device to participate in PIM-SSM, you must perform some fairly simple steps. Before we begin, we must make a few assumptions. The first is that full IP reachability has been established between our multicast requesters and our multicast sources. (S, G) multicast distribution trees are dependent on the ability of each PIM-speaking router in the path to identify an appropriate route to the multicast sources. The second assumption comes in that all routers in the path from channel requesters to channel sources have PIM-SM enabled properly. As mentioned earlier, the use of PIM-SSM is dependent on the use of PIM messaging to create and maintain the (S, G) distribution tree. We will review the basic configuration of PIM-SM in FortiOS during this walk through.

Defining Address Range

When configuring PIM-SSM, we will want to define the range of multicast addresses acceptable for source-specific requests. To do this, use an "access-list." The below example shows an access-list that defines the 232.0.0.0/8 subnet as outlined for use with PIM-SSM in RFCs 3569 and 4607.

```
config router access-list
 edit "PIMSSM"
  config rule
   edit 1
    set prefix 232.0.0.0 255.0.0.0
    set exact-match disable
   next
  end
 next
end
```

Controlling SSM Channel Assignments

By using the "multicast-flow" command we can create channel and control the source and destination pairs that can be joined on each interface using SSM. The following example shows a multicast-flow configured with a single flow from source 10.10.25.125 providing a stream to multicast group 232.10.45.15.

```
config router multicast-flow
 edit "SSMTest"
  config flows
```

```
   edit 1
     set group-addr 232.10.45.15
     set source-addr 10.10.25.125
   next
  end
 next
end
```

It should be understood that the use of the "multicast-flow" option does not negate the need to use multicast policies to allow traffic to flow through the system. The use of multicast firewall polices was covered in an earlier chapter. Multicast firewall policies are also used to provide network address translation of either the source address and/or the multicast group address.

Enabling Multicast Routing

Now that the prep work has been accomplished, we can configure FortiOS to participate in the PIM environment. As we are not concerned with participating in any (*, G) distribution trees, our configuration is very simple.

In the example, we can see that we have enabled multicast routing as well as the use of PIM-SSM. The second SSM option defined in the example is that of the multicast address range allowing use in SSM by referencing the access-list created during our prep work.

```
config router multicast
set multicast-routing enable
 config pim-sm-global
   set ssm enable
   set ssm-range "PIMSSM"
 end
end
```

As we continue this configuration, we will assume that the FortiGate is to route traffic between the "internal" and "wan1" interfaces. We will want to enable PIM-SM on these interfaces for our firewall to participate in the creation of our multicast distribution trees. FortiOS interfaces default to IGMPv3, so we will not need to configure any other option at the interface level.

While there is no further configuration required, we have taken an additional step by applying the "multicast-flow" we defined earlier. As discussed previously, applying this configuration to the interface will restrict the channels that IGMPv3 clients can successfully request. There is no implicit denier when using "multicast-flow," so if there is no "multicast-flow" applied to the interface, there will be no restrictions applied.

```
config router multicast
 config interface
```

```
    edit "internal"
     set pim-mode sparse-mode
     set multicast-flow "SSMTest"
    next
    edit "wan1"
     set pim-mode sparse-mode
    next
   end
 end
```

Monitoring IP Multicast

When ensuring a network environment can support the distribution of multicast streams, many of the tools described earlier in this book will come handy. Full IP reachability must be established before we can properly set up any multicast routing.

Assuming this has been done and all is functioning well, there are a couple of key commands to be familiar with when establishing your IP multicast networking.

PIM Interfaces

One of the first things you may need to verify is that you have enabled PIM-SM on the interfaces as required. The following command will show the interfaces with PIM-SM enabled, which interfaces have PIM neighbors, and the IP address of the PIM designated router on each interface segment.

FWF60C # get router info multicast pim sparse-mode interface

Address	Interface Mode	VIFindex Count	Ver/ Nbr Prior	DR	DR
192.168.1.99	internal	0	v2/S 0	1	192.168.1.99
172.16.50.100	wan1	2	v2/S 1	1	172.16.50.100

PIM Neighbors

For a more detailed view of the health of your neighbor relationship, the following command will show you the IP address of any PIM neighbors, the interface on which they are peered, and the time your neighbor relationship has been established.

FWF60C # get router info multicast pim sparse-mode neighbor

Neighbor Address	Interface	Uptime/Expires Priority/Mode	Ver	DR
172.16.50.1	wan1	02d17h54m/00:01:17	v2	1/

IGMP Interface Verification

While IGMPv3 is the default, the following command can verify that the interface is configured and operating as required working with PIM-SSM.

```
FWF60C # get router info multicast igmp interface
Interface internal (Index 4)
IGMP Enabled, Active, Querier, Configured for version 3
Internet address is 192.168.1.99
IGMP query interval is 125 seconds
IGMP querier timeout is 255 seconds
IGMP max query response time is 10 seconds
Last member query response interval is 1000 milliseconds
Group Membership interval is 260 seconds
Router Alert options not required in IGMP packets
```

IGMP Group Membership

Once we have confirmed configuration, one of the next items is to verify the IGMP group membership requests received by the firewall. The following command will show the groups requested on each interface as well as the address of the requester.

The expiry timer shows when the forwarding of the groups will end if no further updates or continuation requests are seen. The status of "stopped" for group 232.10.45.15 is an IGMPv3 source-specific joint and indicates that this timer does not determine the expiration of this group.

FWF60C # get router info multicast igmp groups

IGMP Connected Group Membership		
Group Address	Interface	Uptime Expires Last Reporter
224.0.1.60	internal	03d20h36m 00:02:48 192.168.1.110
224.0.1.140	internal	03d20h36m 00:02:48 192.168.1.99
232.10.45.15	internal	03d17h52m stopped 192.168.1.110
233.45.17.10	internal	03d20h36m 00:02:44 192.168.1.110
239.255.255.250	internal	03d20h36m 00:02:49 192.168.1.110

Multicast Routing Table

Once we have verified that the expected request is made, we can verify the expected route in the multicast routing table. The following command finds and verifies the entry for the multicast channels being created and distributed correctly.

The table snippet shown below confirms we are receiving for the group and identifies the source or sources. Two important things to verify are the "Asserted" or incoming interface and the "Outgoing" interface of the channel. The "Asserted" interface is determined by the reverse path look up toward the sources. If there is an unexpected result in this field, troubleshoot the normal IP routing table to verify the correct route to the source.

The outgoing interface is created toward any IGMP interfaces with requesting host and/or interface with PIM neighbors that have requested the stream to forward further into the distribution tree.

The trailing address used in this sample is optional. Leaving it off will provide output for the entire IP Multicast routing table.

```
FWF60C # get router info multicast pim sparse-mode table
   232.10.45.15(10.10.25.125, 232.10.45.15)
RPF nbr: 172.16.50.1
RPF idx: wan1
SPT bit: 1
Upstream State: JOINED
Local:
 internal
Joined:
Asserted:
 wan1:
Outgoing:
 internal
```

Debugging PIM-SM Messages

The previous "get" commands will normally provide enough information for you to confirm proper operation or to diagnose any issues you may be experiencing. However, there will always be those times when you must go just a little deeper to determine why things may not be operating as planned.

Debugging PIM events requires first choosing the PIM event output you want to witness. By default, all PIM event message types are enabled. If setting the event level to informational provides too much output, disabling events or message types that are not of interest is advisable. As with any debug-level troubleshooting, the use of the "diag debug enable" command is how you start getting output.

You can see some examples of the commands used and a sample output of PIM events from an information output.

```
FWF60C # diagnose ip router pim-sm level
   critical                    critical level
   error                       error level
   info                        information level
```

```
none                              none level
warn                              warning level

FWF60C # diagnose ip router pim-sm level info
FWF60C # diagnose ip router pim-sm show

Debugging status:
PIM event debugging is on
PIM MFC debugging is on
PIM state debugging is on
PIM packet debugging is on
PIM Hello HT timer debugging is on
PIM Hello NLT timer debugging is on
PIM Hello THT timer debugging is on
PIM Join/Prune JT timer debugging is on
PIM Join/Prune ET timer debugging is on
PIM Join/Prune PPT timer debugging is on
PIM Join/Prune KAT timer debugging is on
PIM Join/Prune OT timer debugging is on
PIM Assert AT timer debugging is on
PIM Register RST timer debugging is on
PIM Bootstrap BST timer debugging is on
PIM Bootstrap CRP timer debugging is on
PIM mib debugging is on
PIM nsm debugging is on
PIM nexthop debugging is on
PIM sparse-mode debug level: INFO

FWF60C # diag debug enable
id=36870 msg="PIM-SM: PIM Assert from 172.16.50.1"
id=36870 msg="PIM-SM: Recv Assert message"
id=36870 msg="PIM-SM: Group: 232.10.45.15/32 (Family 1, Type 0)"
id=36870 msg="PIM-SM: Source: 10.10.25.125 (Family 1, Type 0)"
id=36870 msg="PIM-SM: R-Bit: 0"
id=36870 msg="PIM-SM: Preference: 10"
id=36870 msg="PIM-SM: Metric: 0"
id=36870 msg="PIM-SM: MRIB.pref(10.10.25.125): nexthop 172.16.50.1
   preference 10"
id=36870 msg="PIM-SM: MRIB.metric(10.10.25.125): nexthop 172.16.50.1
   metric 0"
```

```
id=36870 msg="PIM-SM: MRIB.pref(10.10.25.125): nexthop 172.16.50.1
    preference 10"
id=36870 msg="PIM-SM: MRIB.metric(10.10.25.125): nexthop 172.16.50.1
    metric 0"
id=36870 msg="PIM-SM: Receive Acceptable Assert from Current Winner
    for (10.10.25.125, 232.10.45.15) on wan1"
id=36870 msg="PIM-SM: Assert (10.10.25.125, 232.10.45.15) on wan1:
    Restarting AT timer with 180 secs timeout"
id=36870 msg="PIM-SM: PIM Hello packet Recved."
id=36870 msg="PIM-SM: PIM Hello from 172.16.50.1 on wan1"
id=36870 msg="PIM-SM: Recv Hello message"
id=36870 msg="PIM-SM: Holdtime: 105
id=36870 msg="PIM-SM: T-bit: off"
id=36870 msg="PIM-SM: Lan delay: 1"
id=36870 msg="PIM-SM: Override interval: 3"
id=36870 msg="PIM-SM: DR priority: 1"
id=36870 msg="PIM-SM: Gen ID: 1212108891"
id=36870 msg="PIM-SM: Restarting NLT for neighbor 172.16.50.1 on wan1
    with 105 secs timeout from Hello message"
id=36870 msg="PIM-SM: Hello Timer expired on internal"
id=36870 msg="PIM-SM: Restarting Hello Timer on internal with 30 secs
    timeout"
id=36870 msg="PIM-SM: Stopping Triggered Hello Timer on internal"
id=36870 msg="PIM-SM: Hello send to internal"
id=36870 msg="PIM-SM: Send Hello message"
id=36870 msg="PIM-SM: Holdtime: 105"
id=36870 msg="PIM-SM: T-bit: off"
id=36870 msg="PIM-SM: Lan delay: 1"
id=36870 msg="PIM-SM: Override interval: 3"
id=36870 msg="PIM-SM: DR priority: 1"
id=36870 msg="PIM-SM: Gen ID: 128959393"

FWF60C # diag debug disable
FWF60C # diagnose ip router pim-sm level critical
```

Debugging IGMP Messages

Debugging IGMP messaging is nearly identical to that for PIM messages.

Debug-level messages and message types are configured as in the examples. Like the PIM message debug output, the IGMP message debug output can be overly verbose and it can help to enable and disable different message types in addition to setting the debug level.

```
FWF60C # diag ip router igmp show
IGMP Debugging status:
 IGMP Decoder debugging is on
 IGMP Encoder debugging is on
 IGMP Events debugging is on
 IGMP FSM debugging is on
 IGMP Tree-Info-Base (TIB) debugging is on
IGMP debugging level is INFO

FWF60C # diag ip router igmp level info
FWF60C # diag debug enable
id=36870 msg="NSM: [IGMP-ENCODE] Send Gen Query: Sent General Query on
    internal, ret=36"
id=36870 msg="NSM: [IGMP-DECODE] Dec Msg: IGMP Membership Query, Max.
    Rsp. Code 100"
id=36870 msg="NSM: [IGMP-DECODE] Dec Msg: IGMP V3 Membership Report,
    Max. Rsp. Code 0"
id=36870 msg="NSM: [IGMP-DECODE] Dec V3 Grp Rec: Grp 239.255.255.250
    on internal"
id=36870 msg="NSM: [IGMP-FSM] Process Event: I=internal,
    G=239.255.255.250, State: Exclude, Event: Mode Is Exclude"
id=36870 msg="NSM: [IGMP-FSM] State Change: Exclude(2)->Exclude(2)"
id=36870 msg="NSM: [IGMP-DECODE] Dec V3 Grp Rec: Grp 224.0.1.60 on
    internal"
id=36870 msg="NSM: [IGMP-FSM] Process Event: I=internal, G=224.0.1.60,
    State: Exclude, Event: Mode Is Exclude"
id=36870 msg="NSM: [IGMP-FSM] State Change: Exclude(2)->Exclude(2)"
id=36870 msg="NSM: [IGMP-DECODE] Dec Msg: IGMP V2 Membership Report,
    Max. Rsp. Code 0"
id=36870 msg="NSM: [IGMP-DECODE] Dec V2 Report: Grp 224.0.1.140 on
    internal"
id=36870 msg="NSM: [IGMP-FSM] Process Event: I=internal,
    G=224.0.1.140, State: Exclude, Event: Mode Is Exclude"
id=36870 msg="NSM: [IGMP-FSM] State Change: Exclude(2)->Exclude(2)"
id=36870 msg="NSM: [IGMP-DECODE] Dec Msg: IGMP V3 Membership Report,
    Max. Rsp. Code 0"
id=36870 msg="NSM: [IGMP-DECODE] Dec V3 Grp Rec: Grp 232.10.45.15 on
    internal"
```

```
id=36870 msg="NSM: [IGMP-FSM] Process Event: I=internal,
   G=232.10.45.15, State: Include, Event: Mode Is Include"
id=36870 msg="NSM: [IGMP-FSM] State Change: Include(1)->Include(1)"
id=36870 msg="NSM: [IGMP-DECODE] Dec Msg: IGMP V2 Membership Report,
   Max. Rsp. Code 0"
id=36870 msg="NSM: [IGMP-DECODE] Dec V2 Report: Invalid Grp 224.0.0.22
   on internal, Ignoring..."
id=36870 msg="NSM: [IGMP-DECODE] Dec Msg: IGMP V3 Membership Report,
   Max. Rsp. Code 0"
id=36870 msg="NSM: [IGMP-DECODE] Dec V3 Grp Rec: Grp 233.45.17.10 on
   internal"
id=36870 msg="NSM: [IGMP-FSM] Process Event: I=internal,
   G=233.45.17.10, State: Exclude, Event: Mode Is Exclude"
```

REFERENCES

[1] RFC 3569—An Overview of Source-Specific Multicast (SSM).
[2] RFC 4607—Source-Specific Multicast for IP.
[3] RFC 4601—Protocol Independent Multicast-Sparse Mode (PIM-SM): Protocol Specification.
[4] RFC 4604—Using Internet Group Management Protocol Version 3 (IGMPv3) and Multicast Listener Discovery Protocol Version 2 (MLDv2) for Source-Specific Multicast.

Troubleshooting the Project

INTRODUCTION

You probably wonder why we need a "Troubleshooting the Project" Appendix in a technical book. In an ideal world, technical people shouldn't be affected that issues related to budget or timing. However, in the real world, how often have people asked you to do something that should have been completed yesterday? How often have you been asked to find a less-expensive option? If you have ever experienced this, the information here will help you understand how to better deal with potential project management issues.

Chapter 10 discussed several Project Management tips and tricks. Here, we will discuss what to do when things seem to be off track. While there are no rules on tackling these situations, we advise on ways to reduce the impact of problems and how to, if possible, get things back on track.

DEALING WITH COST ISSUES

Cost issues arise when the money available is insufficient to reach the objective within the timeframe. Of course, there are options that are external to the project, such as transferring money from other projects or asking for credits or loans. However, there are alternatives.

The first thing that must be evaluated is how we got into the situation. However, it is important to make it clear to everyone that the idea is not to point fingers or assign guilt. The goal is to prevent the issue from happening again. Here are some common causes:

- *Missing Items:* This arises when the Bill of Materials (BoM) or list of elements to be used on the project lacks an item. Sometimes, it is a license or a contract. An example is support. If you need a contract that lists an Advanced Replacement/24×7 option, and you have Return and Replace/8×5, problems can arise. Sometimes, you will experience hardware issues, such as needing additional hard disks or connectors. These missing items result on additional expenditures, pushing you past your budget.
  - *Suggestions to avoid it:* The best way to avoid this issue is to plan and do a test run in advance. Do this with at least two different people (the 4-eye principle). A good way to avoid surprises here is to have diagrams illustrating physical connections of all the boxes. This way, missing elements as switches, connectors, or modules may become clear. Also, review contracts and ask in advance: "what's the worst situation I could face here"? Do the contracts provide the coverage I need for this environment and its potential failures?
  - *Suggestions to address it:* This is probably the hardest situation you can find, because if you missed your opportunity to request budget for something that is required. However, you have a few options.

    - *Find a Substitute:* Sometimes you may have a spare item somewhere else in the network which can be reused for this project. You might also try to find something that could do on a temporary basis, while you find budget to purchase what you need. A Hard Disk module from another FortiGate that only logging could give you the module, you need to perform WAN Optimization. Another FortiGate might have the fiber transceiver you need and be more feasible to switch from copper to fiber.
    - *Use another element in the network:* Even though it is not desirable, sometimes you can shift workload to other network elements: an additional VLAN could be implemented on a switch or an additional VDOM on an existing FortiGate.
    - *Change the scope:* You can always evaluate the impact of not having the missing piece, and change the expectations to fit the new situation. For example, if you missed the 24×7 support option, some processes could be adopted to ensure support calls would be done only within business hours, and select maintenance windows such that they would fall within business hours. *Note:* this is seldom possible.

- *Undersized models:* It is sadly common for people to undersize their FortiGate selection. They say the project scope is only Web Content Filter+Antivirus, and end up also enabling QoS+Application Control. Perhaps, the number of users is estimated at 2000 with three connections each, but in there are actually 2500 users opening 10 connections each that need inspection. This results on having to spend additional money to upsize the box.

- *Suggestions to avoid it:* This has been addressed by earlier chapters. However, the final two pieces of advice: (1) Always size thinking all the FortiGate features will eventually be enabled. (2) If in doubt, go bigger: it is cheaper to request and spend additional money in the beginning than to attempt to replace a device later.
- *Suggestions to address it:* If the device cannot be replaced with a bigger one, three things should be considered: (1) Maximize performance tuning by leveraging ASICs as much as possible, adjusting content inspection (IPS, WCF, AV) profiles and reducing firewall policies. (2) Reduce load by disabling functions such as routing traffic that needs IPS inspection to another system and disabling IPS on the FortiGate. (3) Do the project in phases and plan to move load to older boxes until they can be replaced.

- *Change of scope:* If the project changes its scope and fewer things that must be accomplished, there is seldom an issue. However, if scope is increased to cover for additional items (more functionality, users, or services) this might affect not only the sizing of the FortiGate, but also the amount of time and human resources needed for the project, adding cost.

  - *Suggestions to avoid it:* The planning phase of the project should consider potential changes of scope and, where possible, associated cost. The best way to do this is to carefully review concurrently running projects and assessing overlap or complementation of the project at hand. This might be difficult, but by looking on what you are trying to achieve, the people involved and services to be offered, it may be easier to ascertain this information.
  - *Suggestions to address it:* Since change of scope will often result in an undersized FortiGate, the earlier advice also applies. A phased project approach is often the best, as the expanded scope can be done in a second phase after the first has been completed, tested, and placed into full production.

DEALING WITH TIMING

Estimating time is one of the most common issues that IT projects face, especially when activities are estimated with little experience. Sometimes projects are planned by people who are not experts in security technologies. Other times unforeseen situations cause activities to be delayed.

Unlike money, time cannot be added to a project. If a deadline was promised and cannot be extended, it is important to review alternatives. In this situation, these alternatives should be considered. One option that is conspicuous in its absence is asking people to work longer or more shifts. This seldom results in success.

- *Parallel Activities:* While this is often planned from the beginning, a careful assessment should be done with the objective of identifying activities that can be performed in parallel, perhaps by different teams. This can result in dividing the current people engaged into the project. This also will require an additional activity (analysis), but as the people doing that already some experience in the project itself, this might help to identify optimizable activities.

- *Adding people:* Consider adding people to the project team. However, even if the people being incorporated have the right technical skills and knowledge to help, this option does add additional overload, as those people must be brought up to speed.
- *Avoid or postpone steps:* There are often activities that can be eliminated or postponed, but doing so may carry risk. An analysis could be conducted to determine if some activities are subject to removal, reduction, or postponing. The most tempting tasks to be eliminated are in the Quality Assurance (QA) phases. However, this often adds substantial risk and should only be considered as a last resort. Postponing documentation activities is less risky, but only so long as the documentation is eventually done.

ENGAGING FORTINET PROFESSIONAL SERVICES

Hiring Professional Services might be a way to save both time and money. When planning the project, it is important to decide if expert advice will be required. The rule of thumb is that if your project is critical to your operation, and you are performing a migration from another technology to Fortinet or if you are implementing a FortiGate series 3000 or 5000, then you probably want to have experts assisting. Consider Fortinet Professional Services and Fortinet Partner Services. Professional Services are not designed to compete against what Fortinet partners provide, but instead, provide another set of expert eyes and hands that can help to accomplish the project with the expected quality within the defined timeframes.

The Fortinet Professional Services team's sole purpose is to assist customers with installations and migrations. This assistance can be either onsite pretty much anywhere in the world or it can be also remote. The intent is to complement what Fortinet Partners provide in terms of installations, setup, and initial configuration. Their experience can help by validating the network design and/or architecture, proposing a configuration options and troubleshooting issues. Professional Services engineers should not be considered as Project Managers, but as resources that can be used when planning and executing an installation.

The Professional Services group works upon request and after often busy. So, requesting their services in advance will help to ensure availability when it is needed. Prior to the engagement, the ProServ group will request information that is contained in a Pre-Engagement Form. This will help to determine the engineer to be assigned, the estimated amount of time the engagement will take (based on previous experience and the information given) and what additional information will be necessary to accomplish the objective.

ENGAGING FORTINET TECHNICAL SUPPORT

When you are implementing a FortiGate, you may find issues and need to open a ticket with Fortinet Technical Support, also known as Technical Assistance Center (TAC). While Appendix B discusses troubleshooting, there are some simple steps you can take to facilitate the TAC's ability to help you.

a. *Define the issue in a clear and specific way.* Remember that problems are contradictions between what you want and what you have. State what you want in a way that can be measured, and then state what you currently have. In other words, make sure the description of the problem has a specific "What". "The FortiGate is failing" and "IPS is not working" are overly vague statements. However, "IPS is not catching a SYN Flood attack", "IPS signature X is not catching traffic that should match it, " "When I enable IPS my latency increases from 5 to 7 milliseconds, " and "My throughput drops by 50% when I enable IPS" are statements that can be proven. One of the best ways to test an accurate statement is to ask to describe the problem to a coworker and verify that they understand it in the same way you do.

b. *If you can replicate the issue, indicate the steps to do so.* The most difficult problems to fix are those that cannot be reproduced. One of the first things that you should mention is whether you can cause the problem to occur. If so, make sure you list the steps to do so, including sequence and duration of the steps. By reproducing the problem, a technical support engineer can use Fortinet's equipment to replicate the issue, isolate it and test the potential fix without affecting your environment. If the problem cannot be reproduced, it may be necessary to wait for reoccurrence of the problem to capture additional information to isolate and diagnose the issue.

c. *Indicate your findings.* If you have already tried remediation steps that didn't work, tell the TAC what you tried. This way, you maximize both your time and theirs. Indicate both what you did and what the result was. If possible have copies of the output so the engineer can see the results.

d. *Clearly Communicate importance.* TAC engineers get many calls every day. Some relate to minor issues. Some of them relate to customers who use a FortiGate as a highly critical component. If your ticket is critical, explain this to the TAC to get appropriate priority.

e. *Clearly communicate contact information.* Make sure appropriate names, e-mails, and cell phone numbers (including country code and city code) are posted in the ticket. If possible, this information should include remote access credentials to the FortiGate. By allowing the TAC engineer to connect to the FortiGate, even in read-only mode, they will better understand the environment and the nature of the issue.

f. *Ask for remote assistance during maintenance windows.* Depending on the support contract you purchased, you may be entitled to ask for remote support during maintenance windows. This way, the TAC engineer can remotely connect and collect troubleshooting information, without having to request it from you.

g. All in all, communication is important to ensure TAC engineers have all the tools to help you determine the problem. Also, never assume anything. If you doubt the TAC engineer understood what you were trying to say, it is better to confirm than find out later there was a misunderstanding. Every misunderstanding will just add unproductive time to the equation.

Troubleshooting Technically

B

INFORMATION IN THIS CHAPTER:

- Introduction
- Resources
- Basic Troubleshooting Overview
  - Troubleshooting Guidelines
- Basic Troubleshooting Tools
  - Get and Exec Commands
  - External Flow Trace
  - Internal Flow Trace
- Advanced Troubleshooting Tools
  - Application Monitoring
  - Application Testing

INTRODUCTION

Troubleshooting borders on art as opposed to science due to the symptom you are observing may actually be far-removed or obfuscating the actual root cause and sometimes it comes down to luck that you notice some telltale CLI diagnostic output that leads you to the real culprit. This Appendix presents some tools and guidelines to try to make the FortiGate troubleshooting process shorter than it otherwise might be.

RESOURCES

A short-list of useful websites to access, download, or search for information to prepare for and during troubleshooting is given in the table below.

Website	Source for...
http://docs.fortinet.com	Administrative and Reference Guides in PDF and HTML formats
https://support.fortinet.com > Firmware Images (Registration & Login required)	Release Notes for product firmware versions
http://kb.fortinet.com	Knowledge Base (tips & tricks)
http://support.fortinet.com/forum	Fortinet Technical Discussion Forum
http://training.fortinet.com	Fortinet Online Training Campus for formal course registration & self-paced (free) modules

One particularly useful document is the Troubleshooting chapter of the FortiOS Handbook available from the Fortinet Documentation website (http://docs.fortinet.com). Be sure to obtain the latest version or one corresponding to the FortiOS firmware running on your FortiGate unit since CLI diagnostic commands and output can vary from version to version of FortiOS.

BASIC TROUBLESHOOTING OVERVIEW

Troubleshooting Guidelines

There is no one right way to perform troubleshooting but there are some important guidelines and questions to always keep in mind.

- What has changed?

An important piece of information is whether anything in the network environment has changed recently. Many organizations have a change control procedure whereby end-users are notified ahead of time, via email or web homepage message, of an upcoming change to the network or installed applications. Firmware updates or upgrades to other networking devices such as switches, routers, and load balancers that are in the network path can be a factor. FortiOS firmware patch, or maintenance release (e.g. 4.0-MR2 to 4.0-MR3) updates, or major release (e.g. 3.0 to 4.0) upgrades applied to a FortiGate unit can also have significant effects on an existing configuration. It is important not to overlook any changes of the client-side as well such as new application installations or updates or new hardware added to the client-PC.

- What do we know?

Defining the problem requires an understanding the current conditions for formulating a starting point for a troubleshooting plan. Review of the FortiGate log messages and system baseline information (CPU, memory, session loading) to help determine the specifics of the problem:

- Is the problem persistent or intermittent? Is the problem reproducible?
- When did the problem occur? Is it periodic or does it occur at a particular time?
- Does it occur to certain users or all users?

It is important to be specific and objective and avoid jumping to conclusions since the current state of information may be incomplete and some of the symptoms misleading and acting as distractions for the root cause.

• Isolate the issue

With the wide range of UTM functionality provided by a FortiGate device, it can be challenging to find the root cause among the observable symptoms. It is key to try to isolate the issue by eliminating possible causes and checking if the problem persists or is affected by the controlled changes in configuration. For example, you can observe the effect on the problem by disabling or enabling a particular feature on the FortiGate unit. Sometimes a change of a parameter on the affected client or server can also provide information about the root cause or help eliminate distractions.

Answering or investigating the above questions as part of the troubleshooting process can be very time consuming. It can often require external coordination or establishing observation points on other perimeter or host devices to assist with the information gathering. The following sections of this Appendix provide just a sampling of the tools and techniques using the CLI for helping to troubleshoot a problem associated with your FortiGate UTM appliance.

BASIC TROUBLESHOOTING TOOLS

A basic set of FortiOS CLI troubleshooting tools are:

    get/exec commands
    Internal flow—diag debug flow
    External flow—diag sniffer packet

These basic CLI tools can help address the information gathering for baselining and problem definition. In addition to the above a "bare metal" system recovery can also be used to restore a system to a last-known good configuration.

Get and Exec Commands

The "get" and "exec" (abbreviated from "execute") CLI commands provide one way to obtain current system states and settings. A "get" command is a passive operation in that only a setting or status is output to the CLI. An "exec" command will invoke a particular action that can be useful for testing connectivity or behavior of a particular function. A selection of some useful commands plus one additional "diag" command, and when their output is useful are given below. The complete descriptive listing of these commands can be found in the FortiOS CLI Reference Guide for the particular version of firmware running on your FortiGate unit.

"COMMAND PARSE ERROR"

"Command fail"

If you see this output and there were no syntax or spelling errors in the command, then you might be in the wrong context to be able to run the command. Some commands must be run at the global level and others from within a VDOM context, while certain commands will only be valid in the Management VDOM context. Try to keep in mind whether the associated function is configured at the system level ("config global") or at the VDOM level ("config VDOM >> edit VDOM"), then it is likely that the "get" or "exec" command will also need to run in that same context. There are a few exceptions but this rule of thumb will usually hold true. One such exception is "exec ping <interface>" which must be run from within a VDOM context, but the configuration through "config system interface" is usually performed in the global context.

CLI command	Troubleshooting purpose	Provides	G/V
get system status	Baselining	Firmware and update package versions, VDOM status & opmode, system time	G, V
get system performance status	Baselining Trouble-shooting—current state	Average CPU & memory load (%), network usage (kB), system uptime	G
get system performance firewall statistics	Baselining		V
get system session list | grep <string-pattern>	Troubleshooting—current state	Brief listing for current VDOM sessions filtered by "grep" string pattern	V
get system arp	Troubleshooting—current state, connectivity	IP address & corresponding MAC address in system ARP cache	V
get router info routing-table <...>	Baselining Troubleshooting	static—all active static routesall—all entries in routing-table	V
get system ha status	Baselining	HA cluster status summary	G
get hardware memory	Baselining	Detailed memory usage	G
get webfilter status	Baselining	FortiGuard Distribution Network available server preference list	G
get system fortiguard-service status	Troubleshooting—licensing	List current update package versions and license expiry	G
diag system top	Baselining Troubleshooting	CPU/memory usage of daemons	G

G/V = Global or VDOM context

CLI command	Troubleshooting purpose	Provides	G/V
exec date exec time	Baselining	Set or verify system date & time	G
exec ping exec traceroute	Troubleshooting—connectivity	Connectivity testing with ping and traceroute	V
exec ping-options	Troubleshooting—connectivity	Change parameters of ICMP echo request	V
exec telnet <ip> <port>	Troubleshooting—connectivity	"TCP-ping" alternative when ping is blocked or destination does not respond to ping.	V
exec update-now	Troubleshooting—connectivity	Force update request from FDS Network	G
exec log filter exec log display	Troubleshooting	View log messages as specified by filter settings	G,V

External Flow Trace

The built-in packet sniffer is useful for investigating the ingress and egress packet flow between interfaces. The "diag sniffer packet" CLI command along with optional filter syntax can show details of the packet headers and payload arriving and leaving the FortiGate interfaces.

The command is well-documented in the FortiOS CLI Reference as well as on the Knowledge Base website (http://kb.fortinet.com; search for "cli sniffer" or try the URL http://kb.fortinet.com/kb/microsites/search.do?cmd=displayKC&externalId=11186). The basic command structure is shown below but it can become very verbose when complex filtering expressions are used.

```
diag sniffer packet <interface> <filter> <verbose> <count> <absolute_
    timestamp>
```

<interface> must be a single physical or virtual (VLAN, tunnel) interface or the keyword "any" to specify all interfaces.

<filter> will accept Unix tcpdump or Berkeley Packet Filtering filter expressions or the keyword "none" or a null string entered as two-consecutive single or double quotation marks to match all traffic.

<verbose> is an integer 1-6 to specify the packet information detail to display. When the interface is "any" then options 4 or 6 are useful since the interface name is printed. The output from option 3 can captured in a text file and then converted to PCAP format using a free PERL script available from the Knowledge Base Packet Sniffer article mentioned earlier.

<count> sets the number of packets for the sniffer to display before stopping. When set to "0" or omitted, the output continues until CTRL-C is entered.

<absolute_timestamp> when set to "a" displays the date and time, while any other value or if omitted will display the relative timestamp from when the command was entered.

A sample of the CLI packet sniffer output at the different <verbose> levels is given below.

```
# Verbose = 1 (IP header only)
FGT-Test (root) # diag sniff packet wan1 "udp and port 4500" 1 1
interfaces=[wan1]
filters=[udp and port 4500]
0.907538 70.71.18.94.4500 -> 208.91.15.10.11548: udp 96
# Verbose = 2 (IP packet header and data)
FGT-Test (root) # diag sniff packet wan1 "udp and port 4500" 2 1
interfaces=[wan1]
filters=[udp and port 4500]
1.927546 70.71.18.94.4500 -> 208.91.15.10.59676: udp 96
0x0000    4500 007c 4bc5 0000 4011 eda0  4647 b75e  E..|K...@...FG.^
0x0010    d05b 730b 1194 e91c 0168 5382  0000 0000  .[s......hS.....
0x0020    bfb1 b2fa 9abd 66e9 d825 9cb1  8057 60a8  ......f..%...W'.
0x0030    0810 0501 66fd be77 0000 005c  8488 fa51  ....f..w...\...Q
0x0040    61b9 f481 0f58 ca5d 1532 1f17  6d3c e032  a....X.].2..m<.2
0x0050    5f3a ee27 ecff c9d9 5b8a 2f69  9640 dd4e  _:.'....[./i.@.N
0x0060    69e8 e548 ef26 37c7 285c e794  0b59 1a85  i..H.&7.(\...Y..
0x0070    8633 12a4 03d5 821d beb6 b61f             .3.........
# Verbose = 3 (Ethernet header and data)
FGT-Test (root) # diag sniff packet wan1 "udp and port 4500" 3 1
interfaces=[wan1]
filters=[udp and port 4500]
2.947540 70.71.18.94.4500 -> 208.91.15.10.61724: udp 96
0x0000    0013 5f07 8fd9 0009 0f45 943a  0800 4500  .._......E.:..E.
0x0010    007c 4bc9 0000 4011 ed9c 4647  b75e d05b  .|K...@...FG.^.[
0x0020    730b 1194 f11c 0168 2138 0000  0000 bfb1  s......h!8......
0x0030    b2fa 9abd 66e9 d825 9cb1 8057  60a8 0810  ....f..%...W'...
0x0040    0501 1011 5f00 0000 005c 6c36  31b1 dac3  ...._....\l61...
0x0050    5b30 62ed c50a 195d 5cf0 9463  3f6d 6d32  [0b....]\..c?mm2
0x0060    0378 2d9b 8c34 2824 1725 d3ea  63f1 4c20  .x-..4($.%..c.L.
0x0070    2583 4da4 fd68 d654 e9d1 0bcc  ce25 bf21  %.M..h.T.....%.!
0x0080    caff 448b ef92 ad60 a984             ..D....'..
# Verbose = 4 (header with interface name)
```

```
FGT-Test (root) # diag sniff packet wan1 "udp and port 4500" 4 1 a
interfaces=[wan1]
filters=[udp and port 4500]
2012-06-26 08:06:38.057583 wan1 -- 70.71.18.94.4500 ->
  208.91.15.10.36124: udp 96
```

Some caveats for the usage of the CLI packet sniffer are:

- the output is CPU generated so sniffing of a high-bandwidth interface may fill the packet buffer and not all packets will be displayed, especially for a 9600 bps serial console connection,
- for traffic that is being hardware accelerated on interfaces with the FortiASIC NP2 or NP4 (depends on FortiGate model) only the initial few packets comprising of the TCP or UDP session will be displayed. In order to display the packets with the sniffer, the so-called fastpath must be disabled: temporarily using `"diag npu <np2|np4> fastpath-sniffer enable <physical_port>"`; on a persistent basis in the firewall security policy `"set auto-asic-offload disable"` which will then be applied to subsequent new sessions,
- if VDOMs are enabled, the command must be run from within a VDOM context (look for the name of the VDOM in the CLI prompt); that is, you will get an error message if you attempt to run this command from the global context,
- when using a remote CLI connection and you are sniffing on the same interface as your CLI management connection be sure to filter out the IP address and TCP ports (e.g. 23 or 22) of your management PC,
- after entering the `"diag sniffer packet"` command the sniffer output will continue until CTRL-C is entered in the CLI session.

Internal Flow Trace

With the CLI sniffer presented above, you have a view of the ingress and egress packet flow through the FortiGate but what occurs to the packets internally? The flow of the packet can be traced with the "diag debug flow" commands. The simple set-up for an internal flow trace is

1. Enable output to the console.
2. Set-up the display filter to follow a specific traffic stream.
3. Set the number of packets to display.
4. Stop the internal flow trace.

The corresponding CLI commands are shown in the example below.

```
1. diag debug enablediag debug flow show console enable
2. diag debug flow filter <option>
3. diag debug flow trace start <count>
4. diag debug flow trace stop
```

<option> can be any one of the parameters below and multiple parameters may be entered with separate "filter" command entry but a parameter may only be specified once. Any later entries of the same parameter results in the latest one taking effect for the flow trace filter. One exception is "clear" which resets all flow filter parameters, and entering a null filter simply displays the current filter settings.

```
FG-VM-Test (root) # diag deb flow filter ?
addr    ip address
clear   clear filter
daddr   dest ip address
dport     destination port
negate     inverse filter
port  port
proto     protocol number
saddr     source ip address
sport source    port
vd     index of virtual domain
```

<count> specifies the number of packets processed to display and to end the flow trace, while the countdown is nonzero the "trace stop" command can be used.

Unlike the sniffer command, the flow trace command runs in the background and returns the CLI prompt so you can enter other CLI commands. But the flow trace output will display somewhat asynchronously as traffic matches the display filter, and it may make the CLI display a bit of a jumble of the output of different CLI commands. A best practise is to open another CLI session window under a different administrative user-ID for entering other CLI commands. It is also advisable to enable the logging or session capture of your terminal client application to save the often verbose output of the flow trace.

A few examples of the flow trace output are given below. Working from the end of the flow trace output: the "msg" indicates the action or function; the session number for this traffic stream in the FortiGate's session table, and the relative direction with respect to session initialization; "trace-id" is the packet count since the first flow trace command after system boot-up; "id" is the process number for this flow trace.

```
FGT-Test (root) # id=36871 trace_id=1 msg="vd-root received a
    packet(proto=6, 10.20.80.31:58532->159.33.16.50:80) from wan1."
id=36871 trace_id=1 msg="Find an existing session, id-000ab64e,
    original direction"
id=36871 trace_id=1 msg="send to ips"
id=36871 trace_id=1 msg="SNAT 10.20.80.31->70.71.18.94:5840"
```

ADVANCED TROUBLESHOOTING TOOLS

The Advanced Troubleshooting Tools are comprised of two groups of diagnostic CLI commands. The first is for monitoring a process daemon at various levels of detail as specified by a "debug-level" number which actually are bit flags for enabling or disabling levels of detail that will vary from one functional daemon to another daemon. The second group is one that can be more intrusive with control and display certain parameters.

Application Monitoring

Monitoring of the various process daemons can be done with `"diag debug application"` group of CLI commands. The general format is

```
diag debug app <daemon-name> <debug-level>
```

`<debug-level>` "0" disables the diagnostic monitoring output while other values range from 1 to 255 (also represented as "−1").

`<daemon-name>` can be one of the names taken from the output of `"diag debug app ?"` and are listed below for FortiOS 4.3.6:

```
FGT-Test (root) # diag debug app ?
alarmd         alarmd daemon
alertmail        alertmail daemon
authd       auth daemon
cauploadd        content archive upload daemon
chassis        chassis daemon
crl-update       crl update daemon
cw_acd        capwap AC daemon
cw_wtpd         capwap WTP daemon
ddnscd        ddns client daemon
dhcp6s        dhcp6 server
dhcpc        DHCP client module
dhcprelay       dhcp relay daemon
dhcps       dhcp server
dialinsvr        dial-in-server daemon
dlp          DLP
dlpfingerprint  DLP fingerprint daemon
dnsproxy       dns proxy module
fdpd        fdpd daemon
fdslogd        fdslogd daemon
fdsmgmt        FortiGuard management daemon
```

```
fgd_alert       FortiGuard alert message
fgfmd     FortiGate/FortiManager communication daemon
flgd      flgd daemon
fnbamd      fortigate non-blocking auth daemon
ftpd      ftp proxy
garpd     VIP gratuitous ARP daemon
hasync      HA synchronization module
hatalk      HA protocol module
http      http proxy
ike      IKE daemon
im     im proxy
imap      imap proxy
ipldbd      ipldbd daemon
ipmc      ipmc
ipsengine      ips sensor
ipsmonitor      ips monitor
l2tp      l2tp daemon
l2tpcd      l2tpcd daemon
lted      usb lte daemon
memuploadd    memory log upload daemon
miglogd      log daemon
modemd      modem daemon
netscan      Netscan
nntp      nntp proxy
ntpd      ntpd daemon
pop3      pop3 proxy
ppp      ppp daemon
pptp      pptp daemon
pptpc      pptp client
proxyacceptor    proxy acceptor
proxydaemon  proxy daemon
proxyworker  proxy workder
quarantine      quarantine daemon
radiusd      radius daemon
radvd     router adv daemon
rsyslogd      rsyslogd daemon
rtmon      ping server
```

```
scanunit     scanunit daemon
sccp     SCCP ALG
scep     SCEP
sessionsync     session sync daemon
sflowd     sflow protocol module
sip     SIP ALG
smbcd     SMB client daemon
smtp     smtp proxy
snmpd     snmp daemon
spamfilter     spamfilter module
sshd     sshd daemon
ssl     ssl daemon
sslvpn     sslvpn
update     update daemon
uploadd     upload daemon
urlfilter     urlfilter daemon
vpd     vpn policy daemon
vrrpd     vrrp daemon
vs     virtual-server
wa_cs     WAN acceleration cs server
wa_dbd     WAN acceleration db server
wad     WAN acceleration proxy
wccpd     wccp daemon
wifi     wifi setting
wpad     port access entity daemon
wpad_dump     dump wpad packet in binary format
zebos     ZebOS
zebos-launcher     ZebOS launcher daemon
```

This application monitoring output provides continuous, real-time event information which will continue until it is explicitly stopped or until the unit is rebooted. The monitoring output can affect system performance and will be continually generated even though output might not be displayed in the CLI console.

The format and type of output from a monitored application daemon varies and it is generally not documented in the FortiOS Handbook and you will usually be directed to a particular command when you have a FortiCare Support Case number working through an issue with the Fortinet TAC.

Some D-I-Y guidance can be obtained from the output of "diag system top" to determine the processes or daemons of interest.

Application Testing

The second group of diagnostic commands can be found with "diag test app ?"entered in the global context. Caution must be exercised with these commands since they can be traffic or system affecting.

```
FGT-Test (global) # diag test app ?
ddnscd          ddnscd daemon
dhcprelay       dhcprelay
dlpfingerprint  dlp fingerprint daemon
dnsproxy        dns proxy
ftpd        ftp proxy
http        http proxy
im      AIM/ICQ/MSN/Yahoo proxy
imap        imap proxy
ipldbd          ipldbd daemon
ipsengine       ips sensor
ipsmonitor      ips monitor
l2tpcd          l2tpcd
lted        usb lte daemon
miglogd         miglog logging daemon
nntp        nntp proxy
pop3        pop3 proxy
pptpcd          pptp client
proxyacceptor   proxy acceptor
proxyworker     proxy worker
radiusd         radius daemon
scanunit        scanning unit
sccp        SCCP ALG
sflowd          sflowd
sip         SIP ALG
smtp        smtp proxy
snmpd       snmpd daemon
ssl         ssl proxy
urlfilter       urlfilter daemon
vs      virtual-server
wa_cs       wan optimization cs server
wa_dbd          wan optimization storage server
wad         wan optimization proxy
```

```
wad_diskd        wan optimization disk access daemon
wccpd     wccp daemon
wpad      wpad
```

The usage of the application testing diagnostic command is

```
diag test app <app-name> <test-number>
```

To view the available test options, enter "0" as the test number. For example, the "urlfilter" test options are shown below. The debug levels shown for this diagnostic command are specific for this command only. Each diagnostic command has its own debug level output and not every command will define its output as explicitly as the diag test app urlfilter.

```
FGT-Test (global) # diag test app urlfilter 0
1.  This menu
2.  Clear WF cache
3.  Display WF cache contents
4.  Display WF cache TTL list
5.  Display WF cache LRU list
6.  Display WF cache in tree format
7.  Toggle switch for dumping unrated packet
8.  Increase timeout for polling
9.  Decrease timeout for polling
10. Print debug values
11. Clear Spam Filter cache
12. Clear AV Query cache
13. Toggle switch for dumping expired license packets
14. Show running timers (except request timers)
144.Show running timers (including request timers)
15. Send INIT requests.
16. Display WF cache contents of prefix type
17. Toggle fast INIT retry interval
99. Restart the urlfilter daemon.
Debug levels:
Warning messages:        1 (0x001)
Block events:        2 (0x002)
Pass events:        4 (0x004)
URL request events:        8 (0x008)
Cache events:        16 (0x010)
Prefix events:        32 (0x020)
```

```
Prefix delete subtree events:          64 (0x040)
Add after prefix events:              128 (0x080)
CMDB events:              256 (0x100)
DNS resolver messages:          512 (0x200)
Keyword search messages:              1024 (0x400)
INIT request messages:          2048 (0x800)
```

When running these application test debug commands, they will execute once and then exit and return the CLI prompt.

Country Codes

AD	Andorra
AE	United Arab Emirates
AF	Afghanistan
AG	Antigua and Barbuda
AI	Anguilla
AL	Albania
AM	Armenia
AN	Netherlands Antilles
AO	Angola
AP	Non-spec Asia Pas Location
AR	Argentina
AS	American Samoa
AT	Austria
AU	Australia
AW	Aruba
AX	Aland Islands
AZ	Azerbaijan
BA	Bosnia and Herzegowina
BB	Barbados
BD	Bangladesh
BE	Belgium
BF	Burkina Faso
BG	Bulgaria
BH	Bahrain
BI	Burundi
BJ	Benin
BM	Bermuda
BN	Brunei Darussalam
BO	Bolivia
BR	Brazil
BS	Bahamas
BT	Bhutan

BW	Botswana
BY	Belarus
BZ	Belize
CA	Canada
CD	Congo The Democratic Republic of The
CF	Central African Republic
CG	Congo
CH	Switzerland
CI	Cote D'ivoire
CK	Cook Islands
CL	Chile
CM	Cameroon
CN	China
CO	Colombia
CR	Costa Rica
CU	Cuba
CV	Cape Verde
CY	Cyprus
CZ	Czech Republic
DE	Germany
DJ	Djibouti
DK	Denmark
DO	Dominican Republic
DZ	Algeria
EC	Ecuador
EE	Estonia
EG	Egypt
ER	Eritrea
ES	Spain
ET	Ethiopia
EU	European Union
FI	Finland
FJ	Fiji
FM	Micronesia Federated States of
FO	Faroe Islands
FR	France
GA	Gabon
GB	United Kingdom
GD	Grenada
GE	Georgia
GF	French Guiana
GG	Guernsey
GH	Ghana

GI	Gibraltar
GL	Greenland
GM	Gambia
GN	Guinea
GP	Guadeloupe
GQ	Equatorial Guinea
GR	Greece
GT	Guatemala
GU	Guam
GW	Guinea-bissau
GY	Guyana
HK	Hong Kong
HN	Honduras
HR	Croatia (Local Name: Hrvatska)
HT	Haiti
HU	Hungary
ID	Indonesia
IE	Ireland
IL	Israel
IM	Isle of Man
IN	India
IO	British Indian Ocean Territory
IQ	Iraq
IR	Iran (ISLAMIC Republic Of)
IS	Iceland
IT	Italy
JE	Jersey
JM	Jamaica
JO	Jordan
JP	Japan
KE	Kenya
KG	Kyrgyzstan
KH	Cambodia
KI	Kiribati
KN	Saint Kitts and Nevis
KP	Korea Democratic People's Republic of
KR	Korea Republic of
KW	Kuwait
KY	Cayman Islands
KZ	Kazakhstan
LA	Lao People's Democratic Republic
LB	Lebanon
LC	Saint Lucia

LI	Liechtenstein
LK	Sri Lanka
LR	Liberia
LS	Lesotho
LT	Lithuania
LU	Luxembourg
LV	Latvia
LY	Libyan Arab Jamahiriya
MA	Morocco
MC	Monaco
MD	Moldova Republic of
ME	Montenegro
MF	Saint Martin
MG	Madagascar
MH	Marshall Islands
MK	Macedonia
ML	Mali
MM	Myanmar
MN	Mongolia
MO	Macau
MP	Northern Mariana Islands
MR	Mauritania
MS	Montserrat
MT	Malta
MU	Mauritius
MV	Maldives
MW	Malawi
MX	Mexico
MY	Malaysia
MZ	Mozambique
NA	Namibia
NC	New Caledonia
NE	Niger
NF	Norfolk Island
NG	Nigeria
NI	Nicaragua
NL	Netherlands
NO	Norway
NP	Nepal
NR	Nauru
NU	Niue
NZ	New Zealand
OM	Oman

PA	Panama
PE	Peru
PF	French Polynesia
PG	Papua New Guinea
PH	Philippines
PK	Pakistan
PL	Poland
PM	St. Pierre and Miquelon
PR	Puerto Rico
PS	Palestinian Territory Occupied
PT	Portugal
PW	Palau
PY	Paraguay
QA	Qatar
RE	Reunion
RO	Romania
RS	Serbia
RU	Russian Federation
RW	Rwanda
SA	Saudi Arabia
SB	Solomon Islands
SC	Seychelles
SD	Sudan
SE	Sweden
SG	Singapore
SI	Slovenia
SK	Slovakia (Slovak Republic)
SL	Sierra Leone
SM	San Marino
SN	Senegal
SO	Somalia
SR	Suriname
SV	El Salvador
SY	Syrian Arab Republic
SZ	Swaziland
TC	Turks and Caicos Islands
TD	Chad
TG	Togo
TH	Thailand
TJ	Tajikistan
TK	Tokelau
TL	Timor-leste
TM	Turkmenistan

TN	Tunisia
TO	Tonga
TR	Turkey
TT	Trinidad and Tobago
TV	Tuvalu
TW	Taiwan; Republic of China (ROC)
TZ	Tanzania United Republic of
UA	Ukraine
UG	Uganda
US	United States
UY	Uruguay
UZ	Uzbekistan
VA	Holy See (Vatican City State)
VC	Saint Vincent and The Grenadines
VE	Venezuela
VG	Virgin Islands (British)
VI	Virgin Islands (US)
VN	Viet Nam
VU	Vanuatu
WF	Wallis and Futuna Islands
WS	Samoa
YE	Yemen
ZA	South Africa
ZM	Zambia
ZW	Zimbabwe

Glossary

ASIC. (Application-Specific Integrated Circuit) A silicon chip which is designed with specific functionalities. Having the ability to process specific functions on a dedicated ASIC chip helps offload the system main processor from having to perform the task.

Packet Fragmentation. IP packets that are fragmented when the packet is larger then the network path maximum transmission unit (MTU). A typical Ethernet network has a 1518 Bytes size MTU.

Jumbo Frame. Ethernet frame sizes that are above 1518 Bytes. A typical jumbo frame size would be 9000 Bytes.

RBL. (Real-Time Black List) An anti-spam database consisting of black listed IP address which servers that is updated frequently.

Attack vector. It is one of the ways or paths that can be used to perform an attack. For example, a worm could spread by exploiting a known vulnerability on a web server, which is via HTTP, but also could spread by attaching itself to an e-mail message (SMTP) or by sending a file containing the propagation code via Instant Messaging (IM). IM, SMTP, and HTTP would all be Attack vectors that can be used by this theoretical worm.

Best practice. Computer Security is a knowledge field where new things arise pretty much every day: new attacks are invented and then new defenses are put in place. A best practice is simply what many people think is the best way to solve a specific problem, and might change from time to time depending on the evolution of technology and common experience. One of the most known best practices is shifting towards longer complex password to avoid brute-force attacks and guessing. Another one is to always use the strongest encryption available to protect sensitive data when handling through a VPN connection.

Bot / Botnet. A bot is type of malware that, once installed on a computer, allows an entity (known as bot master) to control it to perform functions like sending a request to a web server or an e-mail message. While a single computer doing one of these actions seems normal and not harmful, if thousands of them do exactly the same thing in a coordinated way, results can be problematic. A group of bots is called

435

a botnet, and if they launch at the same time a request to a web server, they could potentially overwhelm it, exhaust its network resources, and cause a Denial of Service. If all of them send some invalid messages, a botnet could be an effective way to send spam. One of the most famous botnets is Zeus [1], which has been extensively analyzed [2] by experts around the world, including Fortinet's FortiGuard [3] analysts.

Cluster. It is a group of elements, like servers, gateways, or other network devices that behaves as a single entity to the network, the users, and the applications using its services. The most typical reason to configure a cluster is to increase availability or increase performance. A cluster of servers can be formed to solve a part of a complex math problem, since a single server would take too long to do it. A cluster of web servers could share the load if the amount of users is big and a single server cannot handle all the load. A cluster of firewalls can be configured to ensure there is always at least one firewall available in the event of the failure of a single firewall box.

Control. It is a mechanism to ensure policy compliance. There are many types of control classifications but here you have a couple of examples: depending on their nature they can be physical or logical. Depending on their purpose, they can be preventive, detective, or corrective. A door lock for example is a physical control, and it's both preventive and detective, because it prevents a robbery but you can also tell if a robbery potentially happened if you find the lock broken. A network IPS is a logical control that could be preventive, detective, and corrective at the same time, depending on its configuration. Understanding the nature of controls is important especially when you are assessing and environment to determine compliance with a specific regulation.

Cracker. A computer criminal. Someone with enough computer knowledge to cause harm to another entity.

DMZ. De-Militarized Zone. This is a term that was borrowed from the military, and it implies the existence of a zone that has little or no defense, and thus is not really trusted. In computer network topologies, this is typically the zone where services that will have access from the outside will be placed and therefore the permissions will be more relaxed, which also increases the risk. In the past, a DMZ was truly a zone without defenses, meaning it was not protected by a firewall, IPS or any other security device, mainly because of cost and performance reasons. The meaning was changing with time, and now it simply means a network segment where servers and services will be placed, so they can be accessed from other network segments, and due this additional risk they need to be specifically protected.

Denial of Service. It is the name of an attack against availability. A Denial of Service, as its name implies, takes a service offline. This can be achieved in different ways, such as turning off the computer where the service resides, or launching an overwhelmingly high amount of valid requests against the service in such a way that the resources allocated to the service are exhausted and new valid requests cannot be served properly and in some cases even causes the server being shut down.

Exploit. It is a program that contains code aimed to use a known vulnerability. Typically, exploits are used by security researchers to prove their findings. Exploits are also made available by knowledgeable crackers, so others can simply execute the code to abuse a system. Another way to define them would be "canned attacks" or "attacks on a click."

Fail over. It is a condition that occurs when one of the elements of a cluster goes down and its load is sent to the active members of such cluster. A fail over can be triggered by a failure condition, such as a network disconnection or by a scheduled condition, such as system maintenance.

Hacker. This is probably one of the most commonly misunderstood concept. Hacker, in reality, is someone with deep curiosity and deep knowledge on how computers work, some of them boast this knowledge to the point of becoming arrogant, but certainly not all of them. With the popularization of computers, a hacker culture evolved: there is even a Hacker manifesto [4] that was originally published on a hacker magazine and a How To Become A Hacker [5] document. Due the curious technical curiosity of hackers, sometimes they might go beyond the legal frontier on their experiments, and since several hackers were unfortunately responsible of security incidents, the name eventually got bad reputation and it was confused with a computer criminal. For the effects of this book, we will use the term as someone with deep knowledge but that not necessarily commits bad actions.

Proxy. Generally speaking, a proxy is a system that operates on behalf of another system. If we are talking about network proxies, there are entities that open a connection at application level to perform some kind of action or inspection. Proxy firewalls for example, are firewalls that open a session at application level to decide whether a connection is authorized or not. A Web Proxy Cache in the other side opens web applications to review if the content is stored locally, so it's not grabbed again from the origin, but served locally instead of saving bandwidth and time.

Script. It is a program to automate routine tasks. If the same steps can be done manually, but need to be repeated several times to achieve an objective, a script could be an automated solution to save both time and effort.

Single Sign-On (SSO). It is a technology that allows sharing credentials of a single user among several applications, in such a way that if the user is identified in one place, automatically this user is recognized by other applications without asking the user for authentication again. Single sign-on technologies greatly enhance user experience within an environment, because access to resources is more direct and transparent, saving time and effort.

Social Engineering. It is a form of attack, but instead of exploiting network vulnerabilities, it attempts to exploit the human link in the chain by making a person say or do something that shouldnot. For example an attractive person could ask somebody to help her or him on a situation, and eventually ask for that person's password. Someone on the telephone could impersonate a systems administrator, asking a user to change her password to something the attacker knows. Someone could convince a security analyst the alarm raised by the IPS is perfectly normal due to some tests being conducted. Social Engineering can only be fought with education.

Tunnel. It is a networking concept on which there are two sides on a logical connection and something that enters into one side exits in the other side, regardless where both sides are physically located. Typically this is achieved by establishing a connection between two points, then encapsulating and/or encrypting a packet that travels through a public network, which is decapsulated and/or decrypted by the other side. From the perspective of the processed packet, it only traveled one jump and one network, while in reality it probably traversed several.

Virus. Computer code that can replicate itself by "infecting" clean programs, this is, adding its own code to the code of the infected program. Once a program is infected, the virus is loaded once the valid program is executed, and then in turn can infect other programs. It might have or not a payload, which is a malicious code that is executed once a trigger condition is met. The Jerusalem virus, also known as Friday 13th for example, would delete all the executable program files if the date was Friday 13th.

Wire speed. The speed of a connection if only the wire and nothing else is in place. In other words, this is the maximum speed that can be achieved on a network connection, limited only by the physical connection speed. In networking, the term is used when a device imposed no noticeable delay on connections, and thus the speed reached by such connections is the same with and without the device connected.

Worm. An enhanced type of virus that uses the network to replicate itself. A worm is also typically autonomous, which means it does not require a clean or valid program to attach itself to it. Famous worms are the Morris worm, which replicated by exploiting a vulnerability in the sendmail daemon. The Anna Kournikova worm, one of the first using Social Engineering, since its way of replication was by attaching itself to an email message, which was sent to the entire address book of the victim with a message that was apparently a picture of the famous tennis player. Other widely known worms were Nimda and CodeRed.

References

[1] Analysis on Zeus botnet. <http://fgc.fortinet.com/analysis/zeusanalysis.html>.
[2] Fortinet Blog entry about Zeus. <http://blog.fortinet.com/zeus-botnets-multiplying-at-your-service/>.
[3] FortiGuard Center portal. <http://www.fortiguard.com/>.
[4] Hacker Manifesto. Phrack Magazine. The Mentor. <http://www.phrack.org/issues.html?issue=7&id=3&mode=txt>.
[5] Raymond Eric S. How to become a hacker. <http://catb.org/~esr/faqs/hacker-howto.html>.

Index

A

Access Control List (ACL), 127
Access controls, 385
  cable lines, 387
  distributed retail processing, 385–386
  FortiOS, 386
  network segmentations, 386
Access point (AP), 60, 391
ACL. *See* Access Control List
Active Directory service (AD), 155
AD. *See* Active Directory service
"Add Device" wizard, 328–330
  policy configuration importing process, 330, 331
  selection, 329
  Zone mapping, 329–330
Address group
  address space collision, 397
  objects, 134–135
Address objects, 130
  DNS named objects via FQDN, 131–133
  geography-based, 133
  IP range, 131
  miscellaneous address object options, 134
  network, 131
  system level DNS source-ip, 133
  web UI address object setting, 132
  wildcard, 133–134
Administrative Domain (ADOM), 32, 58, 308
ADOM. *See* Administrative Domain; FortiManager
    Administrative Domain
Advanced Persistence Threat (APT), 202
Advanced rule, 286
  for common items, 289
  "FCT", 287
Advanced Troubleshooting Tools, 423
  Application Monitoring, 423–426
  Application Testing, 426–428
ALG. *See* Application Level Gateways
algorithm parameter, 239
Anomaly detection, 10
anomaly-mode command, 239
AntiSpam, 10–11
  SSL inspection, 193
AntiVirus (AV), 11, 203
  SSL inspection, 191
Any Source Multicast (ASM), 396
AP. *See* Access point
API. *See* Application Programming Interface

Application Control, 10, 224
  See also Endpoint Control; Web Content Filter
    (WCF)
  application list, 227–228
  using areas, 224–225
  list as in GUI, 229–230
  need of, 224
  profile creation, 226–227
  shaping, 189–190
  sizing and design steps, 225–226
  work process, 226
Application Control Licensing, 206
Application information, 370
Application Level Gateways (ALG), 142–143
Application Monitoring, 423–426
Application Programming Interface (API), 66
Application security
  Application Control, 224–230
  Fortiguard, 203–224
    licensing, 205–207
    troubleshooting FDN connectivity, 218–224
    updates, 207–213
    UTM analysis, 213–218
  IPS, 235–243
  Network Antivirus, 230–235
  WCF, 243–247
Application Specific Integrated Circuits (ASIC),
    29, 36
Application Testing, 426–428
APSecure 39, 300
APT. *See* Advanced Persistence Threat
AS. *See* Autonomous System
ASIC. *See* Application Specific Integrated Circuits
ASM. *See* Any Source Multicast
Attack vector, 12–13, 21
Auditing, 8
Authentication, 387
  multiple wireless segments, 387
  password requirements, 388
  remote IPSec VPN users authentication,
    387–388
  splash screen, 388
  splash screen disclaimer web page, 388
  two-factor authentication, 388
  web page redirects, 388, 389
  wireless captive portal disclaimer and login web
    page, 389
Autonomous System (AS), 110
AV. *See* AntiVirus

Printed and bound by CPI Group (UK) Ltd, Croydon, CR0 4YY

03/10/2024

01040340-0008